Working Memory and Neurodevelopmental Disorders

Short-term or working memory – the capacity to hold and manipulate information mentally over brief periods of time – plays an important role in supporting a wide range of everyday activities, particularly in childhood. Children with weak working memory skills often struggle in key areas of learning and, given its impact on cognitive abilities, the identification of working memory impairments is a priority for those who work with children with learning disabilities.

Working Memory and Neurodevelopmental Disorders supports clinical assessment and management of working memory deficits by summarising the current theoretical understanding and methods of assessment of working memory. It outlines the working memory profiles of individuals with a range of neurodevelopmental disorders (including Down syndrome, Williams syndrome, Specific Language Impairment, and ADHD), and identifies useful means of alleviating the anticipated learning difficulties of children with deficits of working memory.

This comprehensive and informative text will appeal to academics and researchers in cognitive psychology, neuropsychology, and developmental psychology, and will be useful reading for students in these areas. Educational psychologists will also find this a useful text, as it covers the role of working memory in learning difficulties specific to the classroom.

Tracy Packiam Alloway is a psychologist at the University of Durham. She has worked with a variety of educational professionals and has published numerous articles on working memory and learning. She has also developed classroom-based tools that are widely used to identify and support children with memory impairments.

Susan E. Gathercole is a psychologist with over 20 years of experience in research on memory during childhood. She has written many articles for psychologists and teachers, is a founding co-editor of the journal *Memory*, and has developed several standardised tests of memory for children.

Working Memory and Neurodevelopmental Disorders

Edited by Tracy Packiam Alloway and
Susan E. Gathercole

Psychology Press
Taylor & Francis Group

HOVE AND NEW YORK

First published 2006
by Psychology Press
27 Church Road, Hove, East Sussex BN3 2FA

Simultaneously published in the USA and Canada
by Psychology Press
270 Madison Avenue, New York, NY 10016

Psychology Press is part of the Taylor & Francis Group, an informa business

Typeset in Times by RefineCatch Limited, Bungay, Suffolk
Printed and bound in Great Britain by
TJ International Ltd, Padstow, Cornwall
Cover design by Hybert Design

British Library Cataloguing-in-Publication Data
A catalogue record for this book is available from the British Library

Library of Congress Cataloging in Publication Data
Working memory and neurodevelopmental disorders / [edited by] Tracy
Packiam Alloway and Susan E. Gathercole.
    p. cm.
Includes bibliographical references and index.
ISBN 1-84169-560-2
1. Short-term memory. 2. Developmental disabilities. 3. Pediatric
neuropsychology. 4. Developmental neurobiology. I. Alloway, Tracy
Packiam. II. Gathercole, Susan E.
    RJ506.D47W67 2006
    618.92′8–dc22
                                    2006004232

ISBN13: 978-1-84169-560-0
ISBN10: 1-84169-560-2

Contents

Contributors

Tracy Packiam Alloway, School of Education, University of Durham, Leazes Road, Durham DH1 1TA, UK.

Lisa M. D. Archibald, Department of Psychology, University of Durham, Science Labs, South Road, Durham DH1 3LE, UK.

Sylvie Belleville, Centre de recherche, Institut Universitaire de Gériatrie de Montréal 4565, Queen Mary, Montréal H3W-1W5, Canada.

Jon Brock, Department of Experimental Psychology, University of Oxford, South Parks Road, Oxford OX1 3UD, UK.

Susan E. Gathercole, Department of Psychology, University of York, York YO10 5DD, UK.

Christopher Jarrold, Department of Experimental Psychology, University of Bristol, 8 Woodland Road, Bristol BS8 1TN, UK.

Carolyn B. Mervis, Department of Psychological and Brain Sciences, 317 Life Sciences Building, University of Louisville, Louisville, KY 40292, USA.

Édith Ménard, Clinique spécialisée des TED-SDI, Hôpital Rivière-des-Prairies, 7070 boul. Perras, Montréal, Québec, Canada H1E 1A4.

Marie-Claude Ménard, Centre de recherche, Institut universitaire de gériatrie de Montréal, 4565, Queen Mary, Montréal, Québec, Canada H3W 1W5.

Laurent Mottron, Université de Montréal, Département de Psychiatrie, C.P. 6128, succusake Centre-Ville, Montréal, Québec, Canada H3C 3J7.

Andrea Muse, American Institutes for Research, 1000 Thomas Jefferson Street, NW Washington, DC 20007-3835, USA.

Maria Chiara Passolunghi, Università di Trieste, Facoltà di Psicologia, via S. Anastasio, 12, 34134 Trieste, Italy.

Susan J. Pickering, University of Bristol, Graduate School of Education, Helen Wodehouse Building, 35 Berkeley Square, Clifton, Bristol BS8 1JA, UK.

Harry R. M. Purser, Department of Experimental Psychology, University of Bristol, 8 Woodland Road, Bristol BS8 1TN, UK.

Steve Roodenrys, Department of Psychology, University of Wollongong, Northfields Ave, Wollongong 2522, Australia.

Melissa L. Rowe, Dept. of Psychological and Brain Sciences, 317 Life Sciences Building, University of Louisville, Louisville, KY 40292, USA.

Linda Siegel, University of British Columbia, Department of Educational and Counselling Psychology, and Special Education, Faculty of Education, 2125 Main Mall, Vancouver, BC V6T 1Z4, Canada.

H. Lee Swanson, Sproul Hall 2127, University of California, Riverside, CA 92521, USA.

Rose K. Vukovic, ECPS, 2125 Main Mall, Vancouver, BC V6T 1Z4, Canada.

Richard K. Wagner, Florida Center for Reading Research, Department of Psychology, Florida State University, Tallahassee, FL 32306-1270, USA.

Figures and Tables

FIGURES

TABLES

Foreword

Over the last 30 years there has been a huge development in our knowledge of the functioning of human memory, a development that has been strongly influenced by the study of memory disorders. This has resulted in the enrichment of basic theory and of its application to clinical problems. In 1995, in combination with two colleagues, Barbara Wilson and Fraser Watts, I agreed to edit a handbook of memory disorders, with the aim of presenting this progress in the application of basic research to the study of memory disorders in a way that would be readily accessible to the practising clinician. Our enthusiasm was shared by our colleagues and we were able to assemble a very impressive list of contributors (Baddeley, Wilson & Watts, 1995). There was however, one area of obvious importance that we were unable to cover, namely developmental disorders of learning and memory.

The term learning disability, reflects the paramount importance of the capacity to learn and remember in normal childhood development. We assumed therefore that this would be an area of very active research, comparable in liveliness to research on language disorders and autism. This seemed not to be the case. There appeared to have been little impact of developments in the cognitive psychology of memory on the study of learning disability. Problems in learning were being studied within a broad educational context, but again, with little interaction with recent developments in the cognitive psychology of memory and learning.

The handbook was a success, being welcomed both by clinicians, and by colleagues with a more academic orientation. As a result, we were invited some years later to produce a revision (Baddeley, Wilson & Kopelman, 2002). By this point, we were able to include three excellent chapters on memory development and its disorders. What had happened in the meantime? The answer is that the huge importance of learning during childhood was finally being reflected in the research literature, which was increasingly being influenced by collaboration between developmental psychologists, practitioners and cognitive psychologists.

I myself was pleased to become a small part of this trend when, on retiring from the directorship of the MRC Applied Psychology Unit in Cambridge, I was able to join Susan Gathercole in Bristol to work on a MRC funded programme grant on working memory and learning disability. It was already becoming clear from research on short-term memory such as that of Ursula Bellugi and her colleagues (Bellugi, Marks, Bihrle & Sabo, 1988) that marked qualitative differences could be demonstrated between different groups of learning disabled people. A particularly clear instance was the dissociation between verbal and spatial STM found when comparing people with Down syndrome and people with Williams syndrome. We were fortunate in attracting two outstanding postdoctoral fellows to work on the project, Susan Pickering, who had previously been working on dyslexia, and Chris Jarrold, a developmental psychologist with experience of research on autism. Our programme aimed to combine the analysis of working memory deficits in people with varying degrees and forms of learning disability, at the same time as further developing the basic theoretical model of working memory.

Why working memory? Working memory is a system for holding and manipulating information during the performance of complex cognitive activities such as reasoning and active learning. As such, it can be regarded as the temporary memory system that underpins coherent thought. If that is the case, then any deficit in working memory may potentially have substantial implications for the ability of an individual to learn and to develop at a normal rate. Working memory is not, however, a simple unitary system. My own approach to the analysis of working memory developed from work carried out with Graham Hitch over 30 years ago (Baddeley & Hitch, 1974). It assumes that working memory can be divided into at least three separable components, namely an attentional control system (the *central executive*), coupled with temporary storage subsystems dealing respectively with verbal/ acoustic material (the *phonological loop*), and with visual and spatial storage and manipulation (the *visuospatial sketchpad*). A fourth component that uses a multidimensional code to allow information to be integrated between the subsystems and long-term memory (the *episodic buffer*) has subsequently been proposed (Baddeley, 2000), but the basic model is essentially unchanged, although over the years it has been considerably developed and elaborated (Baddeley, in press).

We already had some indication that children with specific language impairment might have problems with the phonological loop (Baddeley, Gathercole & Papagno, 1998; Gathercole & Baddeley, 1990), and suspected that deficits in other components of the model might be identified and used as a basis for a more detailed understanding of impaired learning capacity. This proved to be the case for both learning disability (see chapters by Jarrold et al., by Archibald & Gathercole, and by Pickering) and for education more generally (Pickering, 2006).

As the chapters that follow indicate, our own work was just part of a growing body of research on the role of working memory in learning disability; some focus on specific deficits, for example in reading or mathematics, while others approach the problem by studying a range of different aetiologies. At a theoretical level, I suspect that the study of learning disability will prove as fruitful to the analysis of working memory, as the study of amnesia was to the analysis of long-term episodic memory. At a practical level, a thorough understanding of the impact of working memory on learning disability is likely to prove vital to any principled approach to educating and supporting people with an impaired capacity for learning.

Alan Baddeley
Department of Psychology,
University of York

REFERENCES

Baddeley, A. D. (2000). The episodic buffer: A new component of working memory? *Trends in Cognitive Sciences, 4*(11), 417–423.

Baddeley, A. D. (in press). *Working memory, thought and action.* Oxford, UK: Oxford University Press.

Baddeley, A. D., Gathercole, S. E., & Papagno, C. (1998). The phonological loop as a language learning device, *Psychological Review, 105*(1), 158–173.

Baddeley, A. D., & Hitch, G. (1974). Working memory. In G. A. Bower (Ed.), *Recent advances in learning and motivation* Vol. 8 (pp. 47–90). New York: Academic Press.

Baddeley, A., Wilson, B., & Kopelman, M. (Eds.). (2002). *Handbook of memory disorders* (2nd ed.). Chichester, UK: John Wiley.

Baddeley, A. D., Wilson, B. A., & Watts, F. N. (1995). The psychology of memory. In A. Baddeley, B. Wilson, & M. Kopelman (Eds.), *Handbook of memory disorders* (pp. 3–25). Chichester, UK: John Wiley.

Bellugi, U., Marks, S., Bihrle, A., & Sabo, H. (1988). Dissociation between language and cognitive functions in Williams syndrome. In D. Bishop & K. Mogford (Eds.), *Language development in exceptional circumstances* (pp. 177–189). Hillsdale, NJ: Lawrence Erlbaum Associates, Inc.

Gathercole, S. E., & Baddeley, A. D. (1990). Phonological memory deficits in language-disordered children: Is there a causal connection? *Journal of Memory and Language, 29*, 336–360.

Pickering, S. (2006). *Working memory and education.* New York: Academic Press.

1   Introduction

Tracy Packiam Alloway

Working memory has been an extremely influential concept that in the last 30 years has guided empirical investigations and understanding of adult and developmental cognition, and, more recently, developmental disorders. The purpose of this book is to bring together researchers involved in applying and developing understanding of working memory in the context of a variety of developmental disorders, from learning disabilities to Williams syndrome.

Current understanding of working memory stems in large part from the working memory model initially advanced in 1974 by Baddeley and Hitch. At the core of this model is the central executive, responsible for controlling resources and monitoring information processing. A component responsible for integrating information from the subcomponents of working memory and long-term memory, known as the episodic buffer, has been recently proposed (Baddeley, 2000). Other cognitive functions have subsequently been associated with the central executive (Baddeley, 1996). These factors, known as attentional or executive functions, are thought to enable a person to successfully engage in independent and purposeful behaviours. These include the ability to suppress irrelevant information, shifting between multiple tasks, and monitoring and revising information held in working memory. In this volume, executive skills are discussed by Roodenrys with respect to children with attention deficit hyperactivity disorder, by Passolunghi in children with mathematical difficulties, and by Belleville et al. in autistic spectrum disorder.

The central executive is supported by two separate storage systems: The phonological loop functions as a temporary store for phonological information, and the visuospatial sketchpad is where visual and spatial representations are temporarily stored and manipulated. The chapters by Pickering and Alloway discuss the specificities of these storage components and their relationship to children with dyslexia and developmental coordination disorder (also known as dyspraxia), respectively.

Another key conceptualization of working memory has been put forward by Cowan (2005), according to which working memory is not a distinct entity, but rather an activated component of long-term memory. Other models of working memory incorporate concepts of attention in memory (e.g., Engle, Kane, & Tuholski, 1999) and temporal duration in performing memory tasks (e.g., Barrouillet, Bernardin, & Camos, 2004). The chapter by Vukovic and Siegel discusses reading comprehension difficulties in light of different working memory models.

Traditionally, working memory capacity is measured using complex span tasks (also known as dual tasks), which require the individual to engage in some form of immediate processing, such as reading sentences or mental arithmetic (e.g., Daneman & Carpenter, 1980) while maintaining information for recall. In contrast, short-term memory tasks only measure storage capacity. Such tasks include ones where the individual has to immediately recall a sequence of verbal or visuospatial information in the order it was presented. Measures of working-memory capacity are strongly related to performance in complex cognitive activities such as reasoning, grammatical understanding, reading comprehension, and mathematical skills. Children with weak working memory skills often struggle to reach expected levels of attainment in key educational domains such as literacy and mathematics, and may have learning difficulties that are sufficiently severe as to be recognized as having special educational needs.

Given the impact of working memory deficits on the child's abilities to acquire knowledge, develop crucial skills and benefit from formal education, the identification of working memory impairments is a priority for many working with young people with learning disabilities. One of the aims of this edited book is to support clinical assessment and management of working memory deficits by summarizing current theoretical understanding and methods of assessment of working memory, characterizing working memory function in individuals with a range of neurodevelopmental disorders, and identifying useful means of alleviating the anticipated learning difficulties of children with deficits of working memory.

Empirical tools and concepts developed in this dynamic field of research have proven extremely valuable in illustrating the characteristics of developmental disorders. This book also reflects the convergence of interest from different academic and professional groups, such as educators, cognitive psychologists, special needs coordinators, and developmental psychopathologists, in the role of working memory in atypical developmental populations. Drawing from the expertise of leading researchers in this area, this text integrates information from both normal and abnormal development to distinguish the contribution of working memory from general cognitive deficits during childhood.

The chapter by Pickering on dyslexia provides an overview of verbal and visuospatial memory deficits in children with dyslexia. She also discusses assessment tools such as the Working Memory Test Battery for Children (WMTB-C; Pickering & Gathercole, 2001) and the Automated Working Memory Assessment (AWMA; Alloway, Gathercole, & Pickering, 2004) that provide useful diagnostic information on the nature of working memory deficits in a dyslexic cohort.

Wagner and Muse provide a slightly different view of dyslexia. Specifically, they outline how developmental dyslexia is distinguished from acquired dyslexia, and can be characterized by deficits in both phonological short-term memory and phonological awareness. In particular, performance on short-term memory tasks such as nonword repetition is discussed in light of phonological coding skills and lexical knowledge.

In a related topic, Swanson presents meta-analyses of studies on reading disabilities and verbal working memory and short-term memory deficits. The findings indicate that working memory plays a significant role in accounting for individual differences in reading abilities. In particular, children with reading deficits struggle with tasks that place high demands on processing skills such as inhibiting conflicting information and updating relevant information.

A key feature in the literature in reading disabilities is that children can have adequate word reading skills, yet struggle in reading comprehension. Vukovic and Siegel review the research on the role of working memory in this cohort. These children have a generalized working memory deficit, and struggled with verbal working memory tasks that involved both words and numbers. This suggests that it is not purely a language deficit that characterizes children with reading comprehension difficulties, but also difficulty with the simultaneous process of storing and manipulating information.

A learning disability that can cooccur in children with reading problems is arithmetic learning disability. Passolunghi discusses the prevalence and criteria for such a diagnosis. She outlines the associations between working memory and different aspects of mathematical knowledge, such as simple arithmetic computations and arithmetic word problems. In addition, she also addresses executive skills such as inhibition, updating, and shifting in children with arithmetic learning disability.

Children with specific language impairment (SLI) are reliably identified with a short-term memory task, nonword repetition. Archibald and Gathercole extend the current understanding of memory impairments in this population to indicate that marked deficits in both verbal short-term memory and verbal working memory may be even more severe than the language impairments that form the basis for their diagnosis. Implications of these memory deficits for effective learning support for children with SLI and other related learning difficulties are considered.

An area that has received very little attention until recently is the working memory profiles of children with motor coordination difficulties (also known as dyspraxia or developmental coordination disorder). Alloway reviews current research which indicates that this cohort typically has normal verbal IQ scores but exhibits specific deficits in performance IQ tasks. New evidence on working memory skills is also presented. The findings indicate that children with motor coordination difficulties performed poorly in both verbal and visuospatial memory tasks, but had a selective deficit in visuospatial working memory tasks.

Roodenrys reviews differential findings on verbal and spatial working memory impairments in children with attention deficit hyperactivity disorder

(ADHD). He suggests that there is some evidence of a verbal working memory impairment, as well as comorbid reading disability. There is stronger evidence for an impairment in spatial working memory. These findings are discussed in light of research on poor inhibition skills.

Children with autistic spectrum disorder can exhibit a range of differential cognitive patterns. Belleville, Ménard, Mottron, and Ménard assess current models of the cognitive features that characterize autism. An interesting finding is that short-term memory skills among savant persons tend to be higher than in a normal population, using a range of material such as pseudowords, function words, and numerical material. There is some evidence that the ability to shift attention from one task to another is impaired in children with autism.

The chapter by Jarrold, Purser, and Brock illustrates how poor short-term memory skills in children with Down syndrome are manifest in different cognitive tasks. In particular, this chapter reviews vocabulary performance in this cohort and whether performance is constrained by individuals' relatively poor verbal short-term memory, or related factors such as hearing difficulties, speech production problems, and language delay, which are also associated with this condition.

Children with Williams syndrome are often found to have dissociable cognitive profiles in verbal and visual memory. Rowe and Mervis establish the relative strength in verbal short-term memory and language and severe weakness in visuospatial skills in children with Williams syndrome across different studies. This strength in verbal memory abilities is strongly related to grammatical ability and vocabulary ability, and is an association that continues to be significant through adolescence for children with Williams syndrome.

Taken together the chapters illustrate how the concept of working memory has been strongly influenced by not only experimental psychology, but also by clinical and neuropsychological research. It is intended that this volume will present the reader with current research in this area and how it pertains to developmental disorders. In addition, the inclusion of remedial approaches provide a background to emerging research on working memory intervention strategies.

REFERENCES

Alloway, T. P., Gathercole, S. E., & Pickering, S. J. (2004). *The Automated Working Memory Assessment* [Test battery]. Available from authors.

Baddeley, A. D. (1996). Exploring the central executive. *Quarterly Journal of Experimental Psychology, 49A*, 5–28.

Baddeley, A. D. (2000). The episodic buffer: A new component of working memory? *Trends in Cognitive Sciences, 4*, 417–423.

Baddeley, A. D., & Hitch, G. (1974). Working memory. In G. A. Bower (Ed.),

Advances in research and theory: Vol. 8. *The psychology of learning and motivation* (pp. 47–89). New York: Academic Press.

Barrouillet, P., Bernardin, S., & Camos, V. (2004). Time constraints and resource sharing in adults' working memory spans. *Journal of Experimental Psychology: General, 133*, 83–100.

Cowan, N. (2005). *Working memory capacity*. New York: Psychology Press.

Daneman, M., & Carpenter, P. A. (1980). Individual differences in working memory and reading. *Journal of Verbal learning and Verbal Behavior, 19*, 450–466.

Engle, R. W., Kane, M. J., & Tuholski, S. W. (1999). Individual differences in working memory capacity and what they tell us about controlled attention, general fluid intelligence and functions of the prefrontal cortex. In A. Miyake & P. Shah (Eds.), *Models of working memory: Mechanisms of active maintenance and executive control* (pp. 102–134). London: Cambridge Press.

Pickering, S. J., & Gathercole, S. E. (2001). *The Working Memory Test Battery for Children*. London: Harcourt Assessment.

2 Working memory in dyslexia

Susan J. Pickering

OVERVIEW

The focus of this chapter is the nature of immediate memory in developmental dyslexia and the contribution that a dynamic, multi-component model of working memory is able to make to the systematic study of individuals with dyslexia. The chapter begins by outlining some of the reasons why dyslexia is a difficult issue for scientific study: the lack of consensus on definition, cause, and even about who is dyslexic and who is not. There follows a description of a popular conceptualisation of immediate memory (the modal model) and a description of the findings of research investigating immediate verbal and visual memory that was carried out largely in the context of this model.

The second half of the chapter introduces the Baddeley and Hitch (1974) working memory model and argues that although this model has been in existence for over 30 years, it has not been employed in the systematic study of dyslexia until about a decade ago, and studies of this kind are still relatively few in number. Although the early data on immediate verbal and visual memory in dyslexia can be mapped onto the two "slave systems" of working memory (the phonological loop and the visuospatial sketchpad), arguably the most significant contribution of the working memory model to the study of dyslexia has been the suggestion of a central executive component that is involved in the active processing of information in immediate memory and in a number of attentional processes. Evidence from studies that have specifically investigated the central executive functioning of dyslexics (and other poor readers) appears to indicate deficits in this part of the memory system.

The final section of the chapter describes a tool for measuring the working memory performance of children across the three components of the Baddeley and Hitch model. The Working Memory Test Battery for Children (WMTB-C) has been administered to children with dyslexia, and other related developmental disorders, in order to investigate the relative profile of strengths and weaknesses in the three working memory components. Results from a series of small studies of these populations allows the investigation of two important questions: Do individuals with dyslexia have impairments in specific components of working memory, and, if so, do individuals with other developmental disorders show similar or different working memory profiles to the dyslexic population. The findings from these studies are discussed with respect to the theoretical and practical implications of detailed working memory assessment in individuals with developmental learning problems.

INTRODUCTION

When one asks the seemingly simple question: "Do individuals with dyslexia have problems with working memory?" one might expect a fairly simple answer – "yes" or "no". However, answering this question has turned out to be far less simple than one might expect. Many individuals with dyslexia (and those around them) will be very clear that their working memory is poor and that this is a key feature of their dyslexic difficulties. Ask practising psychologists with experience of assessing dyslexia, and they are also likely to agree that many of the individuals that they see have problems with immediate memory, as evidenced by poor scores on the Digit Span sub-tests of the Wechsler Intelligence Scale for Children (Wechsler, 1996), or other similar measures (e.g. Turner, 1997). However, ask a researcher about the nature of working memory in dyslexia, and the issue becomes more complex. Despite over 30 years of investigation in this area, there is still little consensus on the status of working memory in individuals with dyslexia, and whether deficits that are observed play a causal role in the dyslexia syndrome.

Developmental dyslexia is itself a difficult disorder to define. Indeed there is no one agreed definition of the problem, despite over 100 years of attempts to describe and explain it. Many would agree that the striking feature of individuals with dyslexia is their pronounced problems with acquiring and using literacy, despite overall levels of intellectual functioning that are at or above average for the population. The following definition is taken from the Orton Dyslexia Society, USA (1994, cited in Miles, 1995, p. 44):

> Dyslexia is one of several distinct learning disabilities. It is a specific language-based disorder of constitutional origin characterized by difficulties in single word decoding, usually reflecting insufficient phonological processing abilities. These difficulties in single word decoding are often unexpected in relation to age and other cognitive and academic abilities; they are not the result of generalized developmental disability or sensory impairment. Dyslexia is manifested by variable difficulty with different forms of written language, often including, in addition to problems reading, a conspicuous problem with acquiring proficiency in writing and spelling.

The above definition of dyslexia indicates that literacy is a major problem for individuals with dyslexia and places phonological processing difficulties at the heart of the disorder (see also Snowling, 1995). Other definitions of dyslexia exist, as do other explanations of the problem. At the present time there are at least two other major explanations of dyslexia in addition to the view that it is caused by phonological deficits (see Frith, 1997, for a review). One explanation focuses on problems in rapid temporal perception of both auditory and visual information (Miller & Tallal, 1995; Stein & Walsh, 1997) that are dependent upon differences in the magnocellular layers of the brain. The other sees dyslexia as being caused by differences in another part of the brain – the cerebellum (Nicolson & Fawcett, 1995). This theory of dyslexia suggests that dyslexia is characterised by a problem in automatising all skills, with complex multi-component skills, such as reading, creating the most challenges for the dyslexic.

The search for a definitive definition of dyslexia, and an explanation of why it occurs, is made particularly difficult for at least two reasons. The first reason is that individuals with dyslexia appear to manifest a range of characteristics that have been associated with the disorder. In this sense, therefore, the term dyslexia acts like an umbrella term for a syndrome with many different "symptoms". More importantly, however, different individuals with dyslexia may show different patterns of characteristics, meaning that one dyslexic individual may not seem very much like another. The internal variability of dyslexia causes many problems for those attempting to define and explain it, and also for those involved in the identification and assessment of the disorder. Problems in the identification and explanation of dyslexia also arise because many individuals with dyslexic difficulties also manifest characteristics associated with other developmental disorders, such as attention deficits (as found in attention deficit hyperactivity disorder, ADHD) and motor skills problems (as shown by individuals with developmental coordination disorder, or dyspraxia). Thus, one of the major challenges facing researchers and practitioners with an interest in dyslexia is that of establishing who is dyslexic and who is not.

The scientific study of working memory can also be characterised by debate and a lively research tradition. Our understanding of the structure and functioning of human memory continues to increase all the time. An important development in our understanding came during the 1960s when a model of memory known as the "modal model" became popular. This model suggested the existence of a unitary "short-term memory" (STM) with a strong dependence on phonological coding (e.g. Atkinson and Shiffrin, 1968). Information entered short-term memory after being received from the environment via a "sensory buffer", and if maintained in short-term memory long enough, would move to "long-term memory". However, by the early 1970s evidence was starting to build up to challenge this view of memory, particularly with respect to the short-term memory component of the model.

What followed was the beginning of a move towards reconceptualising immediate memory as "working memory", based on the work of Baddeley and colleagues (e.g. Baddeley, 1986; Baddeley & Hitch, 1974). This view that immediate memory can be characterised a dynamic, multi-component system continues strongly today. Research into the structure and function of working memory has been prolific. More recently, the role of working memory in the successful acquisition of a whole range of skills, such as reading, reading comprehension and arithmetic, has been investigated (e.g. Bull, Johnston & Roy, 1999; Cain, Oakhill & Bryant, 2004; McNeil & Johnston, 2004; see also Pickering, 2006).

Given that our understanding of working memory has been developing for 30 years, it is surprising to note how little impact the working memory conceptualisation of immediate memory has had on the study of memory in dyslexia. Studies using such a framework have only been carried out for about a decade, and are relatively small in number. However, the evidence from these studies suggests that investigation of working memory in dyslexia and other reading problems is a worthwhile activity, with much to gain from it.

This chapter presents an evaluation of the question "Do individuals with dyslexia have problems with working memory?" by examining recent research that has been undertaken that draws upon a multi-component view of working memory. In particular, it presents the findings of research carried out using a battery of tests designed to measure the three different components of the Baddeley and Hitch working memory model – the Working Memory Test Battery for Children (WMTB-C; Pickering & Gathercole, 2001). Using this research, two key issues are investigated: (a) Is working memory useful in providing a description of the deficits (and strengths) found in dyslexia? (b) Can working memory inform us about the relationship of dyslexia to other developmental disorders? In this chapter it will be argued that the multi-component working memory conceptualisation of immediate memory has provided those interested in the nature of memory in dyslexia with an extremely valuable tool with which to study dyslexia and the problems associated with it. Before tackling these issues, however, a brief review of some of the early research on the nature of immediate verbal and visual memory in dyslexia is presented.

THE NATURE OF IMMEDIATE VERBAL AND VISUAL MEMORY IN DYSLEXIA

One striking feature of the literature on immediate memory and dyslexia (or literacy problems more broadly) is that almost all studies (certainly until very recently) concerned the verbal aspects of short-term memory performance. This may have been influenced by the existence of the modal model of memory during the early stages of research activity in this area. However, it is also the case that concerted research activity in this field coincided with the development of a view of dyslexia as a language-based disorder. Indeed, many of the early memory studies were carried out by researchers in the highly influential Haskins Laboratories (e.g. Mann, Liberman & Shankweiler, 1980; Shankweiler, Liberman, Mark, Fowler & Fischer, 1979) who were largely responsible for the re-definition of dyslexia as a phonological (rather than visual) problem.

Experimental techniques for measuring immediate verbal memory had been in existence for some time and could be readily applied to children with dyslexia and other reading problems. One of the first verbal memory phenomena to feature in such investigations was the *phonological similarity effect*. When individuals are asked to recall sequences of letters or words, it is found that their performance is significantly worse when the memory items sound similar to one another (e.g. P, G, T, D, C) compared to when the memory items have dissimilar sounds (e.g. R, H, X, W, Y) (e.g. Baddeley, 1966; Conrad & Hull, 1964). It has been suggested that phonologically similar lists are more difficult to recall because information is held in a speech-based (phonological) code in verbal short-term memory, and therefore items with similar codes will be harder to discriminate from one another. Findings from a range of studies contrasting children with literacy difficulties with non-impaired control participants (Mann et al., 1980; Mark, Shankweiler, Liberman & Fowler, 1977; Shankweiler et al., 1979) indicated that poor readers were not as affected by the phonological similarity of the memory items as the controls. Poor readers performed worse than controls overall, but, more importantly, the difference between their scores in the similar and dissimilar conditions was not as great as for the controls. This finding has been interpreted to suggest that poor readers experience problems in accessing phonic representations during the memory task (e.g. Torgesen & Houck, 1980).

Subsequent studies of the phonological similarity effect in poor readers have provided less consistent evidence, however. Some studies have replicated the earlier finding (e.g. Siegel & Linder, 1984); others have not (e.g. Hall, Wilson, Humphries, Tinzmann & Bowyer, 1983; Johnston, 1982; Johnston, Rugg & Scott, 1987). One explanation for the lack of consistency in the findings of these studies is the effect of the age of the participants being studied. For example, Johnston (1993) has suggested that the lack of a phonological similarity effect is only found in younger poor readers, and this is because they find the task as a whole too difficult. In support of this view, Holligan and Johnston (1988) found that significantly increasing task difficulty caused even good readers to perform at comparable levels with both phonologically similar and phonologically dissimilar memory items.

How should the findings from the studies of phonological similarity effects be interpreted? Overall, it appears that poor readers can use phonological codes in short-term memory to some extent (Brady, Mann & Schmidt, 1987; Olson, Davidson, Kliegl & Davies, 1984), although their performance is poorer than that of good readers. When task difficulty is controlled appropriately, poor readers do display sensitivity to the phonological similarity of memory items, suggesting that immediate verbal memory is functioning at least on some level. Similar conclusions have been drawn from studies of *word length effects* (Macaruso, Locke, Smith & Powers, 1996). These effects are found when participants are asked to recall verbal items of differing spoken duration (e.g. "cat" versus "aluminium") (e.g., Baddeley, 1997). Children with dyslexia perform more poorly than controls on such tasks, providing further evidence of their problems with the use of phonological codes in immediate memory.

It has been known for some time that older children and adults typically take active steps to remember memory items during a task of immediate memory (e.g. Gathercole, 1999). Before the age of 7 years, children do not appear to engage in *rehearsal* of the memory items by saying the items to themselves, either overtly or covertly (Gathercole, Adams & Hitch, 1994; Gathercole & Hitch, 1993). The emergence of rehearsal as a strategy for the maintenance of items in immediate memory is associated with increases in performance on such tasks. Do children with dyslexia and other reading problems show evidence of rehearsal when carrying out tasks of immediate memory performance?

For rehearsal to benefit memory performance, it has to be carried out in a cumulative fashion. That is, as each memory item in the sequence is presented, it has to be added to the list of items already presented (and being rehearsed), and the whole list has to be rehearsed again. A study of dyslexic boys by Spring and Capps (1974) found that the dyslexic group were much less likely to carry out cumulative rehearsal than the control group, and the dyslexic group were found to be very poor at recalling all but the most recently presented items in the lists. Macaruso and colleagues (1996) also found that poor readers have problems with rehearsal of phonological information in immediate memory. Their research indicated a breakdown in cumulative phonological rehearsal, particularly in the middle of the memory lists. They have speculated that this may occur because of a switch away from phonological coding, to some other form of coding in memory.

Indeed, there is evidence to suggest that dyslexics and other poor readers are more likely to use non-phonological memory codes to remember information in a phonological memory task (Byrne & Shea, 1979; Hicks, 1980; Rack, 1985). Poor readers in a study by Byrne and Shea (1979) were found to be more likely to use a semantic (meaning-based) code for maintaining information, whereas Rack (1985) found evidence to suggest that poor readers were using visual codes to a greater extent than controls (see also Palmer, 2000a). A recent study by McNeil and Johnston (2004) has provided further evidence on this issue. They presented children who were poor readers (and reading age controls) with memory stimuli that were either pictorial or verbal. They found that the poor readers appeared to rely on visual information in tasks where presented images lent themselves strongly to visual coding and where verbal recoding was not obligatory. However, the poor readers did seem to make use of phonological coding when the memory stimuli were not highly visually codable. Taken together, the findings of these studies suggest that dyslexics and other poor readers may sometimes deal with the problems that they experience with phonological codes in working memory by relying on images, meaning, or both, in order to store memory items for later recall.

The speed that we can articulate words appears to be linked to our capacity to hold information in working memory. Baddeley, Thomson and Buchanan (1975) have suggested that a person's memory span represents the number of items that can be uttered in about 2 seconds. Both memory span and *articulation rate* increase over childhood, and it has been proposed that articulation rate plays an important role in the development of memory across childhood (Hulme, Thomson, Muir & Lawrence, 1984; Nicolson, 1981). Rate of articulation may determine how quickly the phonological rehearsal process can re-present memory items to refresh the steadily decaying contents of verbal immediate memory.

McDougall, Hulme, Ellis and Monk (1994) studied the short-term memory and articulation rate of good, average and poor readers. They found that observed differences in memory performance could be accounted for by differences in articulation rate between the groups. Macaruso and colleagues (1996) have also suggested that speed of articulation may be reduced in children with dyslexia. They argue that the poor performance of dyslexics on immediate memory tasks may stem from a combination of less precise phonological codes (which may be more susceptible to confusion during rehearsal) and reduced speed of articulation (which limits the amount of information that can be rehearsed).

Tests of immediate verbal memory can involve a range of different kinds of stimuli. Tasks that require the recall of words, numbers or other familiar material are thought to draw on information stored in long-term memory as well as placing demands on immediate verbal memory. Stimuli such as numbers and words can be processed semantically and/or visually, also reducing the reliance on the immediate verbal memory system. One approach that has been designed to minimise the effects of long-term memory on immediate verbal recall has involved the use of nonsense words as memory items. By using nonsense words such as "doppelate" or "blonterstaping" (Children's Test of Nonword Repetition; Gathercole & Baddeley, 1996), the contribution of knowledge about one's language stored in long-term memory is significantly reduced, and participants are dependent upon their immediate verbal memory when trying to recall each item. Performance on tests involving nonsense words is usually much worse than for tests involving real familiar words. This phenomenon is referred to as the *lexicality effect* (e.g. Hulme, Maughan & Brown, 1991).

A number of studies have tried to locate mechanisms that might be responsible for the lexicality effect and two important sources of influence have been found. One influential factor is our stored knowledge of words in long-term memory. It has been suggested that partially decayed representations of words in immediate verbal memory can be recovered using a process referred to as *redintegration* (Hulme et al., 1991; Schweikert, 1993). This involves the comparison of the partially decayed trace to words held in long-term memory. The chance of selecting the right output is based upon the status of the decaying memory trace and the number of possible candidates that match it. This process cannot be applied to the recall of unfamiliar nonsense words as there are no candidates in long-term memory with which to compare the partially decayed trace. However, we do appear to have knowledge of the typical sound patterns of our language (known as phonotactics), and this knowledge also seems to play a role in the reconstruction of decaying traces in immediate verbal memory (Gathercole, Pickering, Hall & Peaker, 2001).

Studies that have required dyslexics and other poor readers to recall nonsense words have tended to find significant deficits in performance compared to non-impaired controls (e.g. Snowling, 1981; Snowling, Goulandris, Bowlby & Howell, 1986). Such tasks require the use of phonological codes in immediate memory and do not easily lend themselves to alternative forms of coding or support from long-term memory. Interestingly, a study by Roodenrys and Stokes (2001) found that poor readers appeared to be affected by the lexicality effect in a very similar way to control participants. This provides an indication that the locus of the deficits in verbal memory in dyslexia is the immediate memory system, as long-term memory appears to be working to provide support for immediate memory performance in the same way as for children without reading problems.

The above review provides evidence of a range of ways in which the verbal immediate memory system of children with dyslexia and other reading problems appears to function differently to that of children without such problems. Children with reading problems tend to experience difficulties with using phonological codes in immediate memory, often using other codes in their place. Their ability to recall material that cannot be supported by information in long-term memory (e.g. nonsense words) is significantly impaired. Rehearsal, and in particular the use of a cumulative rehearsal process, also appears to be affected (e.g. Bauer, 1977).

Problems in the use of phonological information in immediate memory fit well with one of the current major theoretical explanations of dyslexia as a disorder *caused* by problems in phonological processing. Indeed, Hulme and Roodenrys (1995) have argued that the verbal short-term memory problems found in poor readers are an index of other phonological deficits, rather than a causal factor in reading disability. Evidence to support the alternative view – that phonological short-term memory plays a role in reading and reading disorders over and above that predicted by more general phonological skills – also exists (e.g. Baddeley & Gathercole, 1992; Rohl & Pratt, 1995). This issue is complex and the subject of some debate. It will be discussed further in the final section of this chapter, in the light of more recent evidence on the working memory performance of individuals with dyslexia.

Dyslexia has not always been conceived as a language-based disorder.

Until the 1970s there was a general view that the deficits experienced by dyslexics were of a visual nature (e.g. Orton, 1937) and correlations between visual immediate memory and reading had been reported by a number of researchers (e.g. Carroll, 1973). This view was strongly refuted by Vellutino and colleagues (Vellutino, Pruzek, Steger, & Meshoulam, 1973; Vellutino, Steger, DeSetto & Phillips, 1975) who found that poor readers and control participants did not differ from one another in their immediate memory for unfamiliar visual items. One factor that did seem to influence performance, however, was the extent to which the visual stimuli could be phonologically recoded (i.e. named). A study by Swanson (1978) provided evidence for this view. In the study, poor readers and control participants were asked to remember a series of nonsense shapes; half of the participants were taught names for the shapes. It was found that while the good readers outperformed the poor readers in the groups that were taught the names of the shapes, the performance of the good and poor readers who were not taught names was equivalent. Overall, these findings suggest that poor readers experience problems on tasks of immediate visual memory only when the stimuli involved can be named (and hence stored as phonological codes).

Other studies have also indicated that dyslexics and other poor readers do not differ from one another in their visual immediate memory. For example, Liberman, Mann, Shankweiler and Werfelman (1982) gave good and poor readers two types of visual stimuli in a recognition task: unfamiliar faces and abstract line drawings, neither type of stimuli lending itself easily to phonological recoding. The performance of the two groups was not found to be significantly different on this task. Similar findings were reported in a study by Katz, Shankweiler and Liberman (1981). When good and poor readers were asked to remember doodle drawings, they performed at equivalent levels to one another. However, when the stimuli were common objects, the good readers significantly outperformed the poor readers. Studies by Hulme (1981) and Vellutino (1979) have produced similar findings, and performance on the Corsi blocks task has also been found to be unimpaired in poor readers (e.g. Gould & Glencross, 1990).

Given that some practitioners and researchers have suggested that dyslexics can be classified as being broadly "auditory", broadly "visual" or "mixed" (e.g. Boder, 1973), one might ask: "Do visual dyslexics experience problems with visual immediate memory?" A study by Howes, Bigler, Lawson and Burlingame (1999) attempted to investigate this issue by giving the Test of Memory and Learning (TOMAL; Reynolds & Bigler, 1994) to children that had been classified as either auditory or visual dyslexics using Boder's criteria. They found that although all of the children showed problems with verbal memory, some children also manifested additional visual memory deficits. Thus for at least some children, visual memory problems may be associated with reading problems. Indeed, evidence from a study by Meyler and Breznitz (1998) suggests that the predominantly verbal nature of immediate memory problems in individuals with reading problems might be associated with the nature of the language used by those individuals. In a study of Hebrew-speaking participants, visual immediate memory was found to be related to reading performance. Clearly, further research is needed to examine the relationships between immediate visual and verbal memory and reading in a range of languages other than English.

THE DEVELOPMENT OF THE CONCEPT OF WORKING MEMORY

Over the last 30 years, there has been an increasing recognition that immediate memory is more than simply verbal and visual short-term storage. By the early 1970s a number of limitations had been identified with the modal model of memory that questioned its validity as an accurate account of human memory processes. One such limitation concerned the view that short-term memory was served by a unitary store, capable of dealing with information in a verbal and visual code. Research by Baddeley and colleagues (Baddeley & Hitch, 1974; Baddeley, Lewis, Eldridge & Thomson, 1984) suggested that short-term memory was composed of more than one component. They found that when a test of short-term memory (a digit span task) was combined with another activity that also required the use of short-term memory (e.g. the comprehension of prose passages), performance on the two tasks was not completely impaired, as would be expected if there were a unitary short-term store. The model that was subsequently proposed to capture the multi-component nature of immediate memory has been referred to as the "working memory model", and been responsible for a vast amount of research since its proposal in 1974.

The working memory model has been modified and fine-tuned since its original conception. The most well known version of the model includes three components: a *central executive* and two slave systems (the *phonological loop* and the *visuospatial sketchpad*). More recently, a fourth component has been added – an *episodic buffer* (Baddeley, 2000). Each modification has come in the context of research findings that have served to challenge the extent to which the model is capable of accounting for the way that immediate memory is found to operate in the real world.

It is also worth noting that the Baddeley and Hitch working memory model is not the only conceptualisation of working memory, a fact that is almost certainly represented across the pages of this book. Other interpretations of the structure and function of working memory exist (see Andrade, 2001). This debate is healthy, and serves to keep the research in this area interesting and alive. It is also important to recognise that, as a consequence of the variation in the conceptualisation of working memory, the way that this aspect of cognition has been investigated with respect to dyslexia has also tended to vary from researcher to researcher.

One of the biggest discrepancies between the theoretical specification of immediate memory as indicated in the modal model, and that emanating from the working memory model, is the inclusion of the central executive component. Prior to the existence of the working memory model, data had already been collected that was subsequently accounted for by the structures and functions of the phonological loop and the visuospatial sketchpad. The phonological loop, for example, a two-sub-component structure for the storage and rehearsal of verbal information, fits well with the data on verbal immediate memory in dyslexia outlined earlier. Although less intensively researched than the phonological loop, the visuospatial sketchpad is the component that is thought to store visual and spatial information for short periods of time. This part of the working memory system is therefore well placed to handle the data on visual immediate memory described above.

However, until relatively recently, the third component of the working memory system had not been systematically investigated with respect to dyslexia – for a number of important reasons. The first of these reasons is that for a long time the central executive had tended to serve as a "useful ragbag" (Baddeley & Logie, 1999, p. 39) containing all of the working memory phenomena that had not been accounted for by other parts of the system. The central executive is thought to carry out a number of different roles (Baddeley, 1996) and in recent years there has been an effort to state explicitly what these roles might be, and to attempt to design techniques for measuring them. This, then, has been another reason why there has been relatively little research attempting to investigate the nature of central executive functioning in dyslexia: Without a clear idea of what this component does, it has been difficult to design tasks to measure it.

So what does the central executive do? This issue is a matter of debate, but some of the suggested functions are described below. In 1999, Baddeley and Logie suggested that the central executive is involved in the control and regulation of the whole working memory system, including the coordination of the slave systems, focusing and switching attention, and activating representations on long-term memory. More recently, however, with the inclusion of the fourth working memory component – the episodic buffer – Baddeley (2000) has suggested that the central executive plays roles that are purely attentional in nature, such as focusing, switching, dividing and inhibiting attention. Some of the tasks previously ascribed to the central executive have now been assigned to the episodic buffer, for example, interfacing with long-term memory (Baddeley, 2001).

The central executive has also been linked to tasks that involve maintaining information in memory while simultaneously manipulating that, or other, information. A number of tasks have been designed to sample this aspect of working memory function. Collectively known as complex span tasks, these tests involve the requirement to hold information in mind while processing other information. In listening or reading span tasks (e.g. Daneman & Carpenter, 1980), participants hear or read sentences and have to respond to the sentences by judging their veracity, or providing a missing word. After hearing or reading a number of sentences, they are then required to recall the last word of each sentence, in the order that they were encountered. Another complex span task, counting span (Case, Kurland & Goldberg, 1982) involves counting arrays of dots and recalling successive dot tallies. These tasks can be extremely taxing, with adults often finding them very demanding.

Regardless of the debate that surrounds the concept of the central executive, this aspect of cognitive functioning has become an extremely popular subject for research in the last decade. By incorporating the central executive into any model of immediate memory we are in a position to go beyond the simple storage of verbal and visual information to consider a dynamic system that is capable of dealing flexibly with information in a range of domains. It is the *working memory model* that will be discussed in the rest of this chapter, therefore, as research on the role of working memory in dyslexia is presented.

WORKING MEMORY AND DYSLEXIA

In the earlier review of immediate verbal and visual memory in dyslexia it was argued that individuals with literacy difficulties appear to experience problems on tasks of phonological short-term memory. Reconceptualising these findings using a working memory framework, we can see that dyslexia, and poor reading more generally, appears to be associated with problems in the phonological loop component of working memory. The phonological loop has been suggested to contain two sub-components: a phonological store and a phonological rehearsal process. Findings from the studies outlined above do not allow us to decide whether the dyslexic problem lies in the storage or rehearsal processes (or both) carried out by this part of the memory system, or indeed, whether the memory problem is secondary to a more general phonological processing deficit that affects all tasks that rely on the use of phonological codes (e.g. Hulme & Roodenrys, 1995).

Despite the general view that immediate visual memory appears unaffected in dyslexia, at least a small amount of evidence leads us to question the generalisability of this conclusion to all individuals with reading problems. Here, too, research concerned with learning more about the structure and processes of the visuospatial sketchpad can be applied usefully to the issue of immediate memory in dyslexia. For example, in the last decade it has been suggested that the visuospatial sketchpad is also made up of two separable sub-components. Although there is some debate as to the specific nature of the sub-components, it has been hypothesised that one sub-component is specialised for dealing with information of a static visual nature and the other component for information of a dynamic spatial kind (Logie, 1995; Pickering, Gathercole, Hall & Lloyd, 2001; see Pickering, 2001, for a review). Evidence to support this fractionation of visuospatial working memory has depended largely on the availability of two tasks: the Visual Patterns Test (Della Sala, Gray, Baddeley & Wilson, 1997) and the Corsi blocks task (e.g., Milner, 1971). Experimental and neuro-psychological studies carried out with these tasks (e.g. Della Sala, Gray, Baddeley, Allamano & Wilson, 1999; Logie & Pearson, 1997) indicate that performance on the two tasks can be dissociated.

Although it was noted above that dyslexics were not found to show deficits on the Corsi blocks task (Gould & Glencross, 1990), the use of this task in isolation does not inform us about the nature of the entire visuospatial sketchpad as it is currently conceptualised. As we continue to research this aspect of the working memory system and learn more about the structures and processes that allow us to hold visual and spatial information in memory, this knowledge can be systematically applied to individuals with dyslexia, to learn more about how and why they perform the way they do.

Over the last decade, a number of researchers have attempted to explore the nature of central executive function in individuals with dyslexia and other reading problems. For example, Swanson and his colleagues have carried out a range of studies in which tasks designed to measure central executive function have been applied to individuals with reading problems (e.g. Swanson, 1992, 1993a, 1993b, 1994, 1999; Swanson & Alexander, 1997; Swanson & Ashbaker, 2000; Swanson, Ashbaker & Lee, 1996).

In one study, Swanson (1994) investigated how central executive function related to literacy in children and adults. Participants in the study were given measures of verbal and visuospatial short-term memory and measures of central executive function, in order to contrast the relative importance of the first two types of cognitive activity (storage of information only) with the third type of cognitive activity (storage and processing of information). Here we can see that the first two types of cognitive activity broadly map onto the processes associated with the phonological loop and visuospatial sketchpad of the Baddeley and Hitch model, with the third type of activity associated with the suggested functions of the central executive. Swanson found that the tasks that involved both storage and processing made the greater contribution to reading recognition. In addition it was found that, although short-term memory processes related to performance in reading comprehension for poor readers, it made no such contribution to the reading comprehension of controls. Two important points therefore arise from this study: The memory deficits of poor readers go beyond short-term memory (i.e. storage only), and different memory processes may be used by individuals with and without reading problems when carrying out reading-related tasks.

Swanson and colleagues have carried out further studies in an attempt to clarify the nature of the observed deficit in central executive function in poor readers. Swanson and Ashbaker (2000), for example, explored the role that articulation rate played in the relationship between executive processing and reading. It was found that both the short-term memory and central executive performance of poor readers was worse than that of both chronological- and reading-age matched control participants, even after the contribution of articulation rate had been removed from the analyses. Additionally, central executive performance was found to predict reading performance independently of the contribution of both short-term memory and articulation rate (see also Cohen & Heath, 1990). Together these findings suggest that poor readers have a deficit in the central executive component of working memory that is independent of any deficits they may have in the phonological loop. Perhaps, therefore, poor readers experience problems in not just one, but two parts of the working memory system: the phonological loop *and* the central executive.

Other studies that have investigated the nature of central executive functioning in dyslexics and other poor readers provide yet further evidence on this issue. For example, a study by Siegel (1994) found that executive processes were related to reading in individuals ranging from 6 to 49 years of age. Isaki and Plante (1997) also found that adults with and without reading problems scored differently on tasks of central executive and short-term memory function. De Jong (1998) reports similar findings, and has subsequently suggested that poor readers' deficits in central executive function reflect a general lack of capacity for simultaneous processing and storage of information, rather than a processing deficiency or specific problem with verbal short-term memory. De Jong suggests that the fundamental problem for poor readers may be their poor ability to store phonological information in short-term memory, and that this problem manifests itself most severely when there is a requirement to manipulate phonological codes dynamically, as in the case of a typical central executive task. By this account, poor readers will exhibit problems with phonological loop function, but these problems will be significantly exacerbated when phonological codes are incorporated into central executive activity. The failure to efficiently store and manipulate information in working memory is likely to have a huge impact on literacy due to the many occasions in which complex cognitive activities – such as storing the phonemes of a word long enough to allow blending, storing the words in a sentence long enough to achieve meaning and remembering the phonological and visual form of a word when writing it down – are essential to the use of written language.

Palmer (2000a) has provided further evidence of central executive deficits in a group of dyslexic teenagers. When asked to carry out a task commonly used to measure an aspect of central executive function related to the ability to switch attention and inhibit responses (the Wisconsin Card Sorting Task), the participants of this study showed signs of preservation errors. Based on these and other findings (e.g. Palmer, 2000b), Palmer has suggested that the central executive plays an important role in the development of literacy because it facilitates the ability to inhibit the use of visual processing strategies in favour of phonological ones during the reading process. Her sample of dyslexic teenagers appeared to be using visual coding strategies during reading at a stage at which this approach is no longer an efficient route to reading success. Thus, we can see that another way in which the central executive may play a role in reading is in the development of phonological strategies for reading to replace the earlier visual strategies that appear to characterise the approach to reading taken by very young children.

As the range of techniques designed to measure the central executive component of working memory increases, the number of studies that apply such tasks to individuals with dyslexia and other reading problems has also slowly increased. At the time of writing this chapter, it is clear to see that the influence of the working memory model conceptualisation of immediate memory has increased significantly. Immediate memory is very rarely (if ever) conceived in terms of the outmoded unitary short-term store. A multi-component dynamic view of memory has provided, and continues to provide, the basis for a range of studies of dyslexia and other reading problems. In my own research, this has been made possible by the translation of the concept of the three components of the working memory model into a coherent test battery – a tool for measuring working memory in children across all three components of the system.

In 1995 Sue Gathercole and I began work on a project designed to create a standardised tests of working memory that could be given to children of school age. Before making a start on the test, we carried out experimental research to increase our knowledge of children's working memory development, in domains in which such knowledge was lacking (e.g. Gathercole, Frankish, Pickering & Peaker, 1999; Pickering, Gathercole & Peaker, 1998; Pickering et al., 2001). By combining the information gained from these studies with what had already been written about working memory in children, we were in a position to choose a set of tests to measure performance in the phonological loop, visuospatial sketchpad and central executive components of working memory. A prototype battery was developed that included a mixture of well-known tests of working memory (such as digit recall) and newer tests that had been developed during our experimental work (such as the word list matching task) (see Table 2.1 for a description of the prototype battery). When the prototype battery was administered to children of 6 and 7 years of age, it was found that performance on the battery was related to performance on standardised tests of vocabulary, literacy and arithmetic (Gathercole & Pickering, 2000a), to scores on National Curriculum assessments at Key Stage 1 (Gathercole & Pickering, 2000b) and to be capable of identifying children with special educational needs from those children without special needs (Gathercole & Pickering, 2001).

Of the 13 sub-tests included in the prototype battery, nine were included in the final version of the working memory test (see Table 2.2 for a description of the WMTB-C sub-tests). A 10th test was standardised at the same time as the nine Working Memory Test Battery for Children (WMTB-C) sub-tests, but not included in the test as such. This extra test, the Visual Patterns Test (Della Sala et al., 1997) had already been published as a neuro-psychological test for adults, and, although very straightforward to administer to children,

Table 2.1 Tests included in the prototype version of the WMTB-C

Digit Recall	Phonological loop	Sequences of digits are presented in spoken format. The child is required to recall each list immediately, in the correct order.
Word List Matching	Phonological loop	Sequences of one syllable words are presented twice in spoken format. The child is asked to detect whether changes in serial order occur in the second presentation of the sequence.
Nonword List Matching	Phonological loop	As for Word List Matching except that stimuli are one-syllable nonsense words.
Word List Recall	Phonological loop	Sequences of one syllable words are presented in spoken format. The child is required to recall each list immediately, in the correct order.
Nonword List Recall	Phonological loop	As for Word List Recall except that stimuli are one-syllable nonsense words.
Matrices Static	Visuo-spatial sketchpad	Abstract patterns composed of black and white squares in a matrix are presented. The child is required to recall the location of the black squares.
Matrices Dynamic	Visuo-spatial sketchpad	Each black square in the matrices pattern is presented one at a time in a special sequence. The child is required to recall the sequence.
Mazes Static	Visuo-spatial sketchpad	Routes through two-dimensional mazes are presented as line drawings. The child is required to draw the route into an empty maze.
Mazes Dynamic	Visuo-spatial sketchpad	Routes through two-dimensional mazes are traced with the experimenter's finger. The child is required to draw the route into an empty maze.
Listening Recall	Central executive	A series of sentences are presented for which the child is required to respond either "true" or "false". Follwing this, the child is required to recall the final word from each sentence, in the order that they were heard.
Counting Recall	Central executive	The child is presented with a series of cards bearing dots. The child counts each card of dots and then recalls the dot totals, in the order that they were encountered.
Backward Digit Recall	Central executive	Sequences of digits are presented in spoken format. The child is required to recall each list immediately, in reverse order.

Table 2.2 Tests included in the WMTB-C

Digit Recall	Phonological loop	See Table 2.1
Word List Matching	Phonological loop	See Table 2.1
Word List Recall	Phonological loop	See Table 2.1
Nonword List Recall	Phonological loop	See Table 2.1
Block Recall	Visuo-spatial sketchpad	The examiner taps sequences on nine identical blocks attached to a board. The child recalls the sequence in the correct order.
Mazes Memory	Visuo-spatial sketchpad	The child is shown a two-dimensional maze containing a route. The maze is removed from view and the child has to recall the route by drawing it in an empty maze.
Visual Patterns Test	Visuo-spatial sketchpad	The child is shown a two-dimensional matrix made up of black and white squares. The child is required to recall the location of the black squares in an empty matrix.
Listening Recall	Central executive	See Table 2.1
Counting Recall	Central executive	See Table 2.1
Backward Digit Recall	Central executive	See Table 2.1

had never been previously standardised on a child population. Thus, norms for the Visual Patterns Test feature in the manual for the WMTB-C.

Modifications to the prototype battery were carried out in order to increase the efficiency of the test. Sub-tests chosen to be included in the WMTB-C were those measures that had proved most useful and reliable in the prototype battery. All sub-tests were designed to have a "span" procedure whereby difficulty level is systematically increased throughout the sub-test. All sub-tests begin at a very low level of difficulty and then difficulty level is increased (usually by increasing the number of memory items by one) every six trials. This feature allows children to continue through the sub-test until performance breaks down significantly (three incorrect trials out of a possible six), at which time the administration of that sub-test is stopped.

The WMTB-C was standardised on 750 children from the City of Bristol and surrounding areas. Norms for the test are available for children ranging in age from 4 years and 6 months to 15 years and 6 months (see Pickering & Gathercole, 2001, for more information). Analysis of data collected during the standardisation indicates that the nine sub-tests included in the battery represent three related, but distinct, aspects of cognition. Specifically, the four sub-tests designed to measure phonological loop function: Digit Recall, Word List Matching, Word List Recall and Nonword List Recall, were all found to load together when investigated with factor analysis, and to separate from the other tests in the battery. The same was found to be true for the two (three) sub-tests measuring visuospatial sketchpad function: Block Recall, Mazes Memory (and the Visual Patterns Test), and the three tests designed to measure central executive function: Listening Recall, Counting Recall and Backward Digit Recall. Thus, the test appeared to provide an assessment of three distinct, but related, aspects of working memory performance. On the basis of this the test was designed in such a way that, in addition to calculating standardised scores for each individual sub-test in the battery, three component scores could also be calculated: one for each of the three components of the working memory system.

The development of a standardised test of working memory that reflects the tripartite structure of the working memory system (as it was conceived at the time of the development of the battery) has provided researchers and practitioners with information that was not previously obtainable. That is, rather than using a series of piecemeal tests of memory, such as measures of digit span, and tests from the experimental literature that had not been standardised, the WMTB-C allowed users to sample across the working memory system to establish a profile of relative performance in the three components of working memory. This information has great potential value, as evidence from a range of sources appears to suggest that the different components of working memory are both functionally separable, and perhaps more importantly, differentially related to performance in particular educational domains (and to learning problems in these domains) (see this volume, and Pickering, 2006).

Thus, one of the questions one might ask of research using such a working memory test battery is: Do different problems with learning have a particular WMTB-C profile associated with them? In other words, is there a "signature" WMTB-C profile associated with dyslexia (or developmental coordination disorder, or ADHD, or SLD . . . and so on)? And if this is so – what implications does it have for our understanding of the nature of dyslexia: What it is, and how best to help individuals who have it? In what follows, I present data from a number of small-scale studies that have attempted to address these questions.

APPLYING THE WMTB-C TO DYSLEXIA

The first study in which we systematically investigated working memory performance in children with dyslexia involved the prototype version of the memory battery. In this study (Pickering & Gathercole, 2005), the 13 tests that made up the prototype battery were administered to 15 children with developmental dyslexia and two groups of 15 control participants: one matched for chronological age, and a younger group matched for reading age. Six tests of phonological loop function were included: Digit Recall, Word List Matching, Nonword List Matching, Word List Recall, Nonword List Recall and the Children's Test of Nonword Repetition. Children received four tests of visuospatial sketchpad performance. These tests were based on experimental work that we had carried out prior to the development of the battery and were a Matrices Task with a static and a dynamic version, and a Mazes Task, also with a static and dynamic version. The three tests of central executive function were the Listening Recall task, the Counting Recall task and Backward Digit Recall.

The first notable finding from this study is that the performance of the children with dyslexia varied across the three components of the working memory system. Performance on the tests of phonological loop function was found to be significantly poorer than that of the children of the same age. In addition, it was found that performance of the dyslexic group on the Children's Test of Nonword Repetition was marginally lower than that for the younger children of the same reading age. This finding supports the view that children with dyslexia have pronounced difficulties with the repetition of unfamiliar phonological forms, and in some cases these are worse than would be predicted based on their reading performance.

In contrast to the poorer performance of the dyslexic group on the tests of phonological loop function, scores on three of the four visuospatial sketchpad tests were comparable to that of the chronological age-matched controls, providing support for the view that, for this group of dyslexics at least, visuospatial memory did not seem to be impaired. The test that did prove more difficult for the dyslexic children was the static version of the Matrices task. The specific reason for this finding is unclear, however previous research with tasks of a similar nature to the Matrices static task has found evidence to suggest that older children and adults might engage in phonological recoding of the visually presented stimuli (Miles, Morgan, Milne & Morris, 1996). Given that children with reading problems appear to experience difficulties with phonological coding in working memory, it is possible that they are not able to employ such a strategy as easily as the controls, or may not benefit as much from its use. Further research is needed to examine these possibilities.

Perhaps of greatest interest to us were the results from the tests of central executive performance. Given that very few studies had been carried out in this area, we were not sure what to expect from the dyslexic group in comparison to the controls. It was found that the performance of the dyslexic group was very poor on two of the three central executive tasks: Counting Recall and Backward Digit Recall. Scores on these two tasks were noticeably lower than those for the younger reading age controls. Somewhat surprisingly, the dyslexic group did not perform any worse than the controls on the Listening Recall task. Again, it is not clear why the children with dyslexia were able to perform so well on a task that is found to be difficult even for unimpaired individuals. One possible explanation is that the dyslexic group employed a different (and perhaps more effective) strategy when carrying out this task. That is, given the highly verbal nature of the task, children *without dyslexia* would be very likely to code the incoming information phonologically, whereas children with phonological coding problems might employ visual and/or semantic strategies to encode and maintain the test stimuli. Anecdotal reports from later studies using this test support this view, however, additional research is required to establish if this explanation is correct.

This initial study of working memory in dyslexia, using the prototype version of the working memory battery, thus provides us with the following information. Children with dyslexia do seem to experience problems with their phonological loop function, however, their performance in this area is not dissimilar to that for the reading age matched controls, suggesting that this aspect of memory functions at levels that would be expected based on the reading ability of the children. As indicated by the earlier studies by Swanson and Vellutino, visuospatial sketchpad function appears to be at chronological age appropriate levels, except in a task where phonological recoding of memory items might have been possible. Finally, using three tests of central executive function that require the ability to simultaneously hold and process information in memory, it was found that performance was very poor on two out of three of the tasks. However, we may also note that when non-phonological coding strategies are available during such a task, performance may not be so severely impaired.

Two further studies have investigated the working memory performance of children with dyslexia using the shorter and more refined Working Memory Test Battery for Children (WMTB-C). In both cases the pattern of results was found to be the same as that described above.

One study (Pickering & Chubb, 2005) administered the WMTB-C to children while attending a local Dyslexia Centre in the South-West of England. The participants: 17 children with developmental dyslexia (mean age 10:5 years, mean reading age 8:7 years), and 17 reading age-matched controls (mean age 7:7 years, mean reading age 8:8 years – recruited from local primary schools), were given the nine sub-tests of the WMTB-C, plus the Visual Patterns Test. Figure 2.1 shows the standardised profile of performance of the two groups on the WMTB-C.

Inspection of Figure 2.1 indicates that the standard scores of the reading age controls were in many cases superior to those of the dyslexic children. This does not, of course, mean that their absolute performance was better – scores for each group have been compared to norms derived from children of their own age. For the WMTB-C, average performance for the population is represented as a standard score of 100 (with a standard deviation of 15). In many cases the control group have performed at above average levels on many of the WMTB-C sub-tests; the performance of the dyslexic group lies either at or below average. Surprisingly, the profile of performance across the three domains of working memory shows lowest scores for the dyslexic group on

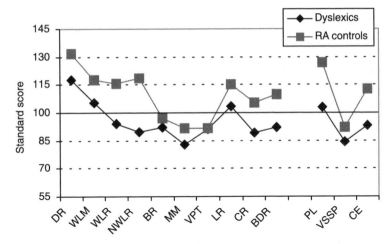

Figure 2.1 Performance of children with dyslexia and reading age controls on the WMTB-C.

the tests of visuospatial sketchpad function. However, we can see that this is also true for the control group. We can also see that the apparent discrepancy between the dyslexic and control groups on the visuospatial sketchpad tests is smaller than that for the other tests in the battery. These discrepancies were therefore investigated more closely. Analysis of the performance of the dyslexic and control group participants for the phonological loop (PL), visuospatial sketchpad (VSSP) and central executive (CE) component scores indicated significant differences for the PL and CE components, but not the VSSP component. The standard scores of the dyslexic group were found to be significantly lower than those for the controls on the Word and Nonword List Recall sub-tests, the Counting Recall sub-test and the Backward Digit Recall sub-test.

Thus, we can see that, although the overall profile of WMTB-C scores for the dyslexic and reading age control groups shows some variability, the points at which the two groups show greatest divergence in their performance is in the tests of phonological loop and central executive function, with no significant differences emerging in their visuospatial sketchpad performance.

A subsequent study replicated this finding in Greek children from Athens and the surrounding area (Pickering & Zacharof, 2005). For this study, a shortened and modified version of the WMTB-C was developed for use with Greek-speaking children. Six sub-tests were included in this battery: Digit Recall and a Greek version of the Nonword Recall test to measure phonological loop function; the Visual Patterns test and Block Recall to measure visuospatial sketchpad function; and Counting Recall and Backward Digit Recall to measure central executive function. The six sub-tests were given to

19 Greek children with a diagnosis of dyslexia (mean age 9:6 years) and 21 chronological age-matched controls (mean age 9:3 years). Figure 2.2 shows the performance of the two groups on the modified WMTB-C. Here we can see that the children with dyslexia performed significantly worse than the controls on the two tests of phonological loop function and the two tests of central executive function. From these findings it is therefore possible to extend our view of this pattern of working memory performance from the English and American children with dyslexia who have tended to provide most data on this issue, to Greek children with the same literacy problems.

In the Introduction to this chapter, it was noted that the conceptualisation of dyslexia was both complex and problematic – a situation not helped by the existence of a great number of children identified as having dyslexia, but also appearing to manifest the characteristics of other developmental disorders. Two major co-morbid conditions often associated with developmental dyslexia are motor coordination problems, such as developmental coordination disorder (DCD), and problems with attention, such as attention deficit hyperactivity disorder (ADHD).

Working memory is an aspect of cognitive functioning that is fundamental to many of the tasks that we carry out in everyday life and appears to be significantly, but selectively, impaired in the children with dyslexia discussed in this chapter. Do children with other developmental disorders show similar problems with working memory? If so, is the pattern of working memory performance in these children similar to that of children with dyslexia, or different? Moreover, what sort of working memory profile can be found in individuals who appear to show the characteristics of more than one type of developmental disorder? The findings of two further studies that have utilised the WMTB-C have helped to shed some light on this issue.

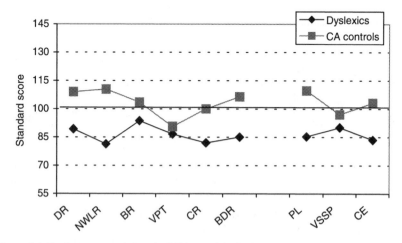

Figure 2.2 Performance of Greek children with dyslexia and chronological age controls on a modified version of the WMTB-C.

In one small-scale study, eight children with dyslexia, but also showing features of DCD (mean age 10:5 years), and six children with DCD, but also showing features of dyslexia (mean age 10:6 years) were administered the WMTB-C. Figure 2.3 shows the performance of the two groups across the subtests of the WMTB-C and the three component scores. In the presence of considerable variability between scores on the different sub-tests, it is possible to identify a broad pattern of performance in the two groups that is different for children identified primarily as having dyslexia, and children identified primarily as having DCD. That is, children with DCD appear to have particular problems with the visuospatial sketchpad tests of the WMTB-C but relatively few problems with phonological loop and central executive tasks. This pattern contrasts with that found for the children identified as dyslexic in this study. Their performance is worse on the tasks designed to measure the central executive component of working memory. Thus, preliminary findings from the application of the WMTB-C to children with characteristics associated with both dyslexia and developmental coordination disorder suggest that these two disorders may be characterised by different patterns of working memory performance. Moreover, if it is the case that one of these disorders might be considered to be the "primary problem" and the other the co-morbid problem, assessment of working memory might be a way of establishing which one is which.

Research by Jeffries and colleagues also provides support for this view (Jeffries & Everatt, 2003, 2004). For example, when Jeffries and Everatt presented adults with a diagnosis of either dyslexia or dyspraxia with a set of tests designed to measure phonological and visuospatial working memory, they found that the dyslexics had impaired performance on phonological working memory tasks, whereas the dyspraxic group performed poorly on the

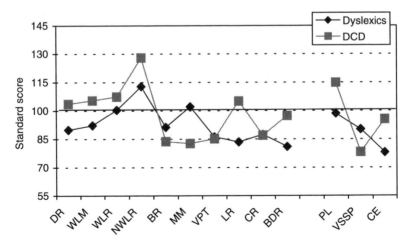

Figure 2.3 Performance of children with dyslexia and developmental coordination disorder (DCD) on the WMTB-C.

visuospatial measures. Clearly, more research is needed to explore the nature of working memory performance in individuals with specific and co-occurring developmental disorders, such as dyslexia and motor coordination problems.

In the final study to be presented in this chapter, the WMTB-C was administered to 18 children with a diagnosis of attention deficit hyperactivity disorder (ADHD) (mean age 9:3 years – all taking medication for their ADHD) and 18 chronological age-matched controls (mean age 9:4 years). Figure 2.4 indicates the performance of the two groups on the WMTB-C sub-tests and component scores.

The profile of performance for the ADHD and controls groups shows a wide range of variation across the different WMTB-C sub-tests. Analysis of the scores from the two groups indicates that the ADHD group significantly under-performed compared to controls across the PL, VSSP and CE components of working memory, although the difference between the components scores is largest for the PL and CE components. Specific sub-tests on which the ADHD group significantly under-performed relative to controls were: Digit Recall, Word List Matching, Block Recall, Listening Recall, Counting Recall and Backward Digit Recall. Interestingly, the only visuospatial sketchpad task on which the ADHD group performed significantly poorly is the Block Recall sub-test. This task is thought to measure the dynamic spatial sub-component of the visuospatial sketchpad, in contrast to the other VSSP subtests, which are more strongly loaded towards the static visual sub-component. Thus, it may be the case that the visuospatial sketchpad deficits found in children with ADHD may be specific to tasks that measure the dynamic spatial aspects of working memory function.

The relatively small amount of literature that has attempted to address the

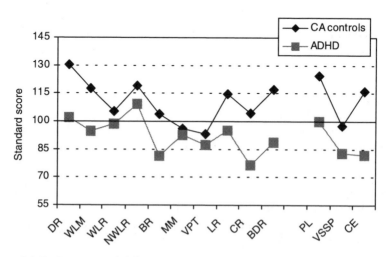

Figure 2.4 Performance of children with ADHD and chronological age controls on the WMTB-C.

nature of working memory in ADHD (e.g. Korkman & Pesonen, 1994) has tended to conclude that while central executive deficits are often found in children with ADHD, performance on tests of phonological loop function is not usually impaired. In this study, 4 of the 18 children with ADHD also had a diagnosis of dyslexia. This may go some way to account for the significantly poorer performance of this group on two of the four tasks of phonological loop functioning. However, further research is clearly needed to establish what, if any, aspects of working memory performance are impaired in children with ADHD (but no other identifiable problems), and children who show the characteristics of ADHD in addition to being identified as having other developmental disorders (see also Roodenrys, chapter 9, this volume).

What then, can we learn about dyslexia from administering a standardised test designed to measure performance across the three components of the working memory system? The first thing that is clear from the profiles of working memory presented in this chapter is that there is a huge degree of variation in the performance of children with and without developmental disorders on these tests. This is not surprising, as we are all individuals, and are likely to vary from one another in the extent to which we have strengths and weaknesses in particular aspects of working memory, and also in the extent to which our experiences with the environment have allowed us to develop these memory skills. This point is especially important with respect to children with particular developmental disorders (such as dyslexia), who tend to be regarded as a homogeneous group, whereas in fact, the opposite tends to be the case. Add to this the natural individual variation in working memory skills experienced by all people, and the patterns of performance that might have been affected by specific remedial approaches used with an individual with dyslexia, and the search for a "signature" working memory profile associated with this condition seems like a rather ambitious task indeed.

Nonetheless, the data presented in this chapter gives us an initial indication that, in spite of the natural variation that we would expect to find amongst individuals with dyslexia, some patterns of working memory performance appear to be associated with dyslexia in a way that they may not be associated with other developmental disorders, even those that show strong co-morbidity with dyslexia.

Thus, the assessment of working memory can provide us with a number of potentially useful outcomes. The first is that, based on the data described above, it seems possible that children with dyslexia as their "primary" problem (but manifesting symptoms of other developmental disorders) may be identifiable on the basis of their performance on the WMTB-C. Across a number of studies in both the UK and abroad, children with dyslexia appear to show particular deficits in their phonological loop, and especially, their central executive, functioning. Children with other developmental disorders, such as DCD, do not seem to show the same pattern of working memory strengths and weaknesses.

Second, assessment of working memory in children with learning problems – of any kind – represents an important step in identifying the nature of one of the child's fundamental cognitive processes, and allows those working with the child to build up a sense of how the relatively unimpaired areas of working memory might be utilised in order to deliver remedial help to the child.

The issue of whether working memory plays a causal role in dyslexia cannot currently be resolved. Whilst providing important information about the working memory performance of children, with and without developmental disorders, the WMTB-C is limited in one respect. That is, the set of tests designed to measure the central executive is restricted to tests that require simultaneous storage and processing of information, and does not include tests designed to measure the other cognitive processes that have been suggested to be attributable to the central executive (e.g. attentional processes). In addition, the design of the Listening Recall, Counting Recall and Backward Digit Recall sub-tests leads them to have a strong verbal component. This limitation stems from the lack of non-verbal tasks of this type available at the time of producing the test battery.

One of the consequences of this limitation is that the data provided regarding the nature of working memory performance in dyslexia does not allow us to choose between two possible accounts of working memory in dyslexia. The first account is that working memory in dyslexia is characterised by poor phonological loop performance, relatively unimpaired visuospatial sketchpad performance and very poor central executive performance. The second account is that working memory in dyslexia is characterised by poor performance on *any task* that requires the storage or manipulation of phonological information. That is, the working memory deficits observed may be the by-product of a basic deficit in phonological skills.

One approach, not available to us at the time of development of the WMTB-C, is to include tests of non-verbal central executive function in a working memory test battery. This approach has now become significantly more feasible, with the development of a number of tests of central executive function that have been designed to minimise or remove the phonological coding component. Some of these tasks have now been included in an automised and extended version of the WMTB-C, called the Automated Working Memory Assessment (AWMA) battery (Alloway, Gathercole & Pickering, 2004). The computer-administered AWMA contains 12 sub-tests in total. An example of a non-verbal central executive task is "Mr X". This requires the child to view two figures on the computer screen, each holding a ball in their hand. The figures may both be in the same position, or one of the figures may be rotated at a point through 360 degrees. The child is asked to say whether the target figure is holding the ball in the same hand as the other figure. Then, both figures are removed from the screen and replaced with a schematic of eight compass points. The child is asked to indicate, using the compass points, the location of the ball that the target figure was holding.

The AWMA provides researchers interested in the nature of working memory in dyslexia with an opportunity to investigate systematically the two accounts described above. By including non-verbal tests of central executive function in the battery, it is possible to see whether children with dyslexia show deficits in their performance on both verbal and non-verbal CE tasks, or only on those tasks that specifically tax their weaker phonological skills. A study by Smith-Spark and colleagues (Smith-Spark, Fisk, Fawcett & Nicolson, 2003) has already provided some evidence to support the first account of working memory deficits in dyslexia. They found that adults with dyslexia showed deficits on a task that required complex active spatial processing in memory, and was unlikely to be amenable to phonological recoding of memory items. Further research using tasks like this one, and those included in the AWMA, will bring us nearer to understanding the nature of working memory in dyslexia, and provide the basis for examining the role that working memory deficits play in dyslexia and other associated developmental disorders.

CONCLUSION

The dynamic, multi-component working memory model proposed by Baddeley and Hitch in 1974 has stimulated a wealth of research over the last 30 years and has significantly increased our understanding of the structures and functions associated with working memory. The application of this knowledge and understanding to learning problems such as dyslexia has much to offer researchers and practitioners concerned with the identification of dyslexia, the description and explanation of the problem, and the development of remedial approaches for those affected by it.

Despite over 30 years of investigation of immediate memory in dyslexia, the pattern of deficits found in this population is still relatively unclear. However, the contribution of the working memory model to this issue has been extremely important in terms of the processes that are thought to be carried out by this aspect of cognition, and the tasks that have been designed to sample them. Strong evidence exists to suggest significant problems with phonological immediate memory, although it is unclear as to whether these deficits are merely the manifestation of a broader problem with language processing. Many individuals with dyslexia do not appear to have problems with the visual and spatial aspects of immediate memory, although when memory items can be named, this can be problematic. Moreover, individuals with "visual" dyslexia, or whose language is not English, may show a greater degree of visuospatial working memory impairment – finding that require further clarification in the coming years.

Perhaps the greatest contribution of the working memory conceptualisation of immediate memory to the study of dyslexia has been the investigation of central executive functioning in this group. Over the last decade there has been a small but increasing body of evidence that this part of the working memory system may cause particular problems for individuals with dyslexia, a suggestion that is consistent with many of the everyday problems reported by dyslexics and those around them.

The identification of dyslexia as distinct from other related developmental disorders remains problematic when many individuals exhibit the characteristics of more than one learning problem. The use of a standardised working memory battery that can sample across the different components of working memory (such as the WMTB-C or AWMA) offers a way of systematically investigating the cognitive functioning of children with different developmental disorders. Early evidence from studies of this kind appears to indicate different patterns of working memory functioning in children with different learning problems. The continuing application of the working memory concept to dyslexia will hopefully provide further evidence on this and other important issues.

REFERENCES

Alloway, T. P., Gathercole, S. E., & Pickering, S. J. (1994). *The Automated Working Memory Assessment* [Test battery]. Available from authors.

Andrade, J. (2001). *Working memory in perspective*. Hove, UK: Psychology Press.

Atkinson, R. C., & Shiffrin, R. M. (1968). Human memory: A proposed system and its control processes. In K. W. Spence (Ed.), *Advances in research and theory: Vol. 2. The psychology of learning and motivation* (pp. 89–195). New York: Academic Press.

Baddeley, A. D. (1966). Short-term memory for word sequences as a function of acoustic, semantic and formal similarity. *Quarterly Journal of Experimental Psychology*, *18*, 362–365.

Baddeley, A. D. (1986). *Working memory*. Oxford, UK: Oxford University Press.

Baddeley, A. D. (1996). Exploring the central executive. *Quarterly Journal of Experimental Psychology*, *49A*, 5–28.

Baddeley, A. D. (1997). *Human memory: Theory and practice*. Hove, UK: Lawrence Erlbaum Associates Ltd.

Baddeley, A. D. (2000). The episodic buffer: A new component of working memory? *Trends in Cognitive Sciences*, *4*, 417–423.

Baddeley, A. D. (2001). Is working memory still working? *American Psychologist*, *56*, 851–864.

Baddeley, A., & Gathercole, S. (1992). Learning to read: The role of the phonological loop. In J. Alegria, D. Holender, J. Juncade Morais, & M. Radeau (Eds.), *Analytic approaches to human cognition* (pp. 153–167). Amsterdam: Elsevier.

Baddeley, A. D., & Hitch, G. (1974). Working memory. In G. A. Bower (Ed.), *Recent advances in learning and motivation, Vol. 8* (pp. 47–90). New York: Academic Press.

Baddeley, A. D., Lewis, V. J., Eldridge, M., & Thomson, N. (1984). Attention and retrieval from long-term memory. *Journal of Experimental Psychology: General*, *113*, 518–540.

Baddeley, A., & Logie, R. (1999). Working memory: The multiple component model.

In A. Miyake & P. Shah (Eds.), *Models of working memory* (pp. 28–61). New York: Cambridge University Press.

Baddeley, A. D., Thomson, N., & Buchanan, M. (1975). Word length and the structure of short-term memory. *Journal of Verbal Learning and Verbal Behaviour, 14,* 575–589.

Bauer, R. H. (1977). Memory processes in children with learning disabilities: Evidence for deficient rehearsal. *Journal of Experimental Child Psychology, 24,* 415–430.

Boder, E. (1973). Developmental dyslexia: A diagnostic screening procedure based on three characteristic patterns of reading and spelling. In B. Bateman (Ed.), *Learning disorders* (pp. 293–321). Seattle, CA: Special Child Publications.

Brady, S. A., Mann, V., & Schmidt, R. (1987). Errors in short-term memory for good and poor readers. *Memory and Cognition, 15,* 444–453.

Bull, R., Johnston, R. S., & Roy, J. A. (1999). Exploring the roles of the visuo spatial sketchpad and central executive in children's arithmetical skills: Views from cognition and developmental neuropsychology. *Developmental Neuropsychology, 15,* 421–442.

Byrne, B., & Shea, P. (1979). Semantic and phonetic memory codes in beginning readers? *Memory and Cognition, 7,* 333–338.

Cain, K., Oakhill, J., & Bryant, P. E. (2004). Children's reading comprehension ability: Concurrent prediction by working memory, verbal ability, and component skills. *Journal of Educational Psychology, 96,* 31–42.

Carroll, J. (1973). Assessment of short-term visual memory and its educational implications. *Perceptual and Motor Skills, 37,* 383–388.

Case, R. D., Kurland, M., & Goldberg, J. (1982). Operational efficiency and the growth of short-term memory span. *Journal of Experimental Child Psychology, 33,* 386–404.

Cohen, R. L., & Heath, M. (1990). The development of serial short-term memory and the articulatory loop hypothesis. *Intelligence, 14,* 151–171.

Conrad, R., & Hull, A. J. (1964). Information, acoustic confusion and memory span. *British Journal of Psychology, 55,* 429–432.

Daneman, M., & Carpenter, P. A. (1980). Individual differences in working memory and reading. *Journal of Verbal Learning and Verbal Behaviour, 19,* 450–466.

de Jong, P. F. (1998). Working memory deficits of reading disabled children. *Journal of Experimental Child Psychology, 70,* 75–96.

Della Sala, S., Gray, C., Baddeley, A., Allamano, N., & Wilson, L. (1999). Pattern span: A tool for unwelding visuospatial memory. *Neuropsychologia, 37,* 1189–1199.

Della Sala, S., Gray, C., Baddeley, A., & Wilson, L. (1997). *Visual Patterns Test.* Bury St Edmunds, UK: Thames Valley Test Company.

Frith, U. (1997). *Brain, mind and behaviour in dyslexia.* In C. Hulme & M. Snowling (Eds.), *Dyslexia: Biology, cognition and intervention.* London: Whurr.

Gathercole, S. E. (1999). Cognitive approaches to the development of short-term memory. *Trends in Cognitive Science, 3,* 410–418.

Gathercole, S. E., Adams, A.-M., & Hitch, G. J. (1994). Do young children rehearse? An individual differences analysis. *Memory and Cognition, 22,* 201–207.

Gathercole, S. E., & Baddeley, A. D. (1996). *The Children's Test of Nonword Repetition.* New York: Psychological Corporation.

Gathercole, S. E., & Hitch, G. J. (1993). Developmental changes in short-term memory: A revised working memory perspective. In A. Collins, S. E. Gathercole, M. A. Conway, & P. E. Morris (Eds.), *Theories of memory* (pp. 189–210). Hove, UK: Lawrence Erlbaum Associates Ltd.

Gathercole, S. E., Frankish, C. R., Pickering, S. J., & Peaker, S. M. (1999). Phonotactic influences on short-term memory. *Journal of Experimental Psychology: Learning, Memory, and Cognition, 25*, 84–95.

Gathercole, S. E., & Pickering, S. J. (2000a). Assessment of working memory in six- and seven-year-old children. *Journal of Educational Psychology, 92*, 377–390.

Gathercole, S. E., & Pickering, S. J. (2000b). Working memory deficits in children with low achievements in the national curriculum at seven years of age. *British Journal of Educational Psychology, 70*, 177–194.

Gathercole, S. E., & Pickering, S. J. (2001). Working memory deficits in children with special educational needs. *British Journal of Special Education, 28*, 89–97.

Gathercole, S. E., Pickering, S. J., Hall, M., & Peaker, S. M. (2001). Dissociable lexical and phonological influences on serial recall and serial recognition. *Quarterly Journal of Experimental Psychology, 54A*, 1–30.

Gould, J. H., & Glencross, D. J. (1990). Do children with a specific reading disability have a general serial-ordering deficit? *Neuropsychologia, 28*, 271–278.

Hall, J. W., Wilson, K. P., Humphries, M. S., Tinzmann, M. B., & Bowyer, P. M. (1983). Phonemic-similarity effects in good vs. poor readers. *Memory and Cognition, 11*, 520–527.

Hicks, C. (1980). The ITPA visual sequential memory task: An alternative interpretation and the implications for good and poor readers. *British Journal of Educational Psychology, 50*, 16–25.

Holligan, C., & Johnston, R. S. (1988). The use of phonological information by good and poor readers in memory and reading tasks. *Memory and Cognition, 16*, 522–532.

Howes, N. L., Bigler, E. D., Lawson, J. S., & Burlingame, G. M. (1999). Reading disability subtypes and the test of memory and learning. *Archives of Clinical Neuropsychology, 14*, 317–339.

Hulme, C. (1981). *Reading retardation and multi-sensory teaching.* London: Routledge & Kegan Paul.

Hulme, C., Maughan, S., & Brown, G. D. A. (1991). Memory for familiar and unfamiliar words: Evidence for a longer term memory contribution to short-term memory span. *Journal of Memory and Language, 30*, 685–701.

Hulme, C., & Roodenrys, S. (1995). Practitioner review: Verbal working memory development and its disorders. *Journal of Child Psychology and Psychiatry, 36*, 373–398.

Hulme, C., Thomson, N., Muir, C., & Lawrence, A. (1984). Speech rate and the development of short-term memory span. *Journal of Experimental Child Psychology, 38*, 241–253.

Isaki, E., & Plante, E. (1997). Short-term and working memory differences in language/learning disabled and normal adults. *Journal of Communication Disorders, 30*, 427–437.

Jeffries, S. A., & Everatt, J. (2004). Working memory: Its role in dyslexia and other specific learning difficulties. *Dyslexia, 10*, 196–214.

Jeffries, S. A., & Everatt, J. (2003). Differences between dyspraxics and dyslexics in sequence learning and working memory. *Dyspraxia Foundation Professional Journal, 2*, 12–21.

Johnston, R. S. (1982). Phonological coding in dyslexic readers. *British Journal of Psychology, 73*, 455–460.

Johnston, R. S. (1993). The role of memory in learning to read, write and spell: A review of recent research. In G. M. Davies & R. H. Logie (Eds.), *Memory in everyday life* (pp. 59–77). Amsterdam: Elsevier.

Johnston, R. S., Rugg, M. D., & Scott, T. (1987). Phonological similarity effects, memory span and developmental reading disorders: The nature of the relationship. *British Journal of Psychology, 78*, 205–211.

Katz, R. B., Shankweiler, D. P., & Liberman, I. Y. (1981). Memory for item order and phonetic recoding in the beginning reader. *Journal of Experimental Child Psychology, 32*, 474–484.

Korkman, M., & Pesonen, A. E. (1994). A comparison of neuropsychological test profiles of children with Attention Deficit-Hyperactivity Disorder and/or learning disorder. *Journal of Learning Disabilities, 27*, 383–392.

Liberman, I. Y., Mann, V. A., Shankweiler, D. P., & Werfelman, M. (1982). Children's memory for recurring linguistic and non-linguistic material in relation to reading ability. *Cortex, 18*, 367–375.

Logie, R. H. (1995). *Visuo-spatial working memory*. Hove, UK: Lawrence Erlbaum Associates Ltd.

Logie, R. H., & Pearson, D. G. (1997). The inner eye and the inner scribe of visuo-spatial working memory: Evidence from developmental fractionation. *European Journal of Cognitive Psychology, 9*, 241–257.

Macaruso, P., Locke, J. L., Smith, S. T., & Powers, S. (1996). Short-term memory and phonological coding in developmental dyslexia. *Journal of Neurolinguistics, 9*, 135–146.

Mann, V. A., Liberman, I. Y., & Shankweiler, D. P. (1980). Children's memory for sentences and word strings in relation to reading ability. *Memory and Cognition, 8*, 329–335.

Mark, L. S., Shankweiler, D. P., Liberman, I. Y., & Fowler, C. A. (1977). Phonetic recoding and reading difficulty in beginning readers. *Memory and Cognition, 5*, 623–629.

McDougall, S., Hulme, C., Ellis, A., & Monk, A. (1994). Learning to read: The role of short-term memory and phonological skills. *Journal of Experimental Child Psychology, 58*, 112–133.

McNeil, A. M., & Johnston, R. S. (2004). Word length, phonemic, and visual similarity effects in poor and normal readers. *Memory and Cognition, 32*, 687–695.

Meyler, A., & Breznitz, Z. (1998). Developmental associations between verbal and visual short-term memory and the acquisition of decoding skill. *Reading and Writing, 10*, 519–540.

Miles, C., Morgan, M. J., Milne, A. B., & Morris, E. D. M. (1996). Developmental and individual differences in visual memory span. *Current Psychology, 15*, 53–67.

Miles, E. (1995). Can there be a single definition of dyslexia? *Dyslexia, 1*, 37–45.

Miller, S. L., & Tallal, P. (1995). A behavioural neuroscience approach to developmental language disorders: Evidence for a rapid temporal processing deficit. In D. Ciccetti & D. J. Cohen (Eds.), *Developmental psychopathology* (pp. 357–390). New York: Wiley.

Milner, B. (1971). Interhemispheric differences in the localisation of psychological processes in man. *British Medical Bulletin, 27*, 272–277.

Nicolson, R. I. (1981). The relationship between memory span and processing speed. In M. Friedman, J. P. Das, & N. O'Connor (Eds.), *Intelligence and learning* (pp. 179–184). New York: Plenum Press.

Nicolson, R. I., & Fawcett, A. J. (1995). Dyslexia is more than a phonological disability. *Dyslexia, 1*, 19–37.

Olson, R. K., Davidson, B. J., Kliegl, R., & Davies, S. E. (1984). Development of phonetic memory in disabled and normal readers. *Journal of Experimental Child Psychology, 37*, 187–206.

Orton, S. (1937). *Reading, writing, and speech problems in children.* New York: W. W. Norton.

Palmer, S. E. (2000a). The retention of a visual encoding strategy in dyslexic teenagers. *Journal of Reading Research, 23*, 28–40.

Palmer, S. E. (2000b). Working memory: A developmental study of phonological recoding. *Memory, 8*, 179–193.

Pickering, S. J. (2001). Cognitive approaches to the fractionation of visuospatial working memory. *Cortex, 37*, 457–473.

Pickering, S. J. (2006). *Working memory and education.* New York: Academic Press.

Pickering, S. J., & Zacharof, C. (2005). Identifiable patterns of working memory performance in Greek children with developmental dyslexia. *Manuscript in preparation.*

Pickering, S. J., & Chubb, R. (2005). Working memory in dyslexia: A comparison of performance of dyslexics and reading age controls on the WMTB-C. *Manuscript in preparation.*

Pickering, S. J., & Gathercole, S. E. (2001). *The Working Memory Test Battery for Children.* London: Psychological Corporation.

Pickering, S. J., & Gathercole, S. E. (2005). Working memory deficits in dyslexia: Are they located in the phonological loop, visuospatial sketchpad or central executive? *Manuscript under revision.*

Pickering, S. J., Gathercole, S. E., Hall, M., & Lloyd, S. A. (2001). Development of memory for pattern and path: Further evidence for the fractionation of visuo-spatial memory. *Quarterly Journal of Experimental Psychology, 54A*, 397–420.

Pickering, S. J., Gathercole, S. E., & Peaker, S. M. (1998). Verbal and visuospatial short-term memory in children: Evidence for common and distinct mechanisms. *Memory and Cognition, 26*, 1117–1130.

Rack, J. (1985). Orthographic and phonetic coding in normal and dyslexic readers. *British Journal of Psychology, 76*, 325–340.

Reynolds, C. R., & Bigler, E. D. (1994). *Test of memory and learning.* Austin, TX: Pro-Ed.

Rohl, M., & Pratt, C. (1995). Phonological awareness, verbal working memory and the acquisition of literacy. *Reading and Writing, 7*, 327–360.

Roodenrys, S., & Stokes, J. (2001). Serial recall and nonword repetition in reading disabled children. *Reading and Writing, 14*, 379–394.

Schweickert, R. (1993). A multinomial processing tree for degradation and redintegration in immediate recall. *Memory and Cognition, 21*, 168–175.

Shankweiler, D. P., Liberman, I. Y., Mark, L. S, Fowler, C. A., & Fischer, F. W. (1979). The speech code and learning to read. *Journal of Experimental Psychology: Human Learning and Memory, 5*, 531–545.

Siegel, L. S. (1994). Working memory and reading: A life-span perspective. *International Journal of Behavioural Development, 17*, 109–124.

Siegel, L. S., & Linder, B. A. (1984). Short-term memory processes in children with reading and arithmetic learning disabilities. *Developmental Psychology, 20,* 200–207.

Smith-Spark, J. H., Fisk, J. E., Fawcett, A. J., & Nicolson, R. I. (2003). Central executive impairments in adult dyslexics: Evidence from visuospatial working memory performance. *European Journal of Cognitive Psychology, 15,* 567–587.

Snowling, M. (1995). Phonological processing and developmental dyslexia. *Journal of Research in Reading, 18,* 132–138.

Snowling, M. (1981). Phonemic deficits in developmental dyslexia. *Psychological Research, 43,* 219–234.

Snowling, M., Goulandris, N., Bowlby, M., & Howell, P. (1986). Segmentation and speech perception in relation to reading skill: A developmental analysis. *Journal of Experimental Child Psychology, 41,* 489–507.

Spring, C., & Capps, C. (1974). Encoding speed, rehearsal, and probed recall of dyslexic boys. *Journal of Educational Psychology, 66,* 780–786.

Stein, J., & Walsh, V. (1997). To see but not to read: The magnocellular theory of dyslexia. *Trends in Neurosciences, 20,* 147–152.

Swanson, H. L. (1978). Verbal encoding effects on the visual short-term memory of learning disabled and normal readers. *Journal of Educational Psychology, 70,* 539–544.

Swanson, H. L. (1992). Generality and modifiability of working memory among skilled and less skilled readers. *Journal of Educational Psychology, 84,* 473–488.

Swanson, H. L. (1993a). Executive processes in learning disabled readers. *Intelligence, 17,* 117–149.

Swanson, H. L. (1993b). Working memory in learning disability subgroups. *Journal of Experimental Child Psychology, 56,* 87–114.

Swanson, H. L. (1994). Short-term memory and working memory: Do both contribute to our understanding of academic achievement in children and adults with learning disabilities? *Journal of Learning Disabilities, 27,* 34–50.

Swanson, H. L. (1999). Reading comprehension and working memory in learning-disabled readers: Is the phonological loop more important than the executive system? *Journal of Experimental Child Psychology, 72,* 1–31.

Swanson, H. L., & Alexander, J. E. (1997). Cognitive processes as predictors of word recognition and reading comprehension in learning-disabled and skilled readers: Revisiting the specificity hypothesis. *Journal of Educational Psychology, 89,* 128–158.

Swanson, H. L., & Ashbaker, M. H. (2000). Working memory, short-term memory, speech rate, word recognition and reading comprehension in learning disabled readers: Does the executive system have a role? *Intelligence, 28,* 1–30.

Swanson, H. L., Ashbaker, M. H., & Lee, C. (1996). Learning-disabled readers' working memory as a function of processing demands. *Journal of Experimental Child Psychology, 61,* 242–275.

Torgesen, J. K., & Houck, D. G. (1980). Processing deficiencies of learning-disabled children who perform poorly on the digit span test. *Journal of Educational Psychology, 72,* 141–160.

Turner, M. (1997). *Psychological assessment of dyslexia.* London: Whurr.

Vellutino, F., Pruzek, R., Steger, J., & Meshoulam, U. (1973). Immediate visual recall in poor and normal readers as a function of orthographic-linguistic familiarity. *Cortex, 9,* 370–386.

Vellutino, F., Steger, J., DeSetto, L., & Phillips, F. (1975). Immediate and delayed recognition of visual stimuli in poor and normal readers. *Journal of Experimental Child Psychology*, *19*, 223–232.

Vellutino, F. (1979). *Dyslexia: Theory and research*. Cambridge, MA: MIT Press.

Wechsler, D. (1996). *Wechsler Intelligence Scale for Children* (Rev. ed.). New York: Psychological Corporation.

3 Short-term memory deficits in developmental dyslexia[1]

Richard K. Wagner and Andrea Muse

OVERVIEW

Developmental dyslexia, reading disability, and reading impairment all refer to unexpected and unexplained poor performance in reading. Expected levels of reading performance can be based on normative data from age-matched peers, or based on an individual child's oral language ability or cognitive ability. Developmental dyslexia is distinguished from acquired dyslexia, with acquired dyslexia referring to impaired reading in formerly normal readers due to brain injury or insult.

THE NATURE OF DEVELOPMENTAL DYSLEXIA

Although most people have heard about dyslexia, its key features are commonly misunderstood (Wagner, 2005). The most common misunderstanding is to view dyslexia as a problem of seeing mirror images of words or letters. This misunderstanding arises from reports that children with dyslexia are reported to read *was* as *saw*, or to confuse the letters "b" and "d." In fact, children with developmental dyslexia who are commonly identified after several years of schooling can be observed reading *was* as *saw* and confusing the letters "b" and "d." But it turns out that normal beginning readers also make similar errors, and there are obvious explanations for these kinds of errors in both beginning normal readers and older impaired readers (Crowder & Wagner, 1991). That words in English are to be read from left to right as opposed to right to left (i.e., the letter sting "s" "a" and "w" should be decoded as *saw* and not *was*) is arbitrary and must be learned. Confusions between letters such as "b" and "d" are explainable in that these letter pairs are both visually confusable (to beginning readers, the letter "b" can be seen as a stick and a ball whereas the letter "d" is a ball and a stick) and similar in sound (i.e., both stop consonants). Careful analysis of reading errors has shown that older readers with dyslexia make no more reversal errors than do younger normal readers who are matched at the same level of reading. What explains the popularity of this mistaken view is that teachers and parents of older readers only see children with reading problems making these errors. Teachers and parents of beginning readers know that such errors are quite common.

Another mistaken idea about reading impairment is that it results from erratic or inefficient eye-movements. Reading requires highly sophisticated and coordinated eye-movements characterized by ballistic movements called saccades and pauses called fixations. During the movements or saccades, little information is available to the eyes beyond a blur. Nearly all information is acquired during fixations. Yet as you read the words on this page, your perception is likely to be that your eyes are moving smoothly across the page. This is an example of a situation where perception does not reflect reality. Try observing a normal reader by having her read directly across from you. Have her hold the book low enough so you can observe her eyes, you will indeed see that the eyes move across the page in a series of small, but observable jerky movements.

Perform the same informal experiment on an individual with reading impairment and it will be apparent that his eyes move much more erratically, even moving in the wrong direction at times. Observations like these resulted in the belief that faulty eye-movements were the origin of reading impairments, and also resulted in interventions based on eye-movement training. It turns out that this view has it backwards. Indeed, the eye-movements of individuals with reading impairments are more erratic than those of normal readers, but the erratic eye-movements are the byproduct, not the cause, of the impaired reading. The eye-movements of individuals with reading impairments do not move across the page as smoothly as do those of normal readers because they are having trouble reading the words. This also explains their greater frequency of backward eye-movements or regressions. Conclusive evidence was provided by careful studies in which normal readers were given material that was as difficult for them to read as is grade-level reading material for individuals with reading impairment, and individuals with reading impairment were given very easy reading material that they could read as well as normal readers could read grade-level material (Crowder & Wagner, 1991; Rayner & Polletsek, 1989). Under these conditions, the eye-movements of normal readers deteriorated to match the previously reported erratic eye-movements of individuals with reading impairment, and the eye-movements of the individuals with reading impairment now looked normal. Additional confirmation came from the results of eye-movement training studies. Although eye-movement training did result in gains performance on eye-movement tasks outside the context of reading, reading performance did not improve.

For the vast majority of individuals with developmental dyslexia, the proximal problem is an inability to decode the individual words on the page accurately and efficiently. Failure to decode words accurately and efficiently secondarily affects comprehension (Torgesen, 1999; Torgesen et al., 2001).

EARLY INTEREST IN THE ROLE OF SHORT-TERM
MEMORY IN DYSLEXIA

Although there has been interest in relations between comprehension and performance on complex span tasks that tap both the executive and phonological store parts of the working memory system, poor performance at the level of decoding individual words – the heart of the problem for individuals with developmental dyslexia – has been linked to poor performance on tasks that tap the phonological part of working memory primarily, such as digit span. Poor performance on phonological memory tasks has been a widely noted feature of individuals with dyslexia since the 1960s (for reviews, see Jorm, 1983, and Torgesen, 1978). Several underlying causes of impaired phonological memory have been proposed.

One proposed cause is inefficiency in the ability of the phonological loop to store information, perhaps because of subtle deficits in articulatory processes (Pickering, chapter 2, this volume). Recall that storage of phonological information is accomplished by replenishing a quickly decaying phonological store by means of covert articulation or rehearsal (Baddeley, 1986). It is hard to demonstrate that deficits exist for covert articulation. However, some evidence exists that children with dyslexia are slower in overt articulation speed when given tasks such as repeat the phrase "pa-ta-ka" as many times as possible in 10 seconds (Spring & Perry, 1983; Wolf & Goodglass, 1986). If slower overt articulation is observed, it is not too great a leap to suspect that individuals with dyslexia might be slower at covert articulation as well.

A second possibility is that children with dyslexia simply are unable or unwilling to use articulatory processes, either covert or overt, to maintain activation of phonological codes when performing short-term memory tasks. This possibility was evaluated in a study of the memory performance of two kinds of children with dyslexia and normal controls (Torgesen, 1996). He identified one group of children with learning (reading) disabilities who had severe problems on verbal short-term memory tasks (LD-S group), a second group of children with learning disabilities whose short-term memory task performance was not impaired (LD-N group), and a comparison group of normal readers (N group). Three kinds of short-term memory tasks were given to the three groups of children. The first kind of task was a visual sequential memory task that involved recall of stimuli that could not easily be coded phonologically. The second kind of task was a sorting-recall task that required semantic memory. Finally, four verbal short-term memory tasks were given. These tasks involved recall of picture sequences, digits presented visually, digits presented auditorially, and sentences. These results are presented in Figure 3.1.

There were minimal differences among the groups for both the visual sequential memory and semantic memory tasks. The poor readers with poor memory span performance performed much more poorly than the other two groups on all four verbal short-term memory tasks. The poor memory

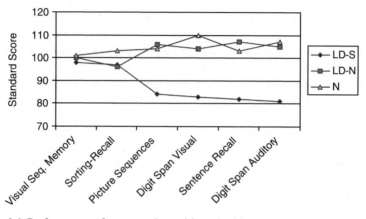

Figure 3.1 Performance of poor readers with and without memory problems on six
memory tasks. Reprinted with permission from Torgesen, J. K. (1996).
A model of memory from an informational processing perspective. In
G. R. Lyon & N. A. Krasnegor (Eds.), Attention, memory, and executive
function. Baltimore: Paul H. Brookes Publishing Co.

performance occurred regardless of whether the verbal material was presented visually or auditorially. Because memory performance was impaired
regardless when presentation of the items to be recalled was visual as well as
auditory, Torgesen (1996) concluded that inability or unwillingness to use
articulatory processes to code incoming auditory information was not an
explanation for the poor performance. Other evidence exists of impaired
short-term memory performance when opportunity for articulatory processing is suppressed. For example, when items are presented so rapidly that
articulation isn't possible, memory differences still exist (Cohen, 1982).

A third possible account of the origin of impaired phonological memory
in dyslexic readers is that they are relying on phonological codes that are
somehow degraded or less well developed as a result of a subtle problem in
speech perception (Brady, 1991; Liberman & Shankweiler, 1991; Torgesen,
1988). This account has been difficult either to refute or to provide conclusive
evidence in favor of it.

THE DEMISE OF A MEMORY DEFICIT ACCOUNT
OF DYSLEXIA

Despite early enthusiasm for memory deficits as a cause of dyslexia, memory
problems have taken a back seat to other kinds of phonological processing
problems. According to the most recent definition of developmental dyslexia proposed by the International Dyslexia Association (Lyon, Shaywitz, &
Shaywitz, 2003), dyslexia is a specific learning disability characterized by
unexpected difficulties in accurate and/or fluent word recognition, decoding,

and spelling. These difficulties are unexpected based on other cognitive abilities and instructional history, are neurobiological in origin, and are attributed to a phonological core deficit that is manifested primarily in poor phonological awareness and poor phonological decoding (e.g., nonword reading) (Morris et al., 1998; Stanovich & Siegel, 1994). Phonological awareness refers to an individual's awareness and access to the sound structure of an oral language (Jorm & Share, 1983; Wagner & Torgesen, 1987). For example, a young child would demonstrate phonological awareness if she could hear that the spoken words "cat," "rat," and "mat" have different initial sounds but sound the same in the middle and end. To an individual with phonological awareness, an alphabetic writing system such as English makes sense. Note the spellings of *cat*, *rat*, and *mat* track the similarities and differences in their pronunciations. They have different initial letters and identical medial and final letters. Poor phonological awareness leads to poor decoding, particularly poor phonological decoding of nonwords.

One reason that memory explanations of dyslexia have taken a back seat to accounts that feature phonological awareness is that measures of phonological awareness are more related to reading than are measures of phonological memory. For example, Wagner et al. (1997) reported a 5-year longitudinal study of several hundred children who were followed from kindergarten through fourth grade. Multiple measures of the constructs of phonological awareness, phonological memory, and rapid naming were obtained, and structural equation modeling was used to test alternative causal models of relations between the development of phonological processing abilities and word-level reading.

Measures of phonological awareness included phoneme elision ("Say the word *cup*. Now tell me what word would be left if I said *cup* without saying /k/."), sound categorization (children were instructed to find the odd one out of sets of words such as *fun, bun, pin, ton*), phoneme segmentation ("Tell me each sound you hear in the word in the order that you hear it."), blending phonemes into words, and blending phonemes into nonwords. Measures of phonological memory included a forward digit span task with multiple trials and a partial credit scoring system to maximize reliability, and a sentence memory task that required verbatim recall. Measures of serial naming included rapid naming of digits and rapid naming of letters. The word-level reading outcome consisted of Word Analysis and Word Attack from the Woodcock Reading Mastery Test–Revised (Woodcock, 1987).

Structural equation models were used to model causal relations for the time periods from kindergarten to second-grade, first-grade to third-grade, and second-grade to fourth-grade. The main results are the structure coefficients presented in Table 3.1. A structure coefficient for a given exogenous (causal) variable represents the predicted change in word-level reading associated with a one-unit change in the exogenous variable, with all other variables in the model held constant. Thus, structure coefficients quantify the unique or independent influence of each causal variable. These coefficients

Table 3.1 Structure coefficients between phonological processing variables and reading. Reprinted with permission from R. K. Wagner et al. (1997), *Developmental Psychology, 33*, 468–479.

Exogenous variable	Time period		
	Kindergarten to 2nd grade	1st to 3rd grade	2nd to 4th grade
Phonological variables			
Phonological awareness	.37***	.29*	.27***
Phonological memory	.12	−.03	.07
Rapid serial naming	.25*	.21*	.07
Control variables			
vocabulary	.10	.22***	−.01
autoregressor	.02	.27*	.57***
Variance accounted for			
Phonological variables	23%	8%	4%
Control variables	25%	56%	73%
Total	48%	64%	77%

are comparable to path coefficients in path analyses, and function similarly to regression coefficients in multiple linear regression. The autoregressive effect refers to the causal effect of word-level reading at an earlier time point on itself at a later time point. The autoregressive effect represents the idea that one potential cause of whether children perform higher or lower than their peers at a time point is where they performed relative to their peers at a previous time point.

There were four important results. First, for all three time periods examined, individual differences in phonological awareness exerted a causal influence on subsequent individual differences in word-level reading. Second, in contrast to the results obtained for phonological awareness, no independent causal influences were observed for phonological memory for any time period. Third, individual differences in serial naming and in vocabulary exerted causal influences on subsequent individual differences in word-level reading initially, but these influences faded over time with the increasing stability of individual differences in word-level reading that are quantified by the autoregressive effect. Fourth, the proportion of variance in word-level reading accounted for by phonological processes decreased over time, whereas that accounted for by the autoregressive effect increased over time. This represents increasing stability of individual differences in word-level reading over time.

The apparent conclusion from this study is that phonological awareness exerts a causal influence on the development of word-level reading skills but phonological memory does not. But is it important to remember that structure coefficients represent the unique variance accounted for by an exogenous variable. Consider the case of ordinary multiple linear regression. For this case, assume there are two highly correlated predictors and a dependent variable. In a simultaneous regression, the independent variable that is even slightly more related to the dependent variable will get the larger regression coefficient, with the other independent variable having a regression coefficient near zero if it makes little additional contribution to prediction, even if it is only negligibly less related to the dependent variable. If phonological awareness and phonological memory are highly correlated, structure coefficients such as those reported in Table 3.1 might not give a complete picture of relations between phonological memory and reading.

RELATIONS BETWEEN PHONOLOGICAL MEMORY AND PHONOLOGICAL AWARENESS

What is the level of correlation between phonological awareness and phonological memory? One informative large-scale dataset comes from a national standardization of the Comprehensive Test of Phonological Processing (CTOPP; Wagner, Torgesen, & Rashotte, 1999). The normative sample consisted of 1265 individuals who were selected to represent the demographic characteristics of the United States. There are two versions of the test. One version is for 5- and 6-year-olds, and the other version is for 7- through 24-year-olds.

Confirmatory factor analyses of the national standardization data were done for each version of the test. For both versions, the measures of phonological memory were Memory for Digits, a forward digit span task with items presented at a rate of two per second to limit time available for rehearsal, and Nonword Repetition, a task requiring repetition of increasingly complex nonwords. For the 5- and 6-year-old version, the measures of phonological awareness were Elision, Sound Matching, and Blending Words. For the 7- through 24-year-old version, the measures of phonological awareness were Elision and Blending Words.

The results for the 5- and 6-year-old version are presented in Figure 3.2. In this figure, the rectangles represent the observed variables or subtests and the ovals represent unobserved or latent variable constructs. The arrows between latent variables and observed variables indicate which observed variables served as indicators for which latent variables. The result of primary interest in the present context is the correlation between latent variables representing the constructs of phonological awareness and phonological memory. For the 5- and 6-year-old version of the CTOPP, this correlation was a remarkably high .88. Results of a confirmatory factor analysis of the 7- through 24-year-old version are presented in Figure 3.3. For this group, the corresponding correlation was .85. These results indicate that a substantial portion of

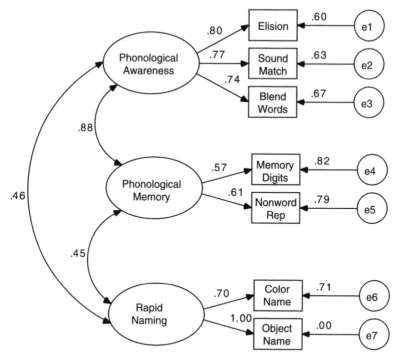

Figure 3.2 Confirmatory factor analysis of the 5- and 6-year-old version of the
CTOPP. Reprinted with permission from R. Wagner et al. (1999). *Comprehensive Test of Phonological Processing*. Austin, TX: Pro-Ed, Inc.

individual differences in phonological memory and in phonological awareness have a common origin, and as is the case of a multiple regression with two correlated variables, this substantial correlation is an explanation for the poor showing of phonological memory in predictive studies that pit it against phonological awareness.

Similar results have been obtained using other samples and other tasks. For example, in a study of preschool children, the correlation between latent variables representing phonological memory and phonological sensitivity (the emergent version of full-blown phonological awareness) was estimated to approach 1.0 (Wagner et al., 1987). Identical results were obtained in a large-scale study of kindergarten children (Wagner, Torgesen, Laughon, Simmons, & Rashotte, 1993). As children develop and learn to read, phonological awareness and phonological memory begin to differentiate, though they remain highly correlated (Wagner, Torgesen, & Rashotte, 1994).

What might explain the pattern of results of phonological memory and phonological awareness being undifferentiable until children learn to read, and also that phonological awareness is more related to word-level reading than is phonological memory? One obvious potential explanation of the

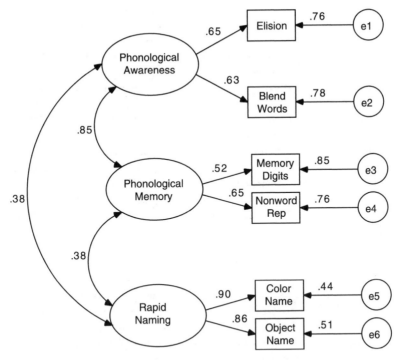

Figure 3.3 Confirmatory factor analysis of the 7- through 24-year-old version of the CTOPP. Reprinted with permission from R. Wagner et al. (1999). *Comprehensive Test of Phonological Processing.* Austin, TX: Pro-Ed, Inc.

strong correlation between phonological memory and phonological awareness is memory demands of phonological awareness tasks. The stimuli are presented auditorially, and the child must keep the stimuli active while carrying out the processing requirements of the specific awareness task to be completed. In fact, one might conceptualize the storage and processing requirements of a phonological awareness task to be similar to a working memory task. Alternatively, the development of phonological awareness and phonological memory performance both may be constrained by subtle deficiencies in the phonological codes used to represent verbal information (Brady, 1991; Liberman & Shankweiler, 1991; Torgesen, 1988).

Learning to read also might change the nature of what is really being assessed by phonological awareness tasks. Given the rough correspondence of letters and speech sounds in alphabetic writing systems such as English, letters can be used to represent phonemes when performing phonological awareness tasks. Indeed, some evidence exists of readers using spelling strategies on phonological awareness tasks. For example, when children who are readers are asked to count the number of phonemes in words, a common error is to report five phonemes in four-phoneme words with five letters such as *pitch* (Bruck, 1992; Ehri & Wilce, 1980; Tunmer & Nesdale, 1985). In fact, one can question whether it is even possible to obtain a pure measure of phonological awareness from individuals who have learned to read. If letter knowledge or other aspects of lexical knowledge are useful in performing phonological awareness tasks, it is not surprising that measures of phonological awareness are more related to word-level reading than are measures of phonological memory.

Although we have been focusing on the fact that phonological awareness measures may be contaminated by individual differences in reading, it is important to note that memory tasks may similarly be affected. Consider an example. Torgesen (1996) reported results from three new samples of children with learning disabilities who had poor verbal short-term memory (LD-S group), children with learning disabilities whose short-term memory task performance was not impaired (LD-N group), and a comparison group of normal readers (N group). The three groups were given span tasks for three different types of material that differed in familiarity: digits, words, and syllables consisting of pronounceable nonwords. Because of their limited number, children have a great deal of experience processing and pronouncing digits as individual units. The words given in the span task were less familiar than digits. Finally, nonword syllables were the least familiar stimuli presented. The results are presented in Figure 3.4. The difference in performance between the short-term memory impaired poor readers and the poor readers without short-term memory impairments varied as a function of stimuli familiarity. Differences were largest for digits, the most familiar kind of stimuli. Smaller differences were found for words, which were intermediate in terms of familiarity. Finally, virtually no differences were found for nonword syllables, the least familiar kind of material. Torgesen concluded that the largest advantage for the most frequent kind of stimuli resulted from the fact that the children without short-term memory impairments had developed more unitary phonological codes for digit names.

It is the rule, rather than the exception, that memory span performance is affected by the familiarity of the stimulus (Wagner, 1996). For example, Hulme, Maughan, and Brown (1991, cited in Cowan, 1993) investigated the relation between speech rate and memory span for a sample of adults who were given stimuli that were words or nonsense words. Speech rate tends to be related to span performance, with individuals who speak faster having better span performance. Hulme et al. found this for their sample as well, but also found that the intercept, or measure of average performance, was higher for words than for nonwords.

One of the more interesting recent measures of phonological memory is nonword repetition (Gathercole & Baddeley, 1990). Asking individuals merely to repeat increasingly complex nonwords appears to be a simple yet effective measure of phonological memory (Archibald & Gathercole, chapter 7, this volume; Brady, 1997; Gathercole, Willis, Baddeley, & Emslie, 1994; Wagner et al., 1999). Nonword repetition is predictive of vocabulary acquisition for

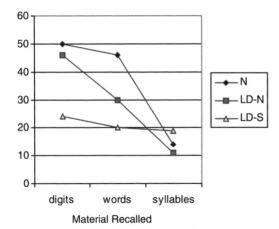

Figure 3.4 Performance of poor readers with and without memory problems as a function of stimulus familiarity. Reprinted with permission from Torgesen, J. K. (1996). A model of memory from an informational processing perspective. In G. R. Lyon & N. A. Krasnegor (Eds.), Attention, memory, and executive function. Baltimore: Paul H. Brookes Publishing Co.

both native and second-language learners (Gathercole & Baddeley, 1989, 1990; Gathercole, Willis, Emslie, & Baddeley, 1992; Hu, 2003; Masoura & Gathercole, 1999; Swanson, Saez, Gerber, & Leafstedt, 2004), and to adults learning novel vocabulary words (Gupta, 2003). Nonword repetition appears to distinguish children with language impairments from children who do not have language impairments (Archibald & Gathercole, chapter 7, this volume; Dollaghan & Campbell, 1998), and performance on these tasks is also highly predictive of the acquisition of letter knowledge in kindergartners (de Jong & Olson, 2004). Nonword repetition is predictive of word-level reading (Muter & Snowling, 1998; Snowling, Goulandris, Bowlby, & Howell, 1986; Stone & Brady, 1995).

Nonword repetition tasks are justifiably considered primarily to be measures of phonological memory, and deficits in nonword repetition have been attributed to difficulties in creating or utilizing phonological codes to encode and store information (Brady, 1991; Elbro, 1996; Hulme & Snowling, 1992; Liberman, Shankweiler, & Liberman, 1989; Torgesen, 1985, 1988). For example, Elbro (1996) has proposed that differences in the distinctiveness of phonological representations play a role in determining performance on phonological tasks. The more distinctive features that separate a representation from its neighbors, the more distinct is the representation and the better it can be retrieved and stored.

However, performance on nonword tasks including nonword repetition can be affected by lexical knowledge. Take Seidenberg and McClelland's (1989) computational model of word recognition, for example. Although the model only has a lexicon of real words to work from, it is able to decode nonwords by relying on patterns of activations of known words that share letters and letter patterns with the nonword to be decoded. The model might correctly pronounce the nonword *doad* by relying on the pattern of activation across real words such as *doe* and *toad*. Treiman, Goswami, and Bruck (1990) provided an empirical demonstration that some nonwords are more "word-like" than others. They had first-grade children, third-grade children, and college students read single syllable, consonant-vowel-consonant (CVC) nonwords. The VC portions of the nonwords were the focus of the study. Half of the stimuli contained VCs that had many "neighbors" in the English language, meaning that there were many words that differed from the nonword by one letter in the initial position of the syllable. The other half had few, if any, neighbors. For example, the nonword "tain" has many neighbors (e.g., main, pain, rain, vain), whereas "goan" has few neighbors (not many real words end in "oan"). Across all three groups of participants, nonwords that had VCs with many neighbors were decoded more accurately than the nonwords that had VCs with few neighbors. An analysis of errors showed more lexicalization errors (i.e., decoding a nonword as if it were a word) for the nonwords that had VCs with many neighbors.

Turning to word recognition in nonword repetition, the current version of a computational model of relations between nonword repetition, word learning, and serial recall (Gupta, 2003; Gupta & MacWhinney, 1997) derives its output jointly from a phonological store and lexical phonological representations. Empirical evidence of lexical processing influencing performance on the nonword repetition task has been provided by Dollaghan, Biber, and Campbell (1993, 1995). They created a nonword repetition task consisting of 24 pairs of nonwords. Each member of a given pair differed only by one phoneme in the stressed syllable, chosen so that one member of the pair had a stressed syllable corresponding to a real word and the other one did not (e.g., bathesis, fathesis). Nonword repetition performance was higher for the nonwords with stressed syllables corresponding to a real word. Presumably, the stressed syllables that corresponded to real words were encoded as word-length units rather than individual phonemes, thereby lessening the memory resources required to remember the nonwords.

Lexical contributions to representations used in short-term memory explain why memory for familiar words is better than memory for unfamiliar words (Hulme et al., 1991). Gathercole (1995) compared relations between nonword repetition and vocabulary for items rated high or low in word likeness. Relations between vocabulary and nonword repetition were stronger for items rated low in word likeness. Gathercole concluded that the items rated low in word likeness provided a purer measure of phonological memory than did items rated high in word likeness.

A growing body of evidence demonstrates that reading disability and language impairment have a genetic basis, and nonword repetition appears to be one of the more promising markers of these genetic origins (Bishop, 2002; Bishop, North, & Donlan, 1996; Chapman et al., 2004; Chapman, Raskind, Thomson, Berninger, & Wijsman, 2003). Raskind, Hus, Berninger, Thomson, and Wijsman (2000) conducted a study to examine the genetic contributions to reading disability. They found that the nonword memory subtest of a prepublication version of the Comprehensive Test of Phonological Processing (CTOPP; Wagner et al., 1999) was one of two tasks that showed correlation patterns in relatives that are strongly supportive of a genetic basis. Similarly, Wijsman et al. (2000) used the same nonword repetition subtest and found the evidence for a genetic basis of nonword repetition performance is quite strong. The results of these studies indicate that nonword repetition measures are good candidates for future genetic studies.

There also is an important practical advantage of nonword repetition. Because the task is so simple, it can be done much more readily by young children than more complicated tasks. Tasks that assess phonological awareness or sensitivity are cognitively complex for very young children. If measures of nonword repetition and phonological sensitivity actually measure identical or very highly overlapping constructs, nonword repetition will prove to be a valuable measure to be used with very young children.

CONCLUSION

In conclusion, interest in phonological memory as an origin of developmental dyslexia has waned from its heyday several decades ago, largely because of the rise of phonological awareness as an explanatory construct. However, the "demise" of interest in phonological memory as an origin of developmental dyslexia was perhaps premature. Large-scale studies indicate that measures of phonological memory and phonological awareness measure nearly the same thing at the preschool level, and very highly related things thereafter. What remains as the key challenge is the development of a theoretical framework that accounts for the high degree of similarity and the modest differences between the constructs of phonological memory and phonological awareness. Simply treating them as two completely distinct constructs flies in the face of compelling data. Interest in phonological memory is on the rise, carried in part by the growing popularity of nonword repetition as a replacement for digit span. Interest in implications of deficits in phonological memory for understanding developmental dyslexia is likely to follow suit.

NOTE

1   Preparation of this manuscript was supported by NICHD Grant HD23340 and by IES Grant R305G030104.

REFERENCES

Baddeley, A. D. (1986). *Working memory*. Oxford, UK: Oxford University Press.

Bishop, D. V. M. (2002). The role of genes in the etiology of specific language impairment. *Journal of Communication Disorders, 35*, 311–328.

Bishop, D. V. M., North, T., & Donlan, C. (1996). Nonword repetition as a behavioural marker for inherited language impairment: Evidence from a twin study. *Journal of Child Psychology and Psychiatry and Allied Disciplines, 37*, 391–403.

Brady, S. A. (1991). The role of working memory in reading disability. In S. Brady & D. Shankweiler (Eds.), *Phonological processes in literacy: A tribute to Isabelle Y. Liberman* (pp. 129–151). Hillsdale, NJ: Lawrence Erlbaum Associates, Inc.

Bruck, M. (1992). Persistence of dyslexics' phonological deficits. *Developmental Psychology, 28*, 874–886.

Chapman, N., Igo, R., Thomson, J. B., Matsushita, M., Brkanac, Z., Hotzman, T., et al. (2004). Linkage analyses of four regions previously implicated in dyslexia: Confirmation of a locus on chromosome 15q. *American Journal of Medical Genetics Part B: Neuropsychiatric Genetics, 131B*, 67–75.

Chapman, N., Raskind, W. H., Thomson, J. B., Berninger, V. W., & Wijsman, E. (2003). Segregation analysis of phenotypic compoments of learning disabilities. II. Phonological decoding. *American Journal of Medical Genetics Part B: Neuro-psychiatric Genetics, 121B*, 60–70.

Cohen, R. L. (1982). Individual differences in short-term memory. *International Review of Research in Mental Retardation, 11*, 43–77.

Cowan, N. (1993). Activation, attention, and short-term memory. *Memory and Cognition, 21*, 162–167.

Crowder, R. G., & Wagner, R. K. (1991). *The psychology of reading*. New York: Oxford University Press.

de Jong, P. F., & Olson, R. K. (2004). Early predictors of letter knowledge. *Journal of Experimental Child Psychology, 88*, 254–273.

Dollaghan, C., Biber, M., & Campbell, T. F. (1993). Constituent syllable effects in a nonsense-word repetition task. *Journal of Speech and Hearing Research, 36*, 1051–1054.

Dollaghan, C., Biber, M., & Campbell, T. F. (1995). Lexical influences on nonword repetition. *Applied Psycholinguistics, 16*, 211–222.

Dollaghan, C., & Campbell, T. F. (1998). Nonword repetition and child language impairment. *Journal of Speech-Language and Hearing Research, 41*, 1136–1146.

Ehri, L. C., & Wilce, L. S. (1980). The influence of orthography on readers' conceptualization of the phonemic structure of words. *Applied Psycholinguistics, 1*, 371–385.

Elbro, C. (1996). Early linguistic abilities and reading development: A review and hypothesis. *Reading and Writing: An Interdisciplinary Journal, 8*, 453–485.

Gathercole, S. (1995). Is nonword repetition a test of phonological memory or long-term knowledge? It all depends on the nonwords. *Memory and Cognition, 23*, 83–94.

Gathercole, S., & Baddeley, A. (1989). Evaluation of the role of STM in the development of vocabulary of children: A longitudinal study. *Journal of Memory and Language, 28*, 200–213.

Gathercole, S., & Baddeley, A. (1990). The role of phonological memory in vocabulary acquisition: A study of young children learning new names. *British Journal of Psychology*, *81*, 439–454.

Gathercole, S., Willis, C., Baddeley, A., & Emslie, H. (1994). The children's test of nonword repetition: A test of phonological working memory. *Memory*, *2*, 103–127.

Gathercole, S., Willis, C., Emslie, H., & Baddeley, A. (1992). Phonological memory and vocabulary development during the early school years: A longitudinal study. *Developmental Psychology*, *28*, 887–898.

Gupta, P. (2003). Examining the relationship between word learning, nonword repetition, and immediate serial recall in adults. *Quarterly Journal of Experimental Psychology: Human Experimental Psychology*, *56A*, 1213–1236.

Gupta, P., & MacWhinney, B. (1997). Vocabulary acquisition and short-term memory: Computational and neural bases. *Brain and Language*, *59*, 267–333.

Hu, C. (2003). Phonological memory, phonological awareness, and foreign language word learning. *Language Learning*, *53*, 429–462.

Hulme, C., Maughan, S., & Brown, G. (1991). Memory for familiar and unfamiliar words: Evidence for a long-term memory contribution to short-term memory span. *Journal of Memory and Language*, *30*, 685–701.

Hulme, C., & Snowling, M. (1992). Deficits in output phonology: An explanation of reading failure? *Cognitive Neuropsychology*, *9*, 47–72.

Jorm, A. F. (1983). Specific reading retardation and working memory: A review. *British Journal of Psychology*, *74*, 311–342.

Jorm, A. F., & Share, D. L. (1983). Phonological recoding and reading acquisition. *Applied Psycholinguistics*, *4*, 103–147.

Liberman, I. Y., & Shankweiler, D. (1991). Phonology and beginning reading: A tutorial. In L. Rieben & C. A. Perfetti (Eds.), *Learning to read: Basic research and its implications* (pp. 27–52). Parkton, MD: York Press.

Liberman, I. Y., Shankweiler, D. P., & Liberman, A. M. (1989). The alphabetic principle and learning to read. In D. P. Shankweiler & I. G. Liberman (Eds.), *Phonology and reading disability* (pp. 1–33). Ann Arbor, MI: University of Michigan Press.

Lyon, G. R., Shaywitz, S. E., & Shaywitz, B. A. (2003). A definition of dyslexia. *Annals of Dyslexia*, *53*, 1–14.

Masoura, E., & Gathercole, S. (1999). Phonological short-term memory and foreign language learning. *International Journal of Psychology*, *34*, 383–388.

Morris, R. D., Stuebing, K. K., Fletcher, J. M., Shaywitz, S. E., Lyon, G. R., Shankweiler, D. P., et al. (1998). Subtypes of reading disability. Variability around a phonological core. *Journal of Education Psychology*, *90*, 347–373.

Raskind, W. H., Hus, L., Berninger, V. W., Thomson, J. B., & Wijsman, E. M. (2000). Familial aggregation of dyslexia phenotypes. *Behavior Genetics*, *30*, 385–396.

Rayner, K., & Pollatsek, A. (1989). *The psychology of reading*. Englewood Cliffs, NJ: Prentice Hall.

Seidenberg, M. S., & McClelland, J. L. (1989). A distributed, developmental model of word recognition and naming. *Psychological Review*, *96*, 523–568.

Snowling, M., Goulandris, N., Bowlby, M., & Howell, P. (1986). Segmentation and speech perception in relation to reading skill: A developmental analysis. *Journal of Experimental Child Psychology*, *41*, 489–507.

Spring, C., & Perry, L. (1983). Naming speed and serial recall in poor and adequate readers. *Contemporary Educational Psychology*, *8*, 141–145.

Stanovich, K. E., & Siegel, L. (1994). Phenotypic performance profile of children with reading disabilities: A regression-based test of the phonological-core variable-difference model. *Journal of Educational Psychology, 86,* 24–53.

Stone, B., & Brady, S. A. (1995). Evidence for phonological processing deficits in less-skilled readers. *Annals of Dyslexia, 45,* 51–78.

Swanson, H. L., Saez, L., Gerber, M., & Leafstedt, J. (2004). Literacy and cognitive functioning in bilingual and nonbilingual children at or not at risk for reading disabilities. *Journal of Educational Psychology, 96,* 3–18.

Torgesen, J. K. (1978). Performance of reading disabled children on serial memory tasks: A selective review of recent research. *Reading Research Quarterly, 14,* 57–87.

Torgesen, J. K. (1985). Memory processes in reading disabled children. *Journal of Learning Disabilities, 18,* 350–357.

Torgesen, J. K. (1988). Studies of children with learning disabilities who perform poorly on memory span tasks. *Journal of Learning Disabilities, 21,* 605–612.

Torgesen, J. K. (1996). The special case of phonological memory. In G. R. Lyon & N. A. Krasnegor (Eds.), *Attention, memory, and executive function* (pp. 157–184). Baltimore: Paul H. Brookes.

Torgesen, J. K. (1999). Phonologically-based reading disabilities. In R. J. Sternberg & L. Spear-Swerling (Eds.), *Perspectives on learning disabilities* (pp. 231–262). New Haven, CT: Westview Press.

Torgesen, J. K., Aleander, A. W., Wagner, R. K., Rashotte, C. A., Voeller, K., Conway, T., & Rose, E. (2001). Intensive remedial instruction for children with severe reading disabilities: Immediate and long-term outcomes from two instructional approaches. *Journal of Learning Disabilities, 34,* 33–58.

Treiman, R., Goswami, U., & Bruck, M. (1990). Not all nonwords are alike: Implications for reading development and theory. *Memory and Cognition, 18,* 559–567.

Tunmer, W. E., & Nesdale, A. R. (1985). Phonemic segmentation skill and beginning reading. *Journal of Educational Psychology, 77,* 417–427.

Wagner, R. K. (1996). From simple structure to complex function: Major trends in the development of theories, models, and measurements of memory. In G. R. Lyon & N. A. Krasnegor (Eds.), *Attention, memory, and executive function* (pp. 139–156). Baltimore: Paul H. Brookes.

Wagner, R. K. (2005). Reading impairment. In P. Strazny (Ed.), *Encyclopedia of psycholinguistics.* New York: Routledge, Taylor, & Francis.

Wagner, R. K., Balthazor, M., Hurley, S., Morgan, S., Rashotte, C. A., Shaner, R., et al. (1987). The nature of prereaders' phonological processing abilities. *Cognitive Development, 2,* 355–373.

Wagner, R., & Torgesen, J. (1987). The nature of phonological processing and its causal role in the acquisition of reading skills. *Psychological Bulletin, 101,* 192–212.

Wagner, R. K., Torgesen, J. K., Laughon, P., Simmons, K., & Rashotte, C. A. (1993). Development of young readers' phonological processing abilities. *Journal of Educational Psychology, 85,* 83–103.

Wagner, R. K., Torgesen, J. K., & Rashotte, C. A. (1994). Development of reading-related phonological processing abilities: New evidence of bi-directional causality from a latent variable longitudinal study. *Developmental Psychology, 30,* 73–87.

Wagner, R., Torgesen, J., & Rashotte, C. (1999). *Comprehensive Test of Phonological Processing.* Austin, TX: Pro-Ed.

Wagner, R. K., Torgesen, J. K., Rashotte, C. A., Hecht, S. A., Barker, T. A., Burgess, S. R., et al. (1997). Changing relations between phonological processing abilities and word-level reading as children develop from beginning to skilled readers: A 5-year longitudinal study. *Developmental Psychology, 33*, 468–479.

Wijsman, E. M., Peterson, D., Leutenegger, A. L., Thomson, J. B., Goddard, K. A., Hsu, L., et al. (2000). Segregation analysis of phenotypic components of learning disabilities: Nonword memory and digit span. *American Journal of Human Genetics, 67*, 631–646.

Wolf, M., & Goodglass, H. (1986). Dyslexia, dysnomia, and lexical retrieval: A longitudinal investigation. *Brain and Language, 28*, 154–168.

Woodcock, R. W. (1987). *Woodcock Reading Mastery Test* (Rev. ed.). Circle Pines, MN: American Guidance Service.

4 Working memory and reading disabilities[1]

Both phonological and executive processing deficits are important

H. Lee Swanson

OVERVIEW

This chapter reviews some of our studies suggesting that children with average intelligence, but reading disabilities (RD), suffer deficits in specific activities of the executive system above and beyond their deficits in the phonological system. We find that their deficits in working memory (WM) manifest themselves as a domain-specific constraint (i.e., the inefficient accessing of phonological representations) and/or a domain general constraint (i.e., capacity limitations in controlled attentional processing). We argue that children with RD suffer WM deficits related to the phonological loop, a component of WM that specializes in the retention of speech-based information. However, we also find that in situations that place high demands on processing, individuals with RD have deficits related to controlled attentional processes (e.g., maintaining task relevant information in the face of distraction or interference) independent of their problems in the phonological system. Although the results suggest that in the domain of reading individuals with RD have smaller general working-memory capacity than their normal achieving counterparts, we have also found evidence that this capacity deficit is *not* entirely specific to reading.

INTRODUCTION

The purpose of this chapter is to review some of our recent work that provides an empirical foundation for the view that reading disabilities reflect a fundamental deficit in working memory. We find, as do others, that children with RD experience considerable difficulty on working memory tasks (e.g., Bull, Johnston, & Roy, 1999; Chiappe, Hasher, & Siegel, 2000; de Beni, Palladino, Pazzaglia, & Cornoldi, 1998; de Jong, 1998; Passolunghi, Cornoldi, & de Liberto, 1999; Siegel & Ryan, 1989). We review evidence that suggests that these deficits, depending on task demands, manifest themselves as a domain-specific constraint (i.e., the inefficient accessing of phonological representations) or a domain general constraint (i.e., capacity limitations in controlled attentional processing). That is, as an extension of research that localizes problems in RD to a phonological system, we think fundamental processing differences also emerge between RD and nonreading disabled (NRD) children that cut across tasks that involve the processing of verbal and visuospatial information. In this chapter we provide a brief quantitative synthesis of the literature suggesting that differences between RD and NRD children are substantial on phonological STM tasks and on verbal and visuospatial WM tasks. How constraints in the executive system operate independently and potentially interact with constraints in the phonological system will also be discussed.

WORKING MEMORY FRAMEWORK

The framework we used to capture WM performance as it applies to reading proficiency is Baddeley's multicomponent model (1986, 1996, 2000). Baddeley (1986; Baddeley & Logie, 1999) describes WM as a limited central-executive system that interacts with a set of two passive storage systems used for temporary storage of different classes of information: the speech-based phonological loop and the visual sketchpad. The phonological loop is responsible for the temporary storage of verbal information; items are held within a phonological store of limited duration, and the items are maintained within the store via the process of articulation. The visual sketchpad is responsible for the storage of visuospatial information over brief periods and plays a key role in the generation and manipulation of mental images. Both storage systems are in direct contact with the central executive system. The central executive system is considered to be primarily responsible for coordinating activity within the cognitive system, but also devotes some of its resources to increasing the amount of information that can be held in the two subsystems (Baddeley & Logie, 1999). A recent formulation of the model (Baddeley, 2000) also includes a temporary multimodal storage component called the *episodic buffer*.

Although the mulitcomponent model of Baddeley was primarily developed from research on adult samples, the model also has an excellent fit to the WM performance of children (Alloway, Gathercole, Willis, & Adams, 2004; Gathercole, Pickering, Ambridge, & Wearing, 2004). Further, there are correlates in the neuropsychological literature that complement the tripartite structure, suggesting that some functional independence exists among the systems (e.g., Jonides, 2000; Ruchkin et al., 1999). Functional magnetic resonance imaging (fMRI) studies suggest separate neural circuitry for the storage and rehearsal components of both the phonological and the visuospatial system, with phonological system activity mainly located in the left hemisphere and visuospatial system activity located primarily in the right hemisphere (Smith & Jonides, 1997). Executive control processes, on the other hand, are associated primarily with the prefrontal cortex (e.g., Reichle,

Carpenter, & Just, 2000; Schretlen et al., 2000; Smith & Jonides, 1999). Baddeley and Logie (1999) review some evidence that the left parietal lobes are associated with verbal WM tasks (i.e., phonological loop), while the right posterior parietal lobe may be one of several locations related to visuo-spatial WM activity. They also suggest that most of the executive functions are linked to the frontal lobes, although it is possible that many other tasks related to central executive processing involve other areas of the brain as well. Neuropsychological evidence also suggests that children with RD experience difficulties related to these structures. Based on the type of task, of course, studies suggest that children with RD have processing difficulties related to regions of the frontal lobe (e.g., Lazar & Frank, 1998), left parietal lobe (e.g., Pugh et al., 2000; Shaywitz et al., 1998), as well as problems related to the interhemispheric transfer and coordination of information across the corpus callosum (e.g., Obrzut, Hynd, Obrzut, & Pirozzolo, 1981; Swanson & Mullen, 1983; Swanson & Obrzut, 1985). Clearly, the biological correlates of the various subcomponents in WM in RD samples are just beginning to be identified with advances in technology. Before discussing the research linking WM to RD, we provide our operational definition of RD and WM.

DEFINITION OF TERMS

The concept of RD rests on two assumptions: (1) Reading difficulties are *not* due to inadequate opportunity to learn, general intelligence, physical or emotional disorders, but to basic disorders in specific psychological processes, and (2) these specific processing deficits are a reflection of neurological, constitutional, and/or biological factors. Although these assumptions may seem straightforward, there is some disagreement in how they should be operationalized. In our studies, we define RD samples by their primary academic difficulties in word recognition and then attempt to isolate problems in psychological processes. Because of the strong correlation between word recognition and comprehension, these children inevitably also suffer deficits in reading comprehension. We operationally defined RD as those children who have general IQ scores on standardized tests above 85 and who have reading scores below the 25th percentile on a standardized reading achievement measure. An IQ-achievement test score discrepancy is not used in our studies because of serious problems with this type of definition of RD (e.g., see Hoskyn & Swanson, 2000, for a review).

Working memory is defined as a processing resource of limited capacity, involved in the preservation of information while simultaneously processing the same or other information (e.g., Baddeley, 1986; Baddeley & Logie, 1999; Engle, Kane, & Tuholski, 1999; Engle, Tuholski, Laughlin, & Conway, 1999; Gathercole & Baddeley, 1993; Just & Carpenter, 1992). Tasks that measure WM assess an individual's ability to maintain task-relevant information in an active state and to regulate controlled processing. For example, individuals performing WM tasks must remember some task elements and ignore, or inhibit, other elements as they complete task-relevant operations. In addition, WM tasks are those that require some inference, transformation and/or monitoring of relevant and irrelevant information (Baddeley & Logie, 1999; Engle, Tuholski, et al., 1999). In our studies, WM tasks typically engage participants in at least two activities after initial encoding: (1) a response to a question or questions about the material or related material to be retrieved, and (2) a response to recall item information that increases in set size. The first part of the task is a distractor of initial encoding items, whereas the second part tests storage.

In contrast, tasks that measure STM typically involve situations that do not vary their initial encoding. That is, participants are not instructed to infer, transform, or vary processing requirements. In those cases, participants are simply asked to recall a sequence of items in the order in which they were presented. Clearly both WM and STM tasks involve sharing some common activities on the participant's part. For example, both STM and WM tasks invoke controlled processes such as rehearsal (e.g., see Gathercole, 1998, for a review). However, controlled processing on WM tasks emerges in the context of high demands on attention (e.g., maintaining a memory trace in the face of interference) and the drawing of resources from the executive system (see Engle, Kane, & Tuholski, 1999, pp. 311–312, for discussion). Instructions in controlled processing emphasize maintaining information in the face of interference. Interference reflects competing memory traces that draw away from the targeted memory trace. In contrast, controlled processing on STM tasks attempts to maintain memory traces above some critical threshold (Cowan, 1995). This maintenance does not directly draw resources from the central executive system. Instructions in controlled processing may emphasize perceptual grouping or chunking skills, skills at phonological coding, and rehearsal speed (see Engle, Kane, & Tuholski, 1999, for a review). We will now briefly review the psychological literature linking RD to components of WM.

EXECUTIVE SYSTEM

The central executive monitors the control processes in WM. There have been a number of cognitive activities assigned to the central executive, including coordination of subsidiary memory systems, control of encoding and retrieval strategies, switching of attention in manipulation of material held related to the verbal and visual spatial systems, and the retrieval of information from LTM (e.g., Baddeley, 1996; Miyake, Friedman, Emerson, Witzki, & Howerter, 2000). Although there is an issue of whether the central executive is a unitary system (Baddeley, 1986) or composed of multiple domain-specific executives (Goldman-Rakic, 1995), there is some agreement that the central executive has some capacity limitations that influence the efficiency of operations. We assume that executive function has separable operations (e.g., inhibition, updating), but these operations may share some underlying commonality (e.g., see Miyake et al., 2000, for a review).

We think that the crucial component of the central executive as it applies to RD is controlled attention. Controlled attention is defined as the capacity to maintain and hold relevant information in "the face of interference or distraction" (Engle, Kane, & Tuholski, 1999, p. 104). Consistent with Engle, Kane, and Tuholski (1999), we have broadly operationalized executive processing as the residual variance in the memory system that influences performance when the influence of STM (storage) has been partialed out of the analysis. We also assume that this residual variance influences performance across verbal and visuospatial task.

We now review some of our studies that have implicated deficits in executive processing for children with RD, particularly as it applies to controlled attention. The involvement of executive processing activities is inferred from three outcomes: (1) poor performance on complex divided attention tasks, (2) poor monitoring, such as an inability to suppress (inhibit) irrelevant information, and (3) depressed performance across verbal and visuospatial tasks that require concurrent storage and processing.

Divided attention

Our results suggest that RD children can be distinguished from average achievers in how they handled attentional demands. For example, in one of our experiments (Swanson, 1993a, Exp. 1), a concurrent memory task, adapted from Baddeley (Baddeley, Eldridge, Lewis, & Thomson, 1984) was administered to RD and skilled readers. The task required subjects to remember digit strings (e.g., 9, 4, 1, 7, 5, 2) while they concurrently sorted blank cards, cards with pictures of nonverbal shapes, or sorting of cards with pictures of items that fit into semantic categories (e.g., vehicles – car, bus, truck; clothing – dress, socks, belt). Demands on the central executive capacity system were manipulated through the level of difficulty (three vs. six digit strings) and type of sorting required (e.g., nonverbal shapes, semantic categories, blank cards). Sorting activities that placed demands on the verbal storage (phonological system) included the categorization of pictures into semantic categories, whereas sorting activities that made demands on the visual store (i.e., visuospatial sketchpad) include discrimination among complex nonverbal shapes. Baddeley et al. (1984) found that in such activities the main task difficulty (sorting) interacts with concurrent memory load, but only with a memory load of six digits. Performance for the six-digit memory load condition places processing demands on the central executive, thereby interfering with the main task. Swanson's (1993a) results indicated a clear effect for memory load. The results showed that RD readers can perform comparably to their chronological age (CA)-matched counterparts on verbal and visuospatial sorting conditions that included three-digit strings (low demands), and that only when the coordination of tasks becomes more difficult (six-digit strings) do ability group differences emerge. More important, the results for the high memory load condition (six-digit strings) showed that RD readers were inferior to the CA-matched readers (and reading matched controls for ordered recall) in their ability to recall digits during both verbal and nonverbal sorting. Because recall performance for RD readers was not restricted to a particular storage system (i.e., verbal storage), compared with the performance of CA-matched skilled readers, one can infer that processes, other than a language-specific system accounted for the results.

Attention to relevant and irrelevant information

We have also explored RD children's selective attention toward features. For example, Swanson and Cochran (1991) compared 10-year-old children with RD with NRD children matched on chronological age on their retrieval of word features within and across the cerebral hemispheres that required dichotic listening. Participants were asked to recall words organized by semantic (e.g., red, black, green, orange), phonological (e.g., sit, pit, hit), and orthographic (e.g., sun, same, seal, soft) features presented to either the left or right ear. The study included two experiments. Experiment 1 compared recall with different orienting instructions to the word lists. One orienting instruction told children about the organizational structure of the words, while the other condition (nonorienting) did not. For the orienting condition, children were told to remember all words, "but to specifically remember words that go with _____" (e.g., colors) or "words that rhyme with ____" (e.g., it) or "words that start with the letter _____" (e.g., s) that the words go with certain categories (such as animals and furniture) or sounds (rhymes). For the nonorienting condition, children were told to remember all words but no mention was made of the distinctive organization features of the words. Experiment 2 extended Experiment 1 by implementing a cued recall condition. In both experiments, children were told they would hear someone talking through the earphone in either the right or left ear. They would also hear words in the other ear. They were told that when they stopped hearing the information in the designated ear and the nondesignated ear, they were to tell the experimenter all the words they could remember.

For both experiments, NRD children had higher levels of target recall and nontargeted recall than RD children. More important, ability group differences emerged in "how specific word features" were selectively attended to. The selective attention index focused on the targeted words in comparison to the background words (targeted word recall minus background word recall) from other lists *within* the targeted ear, as well as background items in the contra lateral ear. Regardless of word features, whether competing word features were presented within ear or across ear conditions, or whether retrieval conditions were non cued or cued, RD readers' selective attention scores were smaller (the different score between targeted items and nontargeted items was closer to zero) than NRD readers. Thus, when compared with RD children, NRD children were more likely to ignore irrelevant information in the competing conditions. Taken together, the results of this study, as well as those of three earlier dichotic listening studies (Swanson, 1986; Swanson & Mullen, 1983; Swanson & Obrzut, 1985) suggest that RD children suffer processing deficits related to resource monitoring (attention to relevant information, suppression of irrelevant information) regardless of the type of word features, retrieval conditions, or ear presentation.

Combined processing and storage demands

Several of our studies (Swanson, 1992; Swanson, 1994, 2003; Swanson & Ashbaker, 2000; Swanson, Ashbaker, & Lee, 1996) have also assessed executive processing via tasks that follow the format of Daneman and Carpenter's (1980) Sentence Span measure – a task strongly related to achievement measures (see Daneman & Merikle, 1996, for a review). This task is assumed to tap central executive processes related to "updating" (Miyake et al., 2000). Updating requires monitoring and coding information for relevance to the task at hand and then appropriately revising items held in WM.

A recent study (Swanson, 2003) compared skilled readers and RD readers across a broad age span. The study compared four age groups (7, 10, 13, 20) on phonological, semantic, and visuospatial WM measures administered under conditions earlier referred to in Swanson et al. (1996): initial (no probes or cues), gain (cues that bring performance to an asymptotic level), and maintenance conditions (asymptotic conditions without cues). This study also explored whether ability groups vary in their WM spans as a function of the type of WM task across age. This study included two verbal WM measures that required the processing of acoustically familiar rhyming words (phonological task, e.g., run, fun, gun; car, star, bar, far) or the processing of semantically related words (semantic task, e.g., pear, apple, prune; car, bus, truck), and a visuospatial WM measure (visual-matrix task) that required the sequencing of dots on a matrix.

The general findings of the Swanson (2003) study were that (a) young adults (20- and 35-year-olds) performed better than children and older adults, (b) skilled readers performed better than RD readers in all processing conditions, and (c) the gain condition improved span performance from initial conditions, but performance declined when maintenance conditions were administered. Perhaps the most important findings of this study were that WM deficits for RD readers across a broad age range reflected a problem in a domain-general capacity system. Three findings lead to this inference. First, the study found that the magnitude of the difference (effect size) between RD and skilled readers increased on gain and maintenance conditions when compared with the initial conditions, suggesting that ability group differences were not eliminated by improving processing efficiency. Second, skilled readers experienced less reduction in performance in the maintenance condition, when compared with the gain condition, than RD readers. Thus, not only did RD readers have smaller WM spans than skilled readers *across* memory conditions, but they also experienced a greater capacity reduction when WM measures were presented under high demand conditions. Finally, RD readers' performance across a large age span was best captured by comparing their performance with adolescents (13-year-old skilled readers) rather than with adult skilled readers who yield the highest WM performance (20- and 35-year-olds).

Prior to leaving this area, we want to report a recent meta-analysis we have completed on WM and RD (Jerman & Swanson, 2005). All studies included in this meta-analysis utilized WM tasks that followed the format (i.e., process and storage question) of the Daneman and Carpenter task (1980). We attempted to address three questions in this synthesis.

1   Are WM differences between RD and NRD children a function of age (i.e., reflect a developmental delay or processing deficit)?
2   Are the deficits generalized (verbal and visual spatial) or specific to a particular domain?
3   Is the magnitude of the difference related to intelligence and reading level?

Articles for this meta-analysis were identified using two methods. A computer literature search of several databases was conducted from 1980 to 2003. To be included in the present analysis each study was required to meet the following criteria:

1   Compare children with RD with NRD readers on at least one measure of WM.
2   Report standardized reading scores below the 25th percentile on RD students and above the 30th percentile for NRD readers.
3   Report standardized intelligence scores for both groups of students indicating that they are in the average range (80–115).

The initial search yielded 75 articles. Out of these 75 studies, several articles were excluded because they failed to report IQ scores, and/or reading scores or effect sizes could not be calculated. Thus, only 28 articles met the criteria for inclusion into the meta-analysis. All 28 studies had RD and NRD readers matched on chronological age and intelligence, and 11 studies also included "reading level" control group – normally achieving younger subjects matched to RD on reading grade level.

The average sample size per study was 42.7 (SD = 27.2; range 8–108) for students with RD; M = 52.8 (SD = 32.0; range 11–121) for average students; and M = 25.3 (SD = 8.46; range 10–38) for the reading-matched students. Within the RD group, the average age was 165.12 months (SD = 64.9; range 65.24–534). Within the NRD group, the mean age was 162.44

months (*SD* = 64.0; range 64.7–534). And within the reading-matched group, the mean age in months was 105.06 (*SD* = 15.95; range 81–144). Though the articles included in this analysis covered kindergarten through adulthood (e.g., Chiappe et al., 2000; Ransby & Swanson, 2003), the majority of studies involved fourth-, fifth-, and sixth-grade students. The most frequently used measure of general cognitive ability across all the studies was the WISC/WISC-R/WISC-III (64.3% of studies) and the most commonly used measures of reading achievement were the WRAT/WRAT-R (46.4%).

The 28 studies produced 208 effect sizes. The overall mean effect size across all studies was –0.81 (*SD* = 0.92). Based on Cohen's criteria, that is a large effect which indicated that the overall mean performance of the RD group was almost one standard deviation below that of the chronologically aged matched NRD group. The mean effect size between RD group and reading-matched group yielded a small effect, –0.14 (*SD* = 1.32).

Table 4.1 provides a review of the age, IQ, reading and math abilities reflected in the meta-analysis articles. There were 14 studies out of 28 that reported math scores. As shown, RD children were close to the cutoff score (91.28) or the 25th percentile. Thus, there are some children who are primarily RD, having math performance in the average range, whereas other studies included samples that shared both reading and math disabilities.

Because the WM tasks varied in content, the measures were divided into six categories as a function of the type of information to be recalled (e.g., tasks that involve digits or counting; tasks that involve visuospatial information). Table 4.2 shows the comparisons among chronologically age-matched as a function of these categories. Using Cohen's cutoff score, .80, as a substantial effect size, it appears that visual/spatial and listening span and the digit counting span approximated Cohen's criterion. Moderate effect sizes were found on the semantic and phonological measures, as well as complex visuospatial measures.

We used a Hierarchical Linear Model (HLM; e.g., Bryk & Raudenbush, 1992) to analyze those variables that best predicted or moderated the magnitude of the effect size between RD and chronologically age-matched IQ-matched peers. Measures were the age, IQ, and reading scores of the RD participants. We narrowed down the previous six categories of WM measures into only two: Tasks that tapped the processing of visual/spatial information and those that tapped the processing of verbal information. We also separated those studies that were in the verbal domain that required greater transformations of information from encoding (semantic association, sentence span) from those that included information more related to the phonological system. For example, the digit counting task and the phonological task seem to be much closer to descriptions of phonological loop. In contrast, those tasks such as listening span and semantic association we assumed to be placing greater demands on the executive system, whereas we assumed that some task could draw more easily from the phonological system.

Table 4.1 Psychometric and demographic information on working memory participants

	Group										
	Control				Reading disabled				Effect size	
	N	M	SD	Range	N	M	SD	Range	M	SD
Age (months)										
CA	27	146.37	42.46	64–318	27	145.75	39.69	64–301	–	–
RL	11	102.58	17.9	81–144					–	–
IQ[A]										
CA	17	106.13	5.79	94–115	27	99.42	4.20	91–111	–0.71	0.60
RL	4	106.92	12.88	92–124					–0.39	1.14
Reading[A]										
CA	24	107.07	7.23	91–118	27	82.41	5.31	66–90	–3.92	4.39
RL	9	101.66	9.49	82–113					–0.89	0.47
Math[A]										
CA	14	109.30	6.93	99–123	27	91.28	8.00	73–113	–1.70	1.37

Notes
N = 28 studies; CA = chronologically age matched average readers; RL = younger children match on reading level; [A] standard scores.

Table 4.2 Effect size as a function of categorical variables when compared to chronological age and IQ matched

Category	Sample size	K	M	SD	Effect size weighted	SE	95% CI for effect size		Homogeneity Q
							Lower	Upper	
1 Listening Sentence span	4,454	53	-1.13	0.75	-1.17	0.14	-1.44	-0.90	23.74
2 Digit/counting	2,428	36	-0.74	0.62	-0.77	0.17	-1.10	-0.43	11.90
3 Visual-spatial	3,240	39	-0.94	0.68	-0.95	0.16	-1.27	-0.64	15.99
4 Complex-visual	1,245	30	-0.44	0.29	-0.45	0.18	-0.80	-0.09	2.38
5 Semantic	1,628	20	-0.65	0.24	-0.65	0.22	-1.09	-0.21	1.03
6 Phonological	1,374	14	-0.66	0.31	-0.66	0.27	-1.19	-0.14	1.13

Table 4.3 Conditional model (N = 28 studies and 207 observations)

Fixed effect	Estimate	SE	t-ratio	p-value
Intercept	−0.85	0.09	−9.11	<.0001
Age LD	−0.001	0.001	−0.72	.47
IQ LD	0.006	0.01	0.39	.69
Reading LD	0.002	0.01	0.23	.82
Verbal vs. visual	−0.06	0.04	−1.29	.19
Executive system vs. phonological system	0.19	0.05	3.25	.001

Random effect (covariance parameter estimates)	Estimate	SE	Z	p-value
Intercept	0.13	0.06	2.23	.01
Residual	0.34	0.04	9.36	<.0001

Table 4.3 shows a conditional model that enters the fixed effects of age, IQ, reading score, and visual versus verbal WM measures. The results indicated that the estimates related to age, IQ, reading level, and verbal versus visuo-spatial measures were no better than chance. However, the effect sizes were better than chance when comparisons were made between those measures that required a large transformation (semantic association, listening span) and those that required less of a transformation. From this meta-analysis, we concluded the following:

1   WM deficits were generalized across visual/spatial and verbal tasks. The results support the notion that ability group differences are related to a domain general system. When we enter reading skill as a variable in our HLM modeling to assess the interaction of domain specificity, we did not find a significant interaction. Thus, we do not think that WM deficits are merely an artifact of the classification variable.
2   The results indicated that age was not related to RD/non-RD effect sizes. In addition, these deficits were independent of effect sizes and reading intelligence between ability groups. Thus, the results support the notion that WM differences in students with RD persist across age.
3   No significant relationship emerged that would suggest that variations in IQ or effect sizes in IQ between RD and NRD are related to the magnitude of differences and effect sizes of WM.

Summary

We have selectively reviewed studies suggesting that RD children's WM deficits may, depending on the task and materials, reflect problems related to the executive processing system. Although our research suggests isolated difficulties related to updating and the suppression of irrelevant information underlies RD, we also want to emphasize that several activities that involve executive processing are very much intact for children with RD. Some of these intact executive processes relate to planning. For example, although planning (such as mapping out a sequence of moves) is considered a component of the executive system (e.g., however, see Miyake et al., 2000, p. 91), we have not found overall solution differences between RD and NRD students on such tasks (see Swanson, 1988, 1993b). For example, studies that have examined performance on complex executive-processing tasks, such as the Tower of Hanoi, have not produced reliable differences between RD and NRD children. In one study, Swanson (1993b) compared RD, average readers, and children with high IQ on the Tower of Hanoi task, as well as two problem-solving tasks (Combinatorial, Pendulum). As expected, an advantage in solution times was found for the intellectually gifted children. In contrast, no significant differences in solution time or number of steps to solution were found between average achievers and RD children (children with reading scores below the 15th percentile) with comparable IQs on the three problem-solving measures. However, "think aloud" protocols revealed that gifted and average achievers placed a heavy emphasis on domain specific strategies, whereas LD children used a more general heuristic (see Swanson, 1993b, p. 883, for a discussion).

In summary, several studies suggest that some participants with RD matched to NRD participants on psychometric IQ measures, are deficient on some tasks that measure specific components of executive processing. Those activities of the executive system that we think are particular candidates for difficulty in individuals with RD are related to updating (e.g., Siegel & Ryan, 1989; Swanson et al., 1996) and the inhibition of dominant or prepotent responses (e.g., Chiappe et al., 2000). Those components of the executive system that are relatively intact (to be reviewed later) are related to planning, self-regulation, or decision making (e.g., Swanson, 1993b). We will now turn our attention to the phonological system.

PHONOLOGICAL LOOP

In Baddeley's model (1986), the phonological loop is specialized for the retention of verbal information over short periods of time. It is composed of both a phonological store, which holds information in phonological form, and a rehearsal process, which serves to maintain representations in the phonological store (see Baddeley, Gathercole, & Papagano, 1998, for an extensive review). Thus, the ability to retain and access phonological representations has been associated with verbal STM – but more specifically the phonological loop. The phonological loop has been referred to as STM (e.g., Baddeley, 1986; Dempster, 1985) because it involves two major components discussed in the STM literature: a speech-based phonological input store and a rehearsal process (see Baddeley, 1986, for a review).

A substantial number of studies (see Vukovic & Siegel, chapter, 5 this volume) support the notion that children with RD in reading experience deficits in phonological processing (e.g., see Stanovich & Siegel, 1994), such as forming or accessing phonological representations of information. This difficulty in forming and accessing phonological representations impairs their ability to retrieve verbal information from STM. Interestingly, this phonological impairment does not appear to have broad effects on general intellectual ability apart from the developmental consequences on language-related functions (see Hohnen & Stevenson, 1999). Several recent studies suggest that deficits in the phonological loop deficit may lie at the root of word learning problems in children with RD (e.g., see Siegel, 1993, for review). These findings build on earlier research that has shown that the manifestations of this phonological deficit are poor word recognition (Siegel, 1993), poor performance on phonological awareness tasks (Bradley & Bryant, 1978), slow naming speed (Denckla & Rudel, 1976), and impaired verbal STM (Nelson & Warrington, 1980). The current research suggests that this deficit (1) predates the acquisition of literacy (Scarborough, 1990), (2) is independent of IQ (Siegel, 1992), and (3) persists over time (Bruck, 1992).

In general, several studies suggest that difficulties in forming and accessing phonological representations impair the ability to learn new words in individuals with RD. We briefly review a quantitative synthesis we did a few years ago, which suggests that deficits in STM are isolated to verbal information and persist across age. A comprehensive meta-analysis was conducted to quantitatively summarize the experimental literature on STM and RD published over approximately a 30-year period (O'Shaughnessy & Swanson, 1998). To be included in the synthesis, each study meet the following criteria: (1) directly compared children with RD and average readers, (2) report standardized reading scores that indicated that RD students are at least 1 year below grade level, and (3) reported intelligence scores for RD students that are in the average range (e.g., 85–115). Although the search resulted in approximately 155 articles on immediate memory and learning disabilities, only 38 studies met the criteria for inclusion. Effect sizes were computed for each experiment; defined as the mean memory score of the RD group minus the mean memory score of the NRD readers group divided by the pooled standard deviation of both groups and then corrected for sample size. Negative effect sizes represent poorer immediate memory performance in the RD group.

Based on a review of the studies included in this analysis, two broad categories were developed to organize the results: studies that use (1) verbal stimuli and/or (2) nonverbal stimuli. In addition, the following subcategories were developed to organize each of the broad categories: (1) free recall and serial recall memory tasks, (2) with and without instruction in mnemonic strategies, (3) auditory and visual presentation, and (4) age (7–8 years, 9–11 years, 12–13 years, 14–17 years, and 18 years and older). An overall average estimate of immediate memory difference was obtained as well as an estimate with outliers removed across all appropriate study outcomes as shown in Table 4.4.

The meta-analysis produced 186 effect sizes from 38 studies. The average sample size per study was 36 (range 8–66; n = 1354) for students with RD, and 42 (range 8–88; n = 1600) for average readers. Within the RD group of subjects, the average age was 11 years with 240 females and 894 males. Within

Table 4.4 Overall magnitude of differences in short-term memory. Adapted from Swanson, Cooney, and O'Shaughnessy (1998). Memory and learning disabilities. In B. Y. Wong (Ed.) *Understanding learning disabilities* (2nd ed.), with permission from Elsevier.

Category	Outliers removed			Total sample		
	K	ES	SD	K	ES	SD
Overall	126	–0.64	0.41	158	–0.68	0.73
Verbal	115	–0.68	0.40	146	–0.72	0.73
Free recall	54	–0.55	0.34	68	–0.52	0.55
Serial recall	63	–0.80	0.48	78	–0.90	0.83
Auditory presentation	41	–0.70	0.52	53	–0.77	0.92
Visual presentation	73	–0.66	0.35	91	–0.69	0.62
With mnemonic instruction	13	–0.54	0.23	18	–0.52	0.32
Without mnemonic instruction	102	–0.71	0.44	128	–0.75	0.77
7–8 years old	10	–0.57	0.48	12	–0.76	0.62
9–11 years old	19	–0.89	0.29	25	–1.01	0.71
12–13 years old	8	–0.78	0.41	10	–0.76	0.49
14–17 years old	3	–0.34	0.49	3	–0.34	0.49
18 years old & older	3	–0.58	0.62	3	–0.58	0.62
Nonverbal (low verbal)	9	–0.15	0.15	12	–0.17	0.50
Free recall	1	0.00	[na]	1	0.00	[na]
Serial recall	8	–0.17	0.15	11	–0.19	0.52
Auditory presentation						
Visual presentation	9	–0.15	0.15	12	–0.17	0.50
With mnemonic instruction						
Without mnemonic instruction	9	–0.15	0.15	12	–0.17	0.50
7–8 years old	2	–0.27	0.03	2	–0.27	0.03
9–11 years old	3	0.35	0.60	3	0.35	0.60
12–13 years old	5	–0.41	0.48	5	–0.41	0.48
14–17 years old	3	–0.34	0.50	3	–0.34	0.50
18 years old & older						

Notes
K = number of dependent measures; ES = effect size between RD and NRD.
Negative effect size indicates poorer performance in RD group. NA indicates not available.
This table is modified and reprinted with permission from Swanson et al. (1998).

the average readers, the average age was 11 with 382 females and 949 males. The majority of studies, 23 out of 38, involved fourth-, fifth-, and sixth-grade students.

As shown in Table 4.4, the results of this synthesis support a large body of clinical research demonstrating that as a group RD exhibit deficits in immediate memory processes compared to average readers students of the same general intelligence. The overall mean effect size across all studies is –0.64 (*SD* = 0.41). Based on Cohen's criteria, this is a moderate effect size. However, as shown in Table 4.4, this effect size varied as further disaggregation occurred within verbal and nonverbal stimuli categories under the subcategories of free recall, serial recall, auditory presentation, visual presentation, with mnemonic or strategy instruction, without mnemonic/strategy instruction, and age. The important findings related to this synthesis were as follows:

1   The RD group performed poorly on tasks requiring memorization of *verbal information* in comparison to average readers (overall mean effect size of –0.68).

2   The mean effects size for visuospatial information was small (overall mean effect size of –0.15).

3   Memory tasks requiring RD readers to recall *exact sequences* of verbal stimuli, such as words or digits, immediately after a series was presented yielded a much greater overall mean effect size (overall mean effect size of –0.80) than nonverbal serial recall tasks (overall mean effect size of –0.17).

4   The overall mean effect size for studies that provided instructions in mnemonic strategies (e.g., rehearsal and sorting items into groups) prior to recall and used verbal stimuli was –0.54; the overall mean effect size for studies that used verbal stimuli but did not provide instructions to students about how to use mnemonic strategies is –0.71.

In summary, there is abundant evidence that participants with RD suffer deficits in STM, a substrate of the phonological system. The quantitative analysis of the literature clearly indicates that children with RD are inferior to their counter parts on measures of STM for verbal information. Most critically, students with RD are at a distinct disadvantage compared to their normal achieving peers when they are required to memorize verbal information in serial order. As in the WM synthesis we also performed hierarchical linear modeling entering variable of age, reading-effect size differences, and verbal IQ effect size difference. None of these variables accounted for the magnitude of effect sizes.

Before we leave this section, a question emerges as to whether verbal STM and verbal WM are comparable constructs. That is, our previous studies show that both STM and WM contributed unique variance to reading problems. Some authors have suggested that verbal STM and verbal WM are synonymous constructs in children. For example, Hutton and Towse (2001) found, via a principal component analysis, that both WM and STM tasks loaded on the same factor for children 8 to 11 years old. In addition, their results also showed that correlations related to WM and STM on measures of reading and math were of the same magnitude (see Table 4.4), suggesting that WM and STM share the same construct (also see Cowan et al., 2003, for a similar finding). As stated by Hutton and Towse "it appears that what holds for WM in adults may not be equally true for children, and vice versa. The study highlights the value of taking account of children's online processing during WM tasks, and in so doing suggests that WM and STM may, at least in some circumstances, be rather equivalent" (p. 392). Our research suggests, however, that a distinction between the two concepts may be necessary in children with RD. Although we assume that verbal WM tasks share some important variance with the phonological loop (STM), we also argue that the verbal WM tasks share important variance with the central system.

VISUOSPATIAL SKETCHPAD

The visuospatial sketchpad is specialized for the processing and storage of visual material, spatial material, or both, and for linguistic information that can be recoded into imaginable forms (see Baddeley, 1986, for a review). Measures of visuospatial WM have primarily focused on memory for visual patterns (e.g., Logie, 1986). A major study by Gathercole and Pickering (2000a, 2000b) found that visuospatial WM abilities, as well as measures of central executive processing, were associated with attainment levels on a national curriculum for children aged 6 to 7 years. Children who showed marked deficits in curriculum attainment also showed marked deficits in visuospatial WM. Thus, there is a strong relationship between visuospatial WM and academic performance in the younger grades. However, the literature linking RD to visuospatial memory deficits is mixed. For example, several studies in the STM literature suggest RD children's visual STM is intact (see Swanson et al., 1998, for a comprehensive review). When visuospatial WM (combined storage and processing demands) performance is considered, however, some studies find that visuospatial WM in students with RD is intact when compared with their same age counterparts (e.g., Swanson et al., 1996, Exp. 1), whereas others suggest problems in various visuospatial tasks (Swanson et al., 1996, Exp. 2). Most studies suggest, however, that depending on the type of academic disability, greater problems in performance are more likely to occur on verbal than visuospatial WM tasks.

We found that the evidence on whether children with RD have any particular advantage on visuospatial WM when compared to their normal achieving counterparts fluctuates with processing demands. Swanson (2000) proposed a model that may account for these mixed findings. There are two parts to this model. The first part of the model assumes that executive processes (domain general system) are used to maintain associations across high demand processing conditions. The maintenance of associations across processing conditions is related to changes, via experimenter feedback (cues or probes), in WM performance. A child with a reading disability has difficulty efficiently maintaining these associations. The predictions of the first part of the model are consistent with current models of executive functions that are called into play only when the activities of multiple components of the cognitive architecture must be coordinated (e.g., Baddeley, 1996; Engle, Cantor, & Carullo, 1992). The second part of the model assumes that when excessive demands are *not* made on the executive system, performance differences between RD and NRD readers are limited to the verbal system. The second part of the model is consistent with earlier work suggesting that the visuospatial system of RD readers is generally intact (see Shankweiler & Crain, 1986, for a review), but when excessive demands are placed on the executive system, their visuospatial performance is depressed compared with chronological age-matched readers (Swanson et al., 1996).

Summary

Taken together, there is evidence that children with RD have problems in various components of the WM system. There is one finding, perhaps, that seems rather paradoxical: Children with specific problems in reading suffer deficits in domain general processes related to the executive system. We now consider four possible explanations in this regard.

Are problems in the executive system merely a manifestation of deficits in the phonological system?

We have addressed this question in four studies (Swanson, 2003; Swanson & Ashbaker, 2000; Swanson & Sachse-Lee, 2001a, 2001b). Our conclusion is that executive processing deficits exist in children with RD independent of their deficits in phonological processing. For example, Swanson and Ashbaker (2000) tested whether the operations related to STM and WM operated independently of one another. In this study, they compared RD and NRD readers and younger reading level-matched children on a battery of WM and STM tests to assess executive and phonological processing, respectively. Measures of the executive system were modeled after Daneman and Carpenter's (1980) WM tasks, whereas measures of the phonological system included those that related to articulation speed, digit span, and word span.

The Swanson and Ashbaker (2000) study yielded two important results. First, although the RD reading group was inferior to NRD readers in WM, verbal STM, and articulation speed, the differences in verbal STM and WM revealed little relation with articulation speed. That is, reading-related differences on WM and STM measures remained when articulation speed was partialed from the analysis. These reading-group differences were pervasive across verbal and visuospatial WM tasks, even when the influence of verbal STM was statistically removed, suggesting that reading-group differences are domain general. Second, WM tasks and verbal STM tasks contributed unique variance to word recognition and reading comprehension beyond articulation speed. These results are consistent with those of Daneman and Carpenter (1980) and others (e.g., Engle, Tuholski et al., 1999) who have argued that verbal STM tasks and WM tasks are tapping different processes. In general, we have found the independent contribution of WM persists in children with RD not only when verbal articulation speed is partialed out in the analysis (Swanson & Ashbaker, 2000), but also when partialing out the influence of verbal STM (Swanson et al. 1996), reading comprehension (Swanson, 1999b), or IQ scores (Swanson & Sachse-Lee, 2001a).

The above findings from Swanson and Ashbaker's (2000) study are consistent with early work on RD samples (Swanson, 1994; Swanson & Berninger, 1995). In a 1994 study, Swanson tested whether STM and WM contributed unique variance to academic achievement in children and adults with RD. He found that STM and WM tasks loaded on different factors. Further, these two factors both contributed unique variance to reading performance.

A study by Swanson and Berninger (1995) also examined potential differences between STM and WM by testing whether STM and WM accounted for different cognitive profiles in RD readers. Swanson and Berninger used a double dissociation design to compare children deficient in reading comprehension (based on scores from the Passage Comprehension subtest of the Woodcock Reading Mastery Test; Woodcock, 1987), and/or word recognition (based on scores from the Word Identification subtest of the Woodcock Reading Mastery Test), on WM and phonological STM measures. Participants were divided into four ability groups: high comprehension/high word recognition, low comprehension/high word recognition, high comprehension/ low word recognition, and low comprehension/low word recognition. The results were straightforward: WM measures were related primarily to reading comprehension, whereas phonological STM measures were related primarily to word recognition. Most critically, because no significant interaction emerged, the results further indicated that the comorbid group (i.e., children low in both comprehension and word recognition) had combined memory deficits. That is, WM deficits were reflective of the poor comprehension-only group and STM deficits were reflective of the poor recognition-only group.

Are the executive processing problems attributed to RD merely a manifestation of attention disorders?

Because executive deficits are manifestations of monitoring attention, it is easy to attribute any executive processing deficits that might arise related to children with RD as manifestations of attention deficit hyperactivity disorder (ADHD). This is because RD and ADHD are comorbid in some epidemiological studies (see Roodenrys, chapter 9, this volume). Further, one can infer

that problems in executive processes overlap with potential problems in attention. A distinction can be made, however, in executive processing related to
the self-monitoring of attention versus constraints in attentional capacity.

Studies that attribute executive deficits to ADHD primarily rely on measures related to various forms of planning, not measures of WM (Barkley,
1997). This distinction partly comes from the literature suggesting that children with ADHD do *not* suffer WM deficits (Siegel & Ryan, 1989; Willcutt,
Pennington, Boada, & Ogline, 2001), whereas those with reading deficits do.
For example, Siegel and Ryan (1989) found that ADHD children's WM span
scores were *not* significantly different from normal achievers. In addition, the
literature is clear that WM problems exist in individuals with RD who do not
suffer from behavioral manifestations (e.g., inability to attend or focus for
long periods, impulsivity) of attention deficits (Siegel & Ryan, 1989).

Thus, we assume that WM measures capture different aspects of executive
functioning when compared to measures used in the clinical literature to
assess executive functioning (i.e., competition for cognitive resources vs.
planning and/or motor inhibition, e.g., Wisconsin Card Sorting task may
reflect motor inhibition, Tower-of-Hanoi Task may reflect planning) (see
Miyake et al., 2000, p. 331). We would argue that the variance related to
poor attention in ADHD are problems related to goal-directed or planning
behaviors (also Roodenrys, chapter 9, this volume), whereas attention problems in children with RD are related to their capacity to maintain and hold
relevant information in the face of interference or distraction (Engle, Kane, &
Tuholski 1999, p. 104). The symptoms attributed to ADHD children's poor
attentional monitoring (impulsivity, distractibility, diminished persistence,
diminished sensitivity to feedback, lack of planning, and lack of judgment)
are intact (or normal) in RD children. In contrast to ADHD children,
research with RD children has shown normal levels of planning and judgment on problem-solving tasks (e.g., Tower of Hanoi; Swanson, 1993b) and
signal detection measures (d') on vigilance tasks show comparable persistence
(although less attentional capacity) as normal achievers in their use of
attentional resources across time (Swanson, 1981, 1983).

Are executive processing deficits secondary disorders to more fundamental problems in reading achievement or a limited knowledge base?

In terms of achievement, a recent subgroup study found that independence
(unique variance) exists between WM and reading achievement. Swanson
and Sachse-Lee (2001b) subgrouped skilled and LD readers on a listening
span measure modeled after Daneman and Carpenter (1980). The subgroups
reflected (1) those children high in executive processing (high listening span),
but with average reading skill, (2) those low in executive processing and
reading, and (3) two additional subgroups of skilled and LD readers who
were matched on listening span (moderate executive processing ability). The

moderate executive processing NRD readers matched the high executive processing group on reading and the two LD subgroups were also matched on poor reading performance. It is also important to note that for the two subgroups matched on moderate WM span, that the poor readers had lower verbal IQ scores than the average readers. These four subgroups were compared on phonological, visuospatial, and semantic WM tasks across noncued and cued WM conditions. As expected, the high executive processing group performed better than the low executive processing, and low executive processing and low reading subgroup underperformed the other subgroups on the phonological, visuospatial, and semantic measures. However, the important results showed that the two reading groups matched on executive processing (moderate ability level) were statistically comparable in performance on phonological, semantic, and visuospatial measures. These findings suggest that executive processing problems operate independently of the influence of reading achievement. These findings complement our other work showing that fundamental processing deficits exist in WM even when reading and/or math ability is partialed from the analysis (see Swanson, 1999b; Swanson & Sachse-Lee, 2001a).

In terms of children's knowledge base, we assume that knowledgeable children can outperform less knowledgeable children on WM tasks. Our work has evaluated the mediating role of accuracy and speed of retrieval of information from LTM on the relationship between WM span and reading comprehension (Swanson, 1999a; see Table 4.4 for a test of the LTM mediation model). In one study (Swanson, 1999b), ability groups (LD, CA-matched, and reading level matched) were statistically matched (standard scores) on measures of fluid intelligence (Raven's Colored Progressive Matrices Test). Ability groups were compared on measures of phonological accuracy and retrieval speed (phonemic deletion, digit naming, pseudoword repetition), measures of LTM accuracy and retrieval speed (semantic, orthographic, and vocabulary) and executive processing (sentence span, counting span, visuospatial span). There were two important findings in this study. First, entering LTM speed and accuracy, and phonological speed and accuracy, before executive processing (WM) in a hierarchical regression model, did not eliminate the significant contribution of executive processing to reading comprehension. Thus, there is important as well as unique variance related to WM measures above and beyond the contribution of LTM and phonological processing. Second, partialing out the influence of achievement (i.e., reading comprehension; see Table 5 in Swanson, 1999b) does *not* eliminate performance differences between LD and CA matched children on measures of speed for accessing phonological information *or* executive processing. Taken together, these findings are not consistent with the view that retrieval of domain specific knowledge from LTM underlies ability group differences in executive processing (c.f., Ericsson & Kintsch, 1995).

Are deficits in executive processing merely a manifestation of differences in fluid intelligence?

This is a particularly complex issue because performance on WM tasks are strongly correlated with fluid intelligence (e.g., Ackerman, Beier, & Boyle, 2002; Engle, Tuholski, et al., 1999; Kyllonen & Christal, 1990; however, see Bayliss, Jarrold, Gunn, & Baddeley, 2003). Kyllonen and Christal (1990), for example, reported a correlation between latent variables for reasoning and WM at approximately .80. Executive processing is seen as a key component linking these two tasks. Thus, it is rather unexpected that RD children with average intelligence will have difficulty on WM tasks. Further, these difficulties in WM are also apparent when such children are carefully matched to normal achieving counterparts on psychometric IQ measures.

Three points must be made in explaining this relationship. First, the relationship between executive processing and fluid intelligence may be indirect in samples with RD. That is, only weak to moderate relations exist between WM and fluid intelligence (performance on the Raven's Colored Progressive Matrices test) in RD samples. Swanson and Alexander (1997) found that the magnitude of the correlations between executive processing and fluid intelligence (Raven's Colored Progressive Matrices Test) varied between .04 and .34 in RD readers and −.05 and .46 in normal readers (see Table 4 in Swanson & Alexander, 1997). We take this as evidence that fluid intelligence, while related to the executive system, is not an exclusive manifestation of such a system.

Further, there are parallel studies to ours in the literature showing that children with average intelligence suffer executive processing deficits (e.g., children with ADHD). In this regard, Crinella and Yu (2000) reviewed literature suggesting a weak relationship between IQ and executive processing with normal achieving children. In reviewing the literature on normal achieving children Crinella and Yu stated "the dissociation of g and specific neurocognitive measures of Executive Function (EF) has been demonstrated in a nodal study by Welsh, Pennington, and Grossier (1991), in which a battery of EF tests was administered to normal children, with subsequent analysis yielding three factors: (1) response speed, (2) set maintenance, and (3) planning. These EF factors were either inversely correlated or not correlated with IQ – a complete dissociation of g and EF" (p. 308). Similarly, the literature on RD clearly shows poor readers with high IQ levels when compared to poor readers with low IQ levels can yield statistically equivalent performance on cognitive measures (e.g., phonological processing; Hoskyn & Swanson, 2000; Siegel, 1992). Further, these commonalities in performance are not isolated to memory or phonological processing measures (see Hosykn & Swanson, 2000; meta-analysis comparing RD and garden variety poor achievers across an array of cognitive measures).

Second, our work on problem solving shows that children with RD may use different routes or processes to problem solve, even though solution accuracy is comparable to CA-matched peers (Swanson, 1988, 1993b). For example, Swanson (1988, 1993b) found RD students successfully set up a series of subgoals for task solution. Further, their problem-solving performance was statistically comparable to their CA-matched peers on a number of fluid measures of intelligence (Picture Arrangement subtest on the WISC-R; Swanson, 1988; Tower of Hanoi, Combinatorial, and Pendulum Task, Swanson, 1993b). However, the studies also found that individuals with RD, in some cases relied on different cognitive routes than did NRD readers in problem solving. For example, on measures of fluid intelligence, problem solving was augmented by "emphasizing problem representation (defining the problem, identifying relevant information or facts given about the problem) rather than procedural knowledge or processes used to identify algorithms" (Swanson, 1993b, p. 864). There is evidence suggesting that performance by individuals with RD on fluid measures of intelligence may involve compensatory processing. This compensation can partially overcome problems in attention allocation (we use the word "partially" because we do not know the threshold where compensatory process are no longer effective) that in turn may allow them to perform in the normal range. However, we recognize that very little research has focused on the compensatory processes that underlie the links between intelligence and executive processing. In general, we argue that compensatory processes play an important role in mediating the relationship between intelligence and WM.

Finally, RD individuals may achieve normal intelligence because the information they experience in their environment does not always place high demands on their WM. A standardized test of WM (S-CPT; Swanson, 1995) shows, for example, that the majority of individuals with RD scored in the 21st percentile on WM measures (scaled scores across 11 subtests hovered around 8, or a standard score of 88 – see Swanson, 1995, p. 167), suggesting they have very weak but adequate WM ability to process information and then store information over the long term. Of course, they may use other experiences by pulling up from LTM things that they already know to help in the processing of information. With the accumulation of LTM links and connections, there is some control over the processing demands of new information. Thus, this control over processing demands may reduce any potential links between fluid intelligence and WM.

RECENT WORK

We will conclude this chapter with an overview of recent work. Some of our recent studies have focused on the importance of WM in predicting children at risk for RD within bilingual samples. A recent study by Swanson, Sáez, Gerber, and Leftstedt (2004) attempted to determine (1) whether the memory processes implicated in reading and second language acquisition extend beyond the phonological domain and (2) whether the cognitive processes that underlie difficulties in second language acquisition are the same as those that underlie difficulties in reading for monolingual students. First-grade bilingual and nonbilingual children were administered a battery of cognitive measures (STM, WM, rapid naming, random letter and number generation, vocabulary, and reading – real word and pseudoword reading) in both Spanish and English. The results showed that English word identification performance was best predicted by a general verbal WM latent factor (factor that reflected loading from both English and Spanish WM measures) and a Spanish speed/ STM factor, whereas English pseudoword reading performance was best predicted by Spanish pseudoword reading and a general WM factor. English vocabulary was best predicted by the general verbal WM factor. The results also showed that WM and STM performance differentiated among children divided into high and low reading.

On the surface, the above results support the notion English vocabulary and English word reading are predicted by a language specific phonological (STM) system (e.g., Thorn & Gathercole, 1999) and a general executive (WM) system. That is, an analysis of latent measures showed that vocabulary and reading group differences emerged on language-specific STM measures and a second-order WM memory factor. However, STM operations may be more important in explaining RD in young second language learners, whereas WM operations may be more important for explaining difficulties in language acquisition. Although children at risk for RD were weak on tasks that drew from a general verbal WM system, these weaknesses were not as pronounced as their weaknesses on language specific STM measures. Thus, both STM and WM play major roles in second language and reading acquisition. However, children at risk for RD are less dependent on a general language system when compared with those children who are only weak in English vocabulary.

We also found that children at risk for RD at different vocabulary levels have a poor cross-language transfer on STM measures. In contrast, children weak in English language acquisition, but not at risk for RD, show a strong cross-language transfer on STM measures (see Swanson et al., 2004, p. 13). For children at risk, poor performance on the Spanish STM factor was unrelated to STM performance in English. However, poor performance on Spanish WM measures was related to poor performance on English WM measures. This pattern of performance differed from children who are relatively weak in second language acquisition. High Spanish/low English children have a significant transfer on both STM and WM operations.

Taken together, we interpret this finding to mean that low or slow acquisition of English word reading evidenced in first grade is not, by itself, a diagnostic feature of reading disability risk among second language learners. The results do add to the current literature highlighting the importance of language-specific knowledge (e.g., Thorn & Gathercole, 1999) and reading skill (e.g., Stanovich & Siegel, 1994; Swanson & Ashbaker, 2000) on memory performance. In terms of language-specific knowledge, the results clearly show that children who score higher in Spanish vocabulary outperform those who score lower in Spanish vocabulary on STM measures for items presented in Spanish. Likewise, children who score higher in English vocabulary perform better than those who score lower in English vocabulary on STM measures for items presented in English. Nevertheless, we did find that cross-language transfer is more likely to occur in STM for some language groups than others. In summary, our findings suggest that variance related to a language-specific STM system and general WM system moderate performance in children with RD. Without doubt, how the source of connection between a general and domain specific system underlies reading deficits in second language learners needs further investigation.

CONCLUSION

We conclude that WM deficits are fundamental problems of children with RD. Although WM is obviously not the only skill that contributes to reading difficulties (e.g., vocabulary and syntactical skills are also important; Siegal & Ryan, 1988), WM does play a significant role in accounting for individual differences. We generally conclude that students with RD suffer WM deficits related to the phonological loop, a component of WM that specializes in the retention of speech-based information. We argue, however, that this sub-system is not the only aspect of WM that is deeply rooted in more complex activities experienced by children with RD. We find that in situations that place high demands on processing, which in turn place demands on controlled attentional processing (such as monitoring limited resources, suppressing conflicting information, and updating information), children with RD are at a clear disadvantage when compared with their chronological-aged counterparts. Further these deficits are sustained when articulation speed, phonological processing, fluid intelligence, and verbal STM are partialed from the analysis. We believe that RD students' executive system (and more specifically monitoring activities linked to their capacity for controlled sustained attention in the face of interference or distraction) is impaired. This impaired capability for controlled processing appears to manifest itself across visuospatial and verbal WM tasks, and therefore reflects a domain-general deficit. RD students' executive processing difficulties may include (1) maintaining task relevant information in the face of distraction or interference, (2) situations in suppressing and inhibiting information irrelevant to the task if necessary, and (3) accessing information from LTM. We also recognize that, although these differences in controlled attention can be domain free, they can, based on the kind of task and processing demands, reflect domain specific codes.

NOTE

1   This chapter draws from previous discussions in Swanson (2003) and Swanson and Siegel (2001a, 2001b); the reader is referred to those sources for additional information.

REFERENCES

Ackerman, P. L., Beier, M. E., & Boyle, M. O. (2002). Individual differences in working memory within a nomological network of cognitive and perceptual speed abilities. *Journal of Experimental Psychology: General, 131,* 567–589.

Alloway, T. P., Gathercole, S. E., Willis, C., & Adams, A.-M. (2004). A structural analysis of working memory and related cognitive skills in young children. *Journal of Experimental Child Psychology, 87,* 85–106.

Baddeley, A. D. (1986). *Working memory.* London: Oxford University Press.

Baddeley, A. D. (1996). Exploring the central executive. *Quarterly Journal of Experimental Psychology, 49A*(1), 5–28.

Baddeley, A. D. (2000). The episodic buffer: A new component of working memory? *Trends in Cognitive Sciences, 4,* 417–422.

Baddeley, A. D., Eldridge, M., Lewis, V. J., & Thomson, N. (1984). Attention and retrieval from long-term memory. *Journal of Experimental Psychology: General, 113,* 518–540.

Baddeley, A. D., Gathercole, S. E., & Papagno, C. (1998). The phonological loop as a language learning device. *Psychological Review, 105,* 158–173.

Baddeley, A. D., & Logie, R. H. (1999). Working memory: The multiple component model. In A. Miyake & P. Shah (Eds), *Models of working memory: Mechanisms of active maintenance and executive control* (pp. 28–61). New York: Cambridge University Press.

Barkley, R. A. (1997). Behavioral inhibition, sustained attention, and executive functions: Constructing a unified theory of ADHD. *Psychological Bulletin, 121,* 65–94.

Bayliss, D. M., Jarrold, C., Gunn, D. M., & Baddeley, A. (2003). The complexities of complex span: Explaining individual differences in working memory in children and adults. *Journal of Experimental Psychology: General, 132,* 71–92.

Bradley, L., & Bryant, P. E. (1978). Difficulties in auditory organization as a possible cause of reading backwardness. *Nature, 271*(5647), 746–747.

Bruck, M. (1992). Persistence of dyslexics phonological awareness deficits. *Developmental Psychology, 28,* 874–886.

Bryk, A., & Raudenbush, S. W. (1992). *Hierarchical linear models.* Newbury Park, CA: Sage.

Bull, R., Johnston, R. S., & Roy, J. A. (1999). Exploring the roles of the visuospatial sketch pad and central executive in children's arithmetical skills: Views from cognition and developmental neuropsychology. *Developmental Neuropsychology, 15,* 421–442.

Chiappe, P., Hasher, L., & Siegel, L. S. (2000). Working memory, inhibitory control, and reading disability. *Memory and Cognition, 28,* 8–17.

Cowan, N. (1995). *Attention and memory: An integrated framework.* Oxford, UK: Oxford University Press.

Cowan, N., Towse, J. N., Hamilton, Z., Saults, J. S., Elliott, E. M., Lacey, J. F., et al. (2003). Children's working memory processes: A response timing analysis. *Journal of Experimental Psychology: General, 132,* 113–132.

Crinella, F. M., & Yu, J. (2000). Brain mechanisms and intelligence. Psychometric *g* and executive function. *Intelligence, 27,* 299–327.

Daneman, M., & Carpenter, P. A. (1980). Individual differences in working memory and reading. *Journal of Verbal Learning and Verbal Behavior, 19,* 450–466.

Daneman, M., & Merikle, P. M. (1996). Working memory and language comprehension: A meta-analysis. *Psychonomic Bulletin and Review, 3,* 422–433.

de Beni, R., Palladino, P., Pazzaglia, F., & Cornoldi, C. (1998). Increases in intrusion errors and working memory deficit of poor comprehenders. *Quarterly Journal of Experimental Psychology: Human Experimental Psychology, 51,* 305–320.

de Jong, P. F. (1998). Working memory deficits of reading disabled children. *Journal of Experimental Child Psychology, 70,* 75–95.

Dempster, F. (1985). Short-term memory development in childhood and adolescence. In C. Brainerd & M. Presseley (Eds.), *Basic processes in memory* (pp. 209–248). New York: Springer-Verlag.

Denckla, M. B., & Rudel, R. G. (1976). Rapid, automatized, naming (R.A.N.): Dyslexia differentiated for other learning disabilities. *Neuropsychological, 14,* 471–479.

Engle, R. W., Cantor, J., & Carullo, J. J. (1992). Individual differences in working memory and comprehension: A test of four hypotheses. *Journal of Experimental Psychology: Learning, Memory, and Cognition, 18,* 972–992.

Engle, R. W., Kane, M. J., & Tuholski, S. W. (1999). Individual differences in working memory capacity and what they tell us about controlled attention, general fluid intelligence, and functions of the prefrontal cortex. In A. Miyake & P. Shah (Eds), *Models of working memory: Mechanisms of active maintenance and executive control* (pp. 102–134). Cambridge, UK: Cambridge University Press.

Engle, R. W., Tuholski, S. W., Laughlin, J. E., & Conway, A. R. A. (1999). Working memory, short-term memory, and general fluid intelligence: A latent-variable approach. *Journal of Experimental Psychology: General, 128,* 309–331.

Ericsson, K. A., & Kintsch, W. (1995). Long-term working memory. *Psychology Review, 102,* 211–245.

Gathercole, S. E. (1998). The development of memory. *Journal of Child Psychology and Psychiatry, 39,* 3–27.

Gathercole, S. E., & Baddeley, A. D. (1993). *Working memory and language.* Hillsdale, NJ: Lawrence Erlbaum Associates, Inc.

Gathercole, S. E., & Pickering, S. J. (2000a). Assessment of working memory in six- and seven-year-old children. *Journal of Educational Psychology, 92,* 377–390.

Gathercole, S. E., & Pickering, S. J. (2000b). Working memory deficits in children with low achievements in the national curriculum at 7 years of age. *British Journal of Education Psychology, 70,* 177–194.

Gathercole, S. E., Pickering, S. J., Ambridge, B., & Wearing, H. (2004). The structure of working memory from 4 to 15 years of age. *Developmental Psychology, 40,* 177–190.

Goldman-Rakic, P. S. (1995). Architecture of the prefrontal cortex and the central executive. *Annals of the New York Academy of Sciences, 769,* 71–83.

Hohnen, B., & Stevenson, J. (1999). The structure of genetic influences on general cognitive, language, phonological, and reading abilities. *Developmental Psychology, 35,* 590–603.

Hoskyn, M., & Swanson, H. L. (2000). Cognitive processing of low achievers and children with reading disabilities: A selective meta-analytic review of the published literature. *School Psychology Review, 29*, 102–109.

Hutton, U. M. Z., & Towse, J. N. (2001). Short-term memory and working memory as indices of children's cognitive skills. *Memory, 9*, 383–394.

Jerman, O., & Swanson, H. L. (2005). Working memory and reading disabilities: A selective meta-analysis of the literature. In T. Scruggs & M. Mastroperi (Eds.), *Advances in learning and behavior disabilities* (pp. 11–31). New York: Elsevier.

Jonides, J. (2000). Mechanism of verbal working memory revealed by neuroimaging studies. In B. Landau et al. (Eds.), *Perception, cognition, and language* (pp. 87–104). Cambridge, MA: MIT Press.

Just, M. A., & Carpenter, P. A. (1992). A capacity theory of comprehension: Individual differences in working memory. *Psychological Review, 99*, 122–149.

Kyllonen, P. C., & Christal, R. E. (1990). Reasoning ability is (little more than) working memory capacity? *Intelligence, 14*, 389–433.

Lazar, J. W., & Frank, Y. (1998). Frontal systems dysfunction in children with attention-deficit/hyperactivity disorder and learning disabilities. *Journal of Neuropsychiatry and Clinical Neurosciences, 10*, 160–167.

Logie, R. H. (1986). Visuo-spatial processing in working memory. *Quarterly Journal of Experimental Psychology, 38A*, 229–247.

Miyake, A., Friedman, N. P., Emerson, M. J., Witzki, A. H., & Howerter, A. (2000). The unity and diversity of executive functions and their contributions to complex frontal lobe tasks: A latent variable analysis. *Cognitive Psychology, 41*, 49–100.

Nelson, H. E., & Warrington, E. K. (1980). An investigation of memory functions in dyslexic children. *British Journal of Psychology, 71*, 487–503.

Obrzut, J., Hynd, G., Obrzut, A., & Pirozzolo, F. (1981). Effect of directed attention on cerebral asymmetries in normal and learning disabled children. *Developmental Psychology, 17*, 118–125.

O'Shaughnessy, T., & Swanson, H. L. (1998). Do immediate memory deficits in students with learning disabilities in reading reflect a developmental lag or deficit? A selective meta-analysis of the literature. *Learning Disability Quarterly, 21*, 123–148.

Passolunghi, M. C., Cornoldi, C., & de Liberto, S. (1999). Working memory and intrusions of irrelevant information in a group of specific poor problem solvers. *Memory and Cognition, 27*, 779–790.

Pugh, K. R., Mencl, W. E., Shaywitz, B. A., Shaywitz, S. E., Fulbright, R. K., Constable, R. T., et al. (2000). The angular gyrus in developmental dyslexia: Task-specific differences in functional connectivity within posterior cortex. *Psychological Science, 11*, 51–56.

Ransby, M. J., & Swanson, H. L. (2003). Reading comprehension skills of young adults with childhood diagnosis of dyslexia. *Journal of Learning Disabilities, 36*, 538–555.

Reichle, E. D., Carpenter, P. A., & Just, M. A. (2000). The neural bases in strategy and skill in sentence-picture verification. *Cognitive Psychology, 40*, 261–295.

Ruchkin, D. S., Berndt, R. S., Johnson, R., Jr., Grafman, J., Rotter, W., & Canoune, H. L. (1999). Lexical contributions to retention of verbal information in working memory: Event-related brain potential evidence. *Journal of Memory and Language, 41*, 345–364.

Scarborough, H. S. (1990). Very early language deficits in dyslexic children. *Child Development, 61*, 1728–1743.

Schretlen, D., Pearlson, G. D., Anthony, J. C., Aylward, E. H., Augustine, A. M.,

Davis, A., & Barta, P. (2000). Elucidating the contributions of processing speed, executive ability, and frontal lobe volume to normal age-related differences in fluid intelligence. *Journal of the International Neuropsychological Society*, *6*, 52–61.

Shankweiler, D. P., & Crain, S. (1986). Language mechanisms and reading disorder. *Cognition*, *24*, 139–168.

Shaywitz, S. E., Shaywitz, B. A., Pugh, K. R., Fulbright, R. K., Constable, R. T., Mencl, W. E., et al. (1998). Functional disruption in the organization of the brain for reading in dyslexia. *Proceedings of the National Academy of Sciences USA*, *95*, 2636–2641. Retrieved from: http://www.pnas.org/cgi/content/full/95/5/2636

Siegel, L. S. (1992). An evaluation of the discrepancy definition of dyslexia. *Journal of Learning Disabilities*, *25*, 618–629.

Siegel, L. S. (1993). Phonological processing deficits as a basis for reading disabilities. *Developmental Review*, *13*, 246–257.

Siegel, L. S., & Ryan, E. B. (1988). Development of grammatical-sensitivity, phonological, and short-term memory skilled in normally achieving and learning disabled children. *Developmental Psychology*, *24*, 28–37.

Siegel, L. S., & Ryan, E. B. (1989). The development of working memory in normally achieving and subtypes of learning disabled. *Child Development*, *60*, 973–980.

Smith, E. E., & Jonides, J. (1997). Working memory: A view from neuroimaging. *Cognitive Psychology*, *33*, 5–42.

Smith, E. E., & Jonides, J. (1999). Storage and executive processes in the frontal lobes. *Sciences*, *283*(5408), 1657–1661.

Stanovich, K. E., & Siegel, L. (1994). Phenotypic performances profile of children with reading disabilities: A regression-based test of the phonological-core variable-difference model. *Journal of Education Psychology*, *86*, 24–53.

Swanson, H. L. (1981). Vigilance deficits in learning disabled children: A signal detection analysis. *Journal of Child Psychology and Psychiatry*, *22*, 393–399.

Swanson, H. L. (1983). A developmental study of vigilance in learning disabled and nondisabled children. *Journal of Abnormal Child Psychology*, *11*, 415–439.

Swanson, H. L. (1986). Do semantic memory deficiencies underline disabled readers encoding processes? *Journal of Experimental Child Psychology*, *41*, 461–488.

Swanson, H. L. (1988). Learning disabled children's problem solving: An information processing analysis of intellectual performance. *Intelligence*, *12*, 261–278.

Swanson, H. L. (1992). Generality and modification of working memory among skilled and less skilled readers. *Journal of Educational Psychology*, *84*, 473–488.

Swanson, H. L. (1993a). Executive processing in learning disabled readers. *Intelligence*, *17*, 117–149.

Swanson, H. L. (1993b). An information processing analysis of learning disabled children's problem solving. *American Education Research Journal*, *30*, 861–893.

Swanson, H. L. (1994). Short-term memory and working memory: Do both contribute to our understanding of academic achievement in children and adults with learning disabilities? *Journal of Learning Disabilities*, *27*, 34–50.

Swanson, H. L. (1995). *S-Cognitive Processing Test*. Austin, TX: Pro-Ed.

Swanson, H. L. (1999a). Reading comprehension and working memory in skilled readers: Is the phonological loop more important than the executive system? *Journal of Experimental Child Psychology*, *72*, 1–31.

Swanson, H. L. (1999b). What develops in working memory? A life span perspective. *Developmental Psychology*, *35*, 986–1000.

Swanson, H. L. (2000). Are working memory deficits in readers with learning disabilities hard to change? *Journal of Learning Disabilities, 33*, 551–566.

Swanson, H. L. (2003). Age-related differences in learning disabled and skilled readers' working memory. *Journal of Experimental Child Psychology, 85*, 1–31.

Swanson, H. L., & Alexander, J. E. (1997). Cognitive processes as predictors of word recognition and reading comprehension in learning disabled and skilled readers: Revisiting the specificity hypothesis. *Journal of Educational Psychology, 89*, 128–158.

Swanson, H. L., & Ashbaker, M. H. (2000). Working memory, STM, articulation speed, word recognition, and reading comprehension in learning disabled readers: Executive and/or articulatory system? *Intelligence, 28*, 1–30.

Swanson, H. L., Ashbaker, M. H., & Lee, C. (1996). Working-memory in learning disabled readers as a function of processing demands. *Journal of Child Experimental Psychology, 61*, 242–275.

Swanson, H. L., & Berninger, V. W. (1995). The role of working memory and STM in skilled and less skilled readers' word recognition and comprehension. *Intelligence, 21*, 83–108.

Swanson, H. L., & Cochran, K. (1991). Learning disabilities, distinctive encoding, and hemispheric resources. *Brain and Language, 40*, 202–230.

Swanson, H. L., Cooney, J. B., & O'Shaughnessy, T. (1998). Memory and learning disabilities. In B. Y. Wong (Ed.), *Understanding learning disabilities* (2nd ed.). San Diego, CA: Academic Press.

Swanson, H. L., & Mullen, R. (1983). Hemisphere specialization in learning disabled readers' recall as a function of age and level of processing. *Journal of Experimental Child Psychology, 35*, 457–477.

Swanson, H. L., & Obrzut, J. (1985). Learning disabled readers' recall as a function of distinctive encoding, hemispheric processing, and selective attention. *Journal of Learning Disabilities, 18*, 409–418.

Swanson, H. L., & Sachse-Lee, C. (2001a). Mathematical problem solving and working memory in children with learning disabilities: Both executive and phonological processes are important. *Journal of Experimental Child Psychology, 79*, 294–321.

Swanson, H. L., & Sachse-Lee, C. (2001b). A subgroup analysis of working memory in children with reading disabilities: Domain general or domain specific deficiency? *Journal of Learning Disabilities, 34*, 249–263.

Swanson, H. L., Sáez, L., Gerber, M., & Leafstedt, J. (2004). Literacy and cognitive functioning in bilingual and nonbilingual children at or not at risk for reading disabilities. *Journal of Educational Psychology, 96*, 3–18.

Thorn, A. S. C., & Gathercole, S. (1999). Language-specific knowledge and short-term memory in bilingual and non-bilingual children. *Quarterly Journal of Experimental Psychology, 52A*, 303–324.

Welsh, M. C., Pennington, B. F., & Grossier, D. B. (1991). A normative developmental study of executive function: A window on prefrontal function in children. *Developmental Neuropsychology, 7*, 131–149.

Willcutt, E. G., Pennington, B. F., Boado, R., & Ogline, J. S. (2001). A comparison of cognitive deficits in reading disability and attention-deficit/hyperactivity disorder. *Journal of Abnormal Psychology, 110*, 157–172.

Woodcock, R. W. (1987). *Woodcock Reading Mastery Test* (Rev. ed.). Circle Pines, MN: American Guidance Service.

5 The role of working memory in specific reading comprehension difficulties[1]

Rose K. Vukovic and Linda Siegel

OVERVIEW

The present chapter reviews the research on the role of working memory in children's reading comprehension abilities, particularly in those children with poor comprehension despite adequate word reading skills. Research in this area has been limited, although it appears that working memory deficits specific to the verbal domain characterize individuals with specific comprehension difficulties. Findings from cross-sectional and longitudinal studies offer support for a relationship between verbal working memory and reading comprehension. The relationship between working memory and reading comprehension, however, does not appear to be restricted to a working memory system for language, as numerical working memory and to a lesser extent visuospatial working memory have been shown to explain unique variance in reading comprehension. More studies with poor comprehenders are needed to understand how working memory contributes to reading comprehension failure over time. The findings of this review suggest that working memory alone does not account for the comprehension deficits in poor comprehenders and that difficulties with lower-level (e.g., phonological abilities, short-term memory) and higher-order (i.e., language processing) processes may also contribute to problems with reading comprehension.

READING COMPREHENSION

In this chapter we review and summarize the research on the role of working memory in children's reading comprehension ability with a particular emphasis on those children with adequate word reading skills but poor comprehension. In the field of learning disabilities (LD), the study of individual differences in working memory has received increased attention as a potential explanation for the individual differences in academic performance. In fact, working memory processes have been implicated in reading and mathematics failure in childhood, adolescence, and adulthood (e.g., Chiappe, Hasher & Siegel, 2000; Daneman & Carpenter, 1980; McDougall, Hulme, Ellis, &

Monk, 1994; Morris et al., 1998; Ransby & Swanson, 2003; Shafrir & Siegel, 1994; Siegel & Ryan, 1989a), and deficits in working memory are implicated in the majority of LD generally (for a review, see Swanson & Siegel, 2001). Less is known, however, about how working memory is involved in reading comprehension difficulties.

The end goal of reading instruction is reading comprehension. Reading comprehension is a complex process that requires both the processing of print and the construction of meaning of what is being read. To gain meaning from text, readers must not only read and understand the individual words on the page, but they must be able to read accurately and fluently, activate the necessary background information, make inferences, hold information in memory, and engage in self-monitoring strategies. Beyond the individual-level cognitive processes involved in reading, factors such as the complexity of the text and reader motivation can also influence reading comprehension.

In the field of LD, two types of comprehension difficulties have been identified: comprehension difficulties with concurrent word reading deficits, and comprehension difficulties in the presence of average word reading skills. The former type of comprehension difficulty is conceptualized as a bottom-up failure such that deficits in lower-level processes (i.e., word recognition) masquerade as comprehension deficits (Perfetti, 1985; Shankweiler, 1989; Swanson & Siegel, 2001; Torgesen, 2000). In other words, bottom-up theories propose that comprehension difficulties are essentially word reading difficulties. It is estimated that word reading difficulties occur in 5–20% of the school-aged population (Lyon, 1995; Shaywitz et al., 1999). In addition, word reading difficulties typically cooccur with arithmetic disabilities in that it is difficult to find children with word reading difficulties who do not also have problems with arithmetic (Siegel & Ryan, 1989a).

The second type of comprehension difficulty is thought to be due to deficits in higher-order cognitive processes, such as working memory. For this type of LD, comprehension failure is thought to be independent of word reading difficulties, as this is a group identified on the basis of good word reading skills yet poor comprehension. That is, those with specific comprehension difficulties are selected to have average word reading skills either based on performance on standardized measures of word recognition (e.g., performance greater than 40th percentile), or by being matched to typically achieving groups on variables such as reading accuracy, sight vocabulary, and reading speed. In contrast to the study of individuals with word reading difficulties, a limited number of studies have examined comprehension failure in those with specific comprehension difficulties – also known as poor comprehenders. It is estimated that poor comprehenders represent approximately 10–15% of school-aged children. It is not clear the extent to which children with specific comprehension deficits have arithmetic difficulties as most investigators of reading difficulties do not report arithmetic levels for their participants.

The purpose of the present review is to evaluate and summarize the research on the relationship between working memory and reading comprehension with a specific focus on how working memory is involved in reading comprehension, independently of word reading ability. The specific role of working memory and its predictive power in explaining reading comprehension ability independent of word reading skills has received minimal attention. Our review was guided by the following questions:

1 What is working memory and how is it hypothesized to affect reading comprehension?
2 What is the evidence that working memory is uniquely involved in reading comprehension?
3 Does working memory contribute to growth in reading comprehension ability?

WHAT IS WORKING MEMORY AND HOW IS IT HYPOTHESIZED TO AFFECT READING COMPREHENSION?

Working memory is conceptualized as a limited resource cognitive system responsible for the temporary storage and processing of information in immediate awareness (Baddeley & Hitch, 1994). Working memory is viewed as being composed of a central executive controlling system and two subsidiary storage systems, namely, the speech-based phonological loop and the visuospatial sketchpad (Baddeley & Hitch, 1994). The central executive is assumed to control and regulate the working memory system, including coordinating the two slave systems, allocating resources between processing and storage demands, activating and retrieving information from long-term memory, and encoding retrieval strategies (Swanson, Cooney, & McNamara, 2004). The central executive uses the resources of its slave systems to assist in the storage and processing of information. The phonological loop is thought to be responsible for the temporary storage of verbal information and is conceptualized as comprising both a phonological store, which holds information in phonological form, and a rehearsal process, which serves to maintain representations in the phonological store. There is debate in the literature as to whether the phonological loop is synonymous with short-term memory (see Swanson et al., 2004; Swanson & Siegel, 2001). The visuospatial sketchpad is assumed to be responsible for the storage of visuospatial information. In general, children with LD have been found to have deficits in aspects of the central executive and phonological store (for a review, see Swanson & Siegel, 2001).

As the working memory system is a limited resource system, there is a limit to the amount of information the central executive can successfully coordinate. Thus, tasks or activities that demand sustained attention or excessive processing draw upon a limited supply of resources in the working memory system, leaving little or no additional resources for the adequate completion of concurrent tasks. Deficits in working memory have implications for performance on a variety of tasks, including reading comprehension. For example, working memory is vital for reading comprehension as the reader must simultaneously decode words, interpret the meaning of the words, integrate the meaning of the text, maintain and remember what has been read, as well as engage in various comprehension strategies, such as making inferences, detecting inconsistencies, self-monitoring, and correcting comprehension errors. Deficits in working memory could contribute to comprehension failure at any point in the comprehension process: A child who struggles to decode words may not have adequate working memory resources left for comprehension; a child whose working memory resources are allocated to interpreting the text may not have additional resources left to remember what has been read.

There are two frameworks used to explain individual differences in working memory: capacity theories and long-term working memory (LT-WM) theory. In the capacity model proposed by Daneman and Carpenter (1980), individual differences in working memory reflect individual differences in processing efficiency. That is, individuals differ in the efficiency with which their central executive processes reading-related material such that individuals with inefficient working memory systems consume a large portion of working memory resources in the execution of reading, leaving little or no capacity for comprehension. Individuals with inefficient processes will have a functionally smaller working memory capacity because their cognitive resources are burdened with processing demands. Thus, this model proposes that people are poor comprehenders because they exert too much effort on the reading process. This theory assumes that working memory deficits are specific to the reading comprehension process as opposed to deficits in a general working memory system independent of reading comprehension.

In the capacity models proposed by Just and Carpenter (1992), and Engle, Cantor, and Carullo (1992), individual differences in working memory can be explained by inherent individual differences in the architecture of working memory such that some individuals simply have a larger working memory capacity than others. Individuals with smaller working memory capacities, therefore, show deficits in tasks that overtax the working memory system because their system cannot handle the volume of information. In terms of reading comprehension, individuals with comprehension difficulties might have a smaller cognitive capacity to hold and manipulate information in working memory and thus have more difficulty simultaneously processing and storing the text for later recall. In contrast to the capacity model proposed by Daneman and Carpenter (1980), these models propose that working memory deficits are not specific to reading comprehension and reflect deficits in a more general working memory system, particularly a working memory system for language.

The second major framework for conceptualizing the working memory system, the long-term working memory (LT-WM) model (Ericsson & Kintsch, 1995), differs fundamentally from capacity theories in that this model proposes an additional component to the working memory system, namely the LT-WM system. The role of LT-WM is the skilled and efficient retrieval of information from long-term memory that can be used to facilitate working memory performance. Much like expert performance on domain specific tasks, an individual's experience and prior knowledge can increase performance on a given task. Through practice, therefore, individuals can become skilled and efficient in storing and retrieving information from long-term memory (i.e., LT-WM) in order to facilitate working memory processes. Ericsson and Kintsch (1995) propose that in skilled activities, a portion of accessible information relevant to the activity (i.e., prior experiences and knowledge) is accessible through retrieval cues in working memory. Thus, increased efficiency in activating such information should increase performance on the task. The LT-WM model avoids the idea of inherent differences in capacity to explain individual differences in reading comprehension (although this does not preclude the idea that there may be some capacity differences). Rather, good readers differ from poor readers because their better comprehension strategies result in more efficient retrieval and encoding processes in LT-WM (Ericsson & Kintsch, 1995). There is no consensus in the field about whether capacity theories or LT-WM best explain the relationship between working memory and reading comprehension.

Working memory is measured by tasks that require the simultaneous processing and storage of information. Consistent with the model of working memory described above, working memory can be assessed through measures involving linguistic or visuospatial information. Typically, linguistic-based working memory is assessed with tasks that involve either verbal or numerical information. Linguistic tasks are divided into verbal and numerical domains in order to examine the differential prediction of these tasks on various outcomes. Specifically, numerical working memory tasks are assumed to involve fewer verbal demands. Thus, studies that find a relationship between numerical working memory measures and outcome variables, such as reading comprehension, can assume that the relationship is not reflective of a working memory system specialized for language, but may indicate a relationship with a more general working memory system.

An example of a verbal working memory task is the listening span test (Daneman & Carpenter, 1980). In this task, participants listen to sets of sentence and after each sentence verify whether the sentence is true or false (processing demands). At the end of each set, participants are required to recall the last word of each sentence in the set (storage demands). Verbal working memory is also often assessed through listening comprehension tasks. An example of a numerical working memory task is the working memory for numbers measure (Siegel & Ryan, 1989a). In this task individuals are required to count aloud (processing demands) the yellow dots from a field of blue and yellow dots arranged in an irregular pattern on sets of index cards.

For example, at the four-number set, participants will count aloud the yellow dots on four separate cards. At the end of each set, participants are asked to recall in the correct order the final number counted on each card of the set (storage demands). In the above example, participants would be required to recall the final number counted on each of the four cards. An example of a visuospatial working memory task is the visual matrix task created by Swanson (1995). In this task, participants are required to remember sequences of dots within a matrix (ranging from 4 squares and 2 dots to 45 squares and 12 dots). After the matrix is removed from viewing, the participant is asked a question about the matrix (processing demand) and is then required to reproduce the pattern of dots on a blank matrix (storage component).

Summary

Working memory is conceptualized as a limited capacity cognitive system responsible for allocating cognitive resources between the processing and storage demands created by the flow of information in immediate awareness. Working memory is hypothesized to be important to reading comprehension because of the complexity of the skills involved in reading comprehension and the need for a system to coordinate the simultaneous processes occurring during reading.

WHAT IS THE EVIDENCE THAT WORKING MEMORY IS UNIQUELY INVOLVED IN READING COMPREHENSION?

Research in three areas can be reviewed to evaluate the evidence for a unique relationship between working memory and reading comprehension: (1) studies that examine the relationship between reading comprehension, working memory, and other variables that have a well-established relationship with reading comprehension; (2) studies that examine the influence of various working memory measures on comprehension; and (3) studies that examine whether working memory deficits characterize poor comprehenders.

Unique contribution of working memory to reading comprehension

In order to demonstrate a unique relationship between working memory and reading comprehension, working memory must be shown not only to be related to reading comprehension, but this relationship must be evident after controlling for variables that have a well-established relationship with reading comprehension. That is, if working memory processes are uniquely involved in comprehension independent of bottom-up processing, working memory should explain unique variance independent of those variables that have a well-established relationship with comprehension, such as word recognition, reading fluency, and vocabulary.

Findings from studies using children across the spectrum of reading ability demonstrate that working memory is an important factor in explaining reading comprehension ability. For example, in a sample of 7- to 8-year-olds ($n = 102$), Cain, Oakhill, and Bryant (2000) found that a task with high verbal working memory demands accounted for 11.4% of the variance in reading comprehension over and above the variance accounted for by age, intelligence scores, vocabulary, and word recognition. Similarly, in a sample of fourth-grade children (mean age 9 years 9 months; $n = 48$), Seigneuric, Ehrlich, Oakhill, and Yuill (2000) found that working memory measures involving sentences, words, and digits each accounted for a significant amount of variance (6%, 10%, and 5%, respectively) in reading comprehension over and above vocabulary and reading fluency. In addition, the working memory measures were correlated as well with reading comprehension as were vocabulary and reading skills.

In a longitudinal study, Cain, Oakhill, and Bryant (2004) found that at each time point in the study (i.e., 7 years old, 8 years old, 10 years old; $n = 100, 92, 80$, respectively), a composite working memory variable (composed of verbal and numerical working memory tasks) explained a significant amount of the variance in reading comprehension over and above the contributions made by vocabulary, verbal abilities, and word recognition. Specifically, when the children were 7 years old, the composite working memory variable uniquely explained 6.9% of the variance; at 8 years old, working memory contributed 5.5%; and at 10 years old, working memory accounted for 5.2% of the variance over and above the other variables in the model. Furthermore, the strength of the association between working memory and reading comprehension was comparable to the relationship between reading comprehension and verbal ability and vocabulary, suggesting that working memory is indeed as important in explaining individual differences in reading comprehension ability as are other factors such as vocabulary knowledge and verbal abilities.

The finding that working memory accounts for unique variance in reading comprehension independent of skills such as word recognition and fluency is consistent with those of a longitudinal study recently conducted in our own lab (Vukovic & Siegel, 2005). This study, however, extends previous findings to demonstrate that working memory plays an important role in explaining reading comprehension ability even after controlling for phonological awareness and rapid naming – two cognitive processes that are implicated in reading failure (e.g., Stanovich & Siegel, 1994; Wolf & Bowers, 1999). The study was designed to examine the reading development from kindergarten to sixth grade of a cohort of children in an entire school district ($n = 572$ followed longitudinally). The children were assessed annually on a battery of reading, phonological awareness, rapid naming, and working memory tasks, including measures of numerical and verbal working memory (interested readers are referred to Chiappe, Siegel, & Wade-Woolley, 2002, and Lesaux & Siegel, 2003, for more information).

Vukovic and Siegel (2005) examined the relationship between reading comprehension and word reading skills, phonological awareness, rapid naming, and working memory in the sample at fifth (mean age 10.89 years) and sixth (mean age 11.82 years) grades. In both grades, verbal working memory contributed unique variance (7.0% and 3.4% in fifth and sixth grade respectively) to reading comprehension over and above word reading skills, phonological awareness, and rapid naming. Furthermore, the correlation between verbal working memory and reading comprehension was comparable to the correlation between reading comprehension and word identification and between reading comprehension and pseudoword reading fluency in both fifth and sixth grades. In fact, with word reading skills controlled, verbal working memory was the only cognitive process that accounted for unique variance in reading comprehension. The findings from this study suggest that working memory, and in particular verbal working memory, is a potential candidate for explaining the comprehension difficulties in poor comprehenders as verbal working memory was found to contribute unique variance in reading comprehension independent of lower-level processes, including word reading skills, phonological processing, and rapid naming.

In sum, these findings indicate that working memory is an important variable in explaining reading comprehension in children from the ages of 7 to 11. In the studies that were reviewed, working memory continued to account for a significant portion of the variance in reading comprehension over and above that variance accounted for by variables such as vocabulary, word reading skills, and underlying cognitive processes such as phonological awareness and rapid naming. It is important to note that the samples in the studies that were reviewed included children with good and poor reading skills. Thus, the specific contribution of working memory to reading comprehension in children with specific comprehension difficulties is not known. Of interest for the current topic is a study that examined the relationship between working memory and reading comprehension in children with word reading difficulties (Swanson & Alexander, 1997). The authors found that reading comprehension was better predicted by a working memory latent variable than by variables such as word recognition, reasoning ability, and performance on a cloze task in which children read a passage with missing words and were required to supply the missing word using contextual cues from the passage. Although the poor readers in the Swanson and Alexander study were not the poor comprehenders that are the focus of the current chapter, their study offers preliminary support for the importance of working memory in explaining comprehension ability in children with reading problems.

Various measures of working memory

The studies reviewed above indicate that working memory shares a unique relationship with reading comprehension. What is not clear from these studies, however, is whether the relationship between reading comprehension and working memory reflects a general working memory system or a working memory system specific for language. Specifically, both verbal working memory and numerical working memory tasks were found to make a unique contribution to working memory (e.g., Cain, Oakhill, & Bryant, 2004; Seigneuric et al., 2000), although in one study only verbal working memory contributed uniquely to reading comprehension (Vukovic & Siegel, 2005). It is important to determine the nature of the relationship between working memory and reading comprehension as deficits in a general versus a language-specific working memory system have different implications for intervention and remediation. Specifically, if a general working memory system is implicated, children with comprehension difficulties will need to be taught strategies to overcome or compensate for their limited capacity systems. On the other hand, deficits in a working memory system for language would suggest that children with specific comprehension difficulties need to be taught strategies for processing and remembering verbal information.

In order to investigate whether the relationship between reading comprehension and working memory reflects a language-based system versus a more general working memory system, researchers directly investigate the relationship between reading comprehension and various measures of working memory, namely, verbal working memory, numerical working memory, and to a lesser extent, visuospatial working memory. In a meta-analysis, Daneman and Merikle (1996) found that in studies of typically achieving readers, tests of working memory involving verbal or numerical information were significantly correlated with standardized and experimental tests of comprehension. However, reading comprehension tended to be more strongly correlated with working memory measures that involved verbal information than with numerical working memory tasks. Similarly, studies generally show that reading comprehension is more strongly related to verbal working memory tasks than to visuospatial working memory, although studies examining the relationship between visuospatial working memory and reading comprehension are limited and the findings mixed (Swanson & Siegel, 2001).

Swanson and Howell (2001) found that reading comprehension was significantly related to a composite linguistic working memory measure (composed of a verbal working memory and numerical working memory task; correlations ranging from .30 to .68) and a composite visuospatial working memory measure (composed of two visuospatial tasks; correlations ranging from .21 to .41) in a cross-sectional study with children aged 9–14 years. The authors also found that linguistic working memory tasks, as well as a working memory latent variable that included overlapping variance between linguistic and visuospatial working memory tasks explained significant portions of variance in reading comprehension. Visual-spatial working memory alone did not consistently explain the variance in reading comprehension. The findings from this study suggest that both a general working memory system and a language-based working memory system may be involved in reading comprehension.

Consistent with the conclusions of Swanson and Howell (2001), Cain, Oakhill, and Bryant (2004) also concluded that a general working memory system seemed to characterize the relationship between working memory and reading comprehension. In a longitudinal study, Cain, Oakhill, and Bryant examined the correlation between reading comprehension and measures of verbal working memory and numerical working memory. In the sample at 7 years of age, reading comprehension was significantly correlated with verbal working memory ($r = .372$) but not numerical working memory. At 8 years old, reading comprehension was significantly correlated with both verbal working memory ($r = .498$) and numerical working memory ($r = .344$). At age 10 years, reading comprehension was significantly correlated only with verbal working memory ($r = .451$). In regression analyses, a composite working memory variable composed of verbal and numerical working memory tasks accounted for a significant amount of variance in reading comprehension beyond the contributions made by vocabulary, verbal abilities, and word recognition. The verbal and numerical working memory tasks in this study were significantly though modestly correlated with each other, suggesting that, although related, the tasks measured different aspects of working memory. This provides support for the tasks sharing a common underlying construct as opposed to both tasks reflecting a specific language-based system. Thus, the authors interpreted the results of this study to indicate that language skills alone cannot account for the relation between reading comprehension and working memory.

It is important to note, however, that Cain, Oakhill, and Bryant (2004) did not examine the influence of the verbal working memory and numerical working memory tasks separately in regression analyses. Furthermore, the numerical working memory task was significantly correlated with reading comprehension only at 8 years old. Thus, without separately investigating the effects of verbal and numerical working memory on reading comprehension, it is not possible to determine whether the relationship between reading comprehension and working memory in this study reflected a generalized working memory system, or whether the strong relationship between verbal working memory and reading comprehension accounted for the significant findings in the regression analyses.

In a study in which various working memory measures were placed in competition with each other, Seigneuric et al. (2000) did not find support for the notion that a general working memory system is involved in reading comprehension. Seigneuric et al. found that reading comprehension was significantly correlated with measures of working memory involving verbal information (correlations between .47 and .56) and measures involving numerical information (correlations between .41 and .45) in a sample of fourth-grade children (age range: 8 years 8 months to 10 years 7 months). A working memory measure involving spatial information was not significantly correlated with comprehension. This pattern was replicated in regression analyses: Working memory measures involving verbal and numerical information accounted for unique variance in reading comprehension, whereas a visuospatial working memory task did not.

When the working verbal and numerical working memory measures were placed in competition with each other in regression models, Seigneuric et al. (2000) found that the relationship between reading comprehension and numerical working memory was not particularly robust. Specifically, numerical working memory did not explain significant portions of the variance in reading comprehension after verbal working memory was controlled, whereas verbal working memory contributed uniquely even after controlling for numerical working memory. In addition, the verbal working memory tasks shared the highest correlation with reading comprehension compared to the other working memory measures. Thus, in contrast to previous studies (e.g., Cain, Oakhill, & Bryant, 2004; Swanson & Howell, 2001), these findings suggest that a language-based working memory system primarily accounts for the relationship between reading comprehension and working memory. Seigneuric et al. speculated that working memory processes involved in reading comprehension are specialized for language processing. In this study, the verbal, numerical, and spatial working memory tasks were significantly, though modestly, correlated with each other (correlations ranging from .37 to .68), suggesting that although related, the tasks were measuring different aspects of working memory.

The findings from the longitudinal study conducted by Vukovic and Siegel (2005) also indicate that the relationship between working memory and reading comprehension reflects a working memory for language system. Vukovic and Siegel found that reading comprehension was significantly correlated with verbal working memory and numerical working memory in both fifth (mean age 10.89 years) and sixth (mean age 11.82 years) grades. As well, the working memory tasks were significantly though modestly correlated with each other ($r = .382$, $r = .428$ in fifth and sixth grades, respectively). However, reading comprehension shared stronger correlations with verbal working memory ($r = .377$ in both grades) than with numerical working memory (correlations ranging from .186 to .252). Furthermore, in regression analyses, numerical working memory did not account for unique variance after controlling for word reading skills, phonological awareness, rapid naming, and verbal working memory, whereas verbal working memory continued to explain unique variance beyond the influence of the other variables. Thus, the findings from this study suggest that a working memory system for language accounts for the relationship between reading comprehension and working memory, and that this relationship remains significant even after controlling for word reading skills, phonological awareness, and rapid naming.

Together, the research in this area indicates that reading comprehension is most strongly related to measures of verbal working memory. Working memory measures involving numerical information have also been shown to be related to reading comprehension, suggesting that a more general working memory system for symbolic information might be involved in reading comprehension. However, in studies in which numerical and working memory measures compete with each other in regression analyses, numerical working memory does not make a unique contribution to reading comprehension after controlling for verbal working memory, whereas verbal working memory continues to contribute uniquely to reading comprehension even after controlling for variables such as word reading skills, phonological awareness, and rapid naming, in addition to numerical working memory. A reliable relationship between visuospatial working memory and reading comprehension has not been established, although latent variables that include the shared variance between linguistic and visuospatial working memory have been found to be very predictive of comprehension. The latter finding suggests that in unselected samples, language skills alone do not account for the relationship between reading comprehension and working memory.

No studies have examined the relationship between reading comprehension and measures of working memory in samples of poor comprehenders. Studies using samples of individuals with concurrent word reading and comprehension difficulties indicate that reading comprehension might be related to a general working memory system in addition to a system specific to the verbal domain (e.g., Swanson & Alexander, 1997; Swanson & Berninger, 1995; Swanson & Sachse-Lee, 2001). Whether this is the case for poor comprehenders remains to be determined. However, the extant research clearly indicates that a working memory system for language is involved in reading comprehension independent of skills such as word reading, reading fluency, vocabulary, phonological awareness, and rapid naming. Thus, in the case of children with specific comprehension deficits, it seems likely that working memory for language certainly plays a role in reading comprehension ability.

The deficits of poor comprehenders

Specific comprehension difficulties are assumed to represent a distinct type of reading problem from word reading difficulties. As such, identification and intervention practices for poor comprehenders are thought to differ from the strategies used for poor readers – that is, readers whose reading comprehension difficulties reflect difficulties in word reading. Specific comprehension difficulties are thought to reflect deficits in higher-order cognitive processes, such as working memory, integrating information in text, making inferences, and the use of metacognitive strategies (Cain & Oakhill, 1999; Cain, Oakhill, & Bryant, 2000; Oakhill, 1993; Oakhill, Yuill, & Parkin, 1986; Yuill, Oakhill, & Parkin, 1989), as opposed to lower-level processes, such as phonological awareness. In order to investigate the cognitive deficits associated with specific comprehension difficulties, researchers compare poor comprehenders to typically achieving peers on a variety of tasks including lower-level and higher-order skills. In addition, some studies include a sample of poor readers to evaluate how the deficits in poor comprehenders compare to the deficits in poor readers.

Cain et al. (2000) found that their sample of 7- to 8-year-old poor comprehenders ($n = 10$–12) performed comparably to a typically achieving group ($n = 10$–12) on most measures of phonological awareness but had difficulty with a phonological task that had high verbal working memory demands. The authors concluded that poor comprehenders do not appear to have deficits in lower-level processes, such as phonological awareness, but appear to have difficulties on tasks that place heavy demand on the working memory system. Poor comprehenders and the skilled readers in this study were matched for reading accuracy, sight vocabulary, and reading speed, thus reducing the likelihood that poor word reading skills were involved in the comprehension difficulties of poor comprehenders. This study did not include a poor reader group so it is not known how the deficits of poor comprehenders compared to the deficits of poor readers.

Siegel and Ryan (1989b) also found that poor comprehenders did not appear to have deficits in phonological skills, but tended to show some difficulties on other lower-level skills, particularly at younger ages. Siegel and Ryan investigated the differences among a cross-sectional sample of poor comprehenders, poor readers, and typically achieving children at younger (6–8 years old; $n = 202$) and older (9–14 years old; $n = 439$) ages on measures of lower-level processes (phonological abilities, short-term memory), and higher-order processes (working memory, language). In younger and older children, poor comprehenders tended to perform more similarly to typical achievers than to poor readers on measures of phonological abilities, which is consistent with the findings of Cain et al. (2000). On phonological short-term memory tasks, however, younger poor comprehenders performed significantly higher than poor readers, but significantly lower than typical achievers, whereas older poor comprehenders performed similarly to typical achievers. These findings indicate that younger poor comprehenders present with phonological short-term memory difficulties, but their difficulties are not as severe as the deficits in the poor reader group. By 9–14 years of age, however, deficits in lower-level processes do not characterize poor comprehenders.

On tasks measuring higher-order processes, Siegel and Ryan (1989b) found that poor comprehenders tended to perform more similarly to typical achievers than to poor readers on working memory but not language tasks. In younger and older children, poor comprehenders did not differ significantly from typical achievers on working memory measures involving numbers, words, or sentences, indicating that poor comprehenders do not present with working memory deficits. On language tasks, younger poor comprehenders had some difficulties with syntactic and morphological aspects of language and vocabulary, although their deficits were not as severe as those in poor readers. In contrast, older poor comprehenders did not differ from typical readers on their performance on language or vocabulary tasks. These findings indicate that younger poor comprehenders present with language deficits, but these deficits are not as severe as in the poor reader group. By 9–14 years of age, however, poor comprehenders perform similarly to typical readers on both language and working memory tasks.

Together, the findings of Siegel and Ryan (1989b) suggest that poor comprehenders do not differ from typical achievers across phonological, short-term memory, working memory, and language tasks. Younger poor comprehenders showed some difficulties on short-term memory and language tasks, but these difficulties were not present in older poor comprehenders. Siegel and Ryan speculated that the reading comprehension difficulties of poor comprehenders might be due to less familiarity with language, as opposed to underlying deficits in phonological processing or working memory. Poor comprehenders in this study were defined as those with below average comprehension and average word reading on the basis of standardized tests; poor comprehenders and typically achieving children were not matched on word recognition.

Vukovic and Siegel (2005) also found that poor comprehenders tended to perform more similarly to typical readers than to poor readers across tasks, although, in contrast to the findings of Siegel and Ryan (1989b), Vukovic and Siegel found that poor comprehenders tended to be characterized by verbal working memory deficits. Vukovic and Siegel examined the characteristics of poor comprehenders, poor readers, and typically achieving children in kindergarten, fifth grade, and sixth grade. Poor comprehenders and typical readers were matched as closely as possible on word reading accuracy and speed of pseudoword reading, thus reducing the likelihood that word reading abilities contributed to the comprehension difficulties of poor comprehenders. In fifth grade, 53 children were identified as poor comprehenders, 15 as poor readers, and 181 as typical readers. In sixth grade, 45 children were identified as poor comprehenders, 14 as poor readers, and 188 as typical readers.

In both fifth grade (mean age 10.89 years) and sixth grade (mean age 11.82 years), poor comprehenders performed similarly to typical readers on measures of phonological awareness, rapid naming, word reading skills (i.e., word identification, decoding accuracy, decoding fluency), and numerical working memory. Yet in both fifth and sixth grade, the poor comprehenders performed below the typical achievers – and similarly to poor readers – on measures of reading comprehension and verbal working memory. In fifth grade poor comprehenders were as impaired as poor readers on verbal working memory, whereas in sixth grade poor comprehenders performed significantly higher than poor readers but significantly lower than typical achievers on the verbal working memory measure. Thus, in the later elementary grades, poor comprehenders appeared to be characterized only by verbal working memory deficits. Poor comprehenders did not have numerical working memory deficits.

In retrospective analyses of the sixth-grade reader groups, Vukovic and Siegel (2005) found that, in kindergarten, poor comprehenders performed below typical achievers and similar to poor readers on measures of phonological awareness, rapid naming, and verbal working memory, although poor comprehenders knew significantly more letters than poor readers (but significantly fewer than typical achievers). That is, poor comprehenders were as depressed on early phonological, rapid naming, and verbal working memory skills as were children with word reading difficulties. These findings indicate that, in kindergarten, poor comprehenders tend to be characterized by deficits in lower-level and higher-order cognitive processes.

The findings from Vukovic and Siegel (2005) are consistent with those studies showing that poor comprehenders do not appear to have deficits in lower-level processes (e.g., Cain et al., 2000; Siegel & Ryan, 1989b), although, in kindergarten, poor comprehenders were characterized by deficits in lower-level processes such as phonological awareness and rapid naming. In later grades, poor comprehenders tend to be characterized by deficits in verbal working memory, which is inconsistent with the findings of Siegel and Ryan, who found that poor comprehenders aged 9–14 years old did not have working memory difficulties. However, these findings are consistent with those of Marshall and Nation (2003) who found that poor comprehenders (mean age 10 years 1 month; $n = 21$) performed lower than typical readers (mean age 10 years 1 month; $n = 20$) on a measure of verbal working memory. The lack of significant differences in the Siegel and Ryan study may be due to floor effects on the working memory tasks. In any case, the findings from the Vukovic and Siegel study suggest that poor comprehenders begin school with deficits in both lower-level and higher-order processes, although, by fifth and sixth grades, the deficits of poor comprehenders tend to be restricted to verbal working memory. In addition, these findings indicate that the working memory difficulties of poor comprehenders reflect working memory difficulties for language, as opposed to a more general working memory system.

Nation, Adams, Bowyer-Crane, and Snowling (1999) also found that poor comprehenders tended to be characterized by working memory deficits specific to the language system, as opposed to a more general working memory system. In this study, poor comprehenders were matched with typical readers as closely as possible for pseudoword reading and nonverbal ability. Nation et al. found that poor comprehenders (mean age 10.83 years; $n = 14$) performed similarly to typical achievers (mean age 10.68 years; $n = 15$) on a visuospatial working memory task, but performed significantly lower than the typical achievers on a measure of verbal working memory. Furthermore, poor comprehenders were found to have average short-term memory skills for concrete words, but recalled significantly fewer abstract words than typical achievers, suggesting a selective short-term memory deficit for tasks that place a heavy burden on semantic processing skills. Nation et al. concluded that poor comprehenders are worse at processing and storing verbal material than typical readers and that poor comprehenders have deficits within the semantic system. Thus, Nation et al. speculated an underlying language deficit in poor comprehenders as opposed to general working memory limitations underlying comprehension deficits in poor comprehenders: that is, Nation et al. speculated that verbal working memory deficits in poor comprehenders reflect underlying language deficits as opposed to working memory deficits causing reading comprehension failure. Siegel and Ryan (1989b) also speculated that the comprehension difficulties of poor comprehenders may reflect underlying language problems as opposed to cognitive processing deficits.

For the most part, thus, it appears that verbal working memory deficits characterize poor comprehenders and that such deficits can affect reading comprehension ability. For example, Cain and Oakhill (1999) studied the ability of 7- to 8-year-old poor comprehenders to make inferences and use their prior knowledge to understand text. In this study children were required to read a passage and then answer questions about the passage from memory. The children were to answer either literal questions based on a passage, make valid inferences based on information provided explicitly in text (text connecting inference), or to use general knowledge to make an inference (gap-filling inference). There were no differences between the poor comprehenders ($n = 29$) and typical readers ($n = 24$) on the ability to answer literal questions from memory, although poor comprehenders had significantly more difficulty making text connecting inferences from memory. However, when the children were provided with the text and told to look through the story again (to answer incorrect questions), poor comprehenders were able to use the information in the text to answer the question correctly and in a manner similar to their normally achieving peers, performed at ceiling. These findings clearly show how weak memory skills can impede poor comprehenders from understanding text as well as typical readers.

Poor comprehenders in the Cain and Oakhill (1999) study also performed significantly below typical readers when answering gap-filling inference questions from memory. With the text available, performance on the gap-filling inference questions improved for all children but did not reach ceiling, and the poor comprehenders continued to demonstrate weaker performance compared to typical readers. When children were explicitly directed to the relevant part of the passage, poor comprehenders continued to have difficulty making gap-filling inferences despite having the adequate general knowledge required to answer the question when further probed by the examiner (Cain & Oakhill). Thus, these findings indicate more general language processing difficulties in poor comprehenders in addition to any memory difficulties. Overall, the findings from this study demonstrate the difficulties poor comprehenders experience with tasks that place a heavy burden on their memory and language skills.

Similarly, Cain, Oakhill, and Lemmon (2004) found that 9- to 10-year-old poor comprehenders ($n = 12$) had difficulty inferring the meaning of novel vocabulary, particularly when processing demands were highest. In this study, participants read a series of stories, each of which used a novel pseudoword whose meaning could be inferred from the context of the story. Of interest was that the context that was needed to infer the vocabulary meaning was placed either near the pseudoword or far from the pseudoword (near and far in terms of intervening sentences). That poor comprehenders were specifically disadvantaged when the useful context was separated from the novel word provides a clear example of how working memory and language difficulties can affect reading comprehension performance in poor comprehenders.

Together, the findings on the nature of poor comprehender's deficits suggest that poor comprehenders tend to have deficits in higher-level processes, including working memory and language processes. The working memory difficulties of poor comprehenders tend to be restricted to verbal working memory tasks, supporting the notion that a language-specific working memory system as opposed to a general working memory system is involved in the comprehension difficulties of poor comprehenders. Yet an unresolved question is whether verbal working memory deficits in poor comprehenders cause poor comprehension, or whether verbal working memory deficits are a consequence of an underlying language deficit in poor comprehenders. Either way, it certainly seems to be the case that weaknesses in a working memory system for language negatively interfere with reading comprehension.

In addition to deficits in higher-order processes, there is also evidence that poor comprehenders show deficits in some lower-level processes. In particular, poor comprehenders were found to perform significantly lower than typical readers on some phonological awareness, rapid naming, and phonological short-term memory tasks, especially at younger ages, although deficits in lower-level processes do not seem to persist over time. These findings suggest that poor comprehenders begin school with general language processing deficits, including deficits in lower-level language processing skills (i.e., phonological processing). Over time poor comprehenders appear to develop lower-level language and phonological skills, although deficits in more complex language skills that tap semantic processing skills – a requirement for reading comprehension – remain. More research is needed to further clarify the lower-level and higher-order processes that characterize poor comprehenders, and how exactly such processes constrain children's reading comprehension.

Summary

Most of the studies reviewed provided evidence that children with specific comprehension difficulties are characterized by verbal working memory deficits. Furthermore, working memory contributes unique variance to reading comprehension even when word reading, vocabulary, and decoding ability are controlled. The relationship between working memory and reading comprehension appears to reflect a language-based relationship as opposed to weaknesses in a general limited capacity system, although more research in this area with poor comprehenders is needed.

DOES WORKING MEMORY CONTRIBUTE TO GROWTH IN READING COMPREHENSION ABILITY?

In order to evaluate whether working memory is involved in the growth of reading comprehension ability, it is important to examine the relationship over time. That is, in order to conclude that the working memory system is important for the development of reading comprehension, working memory performance at younger ages should explain unique variance in reading comprehension at later ages. Few studies, however, have provided a longitudinal perspective on this relationship between reading comprehension and working memory. The few longitudinal studies that are available suggest that working memory – verbal working memory in particular – is uniquely involved in the development of reading comprehension.

The findings from the Cain, Oakhill, and Bryant (2004) longitudinal study previously discussed demonstrated that verbal working memory was significantly correlated with reading comprehension when children were 7, 8, and 10 years old, whereas numerical working memory was correlated with reading comprehension only at 8 years old. The correlation between verbal working memory and reading comprehension was stronger at ages 8 and 10 than at 7 years, indicating a more robust relationship between working memory and comprehension over time. However, in regression analyses, a composite working memory variable (composed of verbal and numerical working memory tasks) accounted for 6.9%, 5.5%, and 5.2% of the variance at 7, 8, and 10 years, respectively, indicating a somewhat stable relationship between working memory and reading comprehension over time. The authors did not investigate whether working memory at 7 or 8 years old, predicted reading comprehension at 10 years old, so it is not known whether working memory processes were uniquely involved in the development of reading comprehension ability. However, these findings do indicate that working memory appears to maintain a consistently strong relationship with reading comprehension over time.

Dufva, Niemi, and Voeten (2001) investigated the development of reading skills in 222 Finnish children from kindergarten to second grade. In kindergarten (6 years old), measures of verbal ability, phonological awareness, and memory were administered. The memory tasks included a measure of listening comprehension as well as measures of word span, digit span, and sentence span. The span tasks were used to create a latent phonological short-term memory variable. At the end of second grade (8 years old), they found that listening comprehension (a verbal working memory task), word recognition, and phonological memory were, in order of importance, critical in the development of reading comprehension skills. Thus, the findings from this study indicate that verbal working memory skills, as well as phonological short-term memory skills, are important in explaining the growth of children's reading comprehension ability, although the influence of phonological memory on reading comprehension may be indirect.

The findings from our own longitudinal study also provide support for verbal working memory as a powerful predictor of reading comprehension (Vukovic & Siegel, 2005). Vukovic and Siegel conducted regression analyses to predict fifth and sixth grade comprehension from kindergarten measures of verbal working memory, phonological awareness, and rapid naming after controlling for word identification and pseudoword reading fluency. With fifth-grade word reading skills controlled, kindergarten verbal working memory explained the most variance in fifth grade comprehension, followed by kindergarten phonological awareness. Kindergarten rapid naming was not found to be important to the model. In the sixth-grade model, kindergarten verbal working memory, kindergarten rapid naming, and kindergarten phonological awareness, were, in relative order, the most important explanatory variables in the model. This study demonstrates that verbal working memory appears to be uniquely involved in the development of reading comprehension ability, even after controlling for word reading skills. Furthermore, of the cognitive processes considered, verbal working memory consistently explained the largest portion of variance in reading comprehension. This study also indicates that lower-level processes – such as phonological awareness and rapid naming – may be important in explaining the development of reading comprehension ability.

Together, the few findings from longitudinal studies suggest that verbal working memory is involved in the growth of children's reading comprehension abilities. In addition, lower-level processes such as phonological awareness, phonological short-term memory, and rapid naming may also be involved in the growth of reading comprehension independent of word reading skills. Studies in this area, however, have been conducted with samples of children across the spectrum of reading ability. Thus, it is unknown whether the same pattern would hold in samples of poor comprehenders followed longitudinally. Previous studies have found that variables such as phonological awareness, rapid naming, and working memory are involved in explaining reading development in children with word reading difficulties (e.g., O'Shaughnessy & Swanson, 1998; Torgesen, Wagner, Rashotte, Burgess, & Hecht, 1997). More studies are needed with poor comprehenders to determine whether lower-level and higher-order cognitive processes are involved in the growth of reading comprehension ability within this group.

Summary

The findings from longitudinal studies indicate that verbal working memory is consistently related to reading comprehension in children between the ages of 5 and 11 years. Longitudinal research is sparse, however, and further research is needed to understand how working memory contributes to reading comprehension failure, particularly in poor comprehenders. The studies reviewed suggest that in addition to working memory, lower-level processes may also be important in the growth of reading comprehension ability.

CONCLUSION

The purpose of this chapter was to review and evaluate the research on the role of working memory in children's reading comprehension abilities, particularly in those children with poor comprehension despite adequate word reading skills. Reading comprehension failure has traditionally been attributed to deficits in lower-level processes, such as deficits in phonological skills and word reading ability, and the fluency with which these skills are executed (e.g., Perfetti, 1985; Shankweiler, 1989; Torgesen, 2000). An alternative hypothesis is that comprehension failure reflects deficits in higher-order skills, such as working memory and language processing (e.g., Nation et al., 1999; Oakhill, 1993; Swanson & Alexander, 1997). The existence of children with poor comprehension despite adequate word reading skills offers support to the notion that comprehension difficulties extend beyond lower-level processing deficits.

A limited number of studies have examined comprehension failure in children with specific comprehension difficulties. Those studies that include samples of poor comprehenders tend to have small sample sizes and the analyses within such studies are restricted to group comparisons rather than longitudinal or regression analyses. Instead, the majority of studies conducted in this area tend to use samples of children across the spectrum of reading ability, which limits the extent to which it can be concluded that working memory is uniquely involved in the reading comprehension abilities of poor comprehenders. Furthermore, there are few longitudinal studies in this area, making it difficult to evaluate the longitudinal relationship between reading comprehension and working memory as it relates to poor comprehenders.

Bearing these caveats, the studies considered in the present review indicate that working memory deficits are involved in the comprehension difficulties of poor comprehenders. The working memory deficits experienced by poor comprehenders appear restricted to the verbal domain, thus indicating that the relationship between reading comprehension and working memory in poor comprehenders reflects deficits in a working memory system for language, as opposed to deficits in a general working memory system. The findings from studies using samples of children across the spectrum of reading abilities indicate that working memory variables involving numerical and visuospatial abilities also contribute unique variance to reading comprehension, thus suggesting that a general-working memory system may be involved in reading comprehension ability. However, no such research has been conducted with samples of poor comprehenders. That numerical and visuo-spatial working memory deficits did not characterize poor comprehenders suggests that these factors may play a different role in poor comprehenders. More studies with poor comprehenders are needed to determine the extent to which the relationship between working memory and reading comprehension reflects a working memory for language system, or a more general working memory system. Also needed are more studies to determine whether the verbal working memory deficits experienced by poor comprehenders cause poor comprehension, or whether such deficits are merely a reflection of underlying language deficits in poor comprehenders (Nation et al., 1999). Such a distinction has important implications for intervention and remediation.

In any case, the findings from the current review suggest that poor comprehenders have difficulties with verbal working memory tasks and that such deficits can and do affect reading comprehension. However, working memory is clearly not the only skill that affects the reading comprehension abilities of poor comprehenders. Language processing skills in particular appear to be an important area to continue to investigate with respect to children with specific comprehension difficulties. Poor comprehenders may also experience deficits in lower-level processes, such as phonological awareness, rapid naming, and phonological short-term memory, especially in the early school years (ages 6–8 years). How such early difficulties are overcome by poor comprehenders is also an important area to continue to investigate. The results from this review are consistent with the conclusions of other researchers that working memory alone does not account for the comprehension deficits in poor comprehenders (Oakhill, 1993; Swanson & Alexander, 1997). Instead reading comprehension appears to depend on the coordination of many lower- and higher-level skills. It may be this very coordination, a function of the working memory system, which is deficient in poor comprehenders.

NOTE

1   This manuscript was supported by a grant from the Natural Sciences and Engineering Research Council of Canada to L. S. Siegel and by grants from the Canadian Institutes of Health Research: Partnering in Community Health Research Program, and the Social Sciences and Humanities Research Council of Canada: Canadian Graduate Scholarship to R. K. Vukovic.

REFERENCES

Baddeley, A. D., & Hitch, G. J. (1994). Development in the concept of working memory. *Neuropsychology*, *8*, 485–493.

Cain, K., & Oakhill, J. (1999). Inference making ability and its relation to comprehension failure in young children. *Reading and Writing, 11*, 489–503.

Cain, K., Oakhill, J., & Bryant, P. (2000). Phonological skills and comprehension failure: A test of the phonological processing deficit hypothesis. *Reading and Writing, 13*, 31–56.

Cain, K., Oakhill, J., & Bryant, P. (2004). Children's reading comprehension ability: Concurrent prediction by working memory, verbal ability, and component skills. *Journal of Educational Psychology, 96*, 31–42.

Cain, K., Oakhill, J., & Lemmon, K. (2004). Individual differences in the inference of word meanings from context: The influence of reading comprehension, vocabulary knowledge, and memory capacity. *Journal of Educational Psychology, 96*, 671–681.

Chiappe, P., Hasher, L., & Siegel, L. S. (2000). Working memory, inhibitory control, and reading disability. *Memory and Cognition, 28*, 8–17.

Chiappe, P., Siegel, L. S., & Wade-Woolley, L. (2002). Linguistic diversity and the development of reading skills: A longitudinal study. *Scientific Studies of Reading, 6*, 369–400.

Daneman, M., & Carpenter, P. A. (1980). Individual differences in working memory and reading. *Journal of Verbal Learning and Verbal Behavior, 19*, 450–466.

Daneman, M., & Merikle, P. M. (1996). Working memory and language comprehension: A meta-analysis. *Psychonomic Bulletin and Review, 3*, 422–433.

Dufva, M., Niemi, P., & Voeten, M. J. M. (2001). The role of phonological memory, word recognition, and comprehension skills in reading development: From preschool to grade 2. *Reading and Writing, 14*, 91–117.

Engle, R. W., Cantor, J., & Carullo, J. J. (1992). Individual differences in working memory and comprehension: A test of four hypotheses. *Journal of Experimental Psychology, 18*, 972–992.

Ericsson, K. A., & Kintsch, W. (1995). Long-term working memory. *Psychological Review, 102*, 211–245.

Just, M. A., & Carpenter, P. A. (1992). A capacity theory of comprehension: Individual differences in working memory. *Psychological Review, 99*, 122–149.

Lesaux, N. K., & Siegel, L. S. (2003). The development of reading in children who speak English as a second language. *Developmental Psychology, 39*, 1005–1019.

Lyon, G. R. (1995). Toward a definition of dyslexia. *Annals of Dyslexia, 45*, 3–30.

Marshall, C. M., & Nation, K. (2003). Individual differences in semantic and structural errors in children's memory for sentences. *Educational and Child Psychology, 20*(3), 7–18.

McDougall, S., Hulme, C., Ellis, A., & Monk, A. (1994). Learning to read: The role of short-term memory and phonological processing skills. *Journal of Experimental Child Psychology, 58*, 112–133.

Morris, R. D., Stuebing, K. K., Fletcher, J. M., Shaywitz, S. E., Lyon, G. R., Shankweiler, D. P., et al. (1998). Subtypes of reading disability: Variability around a phonological core. *Journal of Educational Psychology, 90*, 347–373.

Nation, K., Adams, J. W., Bowyer-Crane, C. A., & Snowling, M. (1999). Working memory deficits in poor comprehenders reflect underlying language impairments. *Journal of Experimental Child Psychology, 73*, 139–158.

Oakhill, J. (1993). Children's difficulties in reading comprehension. *Educational Psychology Review, 5*, 223–237.

Oakhill, J., Yuill, N., & Parkin, A. (1986). On the nature of the difference between skilled and less-skilled comprehenders. *Journal of Research in Reading, 9*, 80–91.

O'Shaughnessy, T., & Swanson, H. L. (1998). Do immediate memory deficits in students with learning disabilities in reading reflect a developmental lag or deficit? A selective meta-analysis of the literature. *Learning Disability Quarterly, 21*, 123–148.

Perfetti, C. A. (1985). *Reading ability*. London: Oxford University Press.

Ransby, M. J., & Swanson, H. L. (2003). Reading comprehension skills of young adults with childhood diagnoses of dyslexia. *Journal of Learning Disabilities, 36*, 538–555.

Seigneuric, A., Ehrlich, M.-F., Oakhill, J. V., & Yuill, N. M. (2000). Working memory resources and children's reading comprehension. *Reading and Writingr, 13*, 81–103.

Shafrir, U., & Siegel, L. S. (1994). Subtypes of learning disabilities in adolescents and adults. *Journal of Learning Disabilities, 27*, 123–134.

Shankweiler, D. P. (1989). How problems of comprehension are related to difficulties in word reading. In D. P. Shankweiler & I. Y. Liberman (Eds.), *Phonology and reading disability: Solving the reading puzzle* (pp. 35–68). Ann Arbor, MI: University of Michigan Press.

Shaywitz, S. E., Fletcher, J. M., Holahan, J. M., Schneider, A. E., Marchione, K. E., Stuebing, K. K., et al. (1999). Persistence of dyslexia: The Connecticut Longitudinal Study at Adolescence. *Pediatrics, 104*, 1351–1359.

Siegel, L. S., & Ryan, E. B. (1989a). The development of working memory in normally achieving and subtypes of learning disabled children. *Child Development, 60*, 973–980.

Siegel, L. S., & Ryan, E. B. (1989b). Subtypes of developmental dyslexia: The influence of definitional variables. *Reading and Writing, 2*, 257–287.

Stanovich, K. E., & Siegel, L. S. (1994). Phenotypic performance profile of children with reading disabilities: A regression-based test of the phonological-core variable-difference model. *Journal of Educational Psychology, 86*, 24–53.

Swanson, H. L. (1995). *S-Cognitive Processing Test*. Austin, TX: Pro-Ed.

Swanson, H. L., & Alexander, J. E. (1997). Cognitive processes as predictors of word recognition and reading comprehension in learning-disabled and skilled readers: Revisiting the specificity hypothesis. *Journal of Educational Psychology, 89*, 128–158.

Swanson, H. L., & Berninger, V. W. (1995). The role of working memory in skilled and less skilled readers' comprehension. *Intelligence, 21*, 83–108.

Swanson, H. L., Cooney, J. B., & McNamara, J. K. (2004). Learning disabilities and memory. In B. Y. L. Wong (Ed.), *Learning about learning disabilities* (3rd ed., pp. 41–92). San Diego, CA: Academic Press.

Swanson, H. L., & Howell, M. (2001). Working memory, short-term memory, and speech rate as predictors of children's reading performance at different ages. *Journal of Educational Psychology, 93*, 720–734.

Swanson, H. L., & Sachse-Lee, C. (2001). A subgroup analysis of working memory in children with reading disabilities: Domain-general or domain-specific deficiency? *Journal of Learning Disabilities, 34*, 249–263.

Swanson, H. L., & Siegel, L. S. (2001). Learning disabilities as a working memory deficit. *Issues in Education, 7*, 1–48.

Torgesen, J. K. (2000). Individual differences in response to early interventions in reading: The lingering problem of treatment resisters. *Learning Disabilities Research and Practice, 15*, 55–64.

Torgesen, J. K., Wagner, R. K., Rashotte, C. A., Burgess, S., & Hecht, S. (1997).

Contributions of phonological awareness and rapid automatic naming ability to the growth of word-reading skills in second- to fifth-grade children. *Scientific Studies of Reading, 1*, 161–185.

Vukovic, R. K., & Siegel, L. S. (2005). *Cognitive processing skills and reading comprehension: The role of phonological awareness, rapid naming, and working memory.* Unpublished manuscript, University of British Columbia.

Wolf, M., & Bowers, P. G. (1999). The double-deficit hypothesis for the developmental dyslexias. *Journal of Educational Psychology, 91*, 415–438.

Yuill, N., Oakhill, J., & Parkin, A. (1989). Working memory, comprehension ability and the resolution of text anomaly. *British Journal of Psychology, 80*, 351–361.

6 Working memory and arithmetic learning disability

Maria Chiara Passolunghi

OVERVIEW

The first part of this chapter presents brief background information on the prevalence and criteria for the diagnosis of arithmetic learning disability (ALD). Moreover, it provides an overview of the relationship between working memory and simple arithmetic computations, as well as more complex tasks such as arithmetic word problems. The following sections focus on our research program as well as on other research that investigates the influence of the different components of working memory in Baddeley's model (1986, 1996), and in particular of the central executive functions, on performance of arithmetic word problems in children with ALD compared to children achieving at normal levels.[1] Altogether the results suggest that complex working memory skills are impaired in children with ALD. In particular the findings suggest a working memory deficit in children with ALD, mainly in the central executive component of Baddeley's model, and, specifically, in the inhibitory and updating processes. However, articulatory processes do not represent a fundamental deficit for children of low mathematical ability when difference in reading is controlled for.

ARITHMETIC LEARNING DISABILITY

Definition of arithmetic learning disability (ALD)

Participants with learning difficulties (LD) are operationally defined as those children and adults who have general IQ scores above 85 and who have scores below the 25th percentile on a standardized achievement measure. In theory, mathematical disability can result from deficits in the ability to represent or process information used in one or all of the many areas of mathematics (e.g., arithmetic, geometry, algebra). Recent studies have focused primarily on mathematical domains including number, counting, and arithmetic (see Geary & Hoard, 2001). In particular, participants with ALD may have an average IQ, but an achievement score lower than the

25th percentile cut off in a standardized maths test (e.g., below 15th, 10th percentile).

It is worth noting that Siegel (1989) argued that learning disabilities should not be defined in terms of IQ-achievement discrepancies. For example, learning disability can be diagnosed when there is a discrepancy between a child's IQ and his achievement. However, this method can lead to over identification of children who have high IQ scores but normal achievement. As such, in this chapter, ALD is defined by cutoff scores in achievement tests consistent with Morrison and Siegel (1991) and Siegel and Ryan (1989), rather than a discrepancy criteria.

Prevalence

Children with learning disorders are characterized by a specific difficulty in mastering reading, spelling and/or calculation, despite adequate instruction, and in the absence of mental retardation. Large-scale epidemiological studies of the prevalence of ALD have not been conducted. However, smaller-scale studies (including about 300 children) indicate that 5–8% of school children suffer from a cognitive or neuropsychological deficit that interferes with their competencies in calculation or word problem solving procedures (Badian, 1983; Gross-Tsur, Manor, & Shalev, 1996; Kosc, 1974).

Comorbidity

Some children with ALD present comorbid attention deficit hyperactivity disorder (ADHD) or reading disability. Gross-Tsur et al. (1996) found that 26% of the children with ALD had symptoms of ADHD, and 17% had difficulties in reading. This is a conservative proportion as some studies have found that as many as half of the children with ALD had comorbid reading difficulties and spelling disability (e.g., Badian, 1983). Children with ALD represent at least two different subgroups: one with difficulties only in arithmetic and one with comorbid reading and spelling disabilities (see Geary, 1993; Geary & Hoard, 2001).

Subtypes of arithmetic learning disabilities

In order to explore the nature of cognitive deficits underlying arithmetic difficulties in children, Geary (1993) identified three subtypes of mathematical disability: procedural, semantic memory, and visuospatial. However, he focused primarily on deficits in simple arithmetic problems (e.g., the basic arithmetic calculations), whereas cognitive deficits in more complex tasks, such as arithmetic word problems have not been fully investigated.

Procedural subtype

Much of the research on children with ALD has focused on the use of a counting procedure to solve simple arithmetic problems (e.g., 5+8) or multistep arithmetic problems (e.g., 238–126). When ALD children solve these problems, they often commit more errors than children achieving at normal levels, and they often used problem-solving procedures that are more commonly used by younger children (e.g., the use of an immature procedure as "counting all"; for example, to solve 3+4, the children lifted the fingers representing the augend and addend. All uplifted fingers were then counted, starting from 1).

In general, children with ALD mainly rely on finger counting, instead of verbal counting, and use a finger strategy for more years than do normally achieving children. The typical errors are miscounting (e.g., undercounting or overcounting by 1), misalignment of numbers, carrying or borrowing errors (Geary, 1993).

Neuropsychological studies of dyscalculia suggest there are neural system deficits underlying the procedural deficits. Individuals with dyscalculia caused by damage to the right hemisphere sometimes show difficulties with the procedural component of counting, especially difficulties with systematically pointing to successive objects that have to be numerated (Seron et al., 1991). Moreover, deficits in the right frontal cortex were found in an individual with procedural difficulties (Temple, 1991). However, Ashcraft, Yamashita, and Aram (1992) suggest that certain procedural deficits might reflect a dysfunction in the left hemisphere. Further research is necessary to better clarify the neural correlates associated with the procedural deficits of children with ALD.

Semantic memory subtype

The main features of this subtype are deficits in the retrieval of the basic arithmetic facts and problems in the memorization of arithmetic tables even after extensive repetition. This pattern suggests that these children have difficulties storing or accessing arithmetic knowledge from long-term memory. However, these children can correctly retrieve some number facts associated with an operation, such as addition, from long-term memory, but cannot correctly retrieve facts associated with another operation (e.g., multiplication).

Children classified in this category are more likely to show comorbid reading disability. Neuropsychological research suggests that this type of deficit may reflect some form of dysfunction involving the posterior region of the left hemisphere (Ashcraft et al., 1992). However, the cognitive and neural mechanisms underlying this deficit are not completely understood. More recent studies suggest that the retrieval deficit of these children may be because of difficulties in inhibiting the retrieval of irrelevant associations from working memory. Barrouillet, Fayol, and Lathulière (1997) found that seventh-grade children with learning disabilities had difficulties in inhibiting the retrieval of irrelevant associations of simple multiplication problems (see Conway & Engle, 1994; Geary, Hamson, & Hoard, 2000, for similar findings). These results suggest that the retrieval deficit may derive from impairment in the areas of the prefrontal cortex that are involved in inhibitory mechanism (Welsh & Pennington, 1988).

Visuospatial subtype

This subtype seems to be associated with a dysfunction of the posterior regions of the right hemisphere (Dahmen, Hartje, Bussing, & Sturm, 1982; Rourke & Finlayson, 1978). The children included in this subtype showed difficulties in spatially representing numerical information (misalignment of numbers in multicolumn arithmetic problems, rotation of numbers, and mis-interpretation of spatially numerical information such as place value errors). However, the relationship between visuospatial competencies and ALD has not been fully explored. In theory, visuospatial deficits should affect perform-ance in some mathematical domains, such as certain areas of complex word problems, but not other domains, such as facts retrieval (Geary, 1993, 1996). Some researchers showed that children with the procedural or semantic sub-type of ALD do not differ from other children in basic visuospatial com-petencies (Geary et al., 2000). An alternative suggestion is that children in the visuospatial subgroup may have a deficit in spatial working memory task (see McLean & Hitch, 1999).

MEMORY DIFFICULTIES IN CHILDREN WITH ALD

The following sections of the chapter focus on the influence of working memory on arithmetic abilities. Several authors found that working memory plays a crucial role both in calculation and in solving arithmetic word prob-lems (Bull & Sherif, 2001; Fuerst & Hitch, 2000; Geary et al., 2000; Hitch, 1978; Lehto, 1995; Logie, Gilhooly, & Wynn, 1994; Passolunghi & Cornoldi, 2000; Passolunghi & Pazzaglia, 2004). Moreover, working memory has been implicated as a central deficit in children with mathematical disability (Geary, 1993; Hitch & McAuley, 1991; Passolunghi, Cornoldi, & de Liberto, 1999; Passolunghi & Siegel, 2001, 2004; Siegel & Ryan, 1989; Swanson, 1993).

The working memory model, originally developed by Baddeley and Hitch (1974) distinguishes a central executive system that is not modality specific and is involved in the control of cognitive activity, from two slave systems that are modality specific: the phonological loop, specialized for storage and rehearsal of verbal information, and the visuospatial sketchpad, specialized for holding visual and spatial information (Baddeley, 1986, 1996).

More recently, Baddeley (2000) added a fourth component to his model, the episodic buffer, which is a limited-capacity system that both integrates and provides temporary storage of information from the two subsystems and long-term memory. Developmental research related to this fourth component is very limited (although see Alloway, Gathercole, Willis, & Adams, 2004), so we focus on the first three components in the current chapter. In particular, in the following two paragraphs, we will focus on the influence of the two slave systems of Baddeley's working memory model on mathematic ability.

Phonological loop and mathematical ability

The phonological loop appears to be involved in counting (Logie & Baddeley, 1987) and in holding information in complex calculations. In addition, Swanson and Sachse-Lee (2001) found that children with arithmetic word problem-solving difficulties showed an impaired performance in phonological processing, assessed by a processing speed task (e.g., the child was requested to orally name randomly ordered digits, as accurately and quickly as possible), phonemic deletion, and digit span forward. However, the phonological loop did not represent a fundamental deficit for children of low mathematical ability when difference in reading was controlled for (Bull & Johnston, 1997; McLean & Hitch, 1999; Passolunghi & Siegel, 2001, 2004).

A separate role for executive and phonological components in mental calculation was shown by Fuerst and Hitch (2000). Using dual task methodology, they found that articulatory suppression impaired the ability to add a pair of briefly verbally presented numbers. Suppression had no effect when the need to store information temporarily was reduced by visually presenting the to be-added numbers. On the other hand, a trail-making task (that taps the executive functions; see Baddeley, 1996) impaired the ability to add visually presented numbers. The performance in the trail task condition progressively declined as the numbers of carry operations in the addition increased. These results suggest that the phonological loop plays a major role when calculation involves storing temporary information, whereas carrying operations put a major demand on the central executive processes.

Logie et al. (1994) reported similar findings: Articulatory suppression produced a smaller decrement in calculation performance, whereas disruption of the central executive, through random letter generation, produced the most errors in mental addition performance (see also de Rammelaere, Stuyven, & Vandierendonck, 1999, 2001). In sum, research studies emphasize that the central executive plays a greater role in mental calculation compared to the phonological loop (de Rammelaere & Vandierendonck, 2001; Kauffman, 2002; Seitz & Schumann-Hengsteler, 2002).

Visual-spatial sketchpad in children with mathematical disability

As described above, one of the three subtypes of learning disabilities in mathematics identified by Geary (1993) involves visuospatial problems. In

Baddeley's (1986, 1996) model, the visuospatial sketchpad (VSSP) is considered to process and store visual spatial information for a short time and to operate on visual images. Heathcote (1994) suggested that the VSSP is used as a mental blackboard where visuospatial material is held while operations are performed on it.

Studies based on clinical samples have suggested that a cognitive deficit in arithmetic can be characterized as a visuospatial deficit and visual motor integration (Hartie, 1987; Rourke, 1993; Rourke & Strang, 1978; White, Moffitt, & Silva, 1992; for a review see Geary, 1993). In addition, studies of dyscalculia – that is, numerical and arithmetical deficits following overt brain injury (e.g., Shalev, Manor, & Gross-Tsur, 1993; Temple, 1991) – reported descriptions of children and adults who have calculation problems (e.g., misalignment of numbers in columns) based on a deficit in visuospatial ability (Heathcote, 1994; Rourke & Conway, 1997; Temple, 1991).

Kyttala, Aunio, Lehto, van Luit, and Hautamaki (2003) examined visuospatial working memory ability of normal developing preschoolers (mean age: 6 years 2 months). They found that an early numeracy skill, more specifically counting, was related to visuospatial abilities. Accordingly, visuospatial disability may be linked to a poor early mathematic skill and, later, to a low mathematic achievement at schools.

While the role of VSSP in counting and calculation is more clear, the relationship between VSSP and more complex math ability, such as problem solving, is not evident. Some studies show no relationship between visuospatial working memory and mathematical ability. In particular, Bull, Johnston, and Roy (1999) found that 7-year-old children of high and low mathematical ability did not differ in visual sequential memory, assessed using Corsi blocks (forward span). Similarly, Swanson, Ashbaker, and Lee (1996, Exp. 1) found that visuospatial working memory in students with learning disabilities was intact when compared with their same-age counterparts. Moreover, Swanson (1993) found that 10-year-old children with learning disabilities, who had either math problems or reading problems, could not be clearly differentiated by performance on verbal or visuospatial working memory: Children with arithmetic disabilities performed as low as children with reading disabilities across verbal and visuospatial working memory tasks (see also Gathercole, Alloway, Willis, & Adams, 2006).

On the other hand, studies focusing on children and adults with nonverbal learning disability (NVLD) support the hypothesis of a relationship between mathematics difficulties and visuospatial ability (Rourke & Conway, 1997; Rourke & Finlayson, 1978). These studies showed that children with NVLD had no impairment in verbal memory (i.e., forward and backward verbal span); however, they had poor performance in visuospatial tasks (see also Cornoldi, Rigoni, Venneri, & Vecchi, 2000). In addition, in a correlational study with young adolescents Reuhkala (2001) found that performances in a visuospatial task (e.g., visual matrix pattern task) and in a mental rotation task were correlated with mathematics test scores.

While there is a debate on the VSSP functions, in a recent study Passolunghi and Sarotti (2005) verified which subsystem of VSSP may play a main role in mathematical ability. Several researchers have highlighted the existence of at least two subsystems of VSSP. A *visual* component that retains material such as shape and color, and a *spatial* component responsible for retaining dynamic information about movement and spatial information such as the location of an object (Quinn & McConnell, 1996; see Baddeley & Logie, 1999, for a review). Passolunghi and Sarotti hypothesized that the spatial component may have a major role in solving arithmetic word problems. Children with mathematics disability, but average intellectual level and reading ability, had a selective impairment in the *spatial* component, but not in the *visual* component of working memory. On the other hand, the children with poor math ability were not impaired in the phonological loop system of the Baddeley working memory model, which is assumed to temporarily store and rehearse linguistic information. These findings are in agreement with the results of McLean and Hitch (1999), who found that children with poor arithmetic had normal phonological working memory (e.g., nonword repetition), but were impaired on spatial working memory (Corsi blocks, forward span).

SPECIFIC INFLUENCE OF WORKING MEMORY COMPONENTS ON MATHEMATICAL DISABILITY

This section of the chapter discusses in detail some questions regarding the relationship between working memory and arithmetic learning disability and examines the results of our study and other research on the role of central executive functions in mathematics. The following questions are addressed:

1   Is the relationship between working memory and learning disability restricted to process numerical information?
2   Does the working memory deficit of children with a learning disability in mathematics extended to short-term memory tasks that rely on a passive storage system?
3   Which component of Baddeley's working memory model is primarily involved in mathematical ability?

In order to address these issues, we investigated the roles of the phonological loop and the central executive in mathematical skills. Our hypothesis was that the central executive could be more specifically and strongly involved in math ability and especially in word problem solution. The involvement of the central executive was measured using working memory tasks that involved both storage and processing of information. In addition, we focused on the fractionation of the central executive components hypothesized by Baddeley (1996) and Miyake, Friedman, Emerson, Witzki, and Howerter (2000). Consequently, we examined the influence of specific central executive functions, such as shifting, inhibition, and updating in mathematical skills.

Working memory deficits in ALD

Some studies have found that children with difficulties in mathematics may have a selective impairment in working memory tasks in which remembering arithmetic information is critical. Indeed, Siegel and Ryan (1989) found that the performance of children with a mathematical learning disability was similar to that of normal achievers in a working memory task involving sentence processing, but impaired on a working memory task requiring processing of numerical information. In a related study, Hitch and McAuley (1991) found that children with specific difficulties in mathematics were impaired in working memory tasks that involve the processing of numerical information, but not in other complex verbal span tasks. On the contrary, Swanson and Sachse-Lee (2001) showed that poor achievers in mathematics had lower scores in complex verbal span tasks (e.g., Listening Span Task).

In order to disentangle this aspect, we have examined the children's performance on working memory tasks that required processing of numerical information as well as tasks that did not (Passolunghi & Siegel, 2001, 2004). In this longitudinal study, working memory skills and problem-solving ability of children with difficulties in mathematics were compared to skills of children who were achieving at normal levels. The two groups were matched for age, gender, and scores in the standardized vocabulary subtest of PMA battery (Thurstone & Thurstone, 1941/1968). Converted to verbal IQ (see Table 6.1), the difference was not significant ($p = .32$). Another criteria was that all children had to perform in the normal range in reading comprehension tests. There was no significant difference ($p > .15$) between the scores of the two groups in reading ability, assessed on an Italian reading comprehension standardized test (Cornoldi & Colpo, 1981), as shown in Table 6.1.

The children in the fourth and fifth grade (respectively 9 years 4 months and 10 years 4 months) were tested on three working memory tasks: (1) the Listening Span Task (Daneman & Carpenter, 1980), in which children listened to sets of increasing numbers of sentences, judged whether the sentences are true or false, then at the end of each set, recalled the last word of each of the sentences; (2) the Listening Span Completion Task (Siegel & Ryan, 1989), in which several sentences with the final word missing were presented and the child had to generate the missing word at the end of the sentence, then had to repeat all the missing words from the sets; (3) the Counting Span Task (Case, Kurland, & Goldberg, 1982; Siegel & Ryan, 1989), in which children counted target dots from an irregular pattern of dots, then recalled the counts of the presented patterns.

The results of the working memory tasks are shown in Table 6.2. The findings indicate that children with specific mathematical difficulties had a persistent deficit in working memory that is not restricted to a numerical

Table 6.1 Descriptive statistics of children with arithmetic difficulties and children achieving at normal levels in studies of Passolunghi and Siegel (2001, 2004) (reprinted from Passolunghi and Siegel, 2004), Working memory and access to numerical information in children with disability in mathematics. *Journal of Experimental Child Psychology, 88,* 348–367, with permission from Elsevier.

	Children with arithmetic difficulties		Children achieving at normal levels	
	M	*SD*	*M*	*SD*
Scores in the fourth grade				
Verbal IQ	119.36	(4.18)	120.67	(4.74)
Standardized Reading test	−0.20	(1.01)	0.18	(0.98)
Standardized Math test	−0.95	(0.20)	0.84	(0.56)**
Scores in the fifth grade				
Standardized Math test	−0.73	(0.55)	0.59	(0.88)**
Standardized Calculation Test (WRAT3)	−0.60	(0.88)	0.48	(0.81)**
Gender	Male	Female	Male	Female
Number	14	13	11	11

Notes

** $p < .001$.

IQ score may be overestimated, since the PMA battery was normed in 1968. This may be due to general cross-generational increase in mean IQ score (Flynn, 1987). Z-scores for Reading, Math, and Calculation tests are reported.

Table 6.2 Mean performance and standard deviations of children with arithmetic difficulties and children achieving at normal levels in the Listening Span Task, Listening Span Completion Task, and Counting Span Task

	Children with arithmetic difficulties		Children achieving at normal levels	
	M	*SD*	*M*	*SD*
Scores in the fourth grade				
Listening Span Task	9.65	(3.04)	11.73	(3.43)*
Listening Span Completion Task	18.74	(5.67)	22.23	(5.80)*
Counting Span Task	35.69	(3.72)	38.23	(3.57)*
Scores in the fourth grade				
Listening Span Task	15.68	(4.47)	18.59	(4.53)*
Listening Span Completion Task	28.36	(3.47)	31.55	(3.75)*
Counting Span Task	35.68	(3.87)	38.48	(3.25)*

Note

* $p < .01$.

working memory task. Indeed, ALD children showed an impairment and lower recall of relevant information in working memory tasks involving both verbal and numerical information.

One possibility is that this deficit should also be related to reading comprehension disability. As children with the mathematical disability may be divided into children with or without reading impairment, in the present study, the ALD children and the age-matched controls did not differ in reading comprehension ability.

Short-term memory tasks and mathematical disability

Another issue to address is whether working memory deficits of children with ALD extend to short-term memory tasks. It is possible to hypothesize a distinction between short-term and working memory tasks. Short-term memory tasks (such as word/digit span forward) rely on a passive storage system and involve the recall of the information without manipulating it in any way (see also Cantor, Engle, & Hamilton, 1991; Cornoldi & Vecchi, 2000; Engle, 2002; Passolunghi & Siegel, 2001; Vecchi & Cornoldi, 1999). On the other hand, working memory tasks (such as Listening Span Task or digit/ word span backward), request more active processes, and are those in which information is temporarily held while being manipulated or transformed. Factor analyses have shown that the measures of short-term memory and measures of working memory loaded onto two different factors (Engle, Cantor, & Carullo, 1992; Swanson, 1994). An implication of these assumptions is that children or adults with learning disabilities may have working memory problems independent of problems in short-term memory.

Several studies have not found a significant difference between ALD children and a control group in forward digit and word span, especially when reading ability was controlled for (Bull & Johnston, 1997; McLean & Hitch, 1999). Similarly, Passolunghi and Siegel (2001; also 2004; Passolunghi et al., 1999; Passolunghi, Marzocchi, & Fiorillo, 2005) found that the performance of ALD children was not significantly different from children with normal achievement in word and digit forward-span tasks. Consequently, it seems likely that children with specific mathematical disability are not impaired in verbal short-term memory tasks associated with the phonological loop component of working memory.

Which components of the working memory model are primarily involved in mathematical ability?

In order to address this question, we compared the roles of the phonological loop and central executive components in ALD. Since solutions to word problems require decoding and comprehension, a lower order failure of phonological processing may mediate difficulties in higher order processes such as word problem solving (Bowey, Cain, & Ryan, 1992; Crain,

Shankweiler, Macaruss, & Bar-Shalom, 1990; Siegel, 1993; Stanovich & Siegel, 1994). The results of Bull and Johnston (1997) support this view, as there were significant differences between groups of children with high and low abilities in mathematics on a measure of syllable speech rate. In addition, Swanson and Sachse-Lee (2001) found that mathematical word problem-solving deficits are mediated by both the phonological and executive components of Baddeley's model. However, when differences in reading skills were controlled for, the functioning of the phonological loop did not represent a fundamental deficit for children of low mathematical ability (Bull & Johnston, 1997).

It is possible that the central executive could be more specifically and strongly involved than phonological loop in math ability and especially in arithmetic word problem solution, even when the written text is still available. Comprehension of a text implies that the incoming information is integrated with the previous information maintained in the working memory system. Furthermore the complete comprehension of the problem requires that the solvers build up a mental representation that involves the holding of relevant information. This activity corresponds with functions of the central executive. Indeed, problem solving does not simply involve the maintenance of given information, but requires its control (e.g., that this information is examined for relevance, selected, or inhibited, according to its relevance or integrated with the previous one, etc.). This view is supported by findings that children with ALD were not impaired in tasks involving the role of the phonological loop, but were impaired only in tasks designed to assess executive processes (Passolunghi & Pazzaglia, 2004; Passolunghi & Siegel, 2001, 2004).

Other recent studies assessed the role of central executive on mathematical skills of school-age children and adolescents. Gathercole and Pickering (2000) evaluated working memory skills of children aged 6 and 7 years by a test battery designed to tap individual components of Baddeley and Hitch's (1974) working memory model. Listening span (Daneman & Carpenter, 1980), counting span (Case et al., 1982), and backwards digit recall were chosen to assess the central executive. The results gave further evidence that central executive plays a crucial role in the acquisition of complex cognitive abilities and skills such as literacy, comprehension, and arithmetic (see also Alloway et al., 2005; Bull & Sherif, 2001; McLean & Hitch, 1999). In particular, McLean and Hitch (1999) assessed 9-year-old children with specific ALD, and comparing them with both age-matched and ability-matched controls. Relative to age-matched controls, children with ALD were impaired on spatial working memory and some aspects of executive processing. However, compared to ability-matched controls, children with ALD were impaired only on one task, the Missing Item Task, designed to assess executive processes for holding and manipulating numeric information in long-term memory.

A related function of working memory refers to the ability to inhibit irrelevant information. Espy et al. (2004) found that this skill was related to emergent mathematical proficiency in preschool children aged between 2 and 5 years. Inhibitory control was measured by tasks that required motor inhibition: statue subtest (NEPSY; Korkman, Kirk, & Kemp, 1998), self-control (e.g., do not touch a gift until the examiner had finished a task), and delayed responses. Overall, given the differences in age range and design between these studies, the relation between the central executive component of working memory and mathematics is well-established.

FRACTIONATION OF THREE EXECUTIVE FUNCTIONS (INHIBITION, UPDATING, AND SHIFTING) AND THEIR ROLE ON MATHEMATICAL ABILITY

Recent research has suggested that the functions of the central executive can be fractionated into at least three separate components: inhibition, updating, and shifting (Miyake et al., 2000; also Miyake & Shah, 1999). Miyake et al. (2000) suggest that even though these three components are clearly distinguishable, they share some underlying commonality. These researchers hypothesized that inhibitory processes (e.g., suppression of irrelevant or unnecessary information) may be a factor underlying this commonality. We now discuss how each of these three executive functions relate to ALD.

Inhibition

Among the description of the inhibitory mechanisms, Nigg (2000) proposed a differentiation between effortful and automatic inhibition. Four types of effortful inhibition have been described: interference controls (usually assessed using the Stroop task), cognitive inhibition (control of nonpertinent information saving working memory or attention), behavioral inhibition (for suppressing prepotent responses), and oculomotor inhibition (effortful control of reflexive saccades). We will focus on cognitive inhibition and its role in ALD, particularly in problem solving.

Previous research has demonstrated a relationship between inhibitory processes and reading comprehension. Specifically, children with reading disabilities perform poorly on working memory tasks that require inhibition of irrelevant information (Chiappe, Hasher, & Siegel, 2000; de Beni, Palladino, Pazzaglia, & Cornoldi, 1998). De Beni et al. (1998) found that poor comprehenders recalled fewer target items and made more intrusion errors in a revised version of the Listening Span Task (LST; Daneman & Carpenter, 1980). These findings confirmed that poor comprehenders' performance in the LST was impaired because they were unable to inhibit irrelevant information adequately, with the consequence of overloading their working memory.

It is possible that the ability to inhibit irrelevant information is also related to the success in problem solving. In both text comprehension and problem solving it is necessary to process a great number of information units. Some of these must be rejected in order to maintain only those that are relevant. In particular, integration of the relevant information into a coherent structure allows a correct and complete mental representation of a text of problem. Passolunghi and Siegel (2001, 2004) found that poor problem solvers had a deficit in their ability to reduce accessibility of nontarget and irrelevant information (see also Passolunghi & Cornoldi, 2000; Passolunghi et al., 1999).

These findings are compatible with Engle's (2002) suggestion that individual differences in working memory capacity are not related to how many items can be stored in memory, but in the difference in ability of controlling attention and maintaining information in an active, quickly retrievable state. Moreover, he argues that attentional control is related to inhibitory deficits, that is, individuals who have difficulty maintaining attentional focus on the task-relevant information are likely to make intrusion errors.

This theory was tested in a study comparing good problem solvers and poor problem solvers on the recall of working memory tasks and word problems (Passolunghi et al., 1999). According to Engle (2002), it is likely that poor problem solvers would have worse recall of relevant information and greater recall of irrelevant information in the recall of the word problems. In word problem recall, the children had to listen to a set of problems and focus on the relevant information (i.e., information that was necessary to solve the problem) included in the problems. At the end of each problem, the children were asked to recall the relevant information. Finally, the children were given a booklet with the set of the word problems presented earlier and were asked to solve them. The results are shown in Table 6.3.

The findings confirmed that poor problem solvers solved fewer problems than the good problem solvers. Analysis of participants' protocols showed that the correctly solved problems corresponded to the problems more

Table 6.3 Mean scores and standard deviations in the poor problem solvers group and in the good problem solvers group in the memorization and solution of word arithmetic problems (reprinted with permission from Passolunghi et al., 1999)

	Poor problem solvers group		*Good problem solvers group*	
	M	*SD*	*M*	*SD*
Relevant information	30.13	9.94	39.94	6.68
Irrelevant information	9.00	6.22	5.17	3.75
Correct problem	2.53	2.64	8.78	2.24
Correct number operation	7.87	3.80	23.67	3.80

Note
The first line indicates the number of relevant elements remembered by the participants, the second line, the number of irrelevant elements recalled, the third line, the number of problems correctly solved, and the fourth line, the number of arithmetic operations correctly indicated by the participants in the word problems.

adequately remembered. In particular, recall was twice as high for correctly solved problems than for unsolved ones. These results support the view of a general impairment in inhibitory ability, which extends to the recall of word problems.

The recall of word problems mirrored the working memory tasks used (e.g., Listening Span Task). In the recall of word problems the participants had to listen to auditory presented information and to recall relevant information. In order to correctly perform the task it was necessary to process all the information. After this initial process, the participants had to select target relevant information and to inhibit irrelevant information. In working memory tasks, the target and nontarget information was clearly defined on the basis of a simple rule (e.g., in the Listening Span Task the target items are the last words in each sentences). However, in the Text Problem Recall Task, the participants had to determine the relevant information themselves. Therefore, the higher number of intrusion errors in poor problem solver groups might be due to their inability to identify the irrelevant information included in the text problem.

Consequently, we tested poor problem solver's capacity to differentiate between the relevant and irrelevant information included in arithmetic word problems. Poor problem solvers and good problem solvers were presented with a series of written problems. The children had to underline the information they considered relevant for the solution. Furthermore, they were asked to write down the problem data, a procedure taught in Italian schools. This inspection showed that poor problem solvers were as able as good problem solvers to differentiate between relevant and irrelevant information included in written word problem. This suggests that the higher number of intrusion errors in poor problem solvers is not due to their inability to identify the irrelevant information in the word problem.

In order to understand the selective effect of different types of irrelevant information on arithmetic word problem solution, we compared problem solving skills of children with arithmetic learning disabilities (ALD), those with attention deficit hyperactivity disorder (ADHD), and a control group (Passolunghi et al., 2005). The groups were age matched and IQ matched. Table 6.4 shows the characteristics of the three groups.

While both ADHD and ALD groups may have inhibitory deficits, they differ in inhibiting irrelevant numerical or literal information. All three groups of children were presented with a battery of arithmetic word problems containing one of two types of irrelevant information: numerical and literal information. The irrelevant numerical information were superfluous numerical items (e.g., 12 grams of vitamins), and the irrelevant literal information (e.g., Mary is very greedy) were redundant sentences not necessary to solve the problem. Both types of information may overload the memory system and interfere with the construction of a mental model of the problem. However, they can affect the process of solving the problem for different reasons. Irrelevant numerical information may elicit the wrong procedure, for

Table 6.4 Clinical characteristics of the sample of children with ADHD, ALD, and children achieving at normal levels (NL) (adapted from Passolunghi et al., 2005)

Variables	ADHD		ALD		NL		One-way ANOVA contrasts
	M	SD	M	SD	M	SD	
Age (range 9–11)	9.80	0.48	9.90	0.52	9.85	0.49	
Full-scale IQ	105.10	12.63	102.10	11.13	107.50	17.14	
Inattention parents (0–27)	13.80	2.10	3.80	2.62	0.90	1.10	ADHD > ALD > NL
Hyperactivity parents (0–27)	9.90	2.81	1.70	1.77	0.60	0.84	ADHD > ALD, NL
Inattention teachers (0–27)	14.90	2.13	4.30	3.86	1.20	1.48	ADHD > ALD, NL
Hyperactivity teachers (0–27)	10.90	2.69	2.60	2.80	0.90	1.20	ADHD > ALD, NL

example the execution of extra arithmetic calculations, that is not requested by the word problem question. Irrelevant literal information requires a more demanding and prolonged processing that is useless in correctly solving the problem.

The results indicate a double dissociation in the role of the irrelevant information (see Table 6.5). Children with ADHD showed greater recall of irrelevant literal information compared to children with ALD and children achieving at normal levels. In contrast, children with ALD were mainly affected by irrelevant numerical information (see also Passolunghi & Siegel, 2001, 2004). As expected, the control group made fewer intrusions than both the ADHD and ALD groups.

These findings support the hypothesis that inhibitory mechanisms may explain an impairment in arithmetic word problem solving. Problem-solving difficulties of children with ADHD and ALD are related to the inability of reducing the memory accessibility of nontarget and irrelevant information. Specifically, the results showed that irrelevant literal or numerical information had a different effect on subtypes of children with learning difficulties. A deficit in the inhibitory processes, mainly evident with literal information, was found in children with ADHD. Conversely, the main difficulty of children with ALD is in processing and discharging irrelevant numerical information.

Updating

Another executive functions associated with the central executive is the updating of the information (Baddeley, 1996; Miyake & Shah, 1999). However, only very recently has the relationship between updating ability and problem solving been specifically investigated. Updating is a complex activity that requires attributing different levels of activation to the items presented, and maintaining a restricted set of elements activated continuously. A typical measure of updating ability is Morris and Jones' Updating Task (1990), which requires participants to listen to several lists of letters of varying length (4 to 10). They are then asked to recall only the final four letters of each list. Since the length of each series was unknown, participants are forced to update the information continuously in order to remember the final four letters only. Palladino, Cornoldi, de Beni, and Pazzaglia (2002) found a relationship between memory updating and reading comprehension using a different memory updating test (Semantic Updating Task), based on that of Morris and Jones. Updating processes in this new task were more similar to those used in reading comprehension. Participants had to listen to lists comprising 12 words, and were asked to recall the words denoting the three (or five) smallest items in each list. Thus, differently from Morris and Jones' task, a semantic criterion was given for updating the relevant information.

We suggest that updating skills are involved in resolving arithmetic word problems. In order to understand word problems, children have to process all

Table 6.5 Memory performance: Recall of relevant and irrelevant information (adapted from Passolunghi et al., 2005)

Variables	ADHD		ALD		NL		One-way ANOVA contrasts
	M	SD	M	SD	M	SD	
Recall of relevant literal information	7.00	0.47	12.20	0.92	12.80	0.42	ADHD < ALD, NL
Recall of irrelevant literal information	3.30	0.82	1.00	0.51	0.20	0.42	ADHD > ALD > NL
Recall of relevant numerical information	11.20	1.62	11.20	1.69	12.10	1.37	
Recall of irrelevant numerical information	5.80	2.93	7.30	2.50	0.80	1.03	ADHD, ALD > NL

information derived from texts. Some information will be inhibited very early because it is not relevant to the solution. Other information will be connected in a coherent model that will be enriched successively by new information. This model will be complete when all the information relevant to solving the question is integrated. Further information concerning other questions will then be processed and structured in different models. Shifting from one model to another requires updating information in working memory, in a fine modulation of the mechanisms of enhancement and inhibition (Passolunghi & Pazzaglia, 2005).

In a recent study, we tested the following hypotheses: (1) Memory updating ability may identify both children with either good or poor word problem solution competence and also those with good or poor computation ability, and (2) and the relationship between memory updating and maths competence might not be due to intellectual ability (Passolunghi & Pazzaglia, 2004). Moreover, we expected that children with a high updating ability would also have good memory of the text of problems, which would foster representation of the mental model of the problem and therefore individuation of the correct solution procedure. Two groups of fourth-grade children (9 years 6 months) with high and low updating ability were tested using a semantic updating task developed by Palladino et al. (2002). The high updating ability group included children whose correct recall in the semantic updating memory test was one standard deviation above the mean score, whereas the low updating ability group had one standard deviation less than the mean score. The two groups had to solve a set of word problems, with high and low suppression request and to recall the relevant information of another set of arithmetic word problems. They were also assessed on measures of verbal intelligence, computation ability (WRAT-R; Jastak & Wilkinson, 1993), and verbal short-term memory (e.g., word/digit span forward).

The findings indicated that the low updating group had a poorer performance in solving the word problems, solving significantly fewer problems than the high updating group. There was also an effect of the number of items that have to be suppressed on the solution of arithmetic word problems. The higher quantity of the to-be-inhibited information embedded in the text problems negatively affected building a mental model of the problem and, therefore, the solution. Furthermore, the results showed that the low memory updating ability group had lower computation ability and recalled less relevant information from the text problems. In contrast, the two groups did not differ in verbal intelligence and verbal short-term memory.

Although the computation ability of school children was assessed by a written calculation test in the study described above, it is possible that updating processes are still important even if the arithmetic operations are presented in written format. Solving a written computation may require less involvement of the temporary information storage. However, in both oral and written multidigit computation it is necessary to process a large body of information (e.g., the numbers and type of operation), but hold only part of it (e.g., the partial results) that must be continuously updated until the final result is reached.

Overall these findings support the hypothesis that a relationship exists between updating and mathematical ability, and between updating and recalling the content of word problems. The good intellectual level of the sample strengthens our results on the specificity of the relationship between math ability and updating, which cannot be explained simply in terms of low intellectual resources at the base of poor performance in problem solving and computation. In accordance with previous research, specific difficulties in problem solving were due neither to a general intelligence deficit nor to an impairment in simple span capacity, but rather, to a difficulty in processing and updating information (cf. Passolunghi & Siegel, 2001, 2004; Passolunghi & Pazzaglia, 2005).

Shifting

Another executive function is the ability to shift back and forth between multiple tasks, operations, or mental sets. The basic tasks that tap the shifting functions are the plus–minus task (see Spector & Biederman, 1976), the number–letter task (see Rogers & Monsell, 1995), and the local global task (e.g., Miyake et al., 2000). On the other hand, among the typical complex tests usually used in cognitive and neuropsychological studies to assess executive function, the Wisconsin Card Sorting Task (WCST) could principally involve testing of the shifting processes. The WCST requires matching a series of target cards presented individually with any one of four reference cards. The participants were aware that the sorting criterion would change, but they were not explicitly told the exact number of correctly sorted cards to be achieved before the criterion shifted. This test is often conceptualized as a set shifting task because of its requirement to shift sorting categories after a certain number of successful trials. It is worth noting that some researchers view this task as requiring inhibitory control to suppress the current sorting category before switching to a new one (e.g., Ozonoff & Strayer, 1997). Miyake et al. (2000) confirmed that skills in shifting or inhibition or both would predict WCST performance, using structural equation modeling analyses on the number of perseverative errors of WCST.

There is very little research on shifting and mathematical ability, and further research is necessary to clarify this issue. Bull et al. (1999) found that 7-year-old children with ALD performed poorly on the WCST. However, their difficulty in the task was restricted to perseverative responses as they struggled with shifting from one sorting set to another. In addition, Bull and Sherif (2001) found that the WCST percentage of perseverative responses was negatively correlated with mathematical ability. They suggested that perseveration might be considered a measure of a child's ability to inhibit a learned strategy. Moreover, perseveration was found to have a strong correlation with inhibition efficiency, tested by the Stroop task, which measures the ability to inhibit prepotent and automatic responses to the stimuli. Bull and Sherif suggested that the findings from the WCST indicated that the main difficulty for children with ALD was with inhibiting a learned strategy and switching to a new strategy.

Interestingly, the results of Espy et al. (2004) showed that shifting or mental flexibility did not contribute to mathematical skills in preschool children. They assessed shifting ability by tasks that require rule-base learning and shifting (e.g., spatial reversal task), presumably similar to WCST. It is possible that mental flexibility may contribute more to mathematical abilities in older children, allowing the child to flexibly apply different mathematical procedures in problem solving and calculation (e.g., borrowing, carrying) to obtain correct mathematical solutions.

CONCLUSION

In this chapter, we have reviewed evidence that working memory deficits are crucial problems in children with ALD. Several findings demonstrated that these children may have normal phonological working memory (e.g., in speech rate), but can be impaired on spatial working memory. Overall, the results suggest a main deficit of children with ALD in the central executive component of Baddeley's model, especially in tasks that require high controlled processing of verbal or numerical information (such as Listening and Counting Span Tasks).

Recent work has aimed to show the relationship between single functions of the central executive (inhibition, updating, and shifting) with mathematical ability and in particular with the ability to solve arithmetic word problems. Our data provide evidence that the working memory deficit of children with ALD is related to inhibitory processes and in particular to an inability to control and to ignore irrelevant or no longer relevant information. Indeed, the high number of intrusion errors in working memory tasks suggests that the poor problem solvers maintained information available in memory, which initially had to be processed, but then had to be suppressed.

Moreover, we showed that the same pattern of results found in working memory tasks of children with ALD is also found in higher order tasks such as the recall of the text of arithmetic word problems (e.g., poor recall of relevant information and high recall of intrusive information). In addition, our research reveals a selective effect of different types of irrelevant information on arithmetic word problem solution in different groups of children with learning difficulties. A deficit in the inhibitory processes was mainly evident with literal information in children with ADHD. Conversely, the main difficulty in children with ALD was in processing and discharging irrelevant numerical information.

Regarding the updating functions, the findings support the hypothesis of a relationship between memory updating and arithmetic problem solving, and between memory updating and recalling problem texts. Children with high updating ability had better performance in solving arithmetic problems, written calculation, and recalling relevant information from the text. These results were further reinforced by showing that the children with high or low updating ability did not differ, as expected, in verbal intelligence.

Finally, there are only few studies regarding the shifting processes and mathematical ability. Bull and Sherif (2001) found that shifting ability is related with mathematical ability; however, the results of Espy et al. (2004) showed that shifting or mental flexibility did not contribute to mathematical skills in preschool children. Further research is therefore necessary to fully understand the possible relationship between mathematical ability and the shifting function of the central executive.

NOTE

1 In the literature, the terms "arithmetic learning disability" and "mathematics learning disability" are often used interchangeably. However, the term "arithmetic" is meant for arithmetic-based operations, whereas the term "mathematic" is more general, comprising all tasks that involve any type of arithmetic. In this chapter, we use these terms equivalently, even if they can be used in these two different ways.

REFERENCES

Alloway, T. P., Gathercole, S. E., Adams, A. M., Willis, C., Eaglen, R., & Lamont, E. (2005). Working memory and other cognitive skills as predictors of progress towards early learning goals at school entry. *British Journal of Developmental Psychology*, *23*, 417–426.

Alloway, T. P., Gathercole, S. E., Willis, C., & Adams, A. M. (2004). A structural analysis of working memory and related cognitive skills in early childhood. *Journal of Experimental Child Psychology*, *87*, 85–106.

Ashcraft, M. H., Yamashita, T. S., & Aram, D. M. (1992). Mathematics performance in left and right brain-lesioned children. *Brain and Cognition*, *19*, 208–252.

Baddeley, A. D. (1986). *Working memory*. Oxford, UK: Clarendon Press.

Baddeley, A. D. (1996). Exploring the central executive. *Quarterly Journal of Experimental Psychology*, *49A*, 5–28.

Baddeley, A. D. (2000). The episodic buffer: A new component of working memory? *Trends in Cognitive Sciences*, *4*, 417–422.

Baddeley, A. D., & Hitch, G. J. (1974). Working memory. In G. H. Bower (Ed.), *Advances in research and theory. Vol. 8: The psychology of learning and motivation* (pp. 47–90). New York: Academic Press.

Baddeley, A. D., & Logie, R. H. (1999). Working memory: The multicomponent model. In A. Miyake & P. Shah (Eds.), *Models of working memory: Mechanisms of active maintenance and executive control* (pp. 28–61). New York: Cambridge University Press.

Badian, N. A. (1983). Dyscalculia and nonverbal disorders of learning. In H. R. Myklebust (Ed.), *Progress in learning disabilities* (Vol. 5, pp. 235–264). New York: Stratton.

Barrouillet, P., Fayol, M., & Lathulière, E. (1997). Selecting between competitors in multiplication tasks: An explanation of the errors produced by adolescents with learning disabilities. *International Journal of Behavioral Developments, 21*, 253–275.

Bowey, J. A., Cain, M. T., & Ryan, S. M. (1992). A reading-level design study of phonological skills underlying fourth-grade children's word reading difficulties. *Child Development, 60*, 973–980.

Bull, R., & Johnston, R. S. (1997). Children's arithmetical difficulties: Contributions from processing speed, item identification, and short-term memory. *Journal of Experimental Child Psychology, 65*, 1–24.

Bull, R., Johnston, R. S., & Roy, J. A. (1999). Exploring the roles of the visuospatial sketch pad and central executive in children's arithmetical skills: Views from cognition and developmental neuropsychology. *Developmental Neuropsychology, 15*(3), 421–442.

Bull, R., & Sherif, G. (2001). Executive functioning as a predictor of children's mathematical ability: Inhibition, switching, and working memory. *Developmental Neuropsychology, 19*, 273–293.

Cantor, J., Engle, R. W., & Hamilton, G. (1991). Short term memory, working memory and verbal abilities: How do they relate? *Intelligence, 15*, 229–246.

Case, R., Kurland, D. M., & Goldberg, J. (1982). Operational efficiency of short-term memory span. *Journal of Experimental Psychology, 33*, 386–404.

Chiappe, P., Hasher, L., & Siegel, L. S. (2000). Working memory, inhibitory control and reading disability. *Memory and Cognition, 28*, 8–17.

Conway, A. R., & Engle, R. W. (1994). Working memory and retrieval: A resource-dependent inhibition model. *Journal of Experimental Psychology: General, 123*, 354–373.

Cornoldi, C., & Colpo, G. (1981). *Prove di lettura MT* [*Reading comprehension test MT*]. Firenze, Italy: Organizzazioni Speciali.

Cornoldi, C., Rigoni, F., Venneri, A., & Vecchi, T. (2000). Passive and active processes in visuospatial memory: Double dissociation in developmental learning disabilities. *Brain and Cognition, 43*, 117–120.

Cornoldi, C., & Vecchi, T. (2000). Mental imagery in blind people: The role of passive and active visuospatial processes. In M. Heller (Ed.), *Touch, representation and blindness* (pp. 143–181). Oxford, UK: Oxford University Press.

Crain, S., Shankweiler, D. P., Macaruss, P., & Bar-Shalom, E. (1990). Working memory and sentence comprehension: Investigation of children and reading disorders. In G. Vallar & T. Shallice (Eds.), *Impairments of short-term memory* (pp. 539–552). Cambridge, UK: Cambridge University Press.

Dahmen, W., Hartje, W., Bussing, A., & Sturm, W. (1982). Disorders of calculation in aphasic patients. Spatial and verbal components. *Neuropsychologia, 20*, 145–153.

Daneman, M., & Carpenter P. A. (1980). Individual differences in working memory and reading. *Journal of Verbal Learning and Verbal Behaviour, 19*, 450–466.

de Beni, R., Palladino, P., Pazzaglia, F., & Cornoldi, C. (1998). Increases in intrusion errors and working memory deficit of poor comprehenders. *Quarterly Journal of Experimental Psychology, 51A*, 305–320.

De Rammelaere, S., Stuyven, E., & Vandierendonck, A. (1999). The contribution of working memory resources in the verification of simple mental arithmetic sums. *Psychological Research, 62*, 72–77.

De Rammelaere, S., Stuyven, E., & Vandierendonck, A. (2001). Verifying simple arithmetic sums and products: Are the phonological loop and the central executive involved? *Memory and Cognition, 29*, 267–273.

De Rammalaere, S., & Vandierendonck, A. (2001). Are executive processes used to solve simple arithmetic production tasks? *Current Psychology Letters: Behavior, Brain and Cognition, 5*, 79–90.

Engle, R. (2002). Working memory capacity as executive attention. *Current Directions in Psychological Science, 11*, 19–23.

Engle, R. W., Cantor, J., & Carullo, J. J. (1992), Individual differences in working memory and comprehension: A test of four hypotheses. *Journal of Experimental Psychology: Learning, Memory, and Cognition, 18*, 972–992.

Espy, K. A., McDiarmid, M. M., Cwik, M. F., Stalets, M. M., Hamby, A., & Senn, T. E. (2004). The contribution of executive functions to emergent mathematic skill in preschool children. *Developmental Neuropsychology, 26*, 465–486.

Flynn, J. R. (1987). Massive IQ gains in 14 nations: What IQ tests really measure. *Psychological Bulletin, 101*, 171–191.

Fuerst, A. J., & Hitch, G. J. (2000). Separate roles for executive and phonological components of working memory in mental arithmetic. *Memory and Cognition, 28*, 774–782.

Gathercole, S. E., Alloway, T. P., Willis, C., & Adams, A. M. (2006). Working memory in children with reading disabilities. *Journal of Experimental Child Psychology, 93*, 265–281.

Gathercole, S. E., & Pickering, S. J. (2000). Working memory deficits in children with low achievements in the national curriculum at 7 years of age. *British Journal of Educational Psychology, 70*, 177–194.

Geary, D. C. (1993). Mathematical disabilities: Cognitive, neuropsychological, and genetic components. *Psychological Bulletin, 114*, 345–362.

Geary, D. C. (1996). Sexual selection and sex differences in mathematical abilities. *Behavioral and Brain Sciences, 19*, 229–294.

Geary, D. C., Hamson, C. O., & Hoard, M. K. (2000). Numerical and arithmetical cognition: A longitudinal study of process and concept deficits in children with learning disability. *Journal of Experimental Child Psychology, 77*, 236–263.

Geary, D. C., & Hoard, M. K. (2001). Numerical and arithmetical deficits in learning-disabled children: Relation to dyscalculia and dyslexia. *Aphasiology, 15*, 645–647.

Gross-Tsur, V., Manor, O., & Shalev, R. S. (1996). Developmental dyscalculia: Prevalence and demographic features. *Developmental Medicine and Child Neurology, 38*, 24–33.

Hartie, W. (1987). The effect of spatial disorders on arithmetic skills. In G. Deloche & X. Seron (Eds.), *Mathematical disabilities: A cognitive neuropsychological perspective* (pp. 121–135). Hillsdale, NJ: Lawrence Erlbaum Associates, Inc.

Heathcote, D. (1994). The role of visuospatial working memory in the mental addition of multi-digit addends. *Current Psychology of Cognition, 13*, 207–245.

Hitch, G. J. (1978). The role of short-term working memory in mental arithmetic. *Cognitive Psychology, 10*, 302–323.

Hitch, G. J., & McAuley, E. (1991). Working memory in children with specific arithmetical learning difficulties. *British Journal of Psychology, 82*, 375–386.

Jastak, S., & Wilkinson, G. S. (1993). *Wide Range Achievement Test* (Rev. ed.) Wilmington, DE: Jastak Associates.

Kauffman, L. (2002). More evidence for the role of the central executive in retrieving arithmetic facts. A case study of severe developmental discalculia. *Journal of Clinical and Experimental Neuropsychology, 24,* 302–310.

Korkman, M., Kirk, U., & Kemp, S. (1998). *NEPSY: A developmental neuropsychological assessment manual.* San Antonio, TX: Psychological Corporation.

Kosc, L. (1974). Developmental dyscalculia. *Journal of Learning Disabilities, 7,* 164–177.

Kyttala, M., Aunio, P., Lehto, J., van Luit, J., & Hautamaki, J. (2003). Visuospatial working memory and early numeracy. *Educational and Child Psychology, 20,* 65–76.

Lehto, J. (1995). Working memory and school achievement in the ninth form. *Educational Psychology, 15,* 271–281.

Logie, R. H., & Baddeley, A. D. (1987). Cognitive processes in counting. *Journal of Experimental Psychology, 13,* 310–326.

Logie, R. H., Gilhooly, K. J., & Wynn, V. (1994). Counting on working memory in arithmetic problem solving. *Memory and Cognition, 22,* 395–410.

McLean, J. F., & Hitch, G. H. (1999). Working memory impairments in children with specific mathematics learning difficulties. *Journal of Experimental Child Psychology, 74,* 240–260.

Miyake, A., Friedman, N. P., Emerson, M. J., Witzki, A. H., & Howerter, A. (2000). The unity and diversity of executive functions and their contributions to complex "frontal lobe" tasks: A latent variable analysis. *Cognitive Psychology, 41,* 49–100.

Miyake, A., & Shah, P. (1999). *Models of working memory: Mechanisms of active maintenance and executive control.* Cambridge, UK: Cambridge University Press.

Morris, N., & Jones, D. M. (1990). Memory updating in working memory: The role of central executive. *British Journal of Psychology, 81,* 111–121.

Morrison, S. R., & Siegel, L. S. (1991). Learning disabilities: A critical review of definitional and assessment issues. In J. Obrzut & G. W. Hynd (Eds.), *Neurological foundations of learning disabilities* (pp. 79–97). San Diego, CA: Academic Press.

Nigg, J. T. (2000). On inhibition/disinhibition in developmental psychopathology: Views from cognitive and personality psychology and a working inhibition taxonomy. *Psychological Bulletin, 126,* 220–246.

Ozonoff, S., & Strayer, D. L. (1997). Inhibitory function in non retarded children with autism. *Journal of Autism and Developmental Disorders, 27,* 59–77.

Palladino, P., Cornoldi, C., de Beni, R., & Pazzaglia F. (2002). Working memory and updating processes in reading comprehension. *Memory and Cognition, 29,* 344–354.

Passolunghi, M. C., & Cornoldi, C. (2000). Working memory and cognitive abilities in children with specific difficulties in arithmetic word problem solving. In T. Scruggs & M. Mastopieri (Eds.), *Advances in learning and behavioral disabilities* (Vol. 14, pp. 155–178). London: Jai Press.

Passolunghi, M. C., Cornoldi, C., & de Liberto, S. (1999). Working memory and inhibition of irrelevant information in poor problem solvers. *Memory and Cognition, 27,* 779–790.

Passolunghi, M. C., Marzocchi, G. M., & Fiorillo, F. (2005). Selective effect of inhibition of literal or numerical irrelevant information in children with attention deficit hyperactivity disorder (ADHD) or arithmetic learning disorder (ALD). *Developmental Neuropsychology, 28,* 731–753.

Passolunghi, M. C., & Pazzaglia, F. (2004). Individual differences in memory updating in relation to arithmetic problem solving. *Learning and Individual Differences,* *14*, 219–230.

Passolunghi, M. C., & Pazzaglia, F. (2005). A comparison of updating processes in children good or poor in arithmetic word problem-solving. *Learning and Individual Differences, 15*, 257–269.

Passolunghi, M. C., & Sarotti, R. (2005). Visuo-spatial working memory and mathematical disability. *Manuscript submitted for publication.*

Passolunghi, M. C., & Siegel, L. S. (2001). Short term memory, working memory, and inhibitory control in children with specific arithmetic learning disabilities. *Journal of Experimental Child Psychology, 80*, 44–57.

Passolunghi, M. C., & Siegel, L. S. (2004). Working memory and access to numerical information in children with disability in mathematics. *Journal of Experimental Child Psychology, 88*, 348–367.

Quinn, J. G., & McConnell, J. (1996). Irrelevant pictures in visual working memory. *Quarterly Journal of Experimental Psychology, 49A*(1), 200–215.

Reuhkala, M. (2001). Mathematical skills in ninth-graders: Relationship with visuospatial abilities and working memory. *Educational Psychology, 21*(4), 387–398.

Rogers, R. D., & Monsell, S. (1995). Costs of a predictable switch between simple cognitive tasks. *Journal of Experimental Psychology: General, 124*, 207–231.

Rourke, B. P. (1993). Arithmetic disabilities, specific and otherwise: A neuro-psychological perspective. *Journal of Learning Disabilities, 26*, 214–226.

Rourke, B. P., & Conway, J. A. (1997). Disabilities of arithmetic and mathematical reasoning: Perspective from neurology and neuropsychology. *Journal of Learning Disabilities, 30*, 34–35.

Rourke, B. P., & Finlayson, M. A. J. (1978). Neuropsychological significance of variations in patterns of academic performance: Verbal and visuospatial abilities. *Journal of Abnormal Child Psychology, 6*, 121–133.

Rourke, B. P., & Strang, J. D. (1978). Neuropsychological significance of variations in pattern of academic performance: Motor, psychomotor, and tactile-perceptual abilities. *Journal of Pediatric Psychology, 3*, 62–66.

Seitz, K., & Schumann-Hengsteler, R. (2002). Phonological loop and central executive processes in mental addition and multiplication. *Psychologische Beitrage, 44*, 275–302.

Seron, X., Deloche, G., Ferrand, I., Cornet, J. A., Frederix, M., & Hirsbrunner, T. (1991). Dot counting by brain damaged subjects. *Brain and Cognition, 17*, 11–137.

Shalev, R. S., Manor, O., & Gross-Tsur, V. (1993). The acquisition of arithmetic in normal children: Assessment by a cognitive model of dyscalculia. *Developmental Medicine and Child Neurology, 35*, 593–601.

Siegel, L. S. (1989). Why we do not need intelligence test scores in the definition an analyses of learning disabilities. *Journal of Learning Disabilities, 22*, 514–518.

Siegel, L. S. (1993). Phonological processing deficits as the basis of a reading disability. *Developmental Review, 13*, 246–257.

Siegel, L. S., & Ryan, E. B. (1989). The development of working memory in normally achieving and subtypes of learning disabled children. *Child Development, 60*, 973–980.

Spector, A., & Biederman, I. (1976). Mental set and mental shift revisited. *American Journal of Psychology, 89*, 669–679.

Stanovich, K. E., & Siegel, L. S. (1994). Phenotypic performance profile of children with reading disabilities: A regression-based test of the phonological-core difference model. *Journal of Educational Psychology*, *86*, 24–53.

Swanson, H. L. (1993). Working memory in learning disability subgroups. *Journal of Experimental Child Psychology*, *56*, 87–114.

Swanson, H. L. (1994). Short-term memory and working memory: Do both contribute to our understanding of academic achievement in children and adults with learning disabilities? *Journal of Learning Disabilities*, *27*, 34–50.

Swanson, H. L., Ashbaker, M. H., & Lee, C. (1996). Working-memory in learning disabled readers as a function of processing demands. *Journal of Experimental Child Psychology*, *61*, 242–275.

Swanson, H. L., & Sachse-Lee, C. (2001). Mathematical problem solving and working memory in children with learning disabilities: Both executive and phonological processes are important. *Journal of Experimental Child Psychology*, *79*, 299–321.

Temple, C. M. (1991). Procedural dyscalculia and number fact dyscalculia: Double dissociation in developmental dyscalculia. *Cognitive Neuropsychology*, *8*, 155–176.

Thurstone, N. L., & Thurstone, T. G. (1941). Factorial studies of intelligence. *Psychometric Monographs*, 2. (Italian trans. PMA-Batteria Primaria di Abilità, Firenze, Italy: Organizzazioni Speciali, 1968)

Vecchi, T., & Cornoldi, C. (1999). Passive storage and active manipulation in visuo-spatial working memory: Further evidence from the study of age differences. *European Journal of Cognitive Psychology*, *3*, 391–406.

Welsh, M. C., & Pennington, B. F. (1988). Assessing frontal lobe functioning in children: Views from developmental psychology. *Developmental Neuropsychology*, *4*, 199–230.

White, J. L., Moffitt, T. E., & Silva, P. A. (1992). Neuropsychological and socio-emotional correlates of specific-arithmetic disability. *Archives of Clinical Neuropsychology*, *7*, 1–16.

7 Short-term memory and working memory in specific language impairment

*Lisa M. D. Archibald and
Susan E. Gathercole*

OVERVIEW

This chapter focuses on the memory impairments that characterize children with specific language impairment (SLI). Individuals with SLI have many cognitive deficits, but the problems they encounter in retaining verbal material over brief periods of time are particularly marked. In this chapter we provide a general overview of SLI and then consider evidence, including new data of our own, that marked deficits in both verbal short-term memory and verbal working memory are characteristic of SLI, and may be even more severe than the language impairments that form the basis for their diagnosis. Implications of these memory deficits for effective learning support for children with SLI and other related learning difficulties are considered.

SPECIFIC LANGUAGE IMPAIRMENT

Joel was born after an uneventful pregnancy, the second child of loving and attentive parents. He was a fairly quiet infant, who learned to sit around 6 months of age and walk around 11 months of age, as most children do. At about 18 months of age, Joel could complete his wooden puzzles without any help, and he loved to build block towers, but he didn't say any words. Joel often pointed at what he wanted, and used a couple of specific gestures like waving "bye-bye". Around the time of his second birthday, Joel could say a few sounds that his parents recognized as words. For example, he would say "ba" for ball and "da" for dog. If his mother asked him to "find his shoes" or "get his cup", he would scamper off to do as she had asked with a big smile on his face. At his annual medical examination, he was found to have normal hearing sensitivity and to be in good general health, developing normally with the possible exception of not talking as much as some children his age.

By 4 years of age, Joel knew lots of words and even spoke in short sentences. His speech was quite clear and his sister no longer had to repeat his sentences so others could understand him. Although typically the message he wanted to convey in his sentences was easily comprehensible, Joel often made errors in word forms and sentences. For example, he would say "hers gotta give me" or "him push me". At preschool, he enjoyed playing at the transport centre and the construction centre. Sometimes, if he became frustrated with other children, he pushed or struck out at them. For example, when his friends tried to explain that they wanted to use all the tracks to build a huge road for all of the cars to go on, Joel stamped on the hand of one of the boys who tried to take his track. His teachers found that Joel was often first to sit down on the carpet, but that was usually because he had only completed one of the tasks that he had been asked to do.

Later in his school years, Joel liked to be the class clown. He would often make a silly remark just when his teacher was coming to the most complex part of the lesson. He struggled with learning to read, and received extra teaching support in school. There were times when his parents still had difficulty following a story he was trying to tell them, except when he was talking about football; he was an expert at football. His dream was to become a professional footballer but his dad thought perhaps Joel should become an electrician like him.

Joel is a child with a specific language impairment (SLI). SLI is a relatively common disorder, estimated to occur in approximately 7% of kindergarten children (Tomblin et al., 1997). It is characterized by a disproportionate difficulty in learning language despite having normal hearing, normal intelligence, and no known neurological or emotional impairment. Not all children with SLI are exactly like Joel: some have more problems in understanding language produced by others, others struggle to produce clear sounds in their own speech, while still others experience some difficulties in finding the words they want to say. Some children will recover from SLI, but for the majority problems with language will persist throughout life and have a dramatic impact on scholastic and socioeconomic achievement.

Children with SLI acquire their first words later than typically developing children, and have a relatively restricted vocabulary at school entry (Leonard, 1998). Parent reports indicate that whereas first words emerge for typically developing children around 11 months of age, they emerge around 23 months for children with SLI (Trauner, Wulfeck, Tallal, & Hesselink, 1995). Children with SLI are also slower in acquiring new words. Studies show that children as young as 2 years of age acquire novel words and facts in as little as one or two exposures (Behrend, Scofield, & Kleinknecht, 2001; Brackenbury & Fey, 2003). Children with SLI, however, have lower levels of comprehension for novel words after only one or two exposures than typically developing children (Rice, Buhr, & Nehmeth, 1990; Rice, Buhr, & Oetting, 1992), and this difference is particularly marked for verb forms (Oetting, Rice, & Swank, 1995; Rice, Oetting, Marquis, Bode, & Pae, 1994).

Efficient retrieval of words is also problematic for children with SLI. A word-finding problem – difficulty in finding a specific word for a known concept – is one of the most frequently cited characteristics of SLI. For example, children with SLI perform poorly on tasks involving generating category exemplars (e.g., Weckerly, Wulfeck, & Reilly, 2001), and also in rapid naming of objects with highly familiar names (e.g., Lahey & Edwards, 1996). They sometimes fill gaps with nonspecific language such as "the thing" or descriptive phrases such as "the red one over there". The result is often a confusing message, loss of the listeners' attention, or overall loss of the intended message.

One of the hallmarks of SLI is a failure to produce grammatical morphemes such as articles (e.g., *the*, *an*), auxiliary verbs (e.g., *"is"* in verb phrases such as *"is jumping"*), and verb inflections (e.g., jump*ed* or jump*ing*). Children with SLI produce fewer grammatical morphemes with a lower degree of consistency than typically developing children of the same age, despite the use of complex syntactic constructions (e.g., Leonard, 1989; Schmauch, Panagos & Klich, 1978; Steckol & Leonard, 1979). The use of verb morphology to mark tense is particularly effective in distinguishing children with SLI and control children (Fletcher & Peters, 1984; Gavin, Klee, & Membrino, 1993). Rice and Wexler (1995) monitored a group of children with SLI and a group of children matched for language level over a 1 year period for their use of the regular past and third-singular inflections, copula and auxiliary forms of "be", and auxiliary "do". The control children showed greater use of these morphemes at each observation point and were approaching mastery levels by 4 years of age, whereas approximately half of the children with SLI showed no change in levels of use over the year. Difficulties with grammatical morphemes in SLI extend to the receptive as well as expressive domains even for children whose difficulties appear to be limited to the expressive domain (e.g., Rice, Wexler, & Redmond, 1999).

Participation in discourse with others is particularly demanding for individuals with SLI. In addition to the language demands for well-constructed sentences, conversational interaction is associated with cognitive demands for organization, planning, and sequencing, as well as psychosocial demands for presupposing the partner's knowledge and language level, and approaching and interacting with a partner. One activity that involves coordinating all of these elements is telling a narrative story. Bishop and Edmundson (1987a) found that the ability to retell a simple story was the best predictor of recovery from SLI in a group of preschool children followed for 1½ years. Children with SLI typically know the intent of the story and include the essential ingredients in an appropriate sequence (Clifford, Reilly, & Wulfeck, 1995), but have difficulty with the global organization of content and the use of linguistic structure (Liles, Duffy, Merritt, & Purcell, 1995).

As a result of their problems with comprehending and producing language, children with SLI often have difficulty interacting with peers. They spend more time talking to adults, and can become aggressive with peers when breakdowns occur. Children with SLI report having fewer friends, lower levels of satisfaction in social relationships, and are identified as less socially skilled by their teachers (Fujiki, Brinton, & Todd, 1996). However, in a quality-of-life assessment, adults with a history of SLI generally reported the same positive attitude about their lives as was expressed by controls (Records, Tomblin, & Freese, 1992).

In many cases, SLI persists into later childhood, adolescence, and, in some cases, adulthood. The results of several studies indicate 40–80% of children with SLI continue to display significant language problems into adolescence (Aram, Ekelman, & Nation, 1984; Aram & Nation, 1980; Bishop & Edmundson, 1987b; Snowling, Adams, Bishop, & Stothard, 2001; Snowling, Bishop, & Stothard, 2000; Stark et al., 1984). The impact of the language deficits can be far reaching. Children with SLI typically go on to have difficulty learning to read, and continue to have lower scholastic achievement throughout their lives. The adult respondents with a history of SLI in Records et al.'s (1992) quality-of-life study reported completing fewer years of education, and receiving lower rates of pay than adult control respondents.

IMPAIRMENTS OF SHORT-TERM MEMORY IN SLI

There has been widespread interest in recent years in the possibility that SLI may be a consequence, in part at least, of developmental deficits in verbal short-term memory – the capacity to retain linguistic material for short periods of time. Verbal short-term memory is typically assessed using serial recall paradigms in which participants are presented with sequences of unrelated verbal elements such as digits, letters or words that they must subsequently attempt to recall in the order in which they were presented. The most influential theoretical account of verbal short-term memory is provided by the working memory model of Baddeley and Hitch (1974), developed subsequently by Baddeley (1986, 2000). According to this model, the short-term retention of verbal material is supported by the phonological loop, a specialized system for storing and retaining phonological material. The phonological loop consists of a short-term store that represents phonological material and is subject to rapid decay, and is supplemented by a subvocal rehearsal process that refreshes decaying traces in the store.

It has been known for at least two decades that children with SLI perform poorly on tests of short-term memory for verbal material (e.g., Kirchner & Klatzky, 1985). However, current interest in short-term memory deficits in SLI has largely been triggered by a report by Gathercole and Baddeley (1990a) that a group of children with SLI showed dramatic impairments in one particular task which they suggested tapped verbal short-term memory: nonword repetition. In this task, participants hear a single unfamiliar verbal item such as "woogalamic" or "loddernaypish" and attempt to repeat it immediately; the accuracy of repetition attempts are scored. Gathercole and Baddeley's key finding was that their group of children with SLI were very poor at repeating nonwords, impaired even when compared with younger typically developing children with equivalent (but age-appropriate) language abilities. The magnitude of the deficit was very marked: although the SLI children as a group had a mean chronological age of about 8 years and a language age of about 6 years, their nonword repetition performance was appropriate for that of the average 4-year-old child.

Gathercole and Baddeley (1990a) argued on a number of grounds that the sizeable nonword repetition deficits of their SLI group reflect an underlying impairment of verbal short-term memory. First, these children also performed poorly on measures of verbal serial recall, consistent with abundant evidence from other developmental and neuropsychological studies that nonword repetition and digit span are highly correlated with one another (see Baddeley, Gathercole, & Papagno, 1998; Gathercole, Willis, Emslie, & Baddeley, 1994, for reviews). Second, this group showed the greatest repetition decrement for the lengthiest nonwords, which were four syllables in length. Similar findings have also been reported by Bishop, North, and Donlan (1996) and Montgomery (1995). Sensitivity to increased spoken duration of memory items is highly characteristic of the phonological loop, in which phonological representations decay rapidly as a function of time either for rehearsal (e.g., Baddeley, Thomson, & Buchanan, 1975) or spoken output (e.g., Cowan, Saults, Winterowd, & Sherk, 1991). In the case of nonword repetition, the increasing decrement for lengthier nonwords could arise either from accelerated rates of decay prior to output, or from increased probabilities of noisy or inaccurate representations in the phonological store.

Third, it was suggested that nonword repetition provides a particularly sensitive measure of verbal short-term memory because the novelty of the phonological forms prevents participants from relying on preexisting lexical knowledge to mediate recall (Gathercole, 1995; Gathercole et al., 1994). When familiar phonological structures (typically, words) are employed in short-term memory tasks, their activated lexical representations aid retrieval via redintegration, the process by which incomplete memory traces are filled in using lexical phonological knowledge (Gathercole, Frankish, Pickering, & Peaker, 1999; Schweikert, 1993). This process is widely believed to result in the substantial recall advantage of words over nonwords in serial recall (e.g., Hulme, Maughan, & Brown, 1991) and other related phenomena such as the superior recall of high over low frequency words (Hulme et al., 1997). As a consequence, recall of familiar items such as words and digit names will be less sensitive to the functional capacity of the phonological loop than nonwords, for which lexical support and hence redintegration is not readily available.

Gathercole and Baddeley's (1990a) finding of impaired nonword repetition in children with SLI has now been replicated in many independent studies. Children with SLI have been found to perform more poorly than their age-matched peers on a variety of nonword repetition tasks (Botting & Conti-Ramsden, 2001; Dollaghan & Campbell, 1998; Edwards & Lahey,

1998; Ellis Weismer et al., 2000; Kamhi & Catts, 1986; Kamhi, Catts, Maurer, Apel, & Gentry, 1988; Montgomery, 2004). A smaller number of studies have shown deficits in children with SLI compared to language-age matched controls (Edwards & Lahey, 1998; Montgomery, 1995). The absence of differences between language-age matched controls and children with SLI can be difficult to interpret as a consequence of their disparate levels of cognitive development (e.g., Ellis Weismer & Hesketh, 1996; Plante, Swisher, Kiernan, & Restrepo, 1993). However, such findings of deficits in SLI children relative to language controls are extremely valuable in identifying areas of disproportional deficit, and can provide important clues as to the aetiology of the disorder.

In a recent study (Archibald & Gathercole, in press-a), we compared the nonword repetition performance of a group of children with SLI and both age- and language-age matched controls. The SLI group and age-matched control children had an average chronological age of 9 years, and the language group consisted of typically developing children with an average age of 6 years. Both groups completed the Children's Test of Nonword Repetition (CNRep; Gathercole & Baddeley, 1996), which involves the repetition of 40 nonwords ranging on length from two to five syllables. Figure 7.1 shows the average group performance at each syllable length, adjusted for differences in nonverbal ability measured by the Progressive Coloured Matrices test (Raven, Court, & Raven, 1986).

The results strongly reinforce earlier reports of disproportionate deficits in nonword repetition in children with SLI. The SLI group performed more poorly on the test at all syllable lengths, but the deficits were most dramatic for the longest nonwords, containing four or five syllables. Interestingly, the

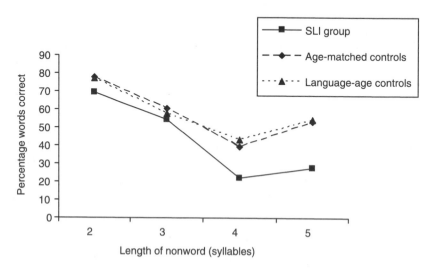

Figure 7.1 Average performance on the Children's Test of Nonword Repetition at each syllable length for participant groups.

two control groups showed comparable performance on the test once the scores had been adjusted statistically for differences in nonverbal ability. In contrast, the SLI group showed a qualitatively distinct pattern of performance that was characterized by an increased sensitivity to nonword length.

Other studies indicate that there is a strong genetic basis to impairments of nonword repetition in SLI. Bishop and colleagues have conducted two twin studies in which at least one member of each twin pair had received a diagnosis of SLI. If nonword repetition deficits are heritable, nonword repetition scores should be lower for cotwins of an affected monozygotic twin than scores for cotwins of an affected dizygotic twin. In both studies this was indeed found to be the case, indicating the characteristic CNRep deficit in SLI was highly heritable (Bishop et al., 1996; Bishop, Bishop, Bright, Delaney, & Tallal, 1999). This conclusion was reinforced further by findings that deficits in nonword repetition persist even in children whose language problems were apparently resolved (Bishop et al., 1996).

Participants in the Bishop et al. (1999) study were tested both on the CNRep (Gathercole & Baddeley, 1996) and on a measure of auditory temporal processing, the Auditory Repetition Test (ART; based on Lincoln, Dickstein, Courchesne, Elmasian, & Tallal, 1992). This comparison is of considerable interest, as one influential account of SLI attributes the disorder to impairments of temporal processing (Tallal, 1976, 2003; Tallal, Merzenich, Miller, & Jenkins, 1998). The study was therefore able to address the key issue of whether both nonword repetition and temporal processing deficits have a common genetic basis, or represent dissociable deficits. In contrast to the CNRep deficit, the ART impairment showed no evidence of heritability. Furthermore, the CNRep was a better predictor of low language scores than the ART. These results suggest that nonword repetition taps a core and relatively specific deficit in SLI that is distinguishable from temporal processing problems. Recently, nonword repetition deficits in SLI have been linked in particular with abnormalities of chromosome 16q (SLI Consortium, 2002).

The consistency of the nonword repetition deficits in SLI has raised interest in the diagnostic utility of the task. Bishop et al. (1996) concluded that the nonword repetition deficit in SLI as measured by CNRep meets the four criteria for phenotypic markers of a disorder (Gershon & Goldin, 1986): (1) CNRep deficit has been demonstrated to be associated with the condition, SLI; (2) CNRep deficit is heritable; (3) CNRep deficit is state independent (i.e., present when the condition itself is no longer manifest); and (4) CNRep deficit occurs within families (i.e., present in those who have the disorder and absent in those who do not). A further important feature of nonword repetition that is consistent with its strong genetic basis is its apparent independence from measures of environmental experiences such as ethnic background (Dollaghan & Campbell, 1998).

Dollaghan and Campbell (1998) designed their own nonword repetition task and administered it both to a large group of school-age children enrolled in language intervention and to typically developing children of the same age.

They found that test scores perfectly discriminated the children with language impairments from controls, with low test scores occurring many times more frequently in the language impaired group. Conti-Ramsden and colleagues recently provided a broader evaluation of potential clinical markers of SLI in a group of 5-year-old children (Conti-Ramsden, 2003) and a group of 11-year-old children with a previous history of SLI (Conti-Ramsden, Botting, & Faragher, 2001). Results indicated that nonword repetition provided a useful clinical marker, although the more difficult task of sentence repetition proved a more useful marker in the older age group.

Although the finding of consistent and substantial deficits in nonword repetition are now widely accepted as characteristic of SLI, interpretation of the underlying deficits tapped by this task remains open to debate. As outlined above, Gathercole, Baddeley and colleagues have argued that the task is highly sensitive to verbal short-term memory skills (Baddeley et al., 1998; Gathercole & Baddeley, 1990a). Other theorists have suggested that nonword repetition is constrained by several other cognitive skills that could potentially lie at the root of SLI. Snowling, Chiat, and Hulme (1991) pointed out that despite the nonlexical nature of nonwords by definition, many nonwords incorporate lexical units and grammatical morphemes of the language. Thus children with more extensive vocabulary knowledge may be at an advantage in nonword repetition because they have a greater repertoire of lexical and sublexical knowledge with which to supplement phonological representations in short-term memory. However, such an account of the nonword repetition deficits in SLI is challenged by findings that deficits in nonword repetition in children with SLI are often greater in magnitude than the vocabulary impairment (Archibald & Gathercole, in press-b; Gathercole & Baddeley, 1990a), a situation that should not arise if the former deficit is a direct consequence of the latter.

It has also been argued that nonword repetition requires the segmentation of phonological forms in order to construct a phonological representation. Bowey (1996, 2001) measured phonological awareness, nonword repetition, and receptive vocabulary in a large sample of 5-year-old children, and found that phonological awareness and nonword repetition shared common associations with receptive vocabulary. In a similar vein, Metsala (1999) found that the association between vocabulary and nonword repetition was mediated by individual differences in phonological awareness. On this basis, Metsala proposed that the crucial pacemaker in vocabulary development is phonological segmentation skills rather than verbal short-term memory, and that these skills also directly benefit the ability to repeat nonwords (see also, Brown & Hulme, 1996).

Recent data of our own (Archibald & Gathercole, in press-b) provides little evidence that poor phonological sensitivity underlies the nonword repetition deficit in SLI. In our study, 15 children with SLI (mean age: 9 years 4 months) completed standardized tests of nonword repetition (CNRep; Gathercole et al., 1994) and phonological awareness (Phonological Assessment Battery,

PhAB; Frederickson, Frith, & Reason, 1997). Table 7.1 presents the average group performance on these measures.

Whereas the SLI group performed on average four standard deviations below the mean on the CNRep test, their mean score fell within one standard deviation of the mean on the phonological awareness measures. And in terms of standard scores, every child performed more poorly on CNRep than the phonological awareness tasks. This finding that nonword repetition ability was much more strongly impaired than phonological awareness skill does not fit well with accounts in terms of a deficit in phonological sensitivity, which should give rise to deficits of comparable magnitude in the two paradigms.

Another factor that can influence nonword repetition accuracy is the adequacy of speech output skills: A child with an impaired phonological system will make inevitably more phonological errors in nonword repetition. Could poor output skills lie at the root of the nonword repetition deficit in SLI? Evidence consistent with this position was reported by Sahlen, Reuterskiold-Wagner, Nettelbladt, and Radeborg (1999), who found that maturity of phonological output processes was strongly associated with nonword repetition scores in a sample of young children with language impairments. The extent to which this factor can account for the full magnitude of the nonword repetition deficit in SLI is, however, unclear. In research studies of SLI, it is conventional to exclude children who have significant articulatory deficits. Nonetheless, more subtle phonological output processes may underpin some of the difficulties SLI children have with nonword repetition.

The most direct way of gauging whether the nonword repetition deficit in SLI results from an underlying impairment of verbal short-term memory is to investigate performance on more conventional serial recall measures. Tasks

Table 7.1 Performance statistics for a group of school-age children with SLI (*n* = 15) on measures of phonological awareness, nonword repetition (CNRep), and short-term and working memory

Measure[a]	Mean	SD	Range (min–max)
Phonological awareness	90.93	7.14	76–103.50
CNRep	51.47	7.09	46–65
Verbal STM			
Digit recall	84.33	11.25	69–104
Word recall	83.93	7.52	71–97
Nonword recall	82.93	13.67	59–101
Working memory composite[b]	74.40	7.07	60–84

Note
[a] All scores are standardized scores with a mean of 100 and standard deviation of 15.
[b] Composite score based on listening recall, counting recall, and backward digit span.
CNRep = Children's Test of Nonword Repetition; STM = short-term memory; WM = working memory.

such as digit span draw upon highly familiar and phonologically redundant stimulus sets, and so are likely to be less sensitive to the other constraints on nonword repetition (differences in vocabulary knowledge, phonological sensitivity, and phonological output processes) considered above. There have been several reports that children with SLI perform more poorly than age-matched controls on such tasks (Gathercole & Baddeley, 1990b; Kamhi et al., 1988; Kirchner & Klatzky, 1985), although direct comparisons of the magnitude of deficits compared with nonword repetition have not been made.

We recently assessed both verbal short-term memory and nonword repetition ability in a group of school-age children with SLI. The verbal short-term memory measures taken from the Working Memory Test Battery for Children (Pickering & Gathercole, 2001) included digit span, word list recall, and nonword list recall. In the list recall measures, the monosyllabic words or nonwords are presented one per second resulting in a slight pause between items. The findings are summarized in Table 7.1. At a group level, scores on all three verbal short-term memory measures were around one standard deviation below the mean. Two thirds of the group scored in the deficit range (defined as below 86) on at least two measures. Although these findings indicate that a verbal short-term memory impairment was evident, it was much less marked and pervasive than that of nonword repetition.

In summary, it is now widely accepted that deficits in nonword repetition are highly characteristic of children with SLI, and the diagnostic utility of this finding is now being exploited across the field. However, interpretations of the core impairments underlying this deficit vary. Our own view is that nonword repetition performance is indeed highly sensitive to the adequacy of verbal short-term memory, and that children with SLI do have impairments in this area (Archibald & Gathercole, in press-b). We do, however, suspect that the greater severity of the deficits in nonword than verbal short-term memory may reflect the multiplicity of cognitive skills that contribute to this task. Nonword repetition may be such an effective discriminator of children with SLI because it taps, to varying degrees, many of the skills known to be impaired in SLI – memory, phonological input and output processes, and vocabulary knowledge. The diagnostic utility of the task may thus exceed its theoretical purity.

IMPAIRMENTS OF WORKING MEMORY IN SLI

In the remainder of this chapter, we consider the working memory abilities of children with SLI. Working memory is a term that is used to refer to the capacity to both store and manipulate information in mind for brief periods of time. Thus, whereas assessments of short-term memory such as digit span involve only the storage of information to be remembered, measures of working memory typically involve the combination of the storage of information with a concurrent processing activity. A classic working memory span task is listening span, in which the participant is asked to make a meaning-based judgement about each of a series of sentences, and then remember the last word of each sentence in sequence (e.g., Daneman & Carpenter, 1980). Other related tasks include counting span (in which the participant counts the number of target objects in a series of arrays and then recalls the totals in sequence; Case, Kurland, & Goldberg, 1982) and backwards digit recall (Morra, 1994).

There are several theoretical models of working memory. One conceptualization corresponds to the central executive component of the working memory model advanced by Baddeley and Hitch (1974), a supervisory cognitive system associated with the control of action and the retrieval of information from long-term memory (Baddeley, 1986; Baddeley, Emslie, Kolodny, & Duncan, 1998). Baddeley and Logie (1999) have suggested that in verbally based working memory tasks such as listening span, the processing component is supported by the central executive, whereas the phonological loop stores the memory items.

An alternative view is that working memory is a functional system that is constrained by a limited attentional resource that is needed to support both the activation of representations and also demanding processing activities (e.g., Case et al., 1982; Daneman & Carpenter, 1980). The most recent and most well developed account of this kind has been advanced by Barrouillet, Bernardin, and Camos (2004). They propose specifically that processing activities involving memory retrievals occupy a central bottleneck and are demanding of attention, and that the activation levels of memory representations decay while attention is diverted in this way. A metric of cognitive load that captures this set of relations, according to which recall performance is influenced by the proportion of time that attention is required to support memory retrievals, was found to be a highly effective predictor of working memory span performance (Barrouillet et al., Exp. 5).

There have been several reports that children with SLI show particularly marked deficits on tasks that impose significant concurrent processing and storage demands (Ellis Weismer, Evans, & Hesketh, 1999; Ellis Weismer & Hesketh, 1993, 1996; Montgomery, 2000). For example, Montgomery (2000) compared performance of individuals with SLI and a group of age-matched control children on three verbal recall tasks: one in which the children were free to recall the words in any order they wished, one in which they were required to output the words ordered by the physical size of the associated concepts (e.g., stimulus: *nut, head, cow, thumb*; response: *nut, thumb, head, cow*), and one in which they had to order recall both by physical size and semantic category. Processing demands clearly increase across these three task manipulations. The SLI group were found to be significantly impaired on recall in the dual constraint condition (size and category), possibly because they were less efficient in performing the memory retrievals required to reorder the memory representations appropriately, and so effectively experienced greater cognitive loads.

In a recent study, we have investigated working memory skills in a group of

SLI children (Archibald & Gathercole, in press-b), using a more conventional set of working memory span tasks: the listening recall, counting recall, and backward digit recall measures from the Working Memory Test Battery for Children (WMTB-C; Pickering & Gathercole, 2001). The same children also completed the tests of verbal short-term memory (including nonword repetition) described above. The results are summarized in Table 7.1. Every one of the 15 children in the sample obtained a standard working memory score (a composite based on scores of the three individual working memory measures, with a mean of 100 and a standard deviation of 15) that was below 85; the mean working memory score of the group was 74, with individual scores ranging from 60 to 84. The severity of this deficit exceeded by far the deficits also found in the verbal short-term memory measures from the WMTB-C (mean = 85) and in phonological awareness (mean = 91).

One issue that we wished to address in this research was whether the working memory deficit in this SLI group is simply a consequence of the more general verbal difficulties they experience, or alternatively represents a marked deficit that exceeds their criterial language impairments. In order to test this, standard working memory scores were recalculated using language age rather than chronological age. The finding that the language-adjusted standard scores fall significantly below the mean of 100 would provide strong support for the claim that the working memory deficit in these children is disproportionate for their age. The results were clear: Whereas performance on the language-adjusted verbal short-term memory and phonological awareness scores did not significantly differ from the expected mean of 100 (91 for verbal short-term memory, 95 for phonological awareness), the language-adjusted working memory score was 86, significantly below the expected mean ($p < .01$). Thus, the working memory deficits of this group were indeed disproportionate even with respect to the language impairment on which the diagnosis of SLI was based.

We have also documented deficits in verbal working memory measures of a comparable magnitude in children with learning difficulties in the areas of both literacy and mathematics (Gathercole, Alloway, Willis, & Adams, 2006a; Pickering & Gathercole, 2004) and in children with learning difficulties that are specific to language according to school records (Pickering & Gathercole, 2004). We suggested that working memory acts as a bottleneck for learning in individual learning episodes, and that children with poor working memory capacities make slow academic progress because of frequent failures to retain sufficient information during key learning episodes (Gathercole, Lamont, & Alloway, 2006b; Gathercole, Pickering, Knight, & Stegmann, 2004). Similarly, it seems likely that the reductions in working memory function that are characteristic of SLI will challenge the ease with which children can actively maintain and integrate linguistic information in working memory, and so make learning relatively difficult (Ellis Weismer et al., 1999).

In a further study, we have investigated the extent to which the substantial working memory deficits that characterize this group of children with SLI are specific to the verbal domain (Archibald & Gathercole, in press-c). Working memory appears to comprise both a domain-general component that extends across verbal and visuospatial tasks (e.g., Bayliss, Jarrold, Gunn, & Baddeley, 2003; Conway & Engle, 1996; Engle, Kane, & Tuholski, 1999; Kane et al., 2004) and also domain-specific components (e.g., Friedman & Miyake, 2000; Handley, Capon, Copp, & Harper, 2002; Jurden, 1995; Morrell & Park, 1993; Shah & Miyake, 1996). In our own laboratory, we have found verbal and visuospatial working memory to have dissociable links with learning and school achievement (Jarvis & Gathercole, 2003), indicating that they play distinct roles in supporting academic learning.

In our study, children with SLI and groups of both age-matched and language-age matched typically developing children were tested on a range of visuospatial working memory tasks. The tasks were all preliminary versions of measures included in the Automated Working Memory Assessment (Alloway, Gathercole, & Pickering, 2005), a PC-based test battery incorporating multiple assessments of both verbal and visuospatial short-term and working memory. In each case, the visuospatial tasks were designed to provide little opportunity for verbal recoding, and required manual rather than verbal responses at recall. In the *odd-one-out* task, the child detects and remembers the location of the one mismatching object in successive arrays of three objects, and at the end of the trial, recalls the locations in order. In the *Mr X* task, over successive screens, the child judges the hand in which the rotating cartoon Mr X is holding a ball, and then attempts to recall positions of the balls in order. In the *spatial span* task, the child compares the orientation of a rotating shape marked with a red ball in each of a series of displays, and then recalls the serial positions of the balls.

The group of children with SLI showed no evidence of impairments in these visuospatial memory tasks, performing at comparable levels to age-matched control children in all cases. These findings contrast markedly with the large and consistent impairments of verbal working memory in the same group (Archibald & Gathercole, in press-b), and clearly indicate that in this group at least, the working memory deficit is highly specific to the verbal domain.

PRACTICAL IMPLICATIONS OF MEMORY DEFICITS IN SLI

Poor working memory function may have important clinical implications. Children learning language and academic skills are faced with the task of storing and manipulating information frequently throughout the day. In a recent observational study of children with poor working memory function, Gathercole et al. (2006b) identified several classroom activities that posed storage and effortful processing on the children including attempting to spell an unfamiliar word while writing a sentence from memory, and carrying out a numerical calculation abstracted from a question coached in everyday language. The researchers suggested that as a consequence of their limited working memory function, these children experienced repeated failures in crucial educational activities. Add to this a layer of language processing difficulty and the failure of the child with SLI may be magnified.

Learning support strategies specific to working memory impairments hinge on the balance of storage and processing demands. The nature of the balance has been discussed in different ways: in terms of capacity, time, and quality. According to interpretations based on capacity, there is a limited workspace in which to complete storage and processing tasks and a resource trade-off between the tasks if they exceed the workspace (Daneman & Carpenter, 1980). Constraints on the time that information can be maintained in the workspace may be a limiting factor with strategies that improve efficiency or refresh information effectively increasing workspace capacity (Kail, 2002). Finally, the quality of phonological representations gaining access into or being maintained in the workspace may limit working memory function (Montgomery, 1995).

Two principles of intervention for working memory deficits in SLI follow from this storage-processing framework. First, storage of new information is effortful and resource-demanding. When storage demands are high, processing demands should be minimized. Activities of this nature occur when the child has to store a considerable amount of material that may be arbitrary in structure (such as a series of numbers, or the precise wording of a fairly lengthy sentence). Second, processing of complex instructions is effortful and resource-demanding. When processing demands are high, storage demands should be minimized. Activities of this nature occur when children have to store material while engaged in another activity that is demanding for them (such as spelling or reading a new word, or making an arithmetic calculation).

From these principles, several learning support strategies can be developed. Many of the strategies for poor working memory function overlap with those commonly employed for language impairment, and form the basis for many "best practices" in teaching. Broadly speaking, two approaches may be considered with respect to the storage of information. First, recognize the storage demands of new or arbitrary information. When introducing information of this nature, the emphasis should be on storing (or learning) the information, rather than on manipulation or processing of the information. Strategies that will facilitate the transfer of the information to long-term memory in a "quality-rich" state should be adopted. Specifically, the initial introduction of new information should include several repetitions of the key words in order to reduce the risk of decay or interference in the phonological short-term store, and the information should be reintroduced repeatedly within a short amount of time. Activities that heighten the awareness of the phonological structure of a word such as counting syllables or listing rhyming words, known to many as phonological awareness activities, will improve the quality of the phonological representation gaining access to long-term memory. In addition, pairing new information with rich contextual information such as hands-on manipulatives or picture stories will facilitate a detailed and complex semantic and syntactic network for the new information once part of long-term memory.

The second approach to managing storage demands is useful when processing demands are inherent to the learning opportunity and cannot be minimized. In these cases, storage demands must be minimized either by using information that is so familiar or automatized as to make storage demands minimal or by providing external aids that make it unnecessary to store the information. Research has shown that when highly familiar information is used in complex working memory span tasks, the familiar information places such a minimal storage demand on the system, that individual variation in the performance is dependent on the variation in processing (e.g., Baddeley, Logie, Nimmo-Smith, Brereton, 1985; Daneman & Carpenter, 1980). Hence, the use of familiar information imposing minimal storage demands, such as familiar vocabulary, spellings, or maths, in processing tasks, such as formulating sentences, or solving word problems in maths, may allow the child to meet the demands of the processing task and succeed in the lesson. Alternatively, the storage demands for information that is not familiar may be sufficiently minimized as to allow the child to concentrate on the processing task in hand. Such strategies would include listing key information in words or pictures, or using number lines or counting blocks.

Approaches analogous to those described above for storage demands may facilitate success with processing tasks as well. Firstly, effort should be made to minimize processing demands. It must be recognized that many children with SLI in mainstream classrooms do not have the linguistic skills to be able to manage many of the complex processing tasks assigned to them everyday including comprehension of complex, multistep instructions, or answering questions about a story. In these cases, the processing demands must be minimized by reducing the complexity of the task, either by simplifying vocabulary (common vs. lower frequency words), syntactic complexity (simple subject-verb-object constructions rather than relative clauses), or length (single step vs. multistep instructions). Alternatively, providing external aids that assist the child to remember the demands of the task may reduce processing demands. Such strategies may include writing out the key steps in a task, setting up complex tasks as part of a classroom routine that is repeated each day, and identifying a person in the classroom of whom the child may request repetitions or explanations of the information.

CONCLUSION

In this chapter, we have reviewed evidence that children with SLI may have two separate deficits of memory that are disproportionate in severity, even compared with their more general language impairments. One deficit is in nonword repetition, and we believe this reflects an underlying impairment of verbal short-term memory and also other phonological and lexical processes. The second deficit is in verbal working memory. It seems likely that the striking deficits of children with SLI in these two key domains of immediate memory – associated more generally with impairments of vocabulary learning (short-term memory) and more general learning abilities (working memory) – make a major contribution to the learning difficulties experienced by these children. Remedial approaches that recognize the temporary storage problems of these children in the context of structured learning activities are strongly recommended, particularly those that seek to minimize task failures due to working memory overload.

REFERENCES

Alloway, T. P., Gathercole, S. E., & Pickering, S. J. (2005). *Automated Working Memory Assessment* [Test battery]. Available from www.york.ac.uk/res/wml

Aram, D. M., Ekelman, B. L., & Nation, J. E. (1984). Preschoolers with language disorders: 10 years later. *Journal of Speech and Hearing Research*, *27*, 232–244.

Aram, D. M., & Nation, J. (1980). Preschool language disorders and subsequent language and academic difficulties. *Journal of Communication Disorders*, *13*, 159–170.

Archibald, L. M. D., & Gathercole, S. E. (in press-a). Nonword repetition: A comparison of tests. *Journal of Speech, Language, and Hearing Research*.

Archibald, L. M. D., & Gathercole, S. E. (in press-b). Short-term and working memory in specific language impairment. *International Journal of Communication Disorders*.

Archibald, L. M. D., & Gathercole, S. E. (in press-c). Visuospatial immediate memory in specific language impairment. *Journal of Speech, Language, and Hearing Research*.

Baddeley, A. D. (1986). *Working memory*. Oxford, UK: Oxford University Press.

Baddeley, A. D. (2000). The episodic buffer: A new component of working memory? *Trends in Cognitive Sciences*, *4*, 417–422.

Baddeley, A. D., Emslie, H., Kolodny, J., & Duncan, J. (1998). Random generation and the executive control of working memory. *Quarterly Journal of Experimental Psychology*, *51A*, 819–852.

Baddeley A. D., Gathercole S. E., & Papagno C. (1998). The phonological loop as a language learning device. *Psychological Review*, *105*, 158–173.

Baddeley A. D., & Hitch, G. (1974). Working memory. In G. Bower (Ed.), *The psychology of learning and motivation* (Vol. 8, pp. 47–90). New York: Academic Press.

Baddeley, A. D., & Logie, R. H. (1999). Working memory: The multiple-component model. In A. Miyake & P. Shah (Eds.), *Models of working memory: Mechanisms of active maintenance and executive control* (pp. 28–61). New York: Cambridge University Press.

Baddeley, A. D., Logie, R., Nimmo-Smith, I., & Brereton, N. (1985). Components of fluent reading. *Journal of Memory and Language*, *24*, 119–131.

Baddeley, A. D., Thomson, N., & Buchanan, M. (1975). Word length and the structure of short-term memory. *Journal of Verbal Learning and Verbal Behavior*, *14*, 575–589.

Barrouillet, P., Bernadin, S., & Camos, V. (2004). Time constraints and resource sharing in adults' working memory spans. *Journal of Experimental Psychology: General*, *133*(1), 83–100.

Bayliss, D. M., Jarrold, C., Gunn, D. M., & Baddeley, A. D. (2003). The complexities of complex span: Explaining individual differences in working memory in children and adults. *Journal of Experimental Psychology: General*, *132*, 71–92.

Behrend, D. A., Scofield, J., & Kleinknecht, E. E. (2001). Beyond fast mapping: Young children's extensions of novel words and novel facts. *Developmental Psychology*, *37*, 698–705.

Bishop, D. V. M., Bishop, S. J., Bright, P., Delaney, T., & Tallal, P. (1999). Different origin of auditory and phonological processing problems in children with language impairment: Evidence from a twin study. *Journal of Speech, Language, and Hearing Research*, *42*, 155–168.

Bishop, D. V. M., & Edmundson, A. (1987a). Language-impaired 4-year-olds: Distinguishing transient from persistent impairment. *Journal of Speech and Hearing Disorders*, *52*, 156–173.

Bishop, D. V. M., & Edmundson, A. (1987b). Specific language impairment as a maturational lag: Evidence from longitudinal data on language and motor development. *Developmental Medicine and Child Neurology*, *29*, 442–459.

Bishop, D. V. M., North, T., & Donlan, C. (1996). Nonword repetition as a behavioural marker for inherited language impairment: Evidence from a twin study. *Journal of Child Psychology and Psychiatry*, *37*, 391–403.

Botting, N., & Conti-Ramsden, G. (2001). Non-word repetition and language development in children with specific language impairment (SLI). *International Journal of Language and Communication Disorders*, *36*, 421–432.

Bowey, J. A. (1996). On the association between phonological memory and receptive vocabulary in five-year-olds. *Journal of Experimental Child Psychology*, *63*, 44–78.

Bowey, J. A. (2001). Nonword repetition and young children's receptive vocabulary: A longitudinal study. *Applied Psycholinguistics*, *22*, 441–469.

Brackenbury, T., & Fey, M. E. (2003). Quick incidental verb learning in 4-year-olds: Identification and generalization. *Journal of Speech, Language, and Hearing Research*, *46*, 313–327.

Brown, G. D. A., & Hulme, C. (1996). Nonword repetition, STM and word age of acquisition: A computation model. In S. Gathercole (Ed.), *Models of short-term memory* (pp. 129–148). Hove, UK: Psychology Press.

Case, R., Kurland, D. M., & Goldberg, J. (1982). Operational efficiency and the growth of short-term memory span. *Journal of Experimental Child Psychology*, *22*, 286–404.

Clifford, J., Reilly, J., & Wulfeck, B. (1995). *Narratives from children with language impairment: An exploration in language and cognition* [Tech. Rep. No. CND-9509] San Diego, CA: Center for Research in Language, University of California at San Diego.

Conti-Ramsden, G. (2003). Processing and linguistic markers in young children with specific language impairment. *Journal of Speech, Language, and Hearing Research*, *46*, 1029–1037.

Conti-Ramsden, G., Botting, N., & Faragher, B. (2001) Psycholinguistic markers for

Specific Language Impairment (SLI). *Journal of Child Psychology and Psychiatry*, *42*, 741–748.

Conway, A. R. A., & Engle, R. W. (1996). Individual differences in working memory capacity: More evidence for a general capacity theory. *Memory*, *4*, 577–590.

Cowan, N., Saults, J. S., Winterowd, C., & Sherk, M. (1991). Enhancement of 4-year-old children's memory span for phonological similar and dissimilar word lists. *Journal of Experimental Child Psychology*, *51*, 30–52.

Daneman, M., & Carpenter, P. A. (1980). Individual differences in working memory and reading. *Journal of Verbal Learning and Verbal Behaviour*, *19*, 450–466

Dollaghan, C., & Campbell, T. F. (1998). Nonword repetition and child language impairment. *Journal of Speech, Language, and Hearing Research*, *41*, 1136–1146.

Edwards, J., & Lahey, M. (1998). Nonword repetitions of children with specific language impairment: Exploration of some explanations for their inaccuracies. *Applied Psycholinguistics*, *19*, 279–309.

Ellis Weismer, S., Evans, J. J., & Hesketh, L. (1999). An examination of working memory capacity in children with specific language impairment. *Journal of Speech, Language, and Hearing Research*, *42*, 1249–1260.

Ellis Weismer, S., & Hesketh, L. (1993). The influence of prosodic and gestural cues on novel word acquisition by children with specific language impairment. *Journal of Speech and Hearing Research*, *36*, 1013–1025.

Ellis Weismer, S., & Hesketh, L. (1996). Lexical learning by children with specific language impairment: Effects of linguistic input presented at varying speaking rates. *Journal of Speech and Hearing Research*, *39*, 177–190.

Ellis Weismer, S., Tomblin, J. B., Zhang, X., Buckwalter, P., Gaura Chynoweth, J., & Jones, M. (2000). Nonword repetition performance in school-age children with and without language impairment. *Journal of Speech, Language, and Hearing Research*, *43*, 865–878.

Engle, R. W., Kane, M. J., & Tuholski, S. W. (1999). Individual differences in working memory capacity and what they tell us about controlled attention, general fluid intelligence, and functions of the prefrontal cortex. In A. Miyake & P. Shah (Eds.), *Models of working memory: Mechanisms of active maintenance and executive control* (pp. 102–134). New York: Cambridge University Press.

Fletcher, P., & Peters, J. M. (1984). Characterising language impairment in children: An exploratory study. *Language Testing*, *1*, 33–49.

Frederickson, N., Frith, U., & Reason, R. (1997). *Phonological Assessment Battery*. Windsor, UK: NFER Nelson.

Friedman, N. P., & Miyake, A. (2000). Differential roles for visuospatial and verbal working memory in situation model construction. *Journal of Experimental Psychology: General*, *129*, 61–83.

Fujiki, M., Brinton, B., & Todd, C. (1996). Social skills with specific language impairment. *Language, Speech, and Hearing Services in Schools*, *27*, 195–202.

Gathercole, S. E. (1995). Is nonword repetition a test of phonological memory or long-term knowledge? It all depends on the nonwords. *Memory and Cognition*, *23*, 83–94.

Gathercole, S. E., Alloway, T. P., Willis, C. S., & Adams, A. M. (2006a). Working memory in children with reading difficulties. *Journal of Experimental Child Psychology*, *93*, 265–281.

Gathercole, S., & Baddeley, A. (1990a). Phonological memory deficits in language disordered children: Is there a causal connection? *Journal of Memory and Language*, *29*, 336–360.

Gathercole, S. E., & Baddeley, A. D. (1990b). The role of phonological memory in vocabulary acquistion: A study of young children learning new names. *British Journal of Psychology, 81*, 439–454.

Gathercole, S. E., & Baddeley, A. D. (1996). *The Children's Test of Nonword Repetition*. London: Psychological Corporation.

Gathercole, S. E., Frankish, C., Pickering, S. J., & Peaker, S. M. (1999). Phonotactic influences on short-term memory. *Journal of Experimental Psychology: Learning Memory, and Cognition, 25*, 84–95.

Gathercole, S. E., Lamont, E., & Alloway, T. P. (2006b). Working memory in the classroom. In S. J. Pickering (Ed.), *Working memory and education* (pp. 219–240). New York: Academic Press.

Gathercole, S. E., Pickering, S. J., Knight, C., & Stegmann, Z. (2004). Working memory skills and educational attainment: Evidence from National Curriculum assessments at 7 and 14 years of age. *Applied Cognitive Psychology, 18*, 1–16.

Gathercole, S. E., Willis, C., Emslie, H., & Baddeley, A. D. (1994). The Children's Test of Nonword Repetition: A test of phonological working memory. *Memory, 2*, 103–127.

Gavin, W. J., Klee, T., & Membrino, I. (1993). Differentiating specific language impairment from normal language development using grammatical analysis. *Clinical Linguistics and Phonetics, 7*, 191–206.

Gershon, E. S., & Goldin, L. R. (1986). Clinical methods in psychiatric genetics: Robustness of genetic marker investigative strategies. *Acta Psychiatric Scandinavia, 74*, 113–118.

Handley, S. J., Capon, A., Copp, C., & Harper, C. (2002). Conditional reasoning and the Tower of Hanoi: The role of verbal and spatial working memory. *British Journal of Psychology, 93*, 501–518.

Hulme, C., Maughan, S., & Brown, G. D. A. (1991). Memory for familiar and unfamiliar words: Evidence for a long-term memory contribution to short-term memory span. *Journal of Memory and Language, 30*, 685–701.

Hulme, C., Roodenrys, S., Schweickert, R., Brown, G. D. A., Martin, S., & Stuart, G. (1997). Word frequency effects on short-term memory tasks: Evidence for a redintegration process in immediate serial recall. *Journal of Experimental Psychology: Learning, Memory, and Cognition, 23*, 1217–1232.

Jarvis, H. L., & Gathercole, S. E. (2003). Verbal and non-verbal working memory and achievements on national curriculum tests at 11 and 14 years of age. *Educational and Child Psychology, 20*, 123–140.

Jurden, F. H. (1995). Individual differences in working memory and complex cognition. *Journal of Educational Psychology, 87*, 93–102.

Kail, R. (2002). Developmental change in proactive interference. *Child Development, 73*, 1703–1714.

Kamhi, A. G., & Catts, H. W. (1986). Toward an understanding of developmental language and reading disorders. *Journal of Speech and Hearing Disorders, 51*, 337–347.

Kamhi, A. G., Catts, H. W., Maurer, D., Apel, K., & Gentry, B. F. (1988). Phonological and spatial processing abilities in language- and reading-impaired children. *Journal of Speech and Hearing Disorders, 53*, 316–327.

Kane, M. J., Hambrick, D. Z., Tuholski, S. W., Wilhelm, O., Payne, T. W., & Engle, R. W. (2004). The generality of working-memory capacity: A latent-variable approach to verbal and visuospatial memory span and reasoning. *Journal of Experimental Psychology: General, 133*, 189–217.

Kirchner, D. M., & Klatzky, R. L. (1985). Verbal rehearsal and memory in language-disordered children. *Journal of Speech and Hearing Research, 28,* 556–565.

Lahey, M., & Edwards, J. (1996). Why do children with specific language impairment name pictures more slowly than their peers? *Journal of Speech and Hearing Research, 39,* 1081–1098.

Leonard, L. (1989). Language learnability and specific language impairment in children. *Applied Psycholinguistics, 10,* 179–202.

Leonard, L. (1998). *Children with specific language impairments.* Cambridge, MA: MIT Press.

Liles, B., Duffy, R., Merritt, D., & Purcell, S. (1995). Measurement of narrative discourse ability in children with language disorders. *Journal of Speech and Hearing Research, 38,* 415–425.

Lincoln, A. J., Dickstein, P., Courchesne, E., Elmasian, R., & Tallal, P. (1992). Auditory processing abilities in non-retarded adolescents and young adults with developmental receptive language disorder and autism. *Brain and Language, 43,* 613–622.

Metsala, J. L. (1999). The development of phonemic awareness in reading disabled children. *Applied Psycholinguistics, 20,* 149–158.

Montgomery, J. (1995). Sentence comprehension in children with specific language impairment: The role of phonological working memory. *Journal of Speech and Hearing Research, 38,* 187–199.

Montgomery, J. (2000). Verbal working memory in sentence comprehension in children with specific language impairment. *Journal of Speech, Language, and Hearing Research, 43,* 293–308.

Montgomery, J. (2004). Sentence comprehension in children with specific language impairment: Effects of input rate and phonological working memory. *International Journal of Language and Communication Disorders, 39,* 115–134.

Morra, S. (1994). Issues in working memory measurement: Testing for M capacity. *International Journal of Behavioural Development, 17,* 143–159.

Morrell, R. W., & Park, D. C. (1993). The effects of age, illustrations, and task variables on the performance of procedural assembly tasks. *Psychology and Aging, 8,* 389–399.

Oetting, J., Rice, M., & Swank, L. (1995). Quick incidental learning (QUIL) of words by school-age children with and without SLI. *Journal of Speech and Hearing Research, 38,* 434–445.

Pickering, S. J., & Gathercole, S. E. (2001). *Working Memory Test Battery for Children.* London: Psychological Corporation.

Pickering, S. J., & Gathercole, S. E. (2004). Distinctive working memory profiles in children with special educational needs. *Educational Psychology, 24*(3), 393–408.

Plante, E., Swisher, L., Kiernan, B., & Restrepo, M. A. (1993). Language matches: Illuminating or confounding? *Journal of Speech and Hearing Research, 36,* 661–667.

Raven, J. C., Court, J. H., & Raven, J. (1986). *Raven's Coloured Matrices.* London: H. K. Lewis.

Records, N., Tomblin, J. B., & Freese, P. (1992). The quality of life of young adults with histories of specific language impairment. *American Journal of Speech-Language Pathology, 1,* 44–53.

Rice, M., Buhr, J., & Nehmeth, M. (1990). Fast mapping word-learning abilities of language-delayed preschoolers. *Journal of Speech and Hearing Disorders, 55,* 33–42.

Rice, M., Buhr, J., & Oetting, J. (1992). Specific-language-impaired children's quick incidental learning of words: The effects of a pause. *Journal of Speech and Hearing Research, 35,* 1040–1048.

Rice, M., Oetting, J., Marquis, J., Bode, J., & Pae, S. (1994). Frequency of input effects on word comprehension of children with specific language impairment. *Journal of Speech and Hearing Research, 37,* 106–122.

Rice, M., & Wexler, K. (1995). *Tense over time: The persistence of optional infinitives in English in children with SLI.* Paper presented at the Boston University conference on Language Development, Boston.

Rice, M., Wexler, K., & Redmond, S. M. (1999). Grammaticality judgments of an extended optional infinitive grammar: Evidence from English-speaking children with specific language impairment. *Journal of Speech, Language, and Hearing Research, 42,* 943–961.

Sahlen, B., Reuterskiold-Wagner, C., Nettelbladt, U., & Radeborg, K. (1999). Non-word repetition in children with language impairment – pitfalls and possibilities. *International Journal of Language and Communication Disorders, 34,* 337–352.

Schmauch, V. A., Panagos, J. M., & Klich, R. J. (1978). Syntax influences the accuracy of consonant production in language-disordered children. *Journal of Communication Disorders, 11,* 315–323.

Schweikert, R. (1993). A multinomial processing tree model for degradation and redintegration in immediate recall. *Memory and Cognition, 21,* 168–175.

Shah, P., & Miyake, A. (1996). The separability of working memory resources for spatial thinking and language processing: An individual differences approach. *Journal of Experimental Psychology: General, 125,* 4–27.

SLI Consortium. (2002). A genomewide scan identifies two novel loci involved in specific language impairment. *American Journal of Human Genetics, 70,* 384–398.

Snowling, M., Adams, J. W., Bishop, D. V. M., & Stothard, S. E. (2001). Educational attainments of school leavers with a pre-school history of speech-language impairments. *International Journal of Language and Communication Disorders, 36,* 173–183.

Snowling, M., Bishop, D. V. M., & Stothard, S. E. (2000). Is pre-school language impairment a risk factor for dyslexia in adolescence? *Journal of Child Psychology and Psychiatry, 41,* 587–600.

Snowling, M., Chiat, S., & Hulme, C. (1991). Words, nonwords and phonological processes: Some comments on Gathercole, Willis, Emslie & Baddeley. *Applied Psycholinguistics, 12,* 369–373.

Stark, R., Bernstein, L., Condino, R., Bender, M., Tallal, P., & Catts, H. W. (1984). Four-year follow-up study of language impaired children. *Annals of Dyslexia, 34,* 49–68.

Steckol, K., & Leonard, L. (1979). The use of grammatical morphemes by normal and language impaired children. *Journal of Communication Disorders, 12,* 291–302.

Tallal, P. (1976). Rapid auditory processing in normal and disordered language development. *Journal of Speech and Hearing Research, 19,* 561–571.

Tallal, P. (2003). Language learning disabilities: Integrating research approaches. *Current Directions in Psychological Science, 12,* 206–211.

Tallal, P., Merzenich, M. M., Miller, S. L., & Jenkins, W. (1998). Language learning impairments: Integrating basic science, technology, and remediation. *Experimental Brain Research, 123,* 210–219.

Tomblin, J. B., Records, N. L., Buckwalter, P., Zhang, X., Smith, E., & O'Brien, M.

(1997). Prevalence of specific language impairment in kindergarten children. *Journal of Speech, Language, and Hearing Research, 40*, 1245–1260.

Trauner, D., Wulfeck, B., Tallal, P., & Hesselink, J. (1995). *Neurologic and MRI profiles of language impaired children* [Tech. Rep. No. CND-9513]. San Diego, CA: Center for Research in Language, University of California at San Diego.

Weckerly, J., Wulfeck, B., & Reilly, J. (2001). Verbal fluency deficits in children with specific language impairment: Slow rapid naming or slow to name? *Child Neuropsychology, 7*, 142–152.

8 Working memory skills in children with developmental coordination disorder

Tracy Packiam Alloway

OVERVIEW

This chapter focuses on the working memory profiles of children diagnosed with developmental coordination disorder (DCD). In order to gain a more detailed understanding of the nature of DCD, we first review the different labels used to classify individuals with this disorder, as well as provide a brief overview on motor and visual deficits that characterize children with DCD. Next, we review research on working memory skills of children with DCD, including findings from a recent study. Deficits in all four areas of working memory function were observed, with a selective deficit in visuospatial working memory tasks. Performance on these tasks was significantly poorer than in verbal working memory and visuospatial short-term memory ones. The consequence of how these deficits will affect their capacity to learn is discussed.

DEVELOPMENTAL COORDINATION DISORDER (DCD)

The volume of research on developmental coordination disorder (DCD) has increased substantially over the last 10 years. This disorder has also been referred to as motor dyspraxia and "clumsy child syndrome". The DSM-IV introduced the term developmental coordination disorder (DCD) to identify children who have "a marked impairment in the development of motor coordination . . . that significantly interferes with academic achievement or activities of daily living" (American Psychiatric Association, 1994, p. 53). DCD is a neurologically based disorder of motor planning that is present from birth. It is believed to be an immaturity of parts of the cortical control processes that prevents messages from being properly transmitted to the body (e.g., Wilson, Maruff, & Lum, 2003). Estimated prevalence of DCD in children aged between 5 and 11 years is about 6% (Mandich & Polatajko, 2003), with more males than females being affected.

Some researchers consider that DCD is a generalized problem that affects movement as well as perception (e.g., Visser, 2003). Observable behaviours in children with DCD include clumsiness, poor posture, confusion about which hand to use, difficulties throwing or catching a ball, reading and writing difficulties, and an inability to hold a pen or pencil properly. Evidence indicates that DCD is not due to a neurological lag, and that the rate of progress in movement may not be made up over time (e.g., Barnett & Henderson, 1992). Findings from longitudinal studies indicate that children with motor deficits experience difficulties throughout their childhood and adolescence (Hellgren, Gillberg, Gillberg, & Enerskog, 1993). It is not uncommon for this condition to persist into adulthood, resulting not only in perceptual and motor difficulties, but also in socioemotional struggles (Cousins & Smyth, 2003).

There are reports of heterogeneity of motor profiles in children with DCD (see Visser, 2003, for a review). For example, while some children are able to outgrow their motor difficulties without any intervention, others struggle with motor deficits even into adulthood. More recently, several studies have reported the emergence of a group of children with generalized motor problems, in contrast with a group of children who exhibited specific difficulties in fine motor tasks, and balance (e.g., Wright & Sugden, 1996). Children with DCD can also have comorbid attentional problems, language impairments, and learning difficulties (see Piek & Dyck, 2004).

While there is emerging research on the cognitive characteristics of children with DCD, very little work has actually investigated the working memory profiles of this group. The first aim of this chapter is to gain a more detailed understanding of the nature of DCD. We review the different labels used to classify individuals with this disorder, as well as provide a brief overview on motor and visual deficits that characterize children with DCD. The second aim of this chapter is to understand the working memory profiles associated with DCD. To this end, we present findings from a recent study and discuss the implications of the findings within the context of a multi-component working memory model (Baddeley, 1996; Baddeley & Hitch, 1974).

OVERVIEW OF DCD

Terms

Labels such as developmental dyspraxia, minimal brain dysfunction, perceptual-motor dysfunction, physical awkwardness, and clumsiness, have all been frequently used to describe individuals with motor difficulties. A key theoretical reason for understanding the variations in terminology for this disorder is that confusion regarding labels can lead to differing inclusion criteria in research, which in turn can lead to inconsistencies in findings. Peters, Barnett, and Henderson (2001) conducted a content analysis of different terms such as clumsiness, dyspraxia, and developmental coordination disorder as used by health and educational professionals in the UK. All participants were familiar with the term *clumsy*, classifying it as a derogatory and nonclinical term which has been replaced with *dyspraxia*. It was also considered as a label for a milder form of dyspraxia. The term *developmental coordination disorder* was less familiar to participants. Those who provided a definition perceived it as a medical condition.

A similar study was conducted in New Zealand by Miyahara and Register (2000), looking at the following terminology: *DCD*, *developmental dyspraxia*, and *clumsy child syndrome*. Parents were most familiar with the term developmental dyspraxia, while clinicians felt that both developmental dyspraxia and DCD were positive and objective terms to describe this disorder. The label of clumsy child syndrome was the least well-received by both parents and clinicians. Although DCD is the recommended label for this disorder (decided by an international consensus in 1999, cf, Polatajko, 1999) and is the term listed in the DSM-IV (American Psychiatric Association, 1994), it is not uncommon for studies to still use other terms such as clumsiness and dyspraxia to identify this disorder. In this chapter, we use the term DCD, but include reviews of studies that use related terminology.

Assessment of DCD

The most commonly used tool for diagnosing DCD is the Movement Assessment Battery for Children, a standardized motor test (M-ABC; Henderson & Sugden, 1992). A cutoff criterion of one standard deviation below the mean warrants a DCD diagnosis. Other assessment tools include the teacher checklist of the Movement ABC (M-ABC; Henderson & Sugden, 1992), an observational checklist that assesses the relationship between the child and the environment in both stationary and dynamic forms, as well as provides a descriptive account of behaviours that may lead to problems with day-to-day movement and coordination skills. The Bruininks-Oseretsky Test of Motor Proficiency (Bruininks, 1978), which includes tests differentiating between gross and fine motor skills, is the most commonly used tool in North America. An additional inclusion criterion for DCD membership is IQ scores in the normal range (see Geuze, Jongmans, Schoemaker, & Smits-Engelsman, 2001, for a review on various inclusionary and exclusionary criteria in DCD studies).

A qualitative analysis often accompanies quantitative criteria. This means that if a child has a medical condition such as cerebral palsy, then a DCD diagnosis based on low test scores on the M-ABC is not appropriate. Further, a diagnosis of DCD is only warranted if the motor impairments of the individual negatively impact his or her daily activities. The qualitative criteria most frequently used are outlined in the DSM-IV, summarized in Table 8.1. In a comparison of the M-ABC, the Bruininks-Oseretsky Test of Motor Proficiency, and other diagnostic questionnaires, Crawford, Wilson, and Dewey (2001) found that the likelihood of an accurate diagnosis of DCD is increased when standardized assessments are combined with clinical observations, such as those based on the DSM-IV criteria.

Table 8.1 The diagnostic criteria for DCD as listed in the DSM-IV (APA, 1994)

A. Performance in daily activities that require motor coordination is substantially below that expected given the person's chronological age and measured intelligence. This may be manifested by marked delays in achieving motor milestones (e.g., walking, crawling, sitting), dropping things, "clumsiness", poor performance in sports, or poor handwriting.

B. The disturbances in Criterion A significantly interferes with academic achievement or activities of daily living.

C. The disturbance is not due to a general medical condition (e.g., cerebral palsy, hemiplegia, or muscular dystrophy) and does not meet the criteria for a pervasive developmental disorder*.

D. If mental retardation is present the motor difficulties are in excess of those usually associated with it.

Note
* This disorder refers to pervasive impairments in several areas of development, and includes disorders such as Autistic disorder, Asperger disorder, and Rett disorder (DSM-IV; APA, 1994).

Motor deficits

It is possible to detect potential motor difficulties from as early as 6 months. By observing developmental milestones, a parent will be able to detect any lag. For example, between 6 and 12 months, a child should be able to sit unaided, roll from back to stomach, and make purposeful arm movements. Indications that a child may be struggling with these gross motor skills include repetitive arm and hand movements, difficulty sitting unaided, and "bottom shuffling". By the time the child begins school, s/he may experience difficulties in writing, drawing, and copying, and engage in stereotypical behaviour such as hand flapping and clapping when excited (see Portwood, 1996, for a full list).

To date, the most comprehensive review of information processing deficits in children with DCD was conducted by Wilson and McKenzie (1998). They carried out a meta-analysis of 50 studies involving close to 2000 children with DCD and controls, aged between 5 and 16 years. Effect sizes were higher for studies that involved active movement (e.g., Hulme, Biggerstaff, Moran, & McKinlay, 1982) than passive movement (e.g., Laszlo & Bairstow, 1983). Other studies have also demonstrated that an active condition of a motor test, rather than a passive one, significantly discriminates DCD children from a control group (e.g., Piek & Coleman-Carman, 1995). Postural control can also be impaired (e.g., Wann, Mon-Williams, & Rushton, 1998).

Visual deficits

Common visual deficits in children with DCD include poor tracking skills and three-dimensional vision (Macintyre, 2001). As a result of poor tracking skills, a child may fail in the following activities: detecting an oncoming ball until it's too late to try to catch it, following the path of a paper aeroplane, or judging the speed or distance of an oncoming vehicle (Macintyre, 2001). With respect to poor three-dimensional vision, this is manifested in misjudging the distance of chairs and tables, and difficulty in finding objects on patterned surfaces.

Two forms of visual tasks are commonly administered to children with DCD. The first are visual tasks that do not include a motor component, such as length discrimination, gestalt completion, and visual integration. The second type of visual tasks is those that include some motor skills, such as block construction tasks and copying of images. Common failures such as inaccuracies in estimating object size (e.g., Lord & Hulme, 1988), and difficulties in locating an object's position in space (Schoemaker et al., 2001) have been reported with respect to both these tasks. Tests such as Block Design and Object Assembly from the WISC-III (Weschler, 1992) are considered as complex visual tasks, and are often good discriminators of children with DCD from controls.

Researchers have demonstrated that extra visual demands of complex movement prove difficult for children with DCD (Smyth, 1991), and that they often fail to draw on visual feedback (e.g., Geuze & Kalverboer, 1987). This results in problems in detecting and correcting movement errors. These findings are consistent with a well-established position that vision is linked with movement control and motor learning (cf, Pew, 1966; Proteau, 1992). Wilson and McKenzie (1998) suggest that "processing of visual information provides the substrate for subsequent processing operations" (p. 835). Hence, it is not unexpected that impairments in visual processing are linked with motor coordination difficulties. On a cautionary note, this relationship has not been established as a causal one. One suggestion is to employ training strategies in order to confirm whether improvements in visual processing will also lead to improvements in motor coordination (see Henderson, 1993).

Although it is agreed that dyspraxic children experience poor motor-coordination and visual skills, the specific links between these deficits are less clear. There are two main views with respect to the types of abnormalities that characterize children diagnosed with DCD. One view is that there is a conjunctive impairment in motor and visual skills (e.g., Hulme, Smart, & Moran, 1982; Sigmundsson, Hansen, & Talcott, 2003; Wilson & McKenzie, 1998). Findings from these studies confirm that children with DCD have an associated impairment in tasks involving visual control. One explanation for why motor deficits are frequently accompanied by visual impairments is the result of impaired cerebellar functions (Lundy-Ekman, Ivry, Keele, & Woollacott, 1991; Sigmundsson et al., 2003).

An alternative view is that motor ability and perceptual skills are dissociable (e.g., Bonifacci, 2004; van Waelvelde, de Weerdt, de Cock, & Smits-Engelsman, 2004). This position is consistent with evidence that visual skills are only minimally impaired in children with DCD (e.g., Schoemaker et al., 2001), particularly in visual tasks that involve a motor component. It is suggested that visual impairments are the consequence of the motor component in these tasks. Others researchers claim that although both visual and motor skills are poor in children with DCD, performance across these two types of tasks is not correlated (e.g., Henderson, Barnett, & Henderson, 1994; also Lord & Hulme, 1988).

An intermediate position was adopted by Parush, Yochman, Cohen, and Gershon (1998). They suggested that motor and visual skills develop independently in a normal population. However, the severity of motor impairments is associated with visual skills. Thus, children with borderline motor difficulties will struggle less on visual tasks compared with children with greater motor difficulties. This view that the relationship between these two components increases in line with severity is consistent with the Atypical Brain Development hypothesis (Gilger & Kaplan, 2001; Kaplan, Wilson, Dewey, & Crawford, 1998). Atypical brain development is a term used to describe a generalized neurodevelopmental condition reflecting underlying neurological abnormalities. The central position of this view is that the brain dysfunctions underlying these abnormalities are not localized, but rather are diffuse (see Visser, 2003, for a discussion).

Working memory deficits

Working memory is the term used to refer to a system responsible for temporarily storing and manipulating information needed in the execution of complex cognitive tasks, such as learning, reasoning, and comprehension. According to Baddeley's model (2000), working memory consists of four components (see also Baddeley & Hitch, 1974). The central executive is responsible for the high-level control and coordination of the flow of information through working memory, including the temporary activation of long-term memory. It has also been linked with control processes such as switching, updating, and inhibition (Baddeley, 1996).

The central executive is supplemented by two slave systems specialized for storage of information within specific domains. The phonological loop provides temporary storage for linguistic material, and the visuospatial sketchpad stores information that can be represented in terms of visual or spatial structure. The fourth component is the episodic buffer, responsible for integrating information from different components of working memory and long-term memory into unitary episodic representations (Baddeley, 2000). This model of working memory has been supported by evidence from studies of children (e.g., Alloway, Gathercole, Willis, & Adams, 2004), adult participants, neuropsychological patients (see Baddeley, 1996; and Gathercole & Baddeley, 1993, for reviews), as well as neuroimaging investigations (see Vallar & Papagno, 2002, for a review).

The key feature of working memory is its capacity both to store and manipulate information. Working memory functions as a mental workspace that can be flexibly used to support everyday cognitive activities that require both processing and storage such as, for example, mental arithmetic. However, the capacity of working memory is limited, and the imposition of either excess storage or processing demands in the course of an ongoing cognitive activity will lead to catastrophic loss of information from this temporary memory system. In contrast, short-term memory refers to the capacity of storing units of information, and is typically assessed by serial recall tasks involving arbitrary verbal elements such as digits or words.

The capacities of verbal short-term and working memory vary widely between individuals, and independently from one another (e.g., Pickering, Gathercole, & Peaker, 1998). Verbal short-term memory skills are much more weakly associated with general academic and cognitive performance than working memory skills (e.g., Daneman & Merikle, 1996). There is, however, a strong and highly specific link between verbal short-term memory and the learning of the sound patterns of new words in both the native language over the early childhood year, and in second language learning at all ages (e.g., Gathercole, Hitch, Service, & Martin, 1997; Service & Craik, 1993; Service & Kohonen, 1995). Children with poor verbal memory skills have specific impairments in the process of learning the phonological structures of new vocabulary items, and so acquire new vocabulary items at a much slower rate than other children (for review, see Baddeley, Gathercole, & Papagno, 1998).

With respect to verbal working memory skills, they are effective predictors of performance in many complex cognitive activities including reading (e.g., de Jong, 1998; Swanson, 1994), mathematics (e.g., Bull & Scerif, 2001; Mayringer & Wimmer, 2000; Siegel & Ryan, 1989), and language comprehension (e.g., Nation, Adams, Bowyer-Crane, & Snowling, 1999; Signeuric, Ehrlich, Oakhill, & Yuill, 2000), as well as attainments in National Curriculum assessments of English and mathematics (Alloway et al., 2005; Gathercole & Pickering, 2000; Gathercole, Pickering, Knight, & Stegmann, 2004; Jarvis & Gathercole, 2003). In particular, marked deficits of verbal working memory correspond with the severity of learning difficulty experienced by a child (Alloway, Gathercole, Adams, & Willis, 2005; Pickering & Gathercole, 2004). Recent research has also established that poor verbal working memory skills are uniquely linked with both reading and mathematical abilities. Corresponding unique associations were not found between either reading or mathematical abilities and fluid intelligence, general verbal abilities or verbal short-term memory. This asymmetry of associations provides a strong basis for identifying working memory as a specific and significant contributor to general learning difficulties.

Previous evidence has established that visuospatial short-term memory plays a role in mathematical skills; however, findings have not been unanimous. Some studies have indicated that visuospatial short-term memory is linked to arithmetic (e.g., Reuhkala, 2001), whereas others have not (e.g., Bull, Johnston, & Roy, 1999; Logie, Gilhooly, & Wynn, 1994).

Until recently all of the complex processing-plus-storage memory span tasks used to assess working memory capacities that are appropriate for use with children were verbal in nature; examples include listening span, counting span, and reading span. However, analogous visuospatial tasks have now been developed (Alloway, Gathercole, & Pickering, 2004, in press). An example is the spatial span task, in which participants have to judge whether each of a series of letters is presented in a normal or mirror-imaged rotation, while remembering their orientation. Using such tasks, Jarvis and Gathercole (2003) found that verbal and visuospatial working memory tasks independently predicted school achievements in English and mathematics at 11 and 14 years of age, and so appear to represent important and distinct cognitive skills to support learning (see Shah & Miyake, 1996, for similar evidence with adults).

There have been very few studies that have looked at the performance of children with DCD on verbal and visuospatial memory tasks. In a small study by Pickering (2004; see also Pickering, chapter 2, this volume, for further details), seven children identified by their schools as requiring additional educational support, as well as diagnosed with DCD, were administered with measures of verbal short-term memory, verbal working memory, and visuospatial short-term memory. Deficits almost two standard deviations below the mean were observed in measures of visuospatial short-term memory. However, performance on tasks of phonological short-term memory and verbal working memory was within age-appropriate levels. This is consistent with the function of the "inner scribe" subcomponent of visuospatial working memory responsible for carrying out activities that might be related to movement planning (Logie, 1995).

Jeffries and Everatt (2004) also explored working memory skills in a cohort of adults with DCD. Participants were presented with a series of sequencing tasks that required either verbal recall or motor recall. An example of a verbal sequencing task was the recall of spoken digits. A motor sequencing task involved the participant recalling a sequence of locations by pointing to them. Compared to a cohort of individuals with dyslexia and a control group, the DCD group performed significantly more poorly on the motor sequencing tasks. However, they performed significantly better than the dyslexic group on the verbal sequencing tasks.

Both of these studies provide a useful starting point for understanding the working memory profiles of individuals with DCD. We recently explored the verbal and visuospatial working memory skills in primary-school-aged children diagnosed with DCD. The key features of this study is that it involves a larger sample than those previously reported and provides a systematic analysis of all four major components of working memory. On the basis that verbal working memory skills may be a critical determinant of the extent and severity of learning difficulties in children of low general abilities (e.g., Gathercole, Pickering, Knight, & Stegmann, 2004), the aim of the present study was to gain a better understanding of the working memory profiles of children with DCD. Of particular interest was whether marked working memory deficits would characterize children with motor difficulties, and whether there would be a degree of specificity in verbal and visuospatial memory impairments.

PRESENT STUDY

Participants

Twenty-four children from primary schools in the North-East of England participated in the study. These children were referred by a medical practitioner at the Durham Local Educational Authority in England, who had identified them as experiencing motor difficulties. There were 16 boys and 8 girls, ages ranged from 5 to 11 years (mean 8.5 years, *SD* 18 months). Parental consent was obtained for each child participating in the study. Information was provided by each child's principal caregiver about maternal educational level (i.e., GCSEs, A levels, vocational training, or higher education) and the age at which the mother left school.

Classroom teachers filled in the Movement Assessment Battery Checklist (M-ABC; Henderson & Sugden, 1996) for each participating child. The scores from this checklist confirmed the severity of the child's movement difficulties. Of the 24 children, 2 children had a marked degree of movement difficulties, and a further 4 children had pervasive movement difficulties that affected their daily physical interactions.

Procedure

Each child was tested individually in a quiet area of the school for a single session lasting up to 40 minutes. All working memory measures were taken from the Automated Working Memory Assessment (AWMA; Alloway, Gathercole, & Pickering, 2004). The tests were administered in a fixed sequence designed to vary task demands across successive tests. All working memory tests were presented on a laptop computer with the screen resolution set to 600×480 pixels. The tests were designed using Borland's C++ Builder 5 (2004). For the spoken presentation of stimuli, audio files were recording using a minidisk player and then edited on the GoldWave program (2004). All picture files were created in Microsoft Powerpoint using the standard shape graphics.

In all of the following working memory tests, the instructions were presented as a sound file while the computer screen was blank. Practice trials followed the instructions. The test trials were presented as a series of blocks; each block consists of six trials. The experimenter recorded the child's response using the right arrow key on the keyboard ($\rightarrow$) for a correct response and the left arrow key on the keyboard ($\leftarrow$) for an incorrect response. The computer program automatically credits a correct trial with a score of 1. According to the "move on" rule, if a child responds correctly to first four trials within a block of trials, the program automatically proceeds to the next block and gives credit for trials that were not administered. However, if three or more errors are made within a block of trials, the program stops the test and automatically returns to the main menu. The score for that test reflects the number of correct responses up to the point at which the test was ended.

Tests

Verbal short-term memory

Three measures were administered. In the *digit recall* task, the child hears a sequence of digits and has to recall each sequence in the correct order. In the *word recall* task, the child hears a sequence of words and has to recall each sequence in the correct order. In the *nonword recall* task, the child hears a sequence of nonwords and has to recall each sequence in the correct order.

Verbal working memory

The following three measures were administered. In the *backwards digit recall* task, the child is required to recall a sequence of spoken digits in the reverse order. Test trials begin with two numbers, and increase by one number in each block, until the child is unable to recall four correct trials at a particular block. In the *listening recall* task, the child is presented with a series of spoken sentences, has to verify the sentence by stating "true" or "false" and recalls the final word for each sentence in sequence. Test trials begin with one sentence, and continue with additional sentences in each block until the child is unable to recall three correct trials at a block. In the *counting recall* task, the child is presented with a visual array of red circles and blue triangles. S/he is required to count the number of circles in an array and then recall the tallies of circles in the arrays that were presented. The test trial begins with one visual array, and increases by an additional visual array in each block, until the child is unable to correctly recall four trials. Each visual array stayed on the computer screen until the child indicated that s/he had completed counting all the circles. The number of correct trials was scored for each child.

Visuospatial short-term memory

Three measures were administered. In the *block recall* task, the child views a video of a series of blocks being tapped, and reproduces the sequence in the correct order by tapping on a picture of the blocks. The blocks were tapped at a rate of one block per second. In the *mazes memory* task, the child views a maze with a red path drawn through it for 3 seconds. S/he then has to trace in the same path on a blank maze presented on the computer screen. The third task is the *dot matrix* task, where the child is shown the position of a red dot in a series of 4 × 4 matrices and has to recall this position by tapping the squares on the computer screen. The position of each dot in the matrix is held on the computer for 2 seconds. The sequences were random with no location being highlighted more than once within a trial.

Visuospatial working memory

The following three measures were administered. The first task was the *odd-one-out* task, where the child views three shapes, each in a box presented in a row, and identifies the odd-one-out shape. At the end of each trial, the child recalls the location of each odd-one-out shape, in the correct order, by tapping the correct box on the screen. Each array is presented on the computer screen for 2 seconds. The second task was the *Mr X* task, where the child is presented with a picture of two Mr X figures. The child identifies whether the Mr X with the blue hat is holding the ball in the same hand as the Mr X with the yellow hat. The Mr X with the blue hat may also be rotated. At the end of each trial, the child has to recall the location of each ball in Mr X's hand in sequence, by pointing to a picture with eight compass points. Both the Mr X figures and the compass points stayed on the computer screen until the child provided a response. In the *spatial span* task, the child views a picture of two arbitrary shapes where the shape on the right has a red dot on it. The child identifies whether the shape on the right is the same or opposite of the shape on the left. The shape with the red dot may also be rotated. At the end of each trial, child has to recall the location of each red dot on the shape in sequence, by pointing to a picture with three compass points. Both the shapes and the compass points stayed on the computer screen until the child provided a response.

IQ tests

Two subtests from the Wechsler Intelligence Scale for Children (3rd UK edition) (WISC-III; Wechsler, 1992) were administered. The Vocabulary subtest is a measure of verbal IQ and the Block Design subtest is a measure of performance IQ.

Results

Descriptive statistics for children with DCD on the principal working memory and IQ measures are shown in Table 8.2. The standard scores for each working memory composite were calculated by summing standard scores of all three measures in each working memory component (i.e., for verbal working memory, standard scores of backwards digit recall, listening recall, and counting recall were summed) and comparing the sum with age-expected levels.

Children performed poorly on all working memory measures. When

Table 8.2 Descriptive statistics of standard scores for working memory measures

Variable	Minimum	Maximum	Mean	SD
Verbal working memory				
Backward digit recall	50	116	80.75	18.84
Counting recall	43	127	82.79	20.68
Listening recall	59	114	75.92	12.38
Composite	45	106	74.46	16.15
Verbal short-term memory				
Digit recall	42	109	78.92	15.29
Word recall	50	110	79.67	15.55
Nonword matching	41	114	77.21	16.70
Composite	48	104	73.13	15.24
Visuospatial working memory				
Odd-one-out	47	118	79.96	13.51
Mr X	48	93	73.83	12.32
Spatial span	40	111	66.42	17.16
Composite	40	107	66.46	15.23
Visuospatial short-term memory				
Block recall	45	116	77.12	16.58
Mazes memory	65	107	82.12	13.31
Dot matrix	32	113	79.17	17.38
Composite	44	100	74.25	14.23
Verbal IQ: Vocabulary	70	110	89.79	10.98
Performance IQ: Block design	55	125	77.71	23.68

comparing the children's performance to the test standardized score of 100, mean scores in all four working memory tasks fell below one standard deviation of the mean (i.e., >15 points from the norm of 100). Performance levels on the visuospatial working memory measures were considerably lower than the other three cognitive skills. Paired sample *t*-tests confirmed that there was a significant difference in performance on the composite scores between the following pairs ($p < .05$): visuospatial and verbal working memory; visuospatial working and short-term memory; but not between visuospatial working memory and verbal short-term memory; or between verbal working and short-term memory. This finding indicates that children with DCD performed significantly worse on visuospatial working memory measures compared to visuospatial short-term memory and verbal working memory tasks.

With respect to the IQ measures, although performance on the vocabulary test was low, it was within age-expected levels. In contrast, performance on the block design, a measure of performance IQ, was markedly worse. A paired sample *t*-test confirmed that deficits in the block design task was significantly worse than the vocabulary task, $t(23) = 2.56$, $p < .05$.

The correlation coefficients between composite scores for all working

Table 8.3 Correlations between working memory scores and IQ measures; partial correlations (controlling for IQ) in upper triangle

	Verbal STM	Verbal WM	VS-STM	VS-WM	V-IQ	P-IQ
1. Verbal STM	—	.57**	.35	.27		
2. Verbal WM	.53**	—	.55**	.33		
3. Visuospatial STM	.29	.59**	—	.39		
4. Visuospatial WM	.21	.41*	.48*	—		
5. Verbal IQ: Vocabulary	−.14	.16	.30	.26	—	
6. Performance IQ: Block design	−.02	.26	.28	.45*	.29	—

Note
*$p < .05$, **$p < .01$.

memory measures and IQ scores are shown in the lower triangle of Table 8.3. Partial correlations with IQ scores partialed out are shown in the upper triangle. Verbal working memory and verbal short-term memory were highly associated with each other ($r = .53$, $p < .01$), as were visuospatial working memory and short-term memory ($r = .48$, $p < .05$). Verbal working memory was also significantly associated with both visuospatial working memory and short-term memory ($r = .41$, and $r = .59$, $p < .05$, respectively). The relationship between visuospatial working memory performance on the Block Design task was significant ($r = .44$, $p < .05$).

In the partial correlation coefficients with variance associated with IQ measures eliminated. Interrcorrelations between some of the working memory components remained high, ranging from. 55 (verbal working memory and visuospatial short-term memory) to .57 (verbal working memory and short-term memory). However, the associations between verbal working memory and visuospatial working memory ($r = .33$), and between visuospatial working memory and short-term memory, were no longer significant ($r = .39$). This finding suggests that performance on the Block Design task contributes to visuospatial working memory skills in children with DCD.

Severity of working memory deficits

Further analyses were performed to identify the rate of incidence of working memory deficits. Composite standard scores for each working memory component of children with DCD were compared with corresponding composite scores for a large unselected sample consisting of 605 children who participated in the standardization sample of the AWMA (Alloway, Gathercole, & Pickering, in press), and for whom schools had not identified special education needs (mean age 9.1 years, $SD = 3.0$).

In order to compare the incidence of this level of working memory performance of special educational needs groups with children in an unselected population, likelihood ratios corresponding to a variety of cutoffs on the

AWMA composite scores were computed. A likelihood ratio is calculated by taking the proportion of participants in the affected group who score at a set criterion on a test and comparing it to the proportion of participants in the unaffected group who score at this level (e.g., Sackett, Haynes, Guyatt, & Tugwell, 1991). The ratio represents the extent to which the incidence of particular profiles of low working memory scores is increased in the DCD group relative to the standardization sample. The likelihood ratios summarized in Table 8.3 were calculated for working memory profiles defined by three cutoff scores: (1) scoring 1 *SD* below the mean (i.e., a standard score of 85 or less), (2) scoring more than 1.25 *SD* below the mean (i.e., a standard score of 80 or less), and (3) scoring more than 1.75 *SD* below the mean (i.e., a standard score of 75 or less).

Likelihood ratios and proportions of children obtaining particular patterns of deficits from the DCD group and standardization (no SEN) sample are shown in Table 8.4. The posttest probability values shown in the table correspond to the proportion of the total group of children comprising each special needs comparison group plus the standardization sample who obtained this particular profile of scores who were members of each of the special needs group.

The incidence of working memory scores below 86 was low for the standardization sample with no special needs, ranging from .10 to .13 for individual components. In contrast, scores at this low level were found for the majority of the children with DCD on all working memory measures, ranging from .75 to .92, with the largest incidence of low scores for visuospatial working memory measures. The corresponding likelihood ratios indicate that children with DCD were at least six times more likely than the standardization sample to achieve scores below 86 (likelihood ratios ranging from 6.30 to 7.32). The percentage of children from the standardization sample obtaining working memory scores below 81 ranges from 4.8% to 6.6%. However, 63–83% of children with DCD obtained scores below 81. The corresponding likelihood ratios indicate that children with DCD were at nine times more likely than the standardization sample to achieve scores below 86 (likelihood ratios ranging from 6.30 to 7.32).

In a final cut off of standard scores below 76, the incidence of working memory scores at this level was very low for the standardization sample with no special needs, ranging from .01 to .03 for individual components. Here again, a large percentage of children with DCD performed at this level, with incidence levels ranging from .50 to .75 (corresponding to likelihood ratios ranging from .94 to .97).

The increase in frequencies of working memory deficits in the children with DCD compared with the standardization sample becomes even more marked when combinations of working memory deficits are considered. Children with DCD were 40 times more likely to obtain scores below 86 than those in an unselected population in all four working memory components. Of the children with DCD, 67% performed below 81 in the verbal memory tasks,

Table 8.4 Likelihood ratios for working memory cutoff scores for children with DCD

Cutoff score	DCD (n = 24)		No SEN (n = 605)		
	No.	Proportion	No.	Proportion	Likelihood ratios
<86					
Verbal WM (VWM)	18	.750	62	.102	7.32 (.88)
Verbal STM (VSTM)	18	.750	72	.119	6.30 (.86)
Visuospatial WM (VS-WM)	22	.917	78	.129	7.11 (.88)
Visuospatial STM (VS-STM)	19	.792	71	.117	6.75 (.87)
Combinations					
Verbal WM & STM	16	.667	21	.035	19.21 (.95)
Visuospatial WM & STM	19	.792	35	.058	13.68 (.93)
Verbal & Visuospatial STM & WM	14	.583	9	.015	39.21 (.98)
<81					
Verbal WM (VWM)	15	.625	29	.048	13.04 (.93)
Verbal STM (VSTM)	15	.625	40	.066	9.45 (.90)
Visuospatial WM (VS-WM)	20	.833	38	.063	13.27 (.93)
Visuospatial STM (VS-STM)	15	.625	36	.060	10.50 (.91)
Combinations					
Verbal WM & STM	16	.667	9	.015	44.81 (.98)
Visuospatial WM & STM	19	.792	16	.026	29.93 (.97)
Verbal & Visuospatial STM & WM	14	.583	2	.003	176.46 (.99)
<76					
Verbal WM (VWM)	12	.500	8	.013	37.81 (.97)
Verbal STM (VSTM)	12	.500	20	.033	15.13 (.94)
Visuospatial WM (VS-WM)	18	.750	19	.031	23.88 (.96)
Visuospatial STM (VS-STM)	12	.500	15	.025	20.17 (.95)
Combinations					
Verbal WM & STM	16	.667	4	.007	100.83 (.99)
Visuospatial WM & STM	19	.792	5	.008	95.79 (.99)
Verbal & Visuospatial STM & WM	14	.583	1	.002	352.92 (1.00)

Note
In parentheses are the posttest probability values using the unselected sample without SEN as comparison (*n* = 605).

79% scored below in the visuospatial memory tasks, and 58% of them scored below in all four areas of working memory function. Similar incidence rates were observed for scores below 76. In the unselected population, only a very small percentage scored below 86 (ranging from 2.6% to 0.3%), and less than 1% scored below 76. The likelihood ratios for these deficits patterns indicate that children with DCD were 176 more likely to score below 81 and 353 more likely to score below 76. They therefore reflect patterns of impairment that are extremely rare in a population of children without special needs.

IMPLICATIONS OF THESE FINDINGS WITHIN THE FRAMEWORK OF THE WORKING MEMORY MODEL

Children with DCD appear to be impaired in all four areas of working memory function, with a selective deficit in visuospatial working memory tasks. Performance on these tasks was significantly poorer than in verbal working memory and visuospatial short-term memory ones. All six visuospatial short-term and working memory tasks involved a motor component in the recall aspect of the task, i.e., the child pointed to the correct spatial locations (dot matrix, block design, odd-one-out, Mr X, spatial span) or routes (mazes memory). Yet, it is interesting to note that performance on the visuospatial short-term memory tasks (all of which involved some motor activity) was not significantly worse than performance on verbal short-term and working memory tasks, which did not involve any motor skills. Indeed, the children performed better on average on the counting recall task, which required them to point and count the circles on the computer screen, compared to the listening recall task and all the verbal short-term memory tasks. This provides support for the view that children with DCD struggle with the memory component of the visuospatial tasks, rather than the motor-coordination aspect. Specifically, it is the added requirement of processing visuospatial information that the children found most difficult. Three key issues need to be addressed in light of these findings.

The first issue is why visuospatial working memory skills were significantly poorer than verbal memory skills? This can be explained in light of research indicating that visuospatial working memory skills are linked with movement planning and control (e.g., Quinn, 1994; Smyth, Pearson, & Pendleton, 1988). For example, Smyth et al. (1988) found that participants' retention of simple movements in sequence was comparable to their retention of verbal information, indicating that visuospatial memory parallels verbal memory. They also found that concurrent spatial activity impaired the recall of movement sequences. This effect is similar to that found in tasks that use articulatory suppression to disrupt verbal processing. Duff and Logie (1999) proposed that certain aspects of visuospatial working memory such as the spatially oriented inner scribe, overlap with cognitive resources allocated to generating movement. The finding from the present study that children who struggle with motor skills also have impaired visuospatial working memory skills fits well with this account of the visuospatial sketchpad.

A related issue regarding the theoretical structure of the visuospatial sketchpad concerns the extent to which it is visual or spatial. While the visual cache is involved in the retention of visual information such as form and colour, the inner scribe is responsible for storing information about movement sequences, as well as planning and executing movement (Logie, 1995). Neuropsychological evidence provides evidence for an impaired spatial but preserved visual memory (Hanley, Young, & Pearson, 1991), and vice versa (Farah, Hammond, Levine, & Calvanio, 1988). Data on selective interference of memory for spatial information with concurrent spatial movements (Baddeley & Lieberman, 1980), and of visual memory with interference by visual items (Quinn & McConnell, 1996) also support this position. Other studies have found differential levels of performance on a block sequence and visual pattern memory tasks, which has been interpreted as supporting a fractionation of visual and spatial working memory (e.g., Logie & Pearson, 1997). In the present study however, there is no support for a dissociation between visual and spatial aspects of the visuospatial sketchpad. Performance on the dot matrix task, which is similar to the Visual Patterns test, and the Block recall task (or Corsi block) is not markedly different (see Table 8.2). There are two possible reasons for this. First, Gathercole (1998) suggested that in practice it is difficult to utilize a task that taps purely visual or spatial components of memory. Second, an alternative explanation for findings that dissociable visual and spatial memory performance could be due to the static versus dynamic presentation formats of the tasks, rather than a visual/spatial distinction (Pickering, Gathercole, Hall, & Lloyd, 2001). Similarly, in the present study, the dynamic presentation of all the visuospatial tasks may have resulted in the undifferentiated performance for the traditionally visual (dot matrix) and spatial (Block recall) tasks.

The marked deficits in the visuospatial working memory tasks in the present study are also consistent with the suggestion that these tasks draw on resources that are distinct from those involved with the phonological loop (Logie, Zucco, & Baddeley, 1990). This view is supported by studies that have demonstrated that a concurrent spatial task negatively affected performance on the spatial version of the Brooks matrix task, but not on the verbal form of the task (Baddeley & Lieberman, 1980).

A further issue that is important to consider is why deficits in the visuospatial working memory tasks were much more pervasive than those in the visuospatial short-term memory tasks. One explanation for this can be drawn from the view that the processing and storage aspects of the visuospatial working memory tasks are supported by different components of the working memory model, the central executive, and the visuospatial sketchpad, respectively. This view is in line with the proposal that working memory capacity is a domain-free construct consists of controlled attention, which is separable from short-term memory capacity (Engle, Tuholski, Laughlin, &

Conway, 1999; also Kane et al., 2004). Controlled attention can be conceived as the ability to allocate attentional resources despite distraction or interference, and is comparable to the central executive system in the Baddeley and Hitch working memory model (1974). There is strong empirical evidence supporting dissociable processing and storage components in verbal memory tasks (e.g., Alloway, Gathercole, Willis, & Adams, 2004; Engle et al., 1999; Gathercole, Pickering, Ambridge, & Wearing, 2004). The view that working memory measures tap something additional to short-term memory tasks is also supported in studies of general intelligence (Conway, Cowan, Bunting, Therriault, & Minkoff, 2002; Engle et al., 1999). Furthermore, verbal working memory measures are better predictors of various complex tasks such as reading comprehension compared with short-term memory measures (Daneman & Carpenter, 1980; Turner & Engle, 1989; see Daneman & Merikle, 1996, for a review). In the present study, the striking visuospatial working memory deficits suggest that children with DCD struggle most with allocating attentional resources when engaged in visuospatial tasks.

A final issue to consider is the contribution of performance IQ (Block Design) to visuospatial working memory skills in the present study as evidenced by the nonsignificant associations between verbal working memory and visuospatial working memory, and between visuospatial working memory and short-term memory once IQ was partialled out of the analysis. First of all, it is important to note that the poor performance on the Block Design test is consistent with research in this area. There are a large number of studies that demonstrate that children with DCD perform below age-expected levels on measures of performance IQ (e.g., Henderson & Hall, 1982; Lord & Hulme, 1988; Piek & Dyck, 2004). This finding has been explained in light of the motor components involved in tasks such as block design, rather than nonverbal intelligence (e.g., Coleman, Piek, & Livesey, 2001). Correspondingly, Bonifacci (2004) found no relationship between motor abilities and nonverbal IQ when the IQ test did not involve motor skills (i.e., a matrices test). One explanation for the low coefficients in the partial correlations in the present study may be due to underlying commonalities between Block Design and the visuospatial working memory manifested by the associated motor components in these tasks.

How does the performance of children with DCD compare with working memory profiles of children with learning difficulties? In a recent study, we compared the working memory skills of children with specific language impairment (SLI) with children with DCD (Alloway, Archibald, & Gathercole, 2005). The findings indicated that although children with SLI obtained relatively low scores on the visuospatial memory tasks, the deficits were not as marked as for phonological loop and central executive. In contrast, children with DCD struggled more with the visuospatial memory tasks than the verbal ones. The dissociation in working memory profiles between children with SLI and DCD is consistent with previous research. The primary function of the phonological loop is to support the acquisition of new words (see

Baddeley et al., 1998), while the inner scribe component of the visuospatial sketchpad is closely linked with planning and execution of movement. On this basis, a deficit in the phonological loop would negatively impact language acquisition, while a deficit in the visuospatial sketchpad would result in a negative effect on motor skills.

IMPLICATIONS FOR LEARNING

An important question to consider is whether such marked working memory deficits found in our sample of children with DCD will affect their capacity to learn. A recent observation study of children with verbal working memory impairments can shed some light on this issue (Gathercole, Lamont, & Alloway, 2006). Children identified as having poor verbal working memory (i.e., standard scores <85) but normal nonverbal IQ in their first year of formal schooling were observed in the classroom 1 year later. These children struggled with tasks involving simultaneous storage and processing of information. Here is an example of such an activity (taken from Gathercole & Alloway, 2004):

> The children in Nathan's class were asked to identify the rhyming words in a text read aloud by the teacher. They had to wait until all four lines had been read before telling the teacher the two words that rhymed: *tie*, and *fly*. This task involves matching the sound structures of a pair of words, and storing them.

Common failures for these children with working memory impairments included forgetting lengthy instructions and place-keeping errors (e.g., missing out letters or words in a sentence). One explanation for these failures is that the concurrent storage and processing demands of the activity were beyond the working memory capacities of these children. Although in isolation, it seems likely the child would be able to meet these storage requirements without difficulty, the added processing demands increased the working memory demands and so led to memory failure.

Based on this observational study, it is likely that children with DCD will experience difficulties in the classroom as well. In the present study, the magnitude of working memory deficits was very high, and in some cases even higher than those observed in a study of children with learning difficulties (Alloway, Gathercole, Adams, & Willis, 2005). Indeed some profiles of severe deficits in three or four components of working memory that were present in a sizeable proportion of the special needs children were never observed in a sample of over 600 children without learning difficulties. Working memory deficits of this severity are clearly very rare in a normal population.

CONCLUSION

This chapter investigated the working memory profiles of children with DCD. This was unique in that very few studies have examined the relationship between working memory performance and motor skills. Further, visuospatial tasks used were limited in being able to assess only short-term memory. However, with the development and standardization of visuospatial working memory measures, the present study provides comprehensive profiles of dissociable skills in children with DCD. The study indicates that children with DCD have working memory deficits in both verbal and visuospatial tasks, but exhibit particularly pervasive deficits in visuospatial working memory tasks. This research is still in its early stages and further studies would be useful in clarifying the extent to which these visuospatial working memory deficits are associated with specific learning problems in numeracy and literacy in children with DCD.

REFERENCES

Alloway, T. P, Archibald, L. M., & Gathercole, S. E. (2005). Are working memory skills dissociable in children with DCD and SLI? *Manuscript in preparation.*

Alloway, T. P., Gathercole, S. E., Adams, A.-M., Willis, C., Eaglen, R., & Lamont, E. (2005). Working memory and phonological awareness as predictors of progress towards early learning goals at school entry. *British Journal of Developmental Psychology, 23*(3), 417–426.

Alloway, T. P., Gathercole, S. E., & Pickering, S. J. (2004). *The Automated Working Memory Assessment* [Test battery]. Available from authors.

Alloway, T. P., Gathercole, S. E., & Pickering, S. J. (in press). Verbal and visuospatial skills in children: Are they dissociable?

Alloway, T. P., Gathercole, S. E., Willis, C., & Adams, A. M. (2004). A structural analysis of working memory and related cognitive skills in early childhood. *Journal of Experimental Child Psychology, 87*, 85–106.

Alloway, T. P., Gathercole, S. E., Adams, A. M., & Willis, C. (2005). Working memory and special educational needs. *Educational and Child Psychology, 22*, 56–57.

American Psychiatric Association. (1994). *Diagnostic and statistical manual of mental disorders* (DSM-IV: 4th ed.). Washington, DC: Author.

Baddeley, A. D. (1996). Exploring the central executive. *Quarterly Journal of Experimental Psychology, 49A*, 5–28.

Baddeley, A. D. (2000). The episodic buffer: A new component of working memory? *Trends in Cognitive Sciences, 4*, 417–423.

Baddeley, A. D., Gathercole, S. E., & Papagno, C. (1998). The phonological loop as a language learning device. *Psychological Review, 105*, 158–173.

Baddeley, A. D., & Hitch, G. (1974). Working memory. In G. A. Bower (Ed.), Advances in research and theory. Vol. 8. *The psychology of learning and motivation* (pp. 47–89). New York: Academic Press.

Baddeley, A. D., & Lieberman, K. (1980). Spatial working memory. In R. S.

Nickerson (Ed.), *Attention and performance VIII* (pp. 521–539). Hillsdale, NJ: Lawrence Erlbaum Associates, Inc.

Barnett, A. L., & Henderson, S. E. (1992). Some observations on the figure drawings of clumsy children. *British Journal of Educational Psychology*, *62*, 341–355.

Bonifacci, P. (2004). Children with low motor ability have lower visual-motor integration ability but unaffected perceptual skills. *Human Movement Science*, *23*, 157–168.

Borland. (2004). *C++ Builder 5*. Borland International.

Bruininks, R. H. (1978). *The Bruininks-Oseretsky Test of Motor Proficiency*. Circle Pines, MN: American Guidance Service.

Bull, R., Johnston, R. S., & Roy, J. A. (1999). Exploring the roles of the visuospatial sketch pad and central executive in children's arithmetical skills: Views from cognition and developmental neuropsychology. *Developmental Psychology*, *15*, 421–442.

Bull, R., & Scerif, G. (2001). Executive functioning as a predictor of children's mathematics ability: Shifting, inhibition and working memory. *Developmental Neuropsychology*, *19*, 273–293.

Coleman, R., Piek, J. P., & Livesey, D. J. (2001). A longitudinal study of motor ability and kinaesthetic acuity in young children at risk of developmental coordination disorder. *Human Movement Science*, *20*, 95–110.

Conway, A. R. A., Cowan, N., Bunting, M. F., Therriault, D. J., & Minkoff, S. R. B. (2002). A latent variable analysis of working memory capacity, short term memory capacity, processing speed, and general fluid intelligence. *Intelligence*, *30*, 163–183.

Cousins, M., & Smyth, M. M. (2003). Developmental coordination impairments in adulthood. *Human Movement Science*, *22*, 433–459.

Crawford, S. G., Wilson, B. N., & Dewey, D. M. (2001). Identifying developmental coordination disorder: Consistency between tests. *Physical and Occupational Therapy in Pediatrics*, *20*, 29–50.

Daneman, M., & Carpenter, P. A. (1980). Individual differences in working memory and reading. *Journal of Verbal learning and Verbal Behavior*, *19*, 450–466.

Daneman, M., & Merikle, P. M. (1996). Working memory and comprehension: A meta-analysis. *Psychonomic Bulletin and Review*, *3*, 422–433.

de Jong, P. F. (1998). Working memory deficits of reading disabled children. *Journal of Experimental Child Psychology*, *70*, 75–96.

Duff, S. C., & Logie, R. H. (1999). Storage and processing in visuospatial working memory. *Scandinavian Journal of Psychology*, *40*, 251–259.

Engle, R. W., Tuholski, S. W., Laughlin, J. E., & Conway, A. R. A. (1999). Working memory, short-term memory and general fluid intelligence: A latent variable model approach. *Journal of Experimental Psychology: General*, *128*, 309–331.

Farah, M. J., Hammond, K. M., Levine, D. N., & Calvanio, R. (1988). Visual and spatial mental imagery: Dissociable systems of representation. *Cognitive Psychology*, *20*, 439–462.

Gathercole, S. E. (1998). The development of memory. *Journal of Child Psychology and Psychiatry*, *39*, 3–27.

Gathercole, S. E., & Alloway, T. P. (2004). Working memory and classroom learning. *Dyslexia Review*, *15*, 4–9.

Gathercole, S. E., & Baddeley, A. D. (1993). *Working memory and language processing*. Hove, UK: Lawrence Erlbaum Associates Ltd.

Gathercole, S. E., Hitch, G. J., Service, E., & Martin, A. J. (1997). Phonological short-term memory and new word learning in children. *Developmental Psychology*, *33*, 966–979.

Gathercole, S. E., Lamont, E., & Alloway, T. P. (2006). Working memory in the classroom. In S. Pickering (Ed.), *Working memory and education* (pp. 219–240). New York: Academic Press.

Gathercole, S. E., & Pickering, S. J. (2000). Working memory deficits in children with low achievements in the National Curriculum at 7 years of age. *British Journal of Educational Psychology, 70*, 177–194.

Gathercole, S. E., Pickering, S. J., Ambridge, B., & Wearing, H. (2004). The structure of working memory from 4 to 15 years of age. *Developmental Psychology, 40*, 177–190.

Gathercole, S. E., Pickering, S. J., Knight, C., & Stegmann, Z. (2004). Working memory skills and educational attainment: Evidence from National Curriculum assessments at 7 and 14 years. *Applied Cognitive Psychology, 18*, 1–16.

Geuze, R. H., Jongmans, M. J., Schoemaker, M. M., & Smits-Engelsman, B. C. M. (2001). Clinical and research diagnostic criteria for developmental coordination disorder: A review and discussion. *Human Movement Science, 20*, 7–47.

Geuze, R. H., & Kalverboer, A. F. (1987) Inconsistency and adaptation in timing of clumsy children. *Journal of Human Movement Studies, 13*, 421–432.

Gilger, J. W., & Kaplan, B. J. (2001). Atypical brain development: A conceptual framework for understanding developmental learning disabilities. *Developmental Neuropsychology, 20*, 465–481.

GoldWave Inc. (2004). *GoldWave Digital Audio Editor Software, Version 5*. St. Johns, Newfoundland. GoldWave Inc.

Hanley, J. R., Young, A. W., & Pearson, N. A. (1991). Impairment of the visuospatial sketchpad. *Quarterly Journal of Experimental Psychology, 43A*, 101–125.

Hellgren, L., Gillberg, C., Gillberg, I. C., & Enerskog, I. (1993). Children with deficits in attention, motor control and perception (DAMP) almost grown up: General health at 16 years. *Developmental Medicine and Child Neurology, 35*, 881–893.

Henderson, S. E. (1993). Motor development and minor handicap. In A. F. Kalverboer, B. Hopkins, R. H. Geuze (Eds.), *Motor development in early and later childhood: Longitudinal approaches* (pp. 286–306). Cambridge, UK: Cambridge University Press.

Henderson, S. E., Barnett, A. L., & Henderson, L. (1994). Visuospatial difficulties and clumsiness: On the interpretation of conjoined deficits. *Journal of Child Psychology and Psychiatry, 35*, 961–969.

Henderson, S. E., & Hall, D. (1982). Concomitants of clumsiness in young school children. *Developmental Medicine and Child Neurology, 24*, 448–460.

Henderson, S. E., & Sugden, D. A. (1992). *Movement Assessment Battery for Children*. Sidcup, UK: Psychological Corporation.

Henderson, S. E., & Sugden, D. A. (1996). *Movement Assessment Battery Checklist*. Sidcup, UK: Psychological Corporation.

Hulme, C., Biggerstaff, A., Moran, G., & McKinlay, I. (1982). Visual, kinaesthetic and cross-modal judgements of length by normal and clumsy children. *Developmental Medicine and Child Neurology, 24*, 461–471.

Hulme, C., Smart, A., & Moran, G. (1982). Visual perceptual deficits in clumsy children. *Neuropsychologia, 20*, 475–481.

Jarvis, H. L., & Gathercole, S. E. (2003). Verbal and nonverbal working memory and achievements on National Curriculum tests at 11 and 14 years of age. *Educational and Child Psychology, 20*, 123–140.

Jeffries, S. A., & Everatt, J. (2004). Working memory: Its role in dyslexia and other specific learning difficulties. *Dyslexia, 10*, 196–214.

Kane, M. J., Hambrick, D. Z., Tuholski, S. W., Wilhelm, O., Payne, T. W., & Engle, R. W. (2004). The generality of working memory capacity: A latent variable approach to verbal and visuospatial memory span and reasoning. *Journal of Experimental Psychology: General, 133*, 189–217.

Kaplan, B. J., Wilson, B. N., Dewey, D. M., & Crawford, S. G. (1998). DCD may not be a discrete disorder. *Human Movement Science, 17*, 471–490.

Laszlo, J. I., & Bairstow, P. J. (1983). Kinesthesis: Its measurement training and relationship to motor control. *Quarterly Journal of Experimental Psychology, 35A*, 411–421.

Logie, R. H. (1995). *Visuo-spatial working memory*. Hove, UK: Lawrence Erlbaum Associates Ltd.

Logie, R. H., Gilhooly, K. J., & Wynn, V. (1994). Counting on working memory in arithmetic problem solving. *Memory and Cognition, 22*, 395–410.

Logie, R. H., & Pearson, D. G. (1997). The inner eye and the inner scribe of visuo-spatial working memory: Evidence from developmental fractionation. *European Journal of Cognitive Psychology, 9*, 241–257.

Logie, R., Zucco, G. M., & Baddeley, A. D. (1990) Interference with visual short-term memory. *Acta Psychologica, 75*, 55–74.

Lord, R., & Hulme, C. (1988). Visual perception and drawing ability in clumsy and normal children. *British Journal of Developmental Psychology, 6*, 1–9.

Lundy-Ekman, L., Ivry, R., Keele, S., & Woollacott, M. (1991). Timing and force control deficits in clumsy children. *Journal of Cognitive Neuroscience, 3*, 367–376.

Macintyre, C. (2001). *Dyspraxia 5–11: A practical guide*. London: David Fulton Publishers.

Mandich, A., & Polatajko, H. J. (2003). Developmental coordination disorder: mechanisms, measurement and management. *Human Movement Science, 22*, 407–411.

Mayringer, H., & Wimmer, H. (2000). Pseudoname learning by German-speaking children with dyslexia: Evidence for a phonological learning deficit. *Journal of Experimental Child Psychology, 75*, 116–133.

Miyahara, M., & Register, G. (2000). Perceptions of three terms to describe physical awkwardness in children. *Research in Developmental Disabilities, 21*, 367–376.

Nation, K., Adams, J. W., Bowyer-Crane, C. A., & Snowling, M. (1999). Working memory deficits in poor comprehenders reflect underlying language impairments. *Journal of Experimental Child Psychology, 73*, 139–158.

Parush, S., Yochman, A., Cohen, D., & Gershon, E. S. (1998). Relation of visual perception and visual motor integration for clumsy children. *Perceptual and Motor Skills, 86*, 291–295.

Peters, J. M., Barnett, A. L., & Henderson, S. E. (2001) Clumsiness, dyspraxia and developmental co-ordination disorder: How do health and educational professionals in the UK define the terms? *Child: Care, Health and Development, 27*, 399–412.

Pew, R. W. (1966). Acquisition of hierarchical control over the temporal organisation of a skill. *Journal of Experimental Psychology, 71*, 764–771.

Pickering, S. J. (2004). Visuo-spatial working memory and learning difficulties. In *Développement cognitif et troubles des apprentissages*. Strasbourg, France: Solal.

Pickering, S. J., & Gathercole, S. E. (2004). Distinctive working memory profiles in children with varying special educational needs. *Educational Psychology, 24*, 393–408.

Pickering, S. J., Gathercole, S. E., Hall, M., & Lloyd, S. A. (2001). Development of memory for pattern and path: Further evidence for the fractionation of visuospatial memory. *Quarterly Journal of Experimental Psychology, 54A*, 397–420.

Pickering, S. J., Gathercole, S. E., & Peaker, S. M. (1998). Verbal and visuospatial short-term memory in children: Evidence for common and distinct perspectives. *Memory and Cognition, 26*, 1117–1130.

Piek, J. P., & Coleman-Carman, R. (1995). Kinaesthetic sensitivity and motor performance of children with developmental co-ordination disorder. *Developmental Medicine and Child Neurology, 37*, 976–984.

Piek, J. P., & Dyck, M. J. (2004). Sensory-motor deficits in children with developmental coordination disorder, attention deficit hyperactivity disorder and autistic disorder. *Human Movement Science, 23*, 475–488.

Polatajko, H. J. (1999). Developmental coordination disorder (DCD): Alias the clumsy child syndrome. In K. Whitmore, H. Hart, & G. Williams (Eds.), *Clinics in developmental medicine: A neurodevelopmental approach to specific learning disorders: The clinical nature of the disorder* (pp. 119–133). London: MacKeith Press.

Portwood, M. (1996). *Developmental dyspraxia: A practical manual for parents and professionals*. Durham, UK: Durham County Council.

Proteau, L. (1992). On the specificity of learning and the role of visual information for movement control. In L. Proteau & D. Elliott (Eds.), *Vision and motor control* (pp. 67–103). Amsterdam: Elsevier.

Quinn, J. G. (1994). Towards a clarification of spatial processing. *Quarterly Journal of Experimental Psychology, 47A*, 465–480.

Quinn, J. G., & McConnell, J. (1996). Irrelevant pictures in visual working memory. *Quarterly Journal of Experimental Psychology, 49A*, 200–215.

Reuhkala, M. (2001). Mathematical skills in ninth-graders: Relationship with visuospatial abilities and working memory. *Educational Psychology, 21*, 387–399.

Sackett, D. L., Haynes, R. B., Guyatt, G. H., & Tugwell, P. (1991). *Clinical epidemiology*. Boston: Little, Brown.

Schoemaker, M. M., van der Wees, M., Flapper, B., Verheji-Janssen, N., Scholten-Jaegers, S., & Geuze, R. H. (2001). Perceptual skills of children with developmental coordination disorder. *Human Movement Science, 20*, 111–113.

Seigneuric, A., Ehrlich, M. F., Oakhill, J. V., & Yuill, N. M. (2000). Working memory resources and children's reading comprehension. *Reading and Writing, 13*, 81–103.

Service, E., & Craik, F. I. M. (1993). Differences between young and older adults in learning a foreign vocabulary. *Journal of Memory and Language, 33*, 59–74.

Service, E., & Kohonen, V. (1995). Is the relation between phonological memory and foreign language learning accounted for by vocabulary acquisition? *Applied Psycholinguistics, 16*, 155–172.

Shah, P., & Miyake, A. (1996). The separability of working memory resources for spatial thinking and language processing: An individual differences approach. *Journal of Experimental Psychology: General, 125*, 4–27.

Siegel, L. S., & Ryan, E. B. (1989). The development of working memory in normally achieving and subtypes of learning disabled children. *Child Development, 60*, 973–980.

Sigmundsson, H., Hansen, P. C., & Talcott, J. B. (2003). Do "clumsy" children have visual deficits? *Behavioural Brain Research, 139*, 123–129.

Smyth, M. M., Pearson, N. A., & Pendleton, L. R. (1988). Movement and working memory: Patterns and positions in space. *Quarterly Journal of Experimental Psychology, 40A*, 497–514.

Smyth, T. R. (1991). Abnormal clumsiness in children: A defect of motor programming? *Child: Care, Health and Development, 17*, 283–294.

Swanson, H. L. (1994). Short-term memory and working memory: Do both contribute to our understanding of academic achievement in children and adults with learning disabilities? *Journal of Learning Disabilities, 27*, 34–50.

Turner, M. L., & Engle, R. W. (1989). Is working memory capacity task dependent? *Journal of Memory and Language, 28*, 127–154.

Vallar, G., & Papagno, C. (2002). Neuropsychological impairments of verbal short-term memory. In A. Baddeley, B. Wilson, & M. Kopelman (Eds.), *Handbook of memory disorders* (pp. 249–270). Chichester, UK: Wiley.

Van Waelvelde, H., de Weerdt, W., de Cock, P., & Smits-Engelsman, B. C. M. (2004). Association between visual perceptual deficits and motor deficits in children with developmental coordination disorder. *Developmental Medicine and Child Neurology, 46*, 661–666.

Visser, J. (2003). Developmental coordination disorder: A review of research on subtypes and comorbidities. *Human Movement Science, 22*, 479–493.

Wann, J. P., Mon-Williams, M., & Rushton, K. (1998). Postural control and coordination disorders: The swinging room revisited. *Human Movement Science, 17*, 491–513.

Wechsler, D. (1992). *Wechsler Intelligence Scale for Children* (3rd UK ed.) London: Psychological Corporation.

Wilson, P. H., Maruff, P., & Lum, J. (2003). Procedural learning in children with developmental coordination disorder. *Human Movement Science, 22*, 515–526.

Wilson, P. H., & McKenzie, B. E. (1998). Information processing deficits associated with developmental coordination disorder: A meta-analysis of research findings. *Journal of Child Psychology and Psychiatry, 39*, 829–840.

Wright, H. C., & Sugden, D. A. (1996). The nature of developmental coordination disorder: Inter- and intragroup differences. *Adapted Physical Activity Quarterly, 13*, 357–371.

9 Working memory function in attention deficit hyperactivity disorder

Steven Roodenrys

OVERVIEW

This chapter reviews recent research on working memory function in children with attention-deficit/hyperactivity disorder (ADHD). Diagnostic criteria and the major theoretical accounts of the disorder are described before a review of the empirical evidence is presented. The review first examines studies that assess working memory capacity by simple and complex span tasks, before going on to consider evidence for impairments in executive working memory functions. It is argued that there is little evidence for an impairment of verbal working memory in ADHD but stronger evidence for an impairment in spatial working memory. Studies of executive working memory functions suggest some functions may show deficits, but it remains unclear whether these deficits might be explained by the well-documented difficulties with inhibition experienced by these children.

ATTENTION DEFICIT HYPERACTIVITY DISORDER

Attention-deficit/hyperactivity disorder is the current label for a well-known disorder characterized by developmentally inappropriate levels of inattention, hyperactivity and impulsivity. This disorder has been given a variety of labels over the last century, many reflecting the putative cause (Spencer, 2002), but the current term emphasizes the diagnostic behavioural features.

Estimates of the prevalence of the disorder vary; however, the DSM-IV (American Psychiatric Association, 1994) puts prevalence rates at 3–5% of children and a ratio between 4:1 and 9:1 of males to females. Ford, Goodman and Meltzer (2003) report the results of a survey of over 10,000 British children and found a rate of 3.6% in boys and 0.85% in girls. The same sample when classified by ICD-10 (World Health Organization, 1993) criteria for hyperkinetic disorder show a prevalence of approximately 1.5% and a male to female ratio of 6:1 (Meltzer, Gatward, Goodman, & Ford, 2000).

To be diagnosed under the DSM-IV the child must have six or more symptoms from the checklist, which have been present for at least 6 months, are severe enough to be maladaptive, have an onset prior to 7 years of age, and are present in two or more settings (such as home and school). There is a list of nine symptoms related to inattention, such as "often fails to give close attention to details and makes careless mistakes in schoolwork, work or other activities" and "is often easily distracted by extraneous stimuli". There is also a list of nine symptoms relating to hyperactivity-impulsivity, such as "often fidgets with hands or feet or squirms in seat", "often talks excessively" and "often has difficulty awaiting turn". If sufficient symptoms from both lists are present the child is diagnosed as attention deficit/hyperactivity disorder, combined type. If there are six or more symptoms from only one of the lists then the child will be diagnosed as either attention-deficit/hyperactivity disorder, predominantly inattentive type or predominantly hyperactive-impulsive type. The ICD-10 has an extremely similar checklist of criteria for a diagnosis of hyperkinetic disorder but requires hyperactive, impulsive and inattentive symptoms to be present, and is only made in the absence of comorbid disorders, hence the lower rate of diagnosis within the same sample reported by Ford et al. (2003).

Comorbidity is a major problem for ADHD research. Tannock (1998) reviewed studies in this area and states that between 50% and 80% of children diagnosed with ADHD have a comorbid disorder (see Tannock, 1998, for a brief review of the theoretical issues related to comorbidity). The most common comorbid disorders are conduct disorder and oppositional defiant disorder; however, substantial proportions also have mood, anxiety or learning disorders.

THEORIES OF ADHD AND HOW THEY RELATE TO WORKING MEMORY

The prevailing view of ADHD is that it is a disorder of behavioural control, particularly in terms of inhibition. The deficit in attention is not seen as a deficit in attentional capacity as ADHD children do not appear to have deficits on tests of divided, selective or sustained attention (see Sergeant & van der Meere, 1990, for a review). Rather, the deficit is seen as one of attentional control due to a failure to inhibit processing of, or responses to, stimuli that are irrelevant to the current task. A number of theories suggest that the central deficit in ADHD is an inability to inhibit or delay behavioural responses (e.g., Barkley, 1997; Quay, 1997).

Probably the most widely cited theory of ADHD is Barkley's (1997) model in which behavioural inhibition is regarded as a mechanism that normally develops early in life and underpins a number of other higher cognitive functions.[1] According to this model, behavioural inhibition is the primary deficit in ADHD, and this gives rise to secondary deficits in four executive functions that require behavioural inhibition in order to develop. These four functions are nonverbal working memory, internalization of speech, self-regulation of affect/motivation/arousal and reconstitution (consisting of the two processes of analysis and synthesis).[2]

Barkley (1997) argues that behavioural inhibition develops in order to allow the child to delay responding. It does so by inhibiting the prepotent response that would otherwise be elicited by a stimulus or event, by allowing the child to interrupt an ongoing behaviour in order to respond to changes in the situation, and by protecting the delay period and any self-generated responses from interference by other distracting events or other responses. The four executive functions require effective behavioural inhibition in order for them to operate efficiently and produce what we think of as organized behaviour. Barkley argues that in the absence of behavioural inhibition, behaviour is controlled by the environment.

In Barkley's (1997) model, working memory is taken to be responsible for more than just keeping stimuli in mind. Its purpose is to allow goal directed behaviour by representing past events and creating hypothetical future events and sequences. It is suggested that working memory allows for vicarious learning and anticipatory set but also underlies self-awareness and our sense of time. Consequently, the tasks Barkley sees as tapping working memory go well beyond the traditional measures of working memory span.

Another of the four executive functions described in Barkley's (1997) model that is relevant to a review of working memory function in ADHD is that of the internalization of speech. This function is also described as verbal working memory, and although it is discussed primarily in terms of its developmental role in the control of behaviour it is also seen as equivalent to the phonological loop component of Baddeley and Hitch's (1974) working memory model.

The relationship between working memory and behavioural inhibition in Barkley's (1997) model has some resonance with theories of working memory function in the adult research literature. For example, it is very similar to Hasher and Zacks (1988) view that working memory capacity is related to attentional selection mechanisms, particularly that inhibitory processes serve to exclude irrelevant information from working memory and remove information from working memory which is no longer required. This is consistent with recent work by Engle and colleagues showing a relationship between working memory capacity and tasks tapping attentional selection mechanisms and/or inhibitory processes (see Engle, 2002, for more detail of this view and a review of the research).

Quay (1997) discusses ADHD in terms of a model of behavioural control developed by Gray (e.g., 1991). Quay suggests that children with ADHD have a deficit in the behavioural inhibition system (BIS) of this model that is responsible for inhibiting ongoing behaviour, increasing arousal and focusing attention. This model is based on neurophysiological evidence and relates the BIS to the septohippocampal system and frontal cortex. It is argued that this system responds to fear stimuli, and conditioned punishment and nonreward stimuli. This is in contrast with the behavioural activating system (BAS) that responds to reward. It is argued that ADHD children are sensitive to punishment but are less responsive to conditioned stimuli, so are less influenced by the possibility of punishment or nonreward contingent upon behaviour.

An alternative view of the inhibitory deficit in ADHD sees it more in motivational terms. Sonuga-Barke (1994) argued that children with ADHD have a motivational deficit in inhibiting immediate responses as they are overly sensitive to delay, finding it more aversive than other children. This leads to problems in delaying gratification (they discount delayed rewards) and behaviour aimed at avoiding the experience of the delay, by filling it with activity. More recently, Sonuga-Barke (2003) has argued against single, core deficit models of ADHD in favour of a dual pathway model in which ADHD symptoms reflect deficits in both an executive attentional control circuit and a reward circuit. He outlines the neural basis for two distinct circuits, which share neuroanatomical and neurochemical elements. Given the heterogeneity in ADHD symptoms and the inconsistency of findings in the research literature on cognitive deficits in ADHD this approach has some appeal.

The Cognitive-Energetic model of ADHD (e.g., Sergeant, 2000) also includes motivational factors in explaining the demonstrated problems ADHD children have on behavioural inhibition tasks. Within this model, behaviour is determined by the combination of executive functions (which includes inhibitory processes) and three energetic pools: effort, arousal and activation. Effort is described as the energy needed to perform a task and includes factors such as motivation and sensitivity to response contingencies. Arousal and activation both refer to physiological activity levels, where arousal signifies a phasic response to a stimulus and activation refers to a tonic level. Like Sonuga-Barke (2003), this model offers an explanation for the heterogeneity of ADHD symptoms in terms of the combined action of different factors rather than a single deficit.

This brief review of the theories of ADHD serves to highlight the central place of an inhibitory deficit in the major theories of the disorder. In Barkley's (1997) model it is suggested that there is a clear reliance on behavioural inhibition for working memory to operate efficiently. In the other models no explicit link is made but, as stated above, research in working memory has also drawn a link between working memory capacity and inhibitory processes. On this basis, deficits in working memory function in ADHD are to be expected.

What follows is a review of studies that either report data from tasks that would be considered standard working memory tasks in the experimental literature, such as memory span, or claim to assess working memory function in ADHD using a variety of tasks that might be less familiar to researchers who study working memory in nonclinical samples. The review is selective so not all tasks labelled working memory tasks in the ADHD literature or tasks relevant to the delay aversion hypothesis will be examined as they seem less relevant to working memory function. The review focuses on more recent research, partly because working memory tasks have become more widespread in the ADHD literature in the last decade, and partly because the earlier literature most related to working memory has been reviewed previously (e.g., see Pennington & Ozonoff, 1996, for a review of executive function deficits).

Any review of the ADHD literature is complicated by differences in reporting, or the lack of reporting, of comorbidity rates and the subtype breakdown for the sample. Comorbidity is a particular problem for attempts to isolate deficits that are specific to ADHD. The review is organized in terms of tasks falling into major groupings according to task structure and stimulus modality, and is restricted to studies reporting data with children as there is a growing literature on adults with ADHD which is additionally complicated by factors such as age of diagnosis and treatment history. For most tasks there is little or no data related to subtypes of ADHD, and there are relatively few studies examining effects of comorbid disorders on the working memory tasks so comment on these factors will only be made when it seems appropriate.

One feature of studies of ADHD that is worth noting at the outset is that on most tasks reported in the literature the ADHD group show greater variability than groups of normal control children and often show greater within-subject variability. This latter factor has been examined explicitly in reaction time measures from the Continuous Performance Task, a vigilance task commonly used in studies of ADHD that reliably shows differences between ADHD children and controls (e.g., Murphy, Barkley & Bush, 2001; Reader, Harris, Schuerholz & Denckla, 1994). The results of many studies show differences in performance favouring the control group, which may not reach significance because of the greater variability. However, the increased variability combined with relatively small differences in performance may also suggest that the ADHD children may not have less capacity when performing the task but may reflect problems with arousal or maintaining focus on the task.

VERBAL SIMPLE SPAN TASKS

Simple span tasks are those that require the subject to recall a short list of stimuli in correct serial order immediately after presentation of the list. Span, or capacity, is most often defined as the maximum length at which all of the lists of that length were successfully recalled, or at which some proportion of the presented lists were recalled. The digit span subtest from the Wechsler Intelligence Scale for Children (WISC) is the most widely reported verbal span task; however, a number of studies have used letters or words as the stimuli.

Many studies have reported normal digit span in ADHD children (Benezra & Douglas, 1988; Korkman & Pesonen, 1994; Lazar & Frank, 1998; Rucklidge & Tannock, 2002; Shue & Douglas, 1992; West, Houghton, Douglas & Whiting, 2002; Williams, Stott, Goodyer & Sahakian, 2000).

Faraone et al. (1993) reported a deficit on digit span in the WISC-R in a sample of 140 ADHD boys, however, this sample scored lower than controls on all of the subtests that were administered. Loge, Staton and Beatty (1990) also found a deficit on the same test but their sample of 20 children also scored lower than controls on several other subtests. Stevens, Quittner, Zuckerman and Moore (2002) have found a deficit in digit span in ADHD children, which failed to remain significant after covarying for differences in IQ. This suggests that there is no specific deficit in digit span, however the WISC digit span subtest combines recall of lists in the forward direction with lists recalled in backwards order. Of those studies that report forward and backward spans separately, most show no difference on either; however, McInnes, Humphries, Hogg-Johnson and Tannock (2003) found a deficit in backward recall in their study, but their sample of 21 ADHD children also scored more poorly than the controls on the block designs subtest and vocabulary tests. Most recently, Siklos and Kerns (2004) report a deficit in backward digit span for a sample of combined type ADHD children who were closely matched to controls on age and IQ as measured by the Raven's Matrices task. However, backward digit span is considered a working memory or complex task because it involves processing as well as storage, whereas forward recall only involves storage of information. This additional processing load is incurred by the demands of having to manipulate the sequence of digits in memory whilst recalling them.

Data from span tasks measuring the forward recall of letters (Benezra & Douglas, 1988; Siegel & Ryan, 1988) or words (Felton & Wood, 1989; Roodenrys, Koloski & Grainger, 2001) also fail to find a deficit in ADHD. These studies have often been focused on the relationship between reading ability and ADHD and show an impairment in serial recall associated with reading ability but no association with ADHD. For example, Felton and Wood (1989, Study 3) used a regression methodology in a study of 358 first-grade children drawn from the school population and found no relationship between ratings on ADHD symptom measures and recall of four-word sequences. Roodenrys et al. (2001) found that children with comorbid ADHD and reading disability were impaired relative to controls on word span, but only to the same degree as a sample of reading disabled only children, suggesting that any deficit was related to the reading disability. This finding may explain the results of Mariani and Barkley (1997) who found a sample of ADHD preschool boys to be impaired relative to controls on a digit span task. However the ADHD boys were also significantly worse on a reading test so the sample may have included children who would go on to be classified as reading disabled.

The above studies provide little evidence for an impairment of simple verbal span performance in ADHD. The exception is the study of Siklos and Kerns (2004) showing impaired backward recall of digits. It is arguable that backward recall may better be termed a complex span task as other processes are involved than in forward recall and the two can be distinguished by factor analysis (Reynolds, 1997). However, several studies have failed to find a significant deficit in backward recall (Benezra & Douglas, 1988; Lazar & Frank, 1998; Rucklidge & Tannock, 2002; Shue & Douglas, 1992).

VISUOSPATIAL SIMPLE SPAN TASKS

The pattern of results of studies measuring performance in a visual span task is more mixed than that for the verbal span task. Although a variety of formats of this task have been used (including computerized versions) the task is a visual analogue of the digit span task and requires the subject to reproduce a sequence of locations on a display demonstrated by the experimenter, with the possible locations being a clearly delimited set. For example, in the case of the Corsi blocks task the locations are indicated by a set of blocks fixed to a board.

Some studies have found lower performance on the spatial span task by children with ADHD compared to control children matched on age and IQ, or after covarying for IQ (Barnett et al., 2001; Kempton et al., 1999). Tripp, Ryan and Pearce (2002) reported an effect on the spatial span task that was not significant after covarying for IQ. However, there was an IQ difference between the ADHD and control children of 20 points and the mean of the ADHD group was 85, so the sample was not typical. McInnes et al. (2003) found their ADHD group was impaired on a spatial span task in comparison to a normal control group but the ADHD group also scored lower on verbal and performance IQ measures and IQ was not included as a covariate in the spatial span task analysis.

Williams et al. (2000) found that a sample of hyperactive children performed significantly worse on a spatial span task than controls matched on IQ, but no worse on a task that presented a sequence of five locations and then sequentially presented a two-alternative forced-choice recognition for each location in the sequence, in reverse order. This would seem to suggest that the ADHD children have difficulty recalling a sequence of locations but are unimpaired at discriminating locations in the sequence from new locations. However, it must be noted that this sample were not formally assessed for ADHD and, although they were above one standard deviation above the mean on the impulsive-hyperactivity subscale of the Conners' Parent Rating Scale (Goyette, Conners & Ulrich, 1978), they did not all meet the usual criteria of one and a half standard deviations above the mean on both the parent and teacher ratings and there was no evaluation by a clinician.

Cohen et al. (2000) examined performance of ADHD children and language impaired children against a control group of children with other psychological disorders on a number of tasks. On a spatial span task in which cells of a 4 × 4 matrix were successively indicated there was no difference between the ADHD children and the controls. All the groups in the study scored below a normative mean derived from Case (1992), 0.73 standard deviations in the case of the ADHD groups, but no statistical comparison to the norms was reported and the normative groups were in 2-year age bands so are not ideal for this purpose. At this point, it seems the most appropriate conclusion is that ADHD children do have a deficit on spatial span tasks that is unrelated to IQ.

Finally, some studies have examined performance in a simple span task within the motor domain. The Kaufman hand movement task requires the subject to repeat a sequence of simple hand movements, such as placing the hand palm downwards followed by a rotation of 90 degrees forming a fist. Several studies report no significant difference between ADHD children and controls on this task (Barkley, Grodzinsky & DuPaul, 1992; Berlin, Bohlin, Nyberg & Janols, 2004; Perugini, Harvey, Lovejoy, Sandstrom & Webb, 2000). However, in a study using preschool children and a larger sample than the other studies, Mariani and Barkley (1997) did find a deficit on this task after controlling for verbal IQ. Lazar and Frank (1998) did not find a deficit on this task in a sample of ADHD children but did find a deficit in comorbid ADHD and learning disabled, and purely learning disabled samples. It may be that Mariani and Barkley's sample included children who would go on to be learning disabled, and that this deficit is associated with learning disability rather than ADHD.

COMPLEX SPAN TASKS

Complex span tasks are those that require ongoing processing and storage of information during presentation followed by sequential recall. The version of the sentence span task originated by Daneman and Carpenter (1980) that has been used most often in studies of ADHD comes from Siegel and Ryan (1989). This task requires participants to read sentences with the last word missing, to generate the last word and remember it for subsequent serial recall after a number of sentences have been read. In most cases the number of sentences/items to be recalled starts low and increases if the subject is successful. In the counting span task the subject is required to count the number of a particular type of stimulus, such as blue squares, on each card in a trial, and then recall the total from each card in the trial, in order of presentation.

Surprisingly, given the impairment of working memory predicted by some theories of ADHD, there are few studies that have examined performance on complex span tasks. Three studies are consistent in showing no impairment in ADHD compared to normal controls on both the sentence span and counting span tasks when participants are matched on IQ (Siegel & Ryan, 1989; Willcutt et al., 2001) or after IQ differences between groups are statistically controlled for (Kunsti, Oosterlaan & Stevenson, 2001). The exception to this pattern is the study by Cohen et al. (2000) described above, where the performance of the ADHD children was below the normative mean but not significantly different from a group of language impaired children and the control group of other psychologically disordered children. All of the groups appear to be below the normative mean on these tasks but in the absence of a statistical evaluation it is not possible to draw a conclusion about this aspect of the study.

Stevens et al. (2002) had participants complete a complex span-type task in which coloured digits appeared successively on a computer screen. The task was to name the colour of each digit when it appeared, and at the end of the trial to recall the digits in order of presentation. A group of ADHD children performed worse than a control group on this task, but not after covarying for IQ.

The complex span tasks described above do not include a heavy spatial component. Only one study has utilized a task that might be considered a complex spatial span task. Cornoldi et al. (2001) presented a task in which the experimenter pointed to a sequence of three cells in a matrix and the subject had to indicate if the three cells formed a line or not. A trial consisted of a number of such sequences and at the end of the trial the subject had to point to the last cell of each sequence in the trial. A sample of ADHD children performed significantly worse on this task than a group of normal control children matched on IQ.

Clearly, this is a very small literature on complex span task performance in ADHD but four of the five studies on nonspatial tasks find no effect of ADHD. It is not clear why the results of Cohen et al.'s (2000) study seem to differ from the others (or even that they do differ, in the absence of explicit testing against the normative mean). In reviewing the studies of simple and complex span tasks above, there appears to be some evidence for a deficit in spatial span tasks, but little evidence for deficits in nonspatial tasks.

NONSPAN WORKING MEMORY TASKS

The ADHD literature includes a number of other studies of what could be called working memory tasks of various types. The *n*-back task is becoming increasingly utilized in behavioural and brain imaging studies of working memory. In this task the subject is presented with a continuous stream of stimuli and the subject must respond to each stimulus indicating whether it is identical to the stimulus *n*-back in the presentation, where *n* varies. When $n = 1$ the comparison is to the immediately preceding stimulus and the larger the *n*, the harder the task. The task requires evaluation of the current stimulus against the contents of memory and the constant updating of the contents of memory.

Only one study has examined the performance of ADHD children on the *n*-back task, that of Shallice et al. (2002) and their procedure was atypical in that the participants only had to respond to particular, cued stimuli. For 20 out of the sequence of 72 digits in each condition, a tone occurred before the digit to indicate that the subject should respond to that item. In the 0-back condition the subject was to respond by pressing a key if the digit was 5, in the 1-back to respond if the digit was the same as the one preceding the tone, and in the 2-back if it was the same as the digit two stimuli before the tone. They divided their participants into two age groups, 7–8 and 9–12 years. The results showed that ADHD participants responded less often than the control participants, and that participants responded less often as the task became more difficult (by increasing n) but there was no interaction. If the ADHD children have a deficit in working memory capacity we would expect this to become more apparent as the working memory load in the task increased, but the lack of interaction means it did not. There was also an effect of age such that the older children responded more often.

Shallice et al. (2002) do not discuss the results of this task but the reaction time data from the correct responses suggests that the ADHD children respond more slowly than controls in the two easier conditions and both groups show a slowing in responses in the 1-back compared to the 0-back condition. However, in the 2-back condition the pattern becomes much more confusing. The older controls show slower responses in the 2-back than the 1-back condition, whereas the younger controls do not, and the ADHD children are just as fast in the 2-back as in the 0-back condition, and as fast as the older controls in the 2-back condition. This suggests that the younger controls and the ADHD group changed strategies for the hardest condition while the older controls did not. The rate of incorrect responses to stimuli that should not have elicited a response (i.e., when the n-back digit did not match the current digit) decreased as the task difficulty increased but showed no other effects so it seems that all the groups responded less frequently as the task became more difficult. The pattern shown by the ADHD children may reflect inattention to the task or a lack of motivation/arousal rather than a deficit in working memory, as they responded quickly but less often in the most difficult condition. They do not appear to be guessing as this would have resulted in more incorrect responses when the two digits did not match, which did not occur.

Another task that requires the constant updating of the contents of memory and additional processing is the Children's Paced Auditory Serial Addition task (CHIPASAT; Johnson, Roethig-Johnson & Middleton, 1988). In this task a series of digits is presented at a fixed rate and the subject must respond to each digit by adding it to the previous digit and give the answer aloud. Thus, each stimulus requires the addition of the stimulus to the previous digit, which is held in memory, then the removal of the previous digit from memory to be replaced by the current digit.

In a study comparing children with ADHD and comorbid reading disability against children with reading disability only and normal controls, Roodenrys et al. (2001) found that the ADHD group performed significantly worse on the CHIPASAT than either of the other groups. Siklos and Kerns (2004) also found a sample of ADHD children to be impaired on the CHIPASAT in comparison to normal controls. Neither of these studies controlled for mathematical ability; however, Roodenrys et al. also measured performance in the memory updating task in which participants are presented with lists of varying length but only have to recall the last few items (e.g., lists of three, five and seven items but only recall the last three). The ADHD group had greater difficulty than the other groups when updating was required, but not when there was no updating necessary. Taken together, these findings suggest that ADHD children do have difficulty in updating the contents of working memory.

Another task that has been examined as a working memory task in a number of studies of ADHD is the self-ordered pointing task of Petrides and Milner (1982), which has been argued to be a relatively selective measure of frontal lobe function (Geurts, Verte, Oosterlaan, Roeyers & Sergeant, 2004). In this task the subject is presented with a series of cards showing a number of objects or patterns, but with the objects rearranged across the cards. The subject must point to one object on each card and avoid pointing to any object more than once across the set of cards. There is an equal number of objects as there are cards and the difficulty of the task is increased by increasing the number of objects/cards. Two different forms of the task are used, one using concrete objects and the other abstract patterns, but, as the location of the stimuli varies across cards and the task is to avoid repetition of stimuli, the task does not have a large spatial processing component.

At first sight, the results of studies using the self-ordered pointing task appear quite mixed. Wiers, Gunning and Sergeant (1998) found that a group of ADHD children made more errors on the abstract design version of this task than a control group but they also scored significantly less on an IQ measure. Van Goozen et al. (2004) recently found no significant differences between a group of comorbid ADHD and oppositional-defiant disorder (ODD) children, a pure ODD group and normal controls on either the object or abstract version of the task. Shue and Douglas (1992) found ADHD children to be impaired relative to control children using object drawings but not with abstract patterns. They also included the requirement that children must not use a strategy of pointing to the same spatial location on each card as they used a matrix to arrange the stimuli. The ADHD children also broke this requirement more often than the controls using the objects but not the abstract patterns. However, they also report that the interaction between the number of items in the set and group was not significant. If the ADHD deficit was due to the working memory demands of the task then it might be expected that the difference between the ADHD and control groups would increase as the task became more difficult with increasing set size. Geurts et al. explicitly suggested this and tested it using abstract stimuli by calculating the slope of the regression relating the number of errors to set size for each subject. Analysis showed no difference between ADHD and controls in the slope of this function but they did not report the actual number of errors. These few studies that have used the self-ordered pointing task provide little evidence for a deficit in performance by ADHD children. If there is a deficit it may well be related to difficulty in following rules or motivational factors rather than a deficit in working memory.

Another task that comes from the neuropsychological literature that has recently been used in studies of ADHD is a self-ordered search task, the spatial working memory task from the Cambridge Neuropsychological Test Automated Battery (CANTAB; Cambridge Cognition, 1992). In this task a number of boxes are shown on a computer screen and the subject is asked to find a token hidden in one of the boxes by selecting boxes one at a time. Once the token is found by the subject it is removed and another token "hidden" with the proviso that tokens are never hidden in the same box twice. Therefore optimal performance involves avoiding boxes where a token has already been found – a between-search error – and the number of such "errors" constitutes one measure of performance. A second measure is the number of within-search errors where a box that has already been checked in the current search is checked again. The test also provides a strategy score, which is a measure of how many searches began with the same box.

Kempton et al. (1999) found that ADHD children made more between-search errors than controls but they did not differ on the strategy score. The interaction between group and task difficulty (the number of boxes in the set) only approached significance. Barnett et al. (2001) also found that ADHD children made more between-search errors but no more within-search errors than control children, and they did marginally worse on the strategy score. These authors examined the effect of task difficulty on between-search errors by breaking the trials into easy (two, three and four boxes) and hard (six and eight boxes). On the easy trials the group difference failed to reach significance but it was significant on the hard trials. Barnett et al. also measured performance on a spatial span task and found a significant impairment in the ADHD group. When the between-search errors were analysed using spatial span as a covariate the effect of group became nonsignificant. This suggests that the ADHD deficit on the self-ordered search task is due to differences in remembering the location of boxes that have already been searched rather than any deficit in strategy use.

One other relevant study by Williams et al. (2000) has used the spatial working memory task from the CANTAB but found no significant differences between groups. However, there are a number of concerns with this study. Williams et al. were primarily interested in the relationship between hyperactivity and specific language impairment and, as described above, although they used one of the ADHD rating scales that is often used (the Connors Parent Rating Scale) their participants did not have a diagnosis of ADHD. More importantly, they relaxed the criterion to one standard deviation above the mean, when the usual criterion is 1.5 standard deviations. In addition, they only had a sample of 10 children in each group and they were all 6 years old, and so might not be expected to show large deficits. Given the limitations with this study, it seems reasonable to accept the conclusion of Barnett et al. (2001) that ADHD children show an impairment in the self-ordered search task that is primarily due to a deficit in spatial span.

Finally, in this section of the review it is worth describing two studies by Barkley and his colleagues that have attempted to discriminate ADHD children from controls on a working memory factor derived from a number of different tasks. Mariani and Barkley (1997) administered a battery of tasks to 64 4- and 5-year-old boys (34 ADHD and 30 controls matched on age but differing in IQ) from which they obtained 25 measures. In a factor analysis a number of tasks loaded on a factor that they labelled "working memory-persistence". These included several tasks from the Kaufman Assessment Battery for Children (Kaufman & Kaufman, 1983) including a spatial memory task that required the recall of the location of pictures within a matrix, a serial recall task using digits, the hand movement task and the arithmetic and reading subtests. A maze task and a task requiring the children to sort coloured chips into separate containers also loaded on this factor along with a measure of hyperactive/off-task behaviour during some of the tasks, such as fidgeting and getting out of the seat. Most of these measures showed significant differences between the groups in univariate analyses so it is probably not surprising that factor scores derived from these tasks were also significantly different between groups.

There are a number of problems with this analysis that argue against interpreting this finding as showing a deficit in working memory in ADHD. Firstly, the number of dependent measures relative to the number of participants is large and likely to make the factor structure unreliable (Tabachnick & Fidell, 1989). Secondly, the total variance accounted for is only 45% and the working memory-persistence factor was the last of four factors extracted and so probably does not account for a lot of variability (the actual amount is not reported). Thirdly, this factor included 8 of the 10 measures that differed significantly between the groups so it might be more appropriate to label it an "ADHD" factor. The authors acknowledged that the validity and content of the factor required more research.

The second study of this type was reported by Barkley, Edwards, Lanari, Fletcher, and Metevia (2001) and used a sample of 101 teenagers diagnosed with comorbid ADHD and ODD and 39 controls matched on age but differing in IQ. The "working memory" factor was dominated by three fluency tasks but also included digit span backwards and a spatial span task which had lower factor loadings. The fluency tasks measured verbal fluency, in which the subject produces as many different words as possible in one minute, all starting with a particular letter, an ideational fluency task of object uses and a form fluency task using shapes to produce representations of objects. Factor scores derived for this factor did not differ significantly between groups. Separate analyses of the tasks are not reported but most of these tasks showed very small differences favouring the control group (between 0 and 0.46 of a standard deviation). Of the fluency tasks only verbal fluency appears to have been studied in ADHD and the results do not provide strong evidence of a deficit. Of the four studies reviewed by Pennington and Ozonoff (1996) only one showed a significant difference; some more recent studies have also failed to find a deficit (Murphy et al., 2001; Shallice et al., 2002).

The factor analytic approach does not seem particularly promising as a method for studying working memory function in ADHD. The very large sample sizes required to extract reliable factors make it impractical and the fact that the factor structure extracted is influenced by the specific tasks, both working memory and other, that are included in the study may also challenge the validity of the factors.

EXECUTIVE PROCESSES, WORKING MEMORY AND ADHD

Currently, the most common approach in the literature to describing the cognitive deficits in ADHD is to refer to executive processes. This approach builds on the apparent similarities between the deficits and behaviour of children with ADHD and those of adult neuropsychological patients with frontal lobe damage, and has been referred to as "the frontal metaphor" view of ADHD (e.g., Pennington & Ozonoff, 1996). The term *dysexecutive syndrome* has sometimes been applied to these patients and it is widely accepted that the frontal lobes play a crucial role in the regulation of behaviour. It is also the case that working memory tasks rely heavily on the prefrontal cortex (see Kane & Engle, 2002, for a review of the evidence for this).

The most extensively investigated executive function in relation to ADHD is inhibition, but as there have been a number of reviews and theoretical papers in this area in recent years (e.g., Nigg, 2001; Sergeant, Geurts, & Oosterlaan, 2002), studies on this function will not be included in the following discussion. It suffices to say that very carefully conducted studies over a number of years have clearly established a deficit in behavioural inhibition in ADHD (see Sergeant et al., 2002, for a review). This term is usually taken to mean the ability to inhibit a motor response, either preventing it from occurring or stopping it after it has been initiated. Studies of inhibitory processes in more cognitive tasks have not been able to demonstrate so unequivocally that a deficit in ADHD exists. In an influential review, Pennington and Ozonoff (1996) concluded that ADHD children may have a core deficit in motor inhibition and an additional impairment in general processing efficiency.

A number of other executive functions, including planning, and maintaining goals and information relevant to the task, have been most investigated in the neuropsychological literature. These executive functions seem to be widely accepted as being part of working memory. In Barkley's (1997) theory of ADHD, for example, some executive functions, such as planning and rule governed behaviour, are described under the heading of working memory. In the multicomponent model of working memory first proposed by Baddeley and Hitch (1974) executive processes were seen as part of working memory but distinct from the other, temporary storage, components. Pennington,

Bennetto, McAleer and Roberts (1996) outlined a view whereby executive function tasks reflect the joint action of inhibition and working memory. The demand for inhibition of a prepotent response and the working memory demands of a task are argued to draw on the same resource pool. Inhibition of competing responses may be due to the increased activation of the working memory processes, so that when the working memory load is not too high these processes are highly activated and effectively inhibit competing responses.

In the model of working memory proposed by Baddeley and Hitch (1974) the central executive component was the most vague aspect of the model. It was described as a general processing resource with some storage capacity. Subsequent revisions of the model dropped the notion of storage capacity and developed the role of the central executive as an attentional control device (Baddeley, 1986); however, it remained somewhat vague and a single entity. Two studies adopting this framework demonstrated that children with ADHD are impaired on the random generation task, which is regarded as relying heavily on the central executive as it requires the inhibition of prepotent responses (Bayliss & Roodenrys, 2000; Roodenrys et al., 2001) so it seems worth considering whether there is other evidence consistent with an impairment of the central executive in ADHD. This model of working memory has not been widely applied to ADHD so studies of ADHD may provide some independent validation of it.

In discussing the problem of how research might proceed to fractionate the executive, Baddeley (1996) suggested four areas that might represent independent functions of a multicomponent executive. These were dual task coordination, selective attention (or ignoring distraction), random generation and the activation of long-term memory. Baddeley (2002) discussed focused attention, divided attention and attention switching as subprocesses of the central executive. There is some evidence relating to the functioning of these processes in ADHD. Studies showing a deficit in random generation performance in ADHD children were described above but tasks tapping some of these other functions have been investigated in ADHD.

There are only a few studies of dual task performance in ADHD. West et al. (2002) found that ADHD children showed only as much dual task decrement as control children using visual search and auditory signal counting as the two tasks despite being marginally worse on the visual search task on its own. Karatekin (2004) combined a simple reaction time task with counting repeatedly from 1 to 9 and with the digit span task with the length of lists set at the child's own span. The ADHD group did not differ from the controls on the reaction time task performed alone or when paired with the counting task, however they were significantly slower when it was paired with the digit span task. Performance on the digit span task did not differ between the groups.

Cornoldi et al. (2001) gave participants a word span task with the dual task requirement that they tap the table whenever an animal noun was presented.

They found that the difference in performance on this task between ADHD and control children was not significant. They also gave participants a complex span task combined with the requirement to tap to animal names. In this task participants heard either two, three or four word lists, and after the lists had been presented they had to recall the last word from each list in the order they were presented. The ADHD children did worse on this task than controls, recalling significantly fewer of the list-final words and incorrectly intruding significantly more animal names, but no more nonanimal words. In fact, the difference in correct recall is more than accounted for by the difference in animal name intrusions. Assuming that the requirement to tap to the animal name results in greater attention to that word, and greater activation, compared to the nonanimal words in the list, this result seems to reflect a difficulty inhibiting irrelevant information rather than a difficulty with dual task performance. It also seems unlikely to be due to difficulties with the complex span task, as the present review suggests ADHD children do not show a deficit in this task, although Cornoldi et al. did not directly test this in their study.

These studies do not provide much evidence for a deficit in dual task coordination in ADHD, although clearly more studies are warranted. However, there is some evidence for difficulties in multitasking in ADHD children. Clark, Prior and Kinsella (2000) and Siklos and Kerns (2004) both looked at performance of ADHD children and controls on modified versions of the six elements task from the Behavioural Assessment of Dysexecutive Syndrome battery (Wilson et al., 1996), which requires the retention of simple rules, and the executive functions of planning and performance monitoring. In the version used by Clark et al. the subject had to carry out six, open-ended tasks over a period of 10 minutes. There were actually only three types of task – telling a story, doing arithmetic and writing down the names of objects pictured on a set of cards – but there were two different sets of materials for each task, grouped together in two stands labelled A and B. The subject was told that they must do at least part of each task and that when they move on from one task (e.g., set A arithmetic), they must not go to the same task in the other set. Siklos and Kerns used six different tasks, such as building an object with blocks or doing mazes, but they were divided into two sets and participants were told not to do two tasks from the one set in a row. Clark et al. and Siklos and Kerns both found that ADHD children performed significantly worse on this test in that they attempted fewer tasks but they did not break any more rules than the control participants.

Arguably, multitasking and performance in the six elements task is more dependent on planning and monitoring than it is on dual-task control as it does not require two tasks to be done at the same time. Siklos and Kerns (2004) also found that ADHD children checked the time less often, suggestive of reduced monitoring of the task goals. Another executive function task drawn from the neuropsychological literature that is described as a planning task is the "tower" task. There are two versions of this task, the Tower of

Hanoi and the Tower of London, that are sufficiently similar to treat them as one. The Tower of Hanoi involves a stack of decreasingly sized discs on one of three pegs. The task is to move all the discs to a target peg by only moving one disc at a time and never placing a larger disc on top of a smaller disc, in as few moves as possible. The Tower of London is broadly similar but generally involves beads of different colours on three pegs and set problems where the beads are in a starting arrangement and must be moved to match a target arrangement in as few moves as possible.

Planning moves ahead in the tower tasks clearly requires some working memory capacity but different versions of the task, and even different problems within a version, may vary in the requirement to inhibit obvious moves in favour of moves more suited to the long-term goal. Tasks commonly used as executive function tasks, such as the Tower of Hanoi, have been criticized because they may tap multiple processes that are ascribed to the prefrontal cortex and a variety of nonprefrontal processes, such as spatial abilities (Pennington & Ozonoff, 1996). Of the three studies reviewed by Pennington and Ozonoff (1996) all found a deficit in the Tower of Hanoi task. More recently, Kempton et al. (1999) reported an ADHD impairment on the Tower of London, and Klorman et al. (1999) found a deficit in ADHD children's performance on the Tower of Hanoi. However, Wiers et al. (1998) did not find a deficit on the Tower of London task with ADHD boys, and van Goozen et al. (2004) did not find a significant difference between ADHD/ODD children and controls on a set problem version of the Tower of Hanoi. Geurts et al. (2004) found no difference between ADHD children and controls in the effect of increasing difficulty in the Tower of London problems. Due to the inconsistent recent findings and the multidetermined nature of these planning tasks more detailed investigation is required in order to determine which component process or processes may be impaired in ADHD.

There has been an explosion of interest in the notion of task switching in the experimental psychology literature in recent years. Often these studies require the switching of attention between different aspects of stimuli as part of a larger change in the processes that might be operating. It has been found that ADHD children have more trouble than controls in shifting their attention to a different stimulus dimension (Cepeda, Cepeda & Kramer, 2000; Kempton et al., 1999; Williams et al., 2000). They also perform more poorly in tasks where they have to switch procedures, when this is operationalized as switching between counting upwards and counting downwards in response to a cue (Bayliss & Roodenrys, 2000; West et al., 2002). Both these studies and the multitasking studies could be argued to reflect a deficit in the ability to inhibit an ongoing behaviour and so would be consistent with Barkley's (1997) view that executive functions depend on the adequate development of inhibitory processes.

This review of executive processes related to working memory in ADHD suggests that children with ADHD are impaired on some tasks but not others. This suggests that ADHD might usefully provide evidence for the independence of the different executive functions; however, the multideter-mined nature of many of these tasks means that more research is required to identify the component processes that are impaired in ADHD.

TREATMENT EFFECTS ON WORKING MEMORY IN ADHD

By far the most common treatment for ADHD, at least in the United States, is stimulant medication, such as methylphenidate. Robison, Sclar, Skaer and Galin (2004) found that for 42% of cases this is the only treatment and for a further 32% this is combined with psychotherapy or counselling. There are many studies of the effects of methylphenidate on ADHD and some of these have reported data on tasks included in the discussion above.

Tannock, Ickowicz and Schachar (1995) reported that methylphenidate improved the performance of ADHD children on the CHIPASAT but not that of a group who had a comorbid anxiety disorder. Cepeda et al. (2000) found that treatment reduced the attention switching cost of the ADHD group to the same level as controls. Barnett et al. (2001), Bedard, Martinussen, Ickowicz and Tannock (2004) and Kempton et al. (1999) all found that medi-cation improved the performance of ADHD children on spatial span, and on the self-ordered search task by reducing the between-search errors. Mehta et al. (2000) showed that in normal adult volunteers methylphenidate reduced the number of between-search errors in this task. Interestingly, among the brain regions that showed a task-related effect of the drug was the dorsola-teral prefrontal cortex. This finding is consistent with the suggestion that the self-ordered search task taps working memory and that working memory is impaired in ADHD.

One additional treatment approach is worth mentioning in the context of this review. Klingberg, Forssberg and Westerberg (2002) and Klingberg et al. (2005) administered a training programme of working memory tasks, such as a spatial span task, backward digit span and a letter span task to ADHD children. The training consisted of performing these tasks for approximately 25 minutes a day for 5 weeks. A control group performed the same tasks with the difficulty set at a very low level. The results show an improvement not only in the working memory tasks themselves but also in measures of rea-soning/fluid intelligence and ratings of ADHD symptoms. The studies did not include a control group of non-ADHD children so it is not known whether the children were impaired on these tasks prior to training. Given that the review above suggests some of these tasks, such as verbal span, may not be impaired in ADHD further investigation is warranted to determine which components of the programme are responsible for the improvement. The long-term efficacy of such treatment remains to be seen but these studies call for the possibility of an effective cognitive training treatment for ADHD to be thoroughly investigated.

An alternative approach to enhancing the learning outcomes for children with ADHD is advocated by Gathercole and Alloway (2006) in their review of the diagnosis and remediation of working memory impairments in children. They argued that there are no well-developed methods for remediating these deficits and learning outcomes may be better facilitated by changing the structure of learning tasks to reduce working memory demands. Although they make a number of suggestions on how to reduce working memory demands some of these are not warranted in the case of ADHD. For example, making instructions briefer and simpler may not be necessary as ADHD children do not appear to have a deficit in verbal working memory. Other suggestions, such as breaking complex tasks down into separate steps, seem more relevant to ADHD where there appears to be some evidence that they have difficulties dealing with complex tasks. A general principle would seem to be that structuring the learning environment to minimize the demands on the impaired systems and providing memory aids and cues are likely to enhance learning outcomes.

CONCLUSION

The strongest conclusion regarding working memory function to come out of this review of the recent literature is that there does not appear to be a general deficit in working memory capacity in ADHD. There is not a deficit in simple verbal span or complex span tasks in the verbal domain. However, there is good evidence for a deficit in the spatial domain in ADHD. The evidence is strong in relation to a deficit in simple span tasks and the only study of a complex spatial span task also reported a deficit. Studies examining the self-ordered search task show that ADHD children are impaired on this task but it may be explained by the deficit in spatial span rather than any more complex working memory processes.

One question that arises from these conclusions is how a specific deficit in spatial working memory can be explained by theories of ADHD that all posit deficiencies in frontal lobe processes or neural circuits involving the frontal lobes and subcortical structures (e.g., Barkley, 1997; Sergeant, 2000; Sonuga-Barke, 2003)? If the core deficit in ADHD is one of inhibition this would suggest that spatial memory is more subject to interference than verbal memory. Hale, Bronik and Fry (1997) provide some evidence that this is true in young children but not older children or adults. They paired verbal and spatial simple memory span tasks with verbal and spatial secondary tasks and found that all groups experienced domain specific interference but the 10-year-old children and adults showed no between-domain interference, whereas an 8-year-old group did. Furthermore, an examination of their data suggests that the interference from the verbal secondary task on the spatial span task was larger than the interference from the spatial secondary task on the verbal span task. Of course this may reflect differences in the difficulty of the two secondary tasks; however, they were both quite simple, in that they required the subject to either say the colour of each stimulus or point to the colour on an accompanying display. Hale et al. argued for a developmental increase in resistance to interference. The deficit in ADHD may reflect a developmental delay in this process, leaving ADHD children more susceptible to interference in the spatial domain.

There is also some evidence for impairment in the "executive" working memory functions but it is not yet clear from what the performance deficits are derived. ADHD children have greater difficulty than controls in updating the contents of working memory, in planning behaviour, in generating random sequences and in switching attention; however, it is not clear whether all of these deficits could be explained in terms of difficulty inhibiting information which is no longer relevant or in inhibiting ongoing behaviour, for which there is strong evidence in the motor domain. More focused research is required using versions of the tasks that vary in their requirement for inhibition.

In conclusion, the evidence for impairments in working memory in ADHD is not as convincing as we might have expected from the prominence it is given in some theories, such as that of Barkley (1997). Any parallel between the phonological loop and the capacity for internalized speech in Barkley's model is not supported as there is very little evidence for an impairment of the phonological loop. However, the main aspect of Barkley's model, a core deficit in inhibitory processes, may still offer the simplest explanation of working memory deficits in ADHD. Different executive (working memory) functions do not seem to be equivalently impaired in ADHD, so further research aimed at specifying the precise nature of the impairments underlying the performance deficits in executive tasks will also shed light on the independence of these processes.

NOTES

1   It should be noted that Barkley (1997) expressly states that this model is not intended to explain the deficits of the predominantly inattentive subtype of ADHD. Quay's (1997) theory is also not intended to apply to this group.
2   Reconstitution is the ability to decompose something like a complex sequence of behaviours into smaller units and to reorganize them into novel sequences.

REFERENCES

American Psychiatric Association. (1994). *Diagnostic and statistical manual of mental disorders*. Washington, DC: Author.

Baddeley, A. D. (1986). *Working memory*. Oxford, UK: Oxford University Press.

Baddeley, A. D. (1996). Exploring the central executive. *Quarterly Journal of Experimental Psychology, 49A*, 5–28.

Baddeley, A. D. (2002). Is working memory still working? *The European Psychologist, 7*, 85–97.

Baddeley, A. D., & Hitch, G. J. (1974). Working memory. In G. A. Bower (Ed.), *Recent advances in learning and motivation* (Vol. 8, pp. 47–90). New York: Academic Press.

Barkley, R. A. (1997). *ADHD and the nature of self-control*. New York: Guilford Press.

Barkley, R. A., Edwards, G., Laneri, M., Fletcher, K., & Metevia, L. (2001). Executive functioning, temporal discounting, and sense of time in adolescents with attention deficit hyperactivity disorder (ADHD) and oppositional defiant disorder (ODD). *Journal of Abnormal Child Psychology, 29*, 541–556.

Barkley, R. A., Grodzinsky, G., & DuPaul, G. J. (1992). Frontal lobe functions in attention deficit disorder with and without hyperactivity: A review and research report. *Journal of Abnormal Child Psychology, 20*, 163–188.

Barnett, R., Maruff, P., Vance, A., Luk, E., Costin, J., Wood, C., & Pantelis, C. (2001). Abnormal executive function in attention deficit hyperactivity disorder: The effect of stimulant medication and age on spatial working memory. *Psychological Medicine, 31*, 1107–1115.

Bayliss, D. M., & Roodenrys, S. (2000). Executive processing and attention deficit hyperactivity disorder: An application of the supervisory attentional system. *Developmental Neuropsychology, 17*, 161–180.

Bedard, A., Martinussen, R., Ickowicz, A., & Tannock, R. (2004). Methylphenidate improves visuospatial memory in children with attention-deficit/hyperactivity disorder. *Journal of the American Academy of Child and Adolescent Psychiatry, 43*, 260–268.

Benezra, E., & Douglas, V. I. (1988). Short-term serial recall in ADDH, normal, and reading-disabled boys. *Journal of Abnormal Child Psychology, 16*, 511–525.

Berlin, L., Bohlin, G., Nyberg, L., & Janols, L. (2004). How well do measures of inhibition and other executive functions discriminate between children with ADHD and controls? *Child Neuropsychology, 10*, 1–13.

Cambridge Cognition. (1992). *Cambridge Neuropsychological Test Automated Battery* [Computer software]. Cambridge, UK: Author.

Case, R. (1992). The role of the frontal lobes in the regulation of cognitive development. *Brain and Cognition, 20*, 51–73.

Cepeda, N. J., Cepeda, M. L., & Kramer, A. F. (2000). Task switching and attention deficit hyperactivity disorder. *Journal of Abnormal Child Psychology, 28*, 213–226.

Clark, C., Prior, M., & Kinsella, G. J. (2000). Do executive function deficits differentiate between adolescents with ADHD and oppositional defiant/conduct disorder? A neuropsychological study using the Six Elements Test and Hayling sentence completion test. *Journal of Abnormal Child Psychology, 28*, 403–414.

Cohen, N. J., Vallance, D. D., Barwick, M., Im, N., Menna, R., Horodezky, N. B., & Isaacson, L. (2000). The interface between ADHD and language impairment: An examination of language, achievement, and cognitive processing. *Journal of Child Psychology and Psychiatry, 41*, 353–362.

Cornoldi, C., Marzocchi, G. M., Belotti, M., Caroli, M. G., de Meo, T., & Braga, C. (2001). Working memory interference control deficit in children referred by teachers by ADHD symptoms. *Child Neuropsychology, 7*, 230–240.

Daneman, M., & Carpenter, P. A. (1980). Individual differences in integrating information between and within sentences. *Journal of Verbal Learning and Verbal Behavior, 19*, 450–466.

Engle, R. W. (2002). Working memory capacity as executive attention. *Current Directions in Psychological Science, 11*, 19–23.

Faraone, S. V., Biederman, J., Lehman, B. K., Spencer, T., Norman, D., Seidman, L. J., et al. (1993). Intellectual performance and school failure in children with attention deficit hyperactivity disorder in their siblings. *Journal of Abnormal Psychology, 102*, 616–623.

Felton, R. H., & Wood, F. B. (1989). Cognitive deficits in reading disability and attention deficit disorder. *Journal of Learning Disabilities, 22*, 3–13.

Ford, T., Goodman, R., & Meltzer, H. (2003). The British Child and Adolescent Mental Health Survey 1999: The prevalence of DSM-IV disorders. *Journal of the American Academy of Child and Adolescent Psychiatry, 42*, 1203–1211.

Gathercole, S. E., & Alloway, T. P. (2006). Practitioner review: Short-term and working memory impairments in neurodevelopmental disorders: Diagnosis and remedial support. *Journal of Child Psychology and Psychiatry and Allied Disciplines, 47*, 4–15.

Geurts, H. M., Verte, S., Oosterlaan, J., Roeyers, H., & Sergeant, J. A. (2004). How specific are executive functioning deficits in attention deficit hyperactivity disorder and autism? *Journal of Child Psychology and Psychiatry, 45*, 836–854.

Goyette, C. H., Conners, C. K., & Ulrich, R. F. (1978). Normative data on Revised Conners' Parent and Teacher Rating Scales. *Journal of Abnormal Child Psychology, 6*, 221–236.

Gray, J. A. (1991). Neural systems, emotion and personality. In J. Madden (Ed.), *Neurobiology of learning, emotion and affect* (pp. 273–306). New York: Raven Press.

Hale, S., Bronik, M. D., & Fry, A. F. (1997). Verbal and spatial working memory in school-age children: Developmental differences in susceptibility to interference. *Developmental Psychology, 33*, 364–371.

Hasher, L., & Zacks, R. T. (1988). Working memory, comprehension and aging: A review and a new view. In G. H. Bower (Ed.), *The psychology of learning and motivation* (Vol. 22, pp. 193–225). San Diego, CA: Academic Press.

Johnson, D. A., Roethig-Johnson, K., & Middleton, J. (1988). Development and evaluation of an attentional test in head injured children: 1. Information processing capacity in a normal sample. *Journal of Child Psychology and Psychiatry, 29*, 199–208.

Kane, M. J., & Engle, R. W. (2002). The role of prefrontal cortex in working-memory capacity, executive attention, and general fluid intelligence: An individual-differences perspective. *Psychonomic Bulletin and Review, 9*, 637–671.

Karatekin, C. (2004). A test of the integrity of the components of Baddeley's model of working memory in attention-deficit/hyperactivity disorder (ADHD). *Journal of Child Psychology and Psychiatry, 45*, 912–926.

Kaufman, A. S., & Kaufman, N. L. (1983). *Kaufman Assessment Battery for Children: Interpretive manual.* Circle Pines, MN: American Guidance Service.

Kempton, S., Vance, A., Maruff, P., Luk, E., Costin, J., & Pantelis, C. (1999). Executive function and attention deficit hyperactivity disorder: Stimulant medication and better executive function performance in children. *Psychological Medicine, 29*, 527–538.

Klingberg, T., Fernell, E., Olesen, P. J., Johnson, M., Gustafsson, P., Dahlstrom, K., et al. (2005). Computerized training of working memory in children with

ADHD – a randomized, controlled trial. *Journal of the American Academy of Child and Adolescent Psychiatry, 44,* 177–186.

Klingberg, T., Forssberg, H., & Westerberg, H. (2002). Training of working memory in children with ADHD. *Journal of Clinical and Experimental Neuropsychology, 24,* 781–791.

Klorman, R., Hazel-Fernandez, L. A., Shaywitz, S. E., Fletcher, J. M., Marchione, K. E., Holahan, J. M., et al. (1999). Executive functioning deficits in attention-deficit/hyperactivity disorder are independent of oppositional defiant or reading disorder. *Journal of the American Academy of Child and Adolescent Psychiatry, 38,* 1148–1155.

Korkman, M., & Pesonen, A. E. (1994). A comparison of neuropsychological test profiles of children with attention deficit-hyperactivity disorder and/or learning disorder. *Journal of Learning Disabilities, 27,* 383–392.

Kuntsi, J., Oosterlaan, J., & Stevenson, J. (2001). Psychological mechanisms in hyperactivity: Response inhibition deficit, working memory impairment, delay aversion, or something else? *Journal of Child Psychology and Psychiatry, 42,* 199–210.

Lazar, J., & Frank, Y. (1998). Frontal systems dysfunction in children with attention-deficit/hyperactivity disorder and learning disabilities. *Journal of Neuropsychiatry and Clinical Neurosciences, 10,* 160–167.

Loge, D. V., Staton, R. D., & Beatty, W. M. (1990). Performance of children with ADHD on tests sensitive to frontal lobe dysfunction. *Journal of the American Academy of Child and Adolescent Psychiatry, 29,* 540–545.

Mariani, M. A., & Barkley, R. A. (1997). Neuropsychological and academic functioning in preschool boys with attention deficit hyperactivity disorder. *Developmental Neuropsychology, 13,* 111–129.

McInnes, A., Humphries, T., Hogg-Johnson, S., & Tannock, R. (2003). Listening comprehension and working memory are impaired in attention-deficit hyperactivity disorder irrespective of language impairment. *Journal of Abnormal Child Psychology, 31,* 427–443.

Mehta, M. A., Owen, A. M., Sahakian, B. J., Mavaddat, N., Pickard, J. D., & Robbins, T. W. (2000). Methylphenidate enhances working memory by modulating discrete frontal and parietal lobe regions in the human brain. *Journal of Neuroscience, 20,* RC65.

Meltzer, H., Gatward, R., Goodman, R., & Ford, T. (2000). *Mental health of children and adolescents in Great Britain.* London: The Stationery Office.

Murphy, K. R., Barkley, R. A., & Bush, T. (2001). Executive functioning and olfactory identification in young adults with attention deficit-hyperactivity disorder. *Neuropsychology, 15,* 211–220.

Nigg, J. T. (2001). Is ADHD a disinhibitory disorder? *Psychological Bulletin, 127,* 571–598.

Pennington, B. F., Bennetto, L., McAleer, O., & Roberts, R. J. (1996). Executive functions and working memory: Theoretical and measurement issues. In G. R. Lyon & N. A. Krasnegor (Eds.), *Attention, memory and executive function* (pp. 327–348). Baltimore: Paul H. Brookes.

Pennington, B. F., & Ozonoff, S. (1996). Executive functions and developmental psychopathology. *Journal of Child Psychology and Psychiatry, 37,* 51–87.

Perugini, E. M., Harvey, E. A., Lovejoy, D. W., Sandstrom, K., & Webb, A. H. (2000). The predictive power of combined neuropsychological measures for attention-deficit/hyperactivity disorder in children. *Child Neuropsychology, 6,* 101–114.

Petrides, M., & Milner, B. (1982). Deficits in subject-ordered tasks after frontal- and temporal-lobe lesions in man. *Neuropsychologia, 20*, 249–262.

Quay, H. C. (1997). Inhibition and attention deficit hyperactivity disorder. *Journal of Abnormal Child Psychology, 25*, 7–13.

Reader, M. J., Harris, E. L., Schuerholz, L. J., & Denckla, M. B. (1994). Attention deficit hyperactivity disorder and executive dysfunction. *Developmental Neuropsychology, 10*, 493–512.

Reynolds, C. R. (1997). Forward and backward memory span should not be combined for clinical analysis. *Archives of Clinical Neuropsychology, 12*, 29–40.

Robison, L. M., Sclar, D. A., Skaer, T. L. & Galin, R. S. (2004). Treatment modalities among US children diagnosed with attention-deficit hyperactivity disorder: 1995–99. *International Clinical Psychopharmacology, 19*, 17–22.

Roodenrys, S., Koloski, N., & Grainger, J. (2001). Working memory function in attention deficit hyperactivity disordered and reading disabled children. *British Journal of Developmental Psychology, 19*, 325–337.

Rucklidge, J. J., & Tannock, R. (2002). Neuropsychological profiles of adolescents with ADHD: Effects of reading difficulties and gender. *Journal of Child Psychology and Psychiatry and Allied Disciplines, 43*, 988–1003.

Sergeant, J. A. (2000). The cognitive-energetic model: An empirical approach to attention-deficit hyperactivity disorder. *Neuroscience and Biobehavioral Reviews, 24*, 7–12.

Sergeant, J. A., & van der Meere, J. J. (1990). Convergence of approaches in localizing the hyperactivity deficit. In B. B. Lahey & A. E. Kazdin (Eds.), *Advances in clinical child psychology* (pp. 207–246). New York: Plenum Press.

Sergeant, J. A., Geurts, H. M., & Oosterlaan, J. (2002). How specific is a deficit of executive functioning for attention-deficit/hyperactivity disorder? *Behavioural Brain Research, 130*, 3–28.

Shallice, T., Marzocchi, G. M., Coser, S., Del Savio, M., Meuter, R. F., & Rumiati, R. I. (2002). Executive function profile of children with attention deficit hyperactivity disorder. *Developmental Neuropsychology, 21*, 43–71.

Shue, K. L., & Douglas, V. I. (1992). Attention deficit hyperactivity disorder and the frontal lobe syndrome. *Brain and Cognition, 20*, 104–124.

Siegel, L. S., & Ryan, E. B. (1988). Development of grammatical-sensitivity, phonological, and short-term memory skills in normally achieving and learning disabled children. *Developmental Psychology, 24*, 28–37.

Siegel, L. S., & Ryan, E. B. (1989). The development of working memory in normally achieving and subtypes of learning disabled children. *Child Development, 60*, 973–980.

Siklos, S., & Kerns, K. A. (2004). Assessing multitasking in children with ADHD using a modified Six Elements Test. *Archives of Clinical Neuropsychology, 19*, 347–361.

Sonuga-Barke, E. J. S. (1994). Annotation: On dysfunction and function in psychological theories of childhood disorder. *Journal of Child Psychology and Psychiatry, 35*, 801–815.

Sonuga-Barke, E. J. S. (2003). The dual-pathway model of AD/HD: An elaboration of neuro-developmental characteristics. *Neuroscience and Biobehavioural Reviews, 27*, 593–604.

Spencer, T. J. (2002). Attention-deficit/hyperactivity disorder. *Archives of Neurology, 59*, 314–316.

Stevens, J., Quittner, A. L., Zuckerman, J. B., & Moore, S. (2002). Behavioral inhibition, self-regulation of motivation, and working memory in children with attention deficit hyperactivity disorder. *Developmental Neuropsychology, 21*, 117–140.

Tabachnick, B. G., & Fidell, L. S. (1989). *Using multivariate statistics.* New York: Harper Collins.

Tannock, R. (1998). Attention deficit hyperactivity disorder: Advances in cognitive, neurobiological, and genetic research. *Journal of Child Psychology and Psychiatry, 39*, 65–99.

Tannock, R., Ickowicz, A., & Schachar, R. (1995). Differential effects of methylphenidate on working memory in ADHD children with and without comorbid anxiety. *Journal of the American Academy of Child and Adolescent Psychiatry, 34*, 886–896.

Tripp, G., Ryan, J., & Peace, K. (2002). Neuropsychological functioning in children with DSM-IV combined type attention deficit hyperactivity disorder. *Australian and New Zealand Journal of Psychiatry, 36*, 771–779.

Van Goozen, S. H. M., Cohen-Kettenis, P. T., Snoek, H., Matthys, W., Swaab-Barneveld, H., & van Engeland, H. (2004). Executvie functioning in children: A comparison of hospitalised ODD and ODD/ADHD children and normal controls. *Journal of Child Psychology and Psychiatry, 45*, 284–292.

West, J., Houghton, S., Douglas, G., & Whiting, K. (2002). Response inhibition, memory, and attention in boys with attention-deficit/hyperactivity disorder. *Educational Psychology, 22*, 533–551.

Wiers, R. W., Gunning, W., & Sergeant, J. A. (1998). Is a mild deficit in executive functions in boys related to childhood ADHD or to parental multigenerational alcoholism? *Journal of Abnormal Child Psychology, 26*, 415–430.

Willcutt, E. G., Pennington, B. F., Boada, R., Ogline, J. S., Tunick, R. A., Chhabildas, N. A., & Olson, R. K. (2001). A comparison of the cognitive deficits in reading disability and attention-deficit/hyperactivity disorder. *Journal of Abnormal Psychology, 110*, 157–172.

Williams, D., Stott, C., Goodyer, I., & Sahakian, B. J. (2000). Specific language impairment with or without hyperactivity: Neuropsychological evidence for frontostriatal dysfunction. *Developmental Medicine and Child Neurology, 42*, 368–375.

Wilson, B. A., Alderman, N., Burgess, P. W., Emslie, H., & Evans, J. J. (Eds.). (1996). *Behavioural assessment of the dysexecutive syndrome.* Bury St. Edmunds, UK: Thames Valley Test Company.

World Health Organization. (1993). *The ICD-10 classification of mental and behavioural disorders: Diagnostic criteria for research.* Geneva, Switzerland: Author.

10 Working memory in autism[1]

Sylvie Belleville, Édith Ménard,
Laurent Mottron, and
Marie-Claude Ménard

OVERVIEW

Autism is an enduring developmental condition characterized by abnormality in the perceptual, cognitive and emotional domains. This chapter will present the current state of empirically based knowledge on the nature and characterization of working memory in autistic persons. The chapter will first present a clinical overview of autism, as well as the current models of the cognitive features that characterize this condition. After describing major theories of working memory, the performance pattern of autistic persons on different components of working memory will be reviewed. Lastly, the impact that special abilities have on the retention of information over the short-term will be analysed. Overall, the chapter will provide a general perspective on the characterization of working memory in autism and it will present critical views on the conclusions that can be drawn from the present findings.

AUTISM

Approximately 85% of the individuals who meet the criteria for autism are diagnosed with "idiopathic" autism. Idiopathic autism is a neurodevelopmental disorder that has a genetic etiology, without additional identifiable neurological or genetic pathologies. In the remaining population of individuals who meet the criteria for autism, the clinical presentation is accompanied by a heterogeneous set of medical, neurological and neurodevelopmental disorders (Volkmar, Lord, Bailey, Schultz & Klin, 2004). As with other genetic conditions, autism may appear in its full symptomatology. However, it can also be milder, with symptoms that do not fulfill all of the criteria for the prototypical condition and that are less marked at a clinical level or developmentally transient. The label "autistic spectrum" encompasses the entire range of autistic symptoms – from persons exhibiting the complete clinical picture to persons almost indistinguishable from their typically developing peers in adulthood. In the DSM-IV (American Psychiatric Association, 1994), the autistic spectrum is divided into three clinical entities: autism per se, Asperger's syndrome and pervasive developmental disorder not otherwise specified (PDD-NOS). All three of these entities are embedded in the broader category of pervasive developmental disorders (PDD). PDDs are typically detected at approximately 18 months of age, but the deviation to the normative phenotype expression diminishes markedly through development, although a marked variation in the final adaptation level is also characteristic of this group.

At a behavioural level, the autistic spectrum is characterized by atypicalities in several apparently unrelated areas (hence, the label "pervasive" for the disorder). Autistic symptoms are conventionally classified into four domains: reciprocal social interactions, communication, imagination, and restricted interests and repetitive behaviours. Various combinations of these domains distinguish the subtypes of PDDs. *Social* symptoms include absent, diminished or atypical spontaneous and reciprocal orientation toward caregivers and peers throughout development. *Communication* symptoms are represented by a complete absence of expressed oral language in a minority of individuals. They can also be represented by atypical reproduction of linguistic material without apparent communicative intent (echolalia), hyperlexia (in the written domain) and diminished ability to recode perceived language (stereotyped language) particularly in older individuals. *Imagination* deficits include the absence of pretend play during childhood and a spontaneous overorientation toward the concrete aspects of the environment at an adult age. *Restricted interests and repetitive behaviours* include repetitive movements such as hand flapping, atypical visual exploratory behaviors for inanimate objects, and focused and inflexible interest in objects or abstract domains of knowledge. Whereas the criteria for autism include the entire set of characteristics mentioned above, the criteria for Asperger's syndrome do not include the presence of a delay in the acquisition of autonomy, language delay or formally repetitive language. In contrast, language is fluent, formal and overly detailed. PDD-NOS is a mixed bag category that shelters subthreshold or incomplete presentations of the syndrome.

There is substantial heterogeneity in the clinical manifestation of autism. One source of heterogeneity is associated with differential aspects of the phenotype through development. Another important source of heterogeneity is the considerable variability in the level of general intelligence associated with the syndrome. Performance by persons with autism ranges from the level of apparent profound mental retardation to that of superior intelligence, and persons with Asperger's syndrome from the level of low intelligence to that of superior intelligence. Mental retardation in autism is characterized by islets of typical information processing (Scheuffgen, Happé, Anderson & Frith, 2000), peaks of ability in certain tasks and sudden improvement of performance in some individuals during key periods of development. Therefore, mental retardation in autism is clearly different from that found in other neurodevelopmental disorders. A classical way to account for this range of performance is to distinguish between high-functioning autism (HFA;

IQ > 70) and low functioning autism (LFA; IQ < 70). However, this distinction is purely descriptive in the current state of knowledge and there is no accepted standard as to what constitutes or distinguishes HFA and LFA in terms of cognitive or genetic mechanisms.

COGNITIVE MODELS OF AUTISM

Attempts to unravel the cognitive underpinnings of autism have led to the so-called "cognitive models" of autism. These models attempt to unify the different signs of autism by finding a single cognitive process, the impairment of which would result in the whole range of behavioral symptoms. In cognitive models, the impaired process would have both a synchronic mechanism of action – it would prevent the normal accomplishment of the cognitive operations relying on its integrity – and a developmental one – it would impede the construction of the systems that rely on its integrity at a given period in development.

One of the first models to account for the cognitive deficits in autism was the theory of mind hypothesis, in which the social peculiarity of autism is explained by an impairment in the ability to detect, identify and manipulate the intentionality of other people (Baron-Cohen, Leslie, & Frith, 1985). Paradoxical superiority in some pattern detection tasks, as well as deficits in processing contextual aspects of linguistic units, led to the weak central coherence model (Frith, 1989/2003). A related model accounts for the absence of a typical bias for global aspects of visual information with a hierarchization deficit hypothesis (Mottron & Belleville, 1993b). An account of preserved versus defective cognitive operations in terms of simple versus complex processing operations is the heart of the complexity hypothesis (Minshew & Goldstein, 1998; Minshew, Goldstein & Siegel, 1997). The enhanced discrimination hypothesis (Plaisted, O'Riordan & Baron-Cohen, 1998) and the enhanced perceptual functioning hypothesis (Mottron & Burack, 2001) focus on preferential/superior processing of "surface" aspects of information, as well as weaknesses in producing and manipulating abstract dimensions. Finally, the executive model (Ozonoff, Pennington & Rogers, 1991) proposes a deficit in generativity, cognitive flexibility and planning, analogous to the one observed in patients with a frontal lobe dysfunction. This is a model that motivated to a large extent the search for a working memory deficit in autism and will therefore be described in more detail than other models, even if it may not be currently the most prevalent model of autism.

A number of authors have suggested an executive function deficit in autistic individuals based on a similarity between the behaviour and cognitive patterns of these people and those of frontal brain damaged persons (Hughes & Russell, 1993; Ozonoff et al., 1991; Pennington & Ozonoff, 1996). This hypothesis attempts to explain the extreme rigidity and repetitiveness found in autistic persons and their need to follow detailed routines (Ozonoff et al., 1991). The presence of an executive deficit in autism is supported by a large number of studies showing cognitive inflexibility and strategic planning problems on tasks sensitive to frontal brain damage, such as the Wisconsin Card Sorting Test, in which participants make conceptual associations between different cards on the basis of feedback given by the examiner, and the Tower of Hanoi, which requires participants to reproduce a model by rearranging balls on pegs using a set of simple rules (Bennetto, Pennington & Rogers, 1996; Ozonoff, 1995; Ozonoff & Jensen, 1999; Ozonoff & McEvoy, 1994; Ozonoff et al., 1991).

Roberts and Pennington (1996) suggest that a working memory deficit could explain the executive deficits reported in autism, and, in particular, the impaired performance of these individuals on the so-called "tower" tests. They argue that the executive tasks failed by autistic persons are those that have heavy working memory demands (Pennington et al., 1997; Roberts & Pennington, 1996). Impairment on tasks such as the Tower of Hanoi would result from difficulty maintaining within working memory the series of movements (subgoals) needed to achieve the final goal (Pennington et al., 1997). This working memory limitation has been conceptualized as a basic deficit that would prevent the development of a large number of domains of abilities, including communication skills and social understanding.

WORKING MEMORY

Working memory is defined as a system involved in the online maintenance of material. In the last few years, there has been considerable theoretical debate about the concept of working memory. Because it is difficult to ground research in such a quickly evolving area, this chapter will reflect both traditional views of working memory and the more recent theoretical contribution to the concept.

One influential view of working memory is the Baddeley and Hitch working memory model (Baddeley, 1986; Baddeley & Hitch, 1974). In this model, memory is conceptualized as a working space for the completion of cognitive activities. Information is maintained over the short term by the interplay of a phonological loop, a visuospatial sketchpad and a central executive. The phonological loop is involved in the maintenance of verbal material and includes a passive phonological store and an active rehearsal. The phonological store would be reflected in the detrimental impact of phonological similarity on immediate serial recall of words or letters. In contrast, rehearsal is responsible for the word length effect whereby shorter words are better recalled than longer words. The visuospatial sketchpad is involved in the retention of images and spatial information. Finally, the central executive is an attention device involved in the management of information among the two slave systems and in the control of attention. The advent of the Baddeley and Hitch working memory model has been extremely fruitful due to its heuristic value. Specifically, it has provided an impetus for working memory research within all fields of cognition. It has also given way to a number of alternative views of working memory, some of which are extensions of the original Baddeley and Hitch model, others that clearly deviate from it.

Working memory capacity has also been defined as the ability to control attention with the goal of keeping information active and easily accessible (Engle, 2002). In this view, working memory is essentially conceived as a system involved in attentional or executive control. Attentional control of action is involved in tasks that are new, demanding or that cannot be performed automatically (Norman & Shallice, 1986; Shallice, 1982). Thus, working memory is envisioned here as an executive attention system used to guide action and maintain or suppress information within the realm of consciousness (Engle, 2002).

Recent theories suggest the existence of different attentional control capacities (e.g., Baddeley, 1996; Belleville, Rouleau, van der Linden & Collette, 2003; Stuss, Shallice, Alexander & Picton, 1995). For example, Baddeley (1996) distinguished between the ability to manipulate information, to select certain pieces of information and reject others (selection and inhibition), to switch retrieval strategies and to coordinate two or more concurrent activities (dual tasking). Our previous work with neurologically impaired persons provided empirical support for the validity of fractionating working memory into at least four components: inhibition, manipulation, updating and divided attention components (Belleville, Peretz & Malenfant, 1996; Belleville, Rouleau et al., 2003; Gilbert, Belleville, Bherer & Chouinard, 2005).

Processing views of working memory argue that retention over the short term is closely linked to the informational domains involved in information processing. In the verbal domain, linguistic models of working memory propose that the reproduction of short series of verbal items, as is done in span tasks, relies on the systems that are involved in the perception and production of language (Allport, 1983, 1985; Belleville, Caza & Peretz, 2003; Martin, Lesch & Bartha, 1999; Martin & Romani, 1994; Martin & Saffran, 1997). Thus, performance on these tasks should be constrained by the same rules and principles. This view was motivated by the finding that lexical and semantic properties of words contribute to immediate serial recall. The processing view is also supported by the finding of an association between the language impairment of aphasic patients and their pattern of performance in immediate serial recall. In their stronger version, processing views of working memory argue that memory for a particular type of information is implemented into the same cognitive and neural systems as those involved in the processing of information (Belleville, Caza & Peretz, 2003; Crowder, 1989; Nairne, 1990, 2002).

WORKING MEMORY IN AUTISM

Because there are numerous ways in which to conceptualize working memory, the presentation of the empirical studies conducted in autism will be guided by combined heuristic approaches. Due to the influence of the Baddeley and Hitch (1974) model on empirical research, this chapter will present findings more or less with reference to that view. However, on occasion, the data will be discussed in relation to other models that are substantiated by findings with autistic persons.

The phonological loop

The phonological loop is implicated in the immediate serial recall of items that can be coded verbally. Persons with autism exhibit normal performance in typical verbal immediate serial recall or verbal span tasks, whether tested with digits (Bennetto et al., 1996; Boucher, 1978) or words (Russell, Jarrold & Henry, 1996). In addition, these individuals show a normal recency effect (Boucher, 1978). However, very few studies have examined whether the verbal span of individuals with autism is supported by the same mechanisms as those of typical persons. For example, a number of linguistic characteristics, such as phonology, word length, and lexical and semantic attributes, have been shown to modulate immediate serial recall and these interact with procedural variables such as modality of presentation, presence of concurrent articulation or nature of the material.

Studies of long-term episodic memory in autistic persons suggest that these persons encode phonological information at a higher level than typical participants matched on chronological age and verbal intelligence, and semantic information to a lesser level (Mottron, Morasse & Belleville, 2001). For example, in a cued recall task, they benefit more than typical adults from phonological orientation and cuing. This suggests that persons with autism encode to a greater extent the surface properties of items, thus exhibiting a shift from deeper to shallower forms of encoding. Considering the importance of surface properties (phonological and articulatory properties) in immediate short-term recall, it is important to examine the extent to which persons with autism use them to support short-term recall.

Only two studies have examined these effects (Ménard, Mottron, Belleville & Limoges, 2001, in preparation-a; Russell et al., 1996). Russell and collaborators have examined the effect of word length on the span of autistic persons by comparing auditory word presentation with two output modes: verbal response and response by pointing to pictures on a board. This study included adolescents (average age = 12 years) with LFA, persons with moderate learning difficulties matched on mental and chronological age and typical controls matched on mental age. Since typical controls were matched on mental age, their average chronological age was only 6 years. When using a pointing response, autistic persons showed a much larger word length effect than both the participants with learning difficulties and the typical controls (but nonsignificantly in this latter case). However, the nature of the control groups may partly explain the larger word length effect obtained in autistic persons. Indeed, the larger word length effect found in autistic persons may be due to the fact that typical controls did not show a word length effect. These participants were 6 years of age on average, which corresponds to a key phase in the development of rehearsal. The use of persons with moderate learning difficulties as mental age matched controls also poses a problem, as some of these individuals may have been dyslexic and it is well known that dyslexia (and moderate learning difficulties) impairs the phonological loop. Thus, it is possible that at least some of the controls did not use rehearsal optimally, explaining the larger effect found in autistic participants.

Importantly however, similar findings were obtained by Ménard, Belleville and Mottron (2001, in preparation-a) with HFA adolescents and adults as compared to age and IQ matched controls. Working with individuals who have HFA allows for the use of typical participants who have a normal IQ in the control group. We measured the word length and phonological similarity effects using visually and auditorily presented words and in both cases, the response was oral. As in Russell et al. (1996), the results indicated a larger word length effect under visual (written) presentation.

Thus, the anomalous word length effect found by Russell and collaborators (1996) in LFA was replicated with a HFA population in which the matching group consisted of normal adolescent/adult participants. Thus, the effect is robust and likely reflects important mechanisms of memorizing in autism. One explanation of this effect may arise from the particular procedure used in the above studies to assess the word length effect. In both studies, the word length effect was measured in paradigms that used images or written words at presentation or recall. One possibility is that such a presentation mode increased the use of semantic and visual features in *typical participants*, thus reducing their reliance on phonoarticulatory parameters. As was found in a previous study on long-term memory, it is possible that autistic persons rely less on semantic features and more on phonological ones than typical participants even when the procedure promotes the use of semantic features (Mottron et al., 2001). Thus, in conditions where control participants increase their use of semantic features (and decrease their use of phonoarticulatory ones), autistic persons continue to rely on phonoarticulatory features. This would result in a larger word length effect in autistic persons than in typical participants not because the condition increases the effect in autistic persons, but because it reduces the effect in typical ones. In support of our interpretation, the word length effect was smaller in the visual than auditory modality in matched controls but not in people with autism, supporting the interpretation that matched controls relied on other properties of the material when it was presented visually. Unfortunately, correlation analyses with speech rate do not support a larger reliance on phonoarticulatory features in autistic participants. Individual articulation rates were not correlated with span in autistic persons, although they were correlated with span in typical children. However, the validity of using correlations between span and speech rate as a direct reflection of rehearsal has been debated recently (e.g., see Nairne, 2002). Thus, this intriguing effect certainly deserves additional investigation. Interestingly, this finding is compatible with processing or feature models of short-term recall (Belleville, Caza & Peretz, 2003; Nairne, 1990; Martin & Saffran, 1997). In these models, all representations, including semantic ones, have the potential to contribute to immediate serial recall. However, their impact depends highly on the nature of the task.

In conclusion, verbal span is typically normal in autistic persons. Nevertheless, there is evidence for an atypical use of phonoarticulatory features in short-term recall. In two studies, a larger word length effect has been found when using visual material at presentation or recall. This may reflect an imbalance between the use and/or impact of phonoarticulatory over semantic features in immediate serial recall.

Visuospatial sketchpad

There is increasing evidence to suggest that aspects of visuospatial working memory are atypical in persons with autism. Minshew, Luna and Sweeney (1999) have measured spatial working memory with the oculomotor delayed-response task. In this task, participants were asked to look (i.e., make a saccade) at the position where a target had occurred 1–8 s previously. This was compared to a visually guided saccade condition in which participants were asked to look at targets that remained on the screen until the saccade was complete. Similar results were found in autistic persons and age matched controls for the visually guided task, where autistic participants exhibited a 1–2 degree increase in the magnitude of saccade error relative to controls in the delayed oculomotor task (Minshew et al., 1999). In addition, this impairment was associated with a decrease in the fMRI activation of the dorsolateral prefrontal cortex and posterior cingulate, two regions that are thought to be involved in spatial working memory (Luna et al., 2002). Koczat, Rogers, Pennington and Ross (2002) have found impairment on a similar task in parents of autistic probants, suggesting that it may act as a genetic marker of autism.

However, it is unclear whether the results reflect the visuospatial nature of the task or whether they are related to the inherent complexity of visual working memory tasks, as it has been shown that visuospatial working memory tasks are mediated to a large extent by executive components (Miyake, Friedman, Rettinger, Shah & Hegarty, 2001). In addition, it is unknown whether ocular movements are inherent components of the working memory deficits in autism or if visuospatial working memory deficits would also be found on tasks that do not rely as much on ocular movement. This point is relevant because autistic persons have been shown to present early atypical exploratory behaviours for animates (Klin, Jones, Schultz, Volkmar &

Cohen, 2002) as well as inanimates (Mottron, Mineau, et al., in press). The impairment observed on the saccade working memory task may reflect the fact that the gaze impairment in autism is more apparent in more sensitive paradigms.

The performance of autistic persons in visuospatial working memory tasks that do not involve saccade measurements has been inconsistent. In the majority of studies, autistic participants exhibit normal performance on span tasks that involve the reproduction of a visuospatial sequence. This is the case when tested with simple visuospatial span procedures, such as the Corsi task or location span tasks. For example, we have used a computerized spatial span task in which participants were presented with a matrix of 16 squares distributed randomly on a computer screen. A series of squares of increasing number was darkened and the participant's task was to point to the box that had been darkened. There were two conditions. One relied on spatial memory, as squares were darkened one after the other and participants were asked to report them in order. The other condition relied on visual/configurational memory as the whole series of squares darkened simultaneously, thus creating a pattern that participants were asked to reproduce by pointing to the appropriate squares. In both conditions, autistic persons performed at the same level as typical persons matched on chronological age and global intelligence (Ménard et al., in preparation-a). Ozonoff and Strayer (2001) also reported a normal visuospatial span in persons with HFA using a task that involved the reproduction of the location of previously presented shapes. However, some studies have reported a tendency for impaired spatial span in autistic children (Geurts, Verté, Oosterlaan, Roeyers, & Sergeant, 2004).

Overall, the use of classical visuospatial span measures has revealed typical performance in autistic persons. Yet, there are indications that positional memory is impaired when using an oculomotor delayed response task, in which participants make a saccade to the position of a previous target.

The attentional component of working memory

The impairment exhibited by autistic persons on executive tasks (Ozonoff et al., 1991; Rumsey, 1985; Rumsey & Hamburger, 1988, 1990; Steel, Gorman & Flexman, 1984) suggests that the attentional controller (or central executive component) of working memory may be particularly sensitive to the disorder. Considering the proposed fractionation of the attentional component of working memory, investigating the pattern of impairments and strengths of fractionated attentional processes may provide indicators of qualitative differences between typical and autistic persons. In this section, we will focus on four of them: inhibition, manipulation, updating and attention sharing.

Inhibition

One important factor influencing the amount of interference in working memory is the ability to select relevant answers and inhibit irrelevant ones (Hasher & Zacks, 1988). This aptitude is selectively impaired in frontal-injured individuals, which explains their increased susceptibility to interference (e.g., Shimamura, Jurica, Mangels, Gershberg & Knight, 1995; van der Linden, Bruyer, Rolland & Schils, 1993). In the Stroop paradigm, participants are presented with colour words that are printed in an incompatible colour of ink (e.g., the word *green* printed in red) and asked to name the colour of the ink. Typical participants are impaired by the incongruence between the word and its colour. The Stroop effect is a classical way to measure inhibition; when tested with it, autistic persons are unimpaired (Bryson, 1983; Ozonoff & Jensen, 1999). Autistic persons also show normal performance on the negative priming task, where participants are asked to identify an item that has been a distractor, i.e., that has been inhibited, in the preceding trial (Ozonoff & Strayer, 1997). This is coherent with our own findings in savant syndrome, which indicate that these individuals can present with normal or better than normal inhibition abilities when tested with linguistic material (Mottron, Belleville, Stip, & Morasse 1998). Similarly, Pennington and Ozonoff (1996) reported that among the different executive capacities, inhibition capacities were left unimpaired by autism.

Notably, there are exceptions to this pattern. First, there are contradictory findings on measures of motor inhibition. In the stop-signal paradigm, participants are asked to respond to repetitive items but, on random trials, a signal occurs to indicate that participants must withhold their response on that trial. Thus, they need to inhibit an ongoing or planned action (Logan, 1994). Using variants of the stop-signal paradigm, one study found normal performance in HFA adolescents (Ozonoff & Strayer, 1997) and another reported impairment in slightly younger HFA persons (mean age = 14 vs. 9 years; Geurts et al., 2004). However, the latter study used a more complex paradigm than the former, as it also implicated a response shift from the participant. As response shifting and cognitive flexibility is typically impaired in autism (Hill, 2004; Pennington & Ozonoff, 1996; Sergeant, Geurts & Oosterlaan, 2002), this added component might actually account for the deficit by increasing the task complexity. Second, the latter study found that whereas performance of HFA was impaired relative to chronological age matched control participants, it was comparable to that of ADHD children. Thus, the impairment is not specific to autism.

Results from the go/no-go paradigm, another task of motor inhibition, are also controversial. In this task, participants are presented with series of stimuli. They are asked to respond to some of them and refrain from responding to others (e.g., press a button when a circle is presented but make no response when the square is presented). Noterdaeme, Amorosa, Mildenberger, Sitter and Minow (2001) failed to find group differences on this task. Ozonoff,

Strayer, McMahon and Filloux (1994) also reported normal performance on the typical go/no-go paradigm in HFA children and adolescents. However, the authors included additional conditions in which autistic persons were impaired. In subsequent blocks, there was a reversal of the stimulus that was responded to and the one that was inhibited. In these conditions, a prepotent response needs to be inhibited and participants are required to switch response sets. Under this circumstance, autistic persons exhibited significant impairment relative to matched healthy controls and persons with Tourette syndrome. Notably, however, autistic persons were able to improve their ability on these conditions when provided with additional trials.

Minshew and collaborators (1999) reported impaired performance in HFA adults on the antisaccade response suppression task. In the antisaccade task, a visual stimulus occurs randomly on either side of a fixation point placed in the centre of a screen. Participants are asked to refrain from looking at the stimulus and to look at the same position in the opposite hemifield. To optimize performance, participants must resist their tendency to shift their gaze to the target and must thus suppress an automatic saccade. Autistic persons show a decrease in their ability to suppress the saccade, a result suggesting that inhibition deficits may occur in autism within the spatial/saccadic domain. These deficits have been interpreted as resulting from anomalies in the circuitry of the prefrontal cortex and its connection with parietal areas (Minshew et al., 1999). HFA adolescents also exhibit impaired performance on an incompatibility task, which bears some resemblance to the antisaccade task (Noterdaeme et al., 2001). In the incompatibility task, participants are presented with arrows located on the left or right side of a central fixation point. They are asked to press the key that corresponds to the direction of the arrow, but to pay no attention to its location in the visual field. On this task, autistic persons were significantly slower than a comparison group matched on chronological age and nonverbal intelligence: They were impaired by the incompatibility between the direction pointed by the arrow and its location in the visual field.

Manipulation

A number of working memory tasks require concurrent manipulation and maintenance of information. Bennetto and collaborators (1996) have reported impaired performance on a sentence span task (Daneman & Carpenter, 1980) in which participants were asked to generate the last word of a sentence and report the generated words at the end of a set of two–six sentences. They also found impairment on a counting span task in which participants were asked to count aloud dots printed on cards, and then report the numbers corresponding to a set of two–six cards. Participants were adolescents with HFA and adults with an average IQ in the low range (82). They were compared with a group of persons with various developmental disorders, the majority of whose members were dyslexic, and matched on chronological age and verbal intelligence. On the basis of these findings, Bennetto and collaborators proposed the presence of a general working memory deficit in autism. These authors proposed that a working memory deficit prevents individuals with autism from solving context-specific problems that require integration of multiple pieces of information over space and time. Specifically, they suggested that the working memory impairment is related to more global aspects of social impairment, such as the failure to integrate highly loaded information over time.

However, in sentence and counting span tasks, storage and processing are performed concurrently and the task thus requires both storage capacities and processing capacities. The normal short-term memory capacities shown by persons with HFA on span tasks suggests that they do not have to struggle with the storage aspect of the task. However, impairment of processing efficiency or the ability to perform sentence comprehension and/or counting operations may produce deficits on these working memory tasks. In this particular case, it is possible that persons with autism had more difficulty with the sentence span task because of the requirement to generate a relevant word. Alternatively, impairment on the counting span task may result from slower scanning of the visually presented material. Increasing the processing load of the task could result in a smaller maintenance capacity. Thus, it is possible that the deficits in sentence and counting span do not actually reflect true working memory impairment.

Importantly, the working memory impairment reported by Bennetto and collaborators (1996) has not been supported by other studies. Russell and collaborators (1996) tested persons with LFA (mean age = 12) on similar paradigms. The comparison groups included younger children and children with moderate learning difficulties. Participants were tested on three tasks of working memory: a counting task, a sum task and an odd-man-out task. All three included a simple and complex version. The counting span task was similar to that described above, but the presentation was canonical (similar to that seen on dice) in the simple condition or in a random visual array in the complex condition. In the odd-man-out task, participants were asked to identify the position of a black dot that appeared in one of three positions (simple condition). In the complex version of the task, the participant was asked to locate among three patterns the one that differed from the other two. He or she was then asked to recall the position of the located patterns. In the sum task, participants were asked to recall the results of a set of additions that were either simply read out loud (simple condition) or that were actually produced by the child (complex condition). In this study, processing time (for example, the time it took to count the items) was also measured and used as a covariate in the analysis. Russell and collaborators found that autistic persons performed more poorly than chronological age matched typical participants, but did not differ from a group of mental age matched persons with moderate learning difficulties. Processing time was related to performance but did not modify the nature of the effect when used as a covariate. The authors proposed that working memory impairment, as measured with complex span, was not a specific marker of autism but could represent a marker of mental handicap. They also concluded that the planning deficits exhibited by autistic individuals could not be readily accounted for by an inability to maintain the task components in working memory space.

Recently, we used two tasks that measured concurrent manipulation and retention, and our findings supported the Russell et al. (1996) data (Ménard, Belleville & Mottron, 1998; Ménard, Belleville & Mottron, in preparation-b). In the Alpha Span Task (Belleville, Rouleau & Caza, 1998), participants are asked to report a series of words in their correct order or in alphabetical order. In this latter condition, participants must both maintain and mentally rearrange the words. The task takes into account the storage capacity of each individual by using sequence lengths that correspond to each person's span. Furthermore, difficulty level was manipulated by presenting series the size of which corresponded to the span of each participant, and series corresponding to the span of each participant plus one item. This task has been shown to recruit the bilateral prefrontal dorsolateral cortex (Collette et al., 1999) and thus corresponds to Petrides' (1995) manipulation and monitoring component of working memory. Participants were also tested with the letter number sequencing task of the WAIS-III (Wechsler, 1997), which involves rearranging a series of digits and letters in numerical/alphabetical order. In both tasks, persons with HFA performed in a similar manner as chronological age and global intelligence matched controls.

Updating

The *n*-back task can be used to measure the autistic person's ability to continuously update the contents of their working memory. In this task, individuals are presented with series of items and are asked to report whether the item presented is the same as that presented one to three items earlier. Ozonoff and Strayer (2001) have used a 1-back and 2-back condition with geometrical shapes in HFA adolescents (IQ = 95; age = 155 months), persons with Tourette syndrome and typical controls matched on chronological age, and verbal performance and global intelligence. No group difference was found on the task with either RT or accuracy as a dependent variable (Ozonoff & Strayer, 2001). We have also found intact performance on the *n*-back task using verbal material (consonants), even when increasing the difficulty level by including the 3-back condition (Ménard et al., in preparation-b).

Autistic persons also perform normally on the self-ordered pointing task, a task that requires pointing to different items from a series on each trial, as well as the manipulation and updating of information (Geurts et al., 2004). Normal performance was found in a spatial variant of the self-ordered pointing task, the box search task, in which participants were asked to explore a set of boxes placed in different locations with the constraint of never returning to the same box (Ozonoff & Strayer, 2001).

Dual tasking

Baddeley (1996) conceptualized the working memory component of the central executive as a system that has, among other functions, the capacity to allocate one's attentional resources between two competing tasks. Although a divided attention dysfunction is supported by observations of overselectivity of attention and shifting difficulties in individuals with autism, only a few studies have examined their capacity in dual tasking.

Ciesielski, Knight, Prince, Harris and Handmaker (1995) were interested in the pattern of brain activity in adolescents and young adults with HFA in the context of a crossmodal divided attention task. They recorded ERPs (event-related potentials) in conditions of focused and divided attention. Participants were asked to respond to a visual target (visual focused condition), a target sound (auditory focused condition) or to both stimuli (divided attention condition). The results on the behavioural measures were not compelling. However, in both the focused and divided attention conditions, autistic persons had a lower discrimination rate than typical participants matched on handedness and chronological age. Thus, the task was globally more difficult for autistic participants. Autistic participants also had a higher false alarm rate in the focused than divided attention condition, contrary to what would be expected in the presence of an attentional impairment. On ERP measures, the study indicated that the clinical group did not show the task modulation effect on the Slow Negative Wave (a large frontally distributed wave) found in typical participants. This wave indexes a general attentional resource system. The pattern of results (unimpaired divided attention with absence of SNW modulation) was interpreted as reflecting the use in autistic persons of an automatic and rapid switching of attention between the two tasks. Note that one important problem in this study is that the groups differed significantly in IQ, with the clinical group having a lower intelligence level. Thus, the group effect on ERPs could be accounted for by IQ differences.

A deficit in divided attention was found by Casey, Gordon, Mannheim and Rumsey (1993). They tested adults with autism and persons with PDD-NOS who displayed savant skills in calendar calculation. The paradigm combined a selective attention task with visual (letter detection) and auditory (tone detection) stimuli. In the divided attention condition, autistic persons detected fewer targets than controls, regardless of the modality. The authors noted a tendency to focus on one modality at the expense of the other, suggesting the possibility of a trade-off effect. Autistic persons also showed a modest but significant decrement on both tasks in the focused attention condition. The authors interpreted their results as arising from deficient orienting responses: Autistic persons experience a depletion of attentional resources for incoming stimulation when they are engaged in an attention-demanding task. The decrement in dual task performance is thought to result from this deficit in flexible shifting of attention (Casey et al., 1993).

One problem in interpreting some of the aforementioned findings is that the difficulty level of the individual tasks combined in the divided attention condition was not adjusted to the capacity of each individual. In both studies, autistic persons were impaired relative to chronological age matched controls when performing the task in *focused* attention. If autistic persons were at a disadvantage in performing one of the tasks in isolation, this would obviously result in a higher level of difficulty than that for controls when asked to combine the tasks.

In our laboratory, this was controlled by using a dual task taken from the Côte-des-Neiges computerized memory assessment battery (*Batterie d'évaluation de la mémoire de Côte-des-Neiges*; Belleville et al., 1992; Chatelois et al., 1992) and inspired by Baddeley, Logie, Bressi, Della Sala and Spinnler (1986). The dual task paradigm combines a visuomotor tracking task and a digit recall task. Blocks of focused and divided attention conditions were alternated using an ABBA design. The speed of the tracking task and the number of digits to recall was individually adjusted to equalize the difficulty level of individual tasks across participants. There were two difficulty levels: one in which digit recall was tested with series lengths corresponding to each participant's span, and one in which it was tested with series corresponding to each participant's span plus one item. In the divided attention condition, participants with HFA did not differ on the percent of digits correctly recalled. On the tracking task, participants with HFA performed more poorly than the controls who were matched on chronological age and global intelligence in the first divided attention block, but their performance was comparable to that of controls on the second block (Ménard et al., in preparation-b; Ménard, Belleville & Fecteau, 1999). These results may indicate that persons with HFA have difficulties allocating attention when two tasks must be performed simultaneously. However, practice improved their ability and increased their adjustment to the task demand, rendering them capable of attaining an optimal performance level.

In a recent study, Hoeksma, Kemner, Verbaten and van Engeland (2004) provided ERP findings suggesting a difficulty in attentional shifting. HFA children and adolescents performed an auditory task (primary task), combined with the visual presentation of irrelevant probes (passive secondary task). The authors examined whether performing a primary task of increasing difficulty reduced the attentional capacity that was devoted to the irrelevant task. Thus, there were two difficulty levels for the primary task. The easy condition was a go/no-go task with animal sounds. In the difficult condition, participants were also asked to compare consecutive sounds. The visual probes were presented between the auditory stimuli and no response was required. All participants performed at a comparable level on those tasks. However, ERP data for autistic children indicated that the attention devoted to the irrelevant stimuli was not reduced by the accomplishment of a concurrent complex task. Contrary to age matched typical persons, the amplitude evoked by irrelevant probes was not diminished in the hard condition relative to the easy condition. A reduction in the amplitude elicited by the irrelevant sound indicates that the attentional or processing capacity that is devoted to the irrelevant task must be transferred to perform the primary task. The authors suggest that the differences between autistic and typical participants arise from difficulties experienced by people with autism in allocating attention flexibly to the most salient and relevant events. Importantly, the anomalous ERP pattern was not found in adolescent HFA, indicating that this allocation difference is developmentally transient.

Summary

Autistic persons exhibit only partial impairment on tasks of attentional control. These individuals perform at a normal level on updating tasks. Although the results of one experiment revealed impairment in manipulation tasks, this finding was not replicated in at least two other studies. Performance on classical inhibition tasks such as the Stroop task or negative priming test is normal. Response inhibition, as measured by the stop-signal or the classical go/no-go procedure, is also normal. However, autistic persons exhibit difficulties in the go/no-go procedure when there is a switch in the stimulus that is associated with response inhibition. Furthermore, there are indications for inhibition impairments when using antisaccade-type procedures. In the majority of studies, divided attention is normal at the behavioural level. Nonetheless, some studies have provided data suggesting differences in the way autistic persons allocate their resources as a function of task demand.

WORKING MEMORY IN SPECIAL ABILITIES

Persons with autism show a characteristic cognitive profile marked by strengths in certain areas and weaknesses in others (Rumsey & Hamburger, 1988). The most fascinating aspect of this polarity is undoubtedly the "special abilities" displayed by certain autistic individuals. These are defined as abilities in which levels of performance far exceed expectations based on a participant's IQ. In some cases, the level of performance reached by persons with a special ability attains or exceeds the level reached by experts in the same field. Special abilities are generally found in the domains of music, memorization of lists, three-dimensional drawing, reading (hyperlexia), and calendar and mental calculation. Special abilities have been proposed to represent a means of understanding the autistic cognitive deficit (Mottron & Belleville, 1993a). They can also be used as a way of understanding the interaction between expertise, cognition and memory. An important question regarding special abilities is whether they are reached by means of memory and whether they rely on the same mechanisms as those seen in typical experts (Mottron, Lemmens, Gagnon & Seron, 2006). Another question is whether the knowledge base underlying the expertise increases working memory performance for the domain in which autistic savants have developed their particular level of expertise.

Charness, Clifton and MacDonald (1988) examined short-term memory in a savant LFA musician. His short-term memory for musical material was comparable to that of typical musicians and was sensitive to the same musical dimensions (e.g., rhythmic grouping, scale), suggesting that the underlying memory processes are not atypical or qualitatively different in autistic savant musicians and typical musicians.

Studies comparing the intellectual profile of autistic persons with and without special abilities have found a significant superiority for savant individuals in the digit span subtest of the WAIS-R (Bölte & Poustka, 2004; Steel et al., 1984; Stevens & Moffitt, 1988). This result suggests that short-term memory may be enhanced in this population and, consequently, may be linked to special abilities. However, because the majority of savants in these studies were calculators, the enhanced short-term memory capacity may be material specific, that is, restricted to digits. Heavey, Pring and Hermelin (1999) have assessed the digit and word span recall of eight calendar calculators. There was no significant difference between individuals with and without special abilities. However, a simple effects analysis revealed that the savants demonstrated an advantage with digits, a type of stimuli more related to their ability. Thus, calendar calculators may have an enhanced short-term memory that is restricted to digit material.

In a recent study, we examined whether similar results were found for different skills. We evaluated the short-term memory of savants who possess different special abilities to examine whether different skills would be accompanied by enhanced memory in the same domain. Four persons with pervasive developmental disorder (autism or Asperger's syndrome) were tested, each of them having a particular ability: a calendar calculator, a savant calculator, a musician with absolute pitch (capacity to identify or produce a note without a reference note) and a hyperlexic child. Short-term memory was evaluated with several materials to examine whether these memory abilities were specific to the domain of expertise, of whether they generalized to other materials. Recognition tasks were used with four types of material: musical (notes), phonological (pseudowords), lexical (grammatical items) and numerical. Binary sequences of items were created by combining two items from each domain (e.g., 9–5–5–9). Musical sequences were made by combining a low pitch note (C^4) and a high pitch note (C^5). Two nonsense syllables ("RAN-BIJ" in French) served to construct the phonological sequences. When presented in isolation, function words can reflect the contribution of lexical representations because they have little semantic content (Caza & Belleville, 1999). Thus, two French function words ("tel – donc" in French) were used to construct lexical sequences. Finally, the numerical sequences were constructed by combining the digits 5 and 9. The length of the sequences varied between two and eight randomly presented items. Each target sequence was immediately followed by a comparison sequence. Participants performed a yes/no recognition judgement of the comparison sequence. Notably, the sequences were binary, which means that they were composed of only two items repeated in the sequence. This likely increased the impact of the memory for the order of the stimuli relative to memory for their identity. As a result, it may have reduced the specific impact of material type on memory.

The results confirmed that short-term memory is not impaired in autistic persons and also that persons with savant syndrome generally perform above IQ matched participants, and therefore above their IQ level, on short-term memory tasks, thus supporting previous findings (Bölte & Poustka, 2004; Steel et al., 1984; Stevens & Moffitt, 1988). However, this increased performance was particularly striking in the calendar calculator and in the savant calculator (who performed 4 *SD* and almost 2 *SD* above controls, respectively, when using function words). Furthermore, this pattern was not specific to numerical sequences. The calendar calculator performed well with pseudowords, function words and numerical material, and the savant calculator performed well on lexical sequences (function words). Thus, contrary to the savants described in Heavey et al. (1999), enhanced short-term memory was found in a range of domains larger than their apparent area of expertise and overtraining. This may be due to the particular procedure used here. Heavey and collaborators used words, but we used pseudowords and function words, both types of items being devoid of semantic content.

In spite of apparent differences, the materials on which the calculators outperformed their comparison group (memorizing a sequence of function words) share some "abstract" properties with their savant capabilities (numbers and calendrical information). First, the units are devoid of semantic content, as are numbers, digits and calendrical information (months, days). The type of network representing digits and calendar units clearly differs from those composing semantic memory. Second, the units composing the sequences are roughly the same size (a few letters) and composed of the same subunits (phonological representations). Third, the level of complexity of the task (memorizing chains of unitary representations) is similar. Fourth, calendar calculators and calculators in general rely heavily on order representations as they memorize sequences of dates, days, months and years and/or highly organized numerical patterns, and our tasks clearly stressed memory of item order. It is possible that the similarity between the tasks on which calendar calculators are overtrained and the tasks used here are responsible for participants' strong performance.

CONCLUSION

The impairment exhibited by autistic persons in classical measures of executive functions motivated the suggestion of an executive deficit hypothesis. In this realm, the presence of a working memory impairment has been proposed as representing a key component that explains the cognitive pattern exhibited by autistic persons. Because working memory is involved in such a wide range of human activities, its impairment is viewed as a potential source of the pervasive aspect of the autistic symptomatology.

Clearly, working memory is not a single homogeneous system and studies on its impairment in autism must take into account its complexity, as well as the different views that now exist to conceptualize this system. When reviewing the existing literature and using a rather broad definition of working memory, a relatively clear pattern of intact and impaired processes arises. First, there is a range of intact processes. Central inhibition or inhibition of well known schemas, such as those measured by the Stroop task or by negative priming, is intact. The majority of studies indicate normal abilities by persons with autism in the manipulation and updating of information.

There are also atypicalities in some aspects of working memory. The phonological loop is generally normal, as is the verbal span, although the presence of a savant syndrome in autistic participants appears to modulate this effect by increasing span in savant persons, particularly calculators. However, a larger word length effect has been reported in autistic than typical individuals when tested with visual material. This appears not as a deficit *per se*, but could be interpreted as a mandatory use of superficial level of information in tasks where typical participants rely more on semantic features. Autistic persons exhibit normal performance on visuospatial span tasks, which reflect some aspects of the visuospatial sketchpad. However, visuospatial working memory is impaired when tested with visual saccades (delayed oculomotor task). An inhibition impairment is found when tested with the antisaccade and incompatibility tasks and autistic persons show difficulties in inhibiting a prepotent response and/or in shifting response sets in a go/no-go paradigm. Finally, the performance on task sharing is better described as qualitatively different rather than impaired per se. The anomalies reported are relatively modest at the behavioural level, as some of them can be overcome with practice and there are indications that they are developmentally transient.

Is there a manner in which this particular pattern of preserved and impaired performance can be reconciled? There is in fact little evidence for a general working memory impairment in autism. In addition, the pattern of performance is not easily explained in terms of impairment of a particular attentional control component of working memory, such as divided attention or inhibition. Inhibition is impaired, but only when using antisaccade types of paradigms or switching procedures. Divided attention capacities are only modestly reduced. Notably, performance on many tasks that include a switching component are found to be deficient or anomalous in autistic persons, suggesting that allocation strategies or shifting capacities may be different in this population. This is an interesting hypothesis that needs to be tested directly using formal switching tasks.

Another question is whether the pattern of impaired and intact functions is more easily interpreted as reflecting impairments in particular processing domains rather than in a particular controlled process. For example, autistic persons are particularly impaired when using tasks involving saccade responses. This has been found in two relatively different tasks (delayed recall and inhibition of a saccade). There is increasing evidence that gaze processing is atypical in autistic persons. These anomalies may be accompanied by an impairment in the ability to perform working memory tasks that rely on these processes and there may not be something specific to working memory in this particular impairment. Thus, the nature of the material used or the type of response may stand out as a significant factor in determining the presence and nature of the working memory deficit in autism.

One last issue that is worthy of discussion concerns the inherent complexity in finding the appropriate comparison group and its impact on the interpretation of the data. Autistic savants often have a lower IQ than the typical population and this has led researchers to use comparison groups of a younger age and/or with other neurological disorders. However, this is a rather simplistic conception of how developmental and/or neurodevelopmental disorders affect cognition. Specifically, this approach promotes the view that differences in development or neurodevelopment only have quantitative and linear effects on cognition. Yet, we know that both younger age and neurological disorders can yield qualitative modifications in the cognitive processes, rendering their use as comparison groups extremely problematic. In addition, the use of developmental age as a current matching procedure suggests that variation in intelligence is amenable to variations in age and that persons with a lower IQ necessarily perform in a similar way as younger persons. Obviously, this may not be the case for all cognitive processes. Testing autistic persons with normal intelligence simplifies the choice of a comparison group because typical persons can then be used. However, some researchers have suggested that work on autism must be conducted in both HFA and LFA persons to allow for a true generalization to the disorder (Mottron, 2004). The problem of IQ comparison is particularly relevant within an approach that investigates working memory. Engle, Tuholski, Laughlin and Conway (1999) have shown that complex working memory tasks (but not simple span tasks) are high predictors of fluid intelligence, and both complex working memory and fluid intelligence are mediated by the prefrontal cortex (see Conway, Kane & Engle, 2003, for a discussion). Thus, although fluid intelligence and working memory are not similar constructs, they do have considerable overlap. This observation raises concerns regarding the choice of an appropriate IQ matching strategy when investigating working memory in autism.

To conclude, there are exciting questions that remain to be answered in the field of working memory and autism. One is the particular role that different verbal properties have on immediate serial recall, particularly given the intriguing finding of a larger word length effect in these individuals. Another question is how savant syndrome actually reconfigures the cognitive system to yield improved performance on such a simple test as span. Another challenge is to use our knowledge on working memory to devise cognitive interventions that could help to improve the ways in which this system functions in autistic persons. Finally, persons with autism are less homogeneous in terms of expertise than are typical individuals (i.e., their repetitive life experiences result in an overexposure to some types of material and to over-practice effects for some cognitive operations). Therefore, the somewhat inconsistent pattern of findings presented here remains to be abstracted in a formulation independent of the specific type of training received by the participant.

NOTE

1   Writing of this chapter was supported by grants from SSHRC and CIHR to LM and SB, by a grant from NSERC to SB and LM, by an FRSQ Chercheur-boursier fellowship to LM, an FRSQ Chercheur national fellowship to SB and by an NSERC summer student award to MCM. We would like to thank Janet Boseovski for revising the manuscript.

REFERENCES

Allport, D. A. (1983). Auditory-verbal short-term memory and conduction aphasia. In H. Bouma & D. G. Bouwhuis (Eds.), *Attention and performance X: Control of language processes* (pp. 313–325). London: Lawrence Erlbaum Associates Ltd.

Allport, D. A. (1985). Distributed memory, modular subsystems and dysphasia. In S. Newman & R. Epstein (Eds.), *Current perspective in dysphasia* (pp. 32–60). London: Churchill Livingstone.

American Psychiatric Association. (1994). *Diagnostic and statistical manual of mental disorders* (4th ed.). Washington, DC: Author.

Baddeley, A. D. (1986). *Working memory*. Oxford, UK: Clarendon Press.

Baddeley, A. D. (1996). Exploring the central executive. *Quarterly Journal of Experimental Psychology, 49A,* 5–28.

Baddeley, A. D., & Hitch, G. (1974). Working memory. In G. Bower (Ed.), *The psychology of learning and motivation* (Vol. 8, pp. 47–90). New York: Academic Press.

Baddeley, A. D., Logie, R., Bressi, S., Della Sala, S., & Spinnler, H. (1986). Dementia and working memory. *Quarterly Journal of Experimental Psychology, 38A,* 603–618.

Baron-Cohen, S., Leslie, A. M., & Frith, U. (1985). Does the autistic child have a "theory of mind"? *Cognition, 21,* 37–46.

Belleville, S., Caza, N., & Peretz, I. (2003). A neuropsychological argument for a processing view of memory. *Journal of Memory and Language, 48,* 686–703.

Belleville, S., Chatelois, J., Fontaine, S. F., Lussier, I., Peretz, I., Pineau, H., et al. (1992). *Batterie d'évaluation de la mémoire Côte-des-Neiges.* Montréal, Canada: Centre de recherche du Centre Hospitalier Côte-des-Neiges.

Belleville, S., Peretz, I., & Malenfant, D. (1996). Examination of the working memory components in normal aging and in dementia of the Alzheimer type. *Neuropsychologia, 34*, 195–207.

Belleville, S., Rouleau, N., & Caza, N. (1998). Effect of normal aging on the manipulation of information in working memory. *Memory and Cognition, 26*, 572–583.

Belleville, S., Rouleau, N., van der Linden, M., & Collette, F. (2003). Effect of manipulation and irrelevant noise on working memory capacity of patients with Alzheimer's dementia. *Neuropsychology, 17*, 69–81.

Bennetto, L., Pennington, B. F., & Rogers, S. J. (1996). Intact and impaired memory functions in autism. *Child Development, 67*, 1816–1835.

Boucher, J. (1978). Echoic memory capacity in autistic children. *Journal of Child Psychology and Psychiatry, 19*, 161–166.

Bölte, S., & Poustka, F. (2004). Comparing the intelligence profiles of savant and nonsavant individuals with autistic disorder. *Intelligence, 32*, 121–131.

Bryson, S. E. (1983). Interference effects in autistic children: Evidence for the comprehension of single stimuli. *Journal of Abnormal Psychology, 92*, 250–254.

Casey, B. J., Gordon, C. T., Mannheim, G. B., & Rumsey, J. M. (1993). Dysfunctional attention in autistic savants. *Journal of Clinical and Experimental Neuropsychology, 15*, 933–946.

Caza, N., & Belleville, S. (1999). Semantic contribution to immediate serial recall using an unlimited set of items: Evidence for a multi-level capacity view of short-term memory. *International Journal of Psychology, 34*, 334–338.

Charness, N., Clifton, J., & MacDonald, L. (1988). Case study of a musical mono-savant. In L. K. Obler & D. A. Fein (Eds.), *The exceptional brain: Neuropsychology of talent and special abilities* (pp. 277–293). New York: Guilford Press.

Chatelois, J., Pineau, H., Belleville, S., Peretz, I., Lussier, I., Fontaine, F., & Renaseau-Leclerc, C. (1992). Batterie informatisée d'évaluation de la mémoire inspirée de l'approche cognitive. *Psychologie Canadienne, 34*, 45–63.

Ciesielski, K. T., Knight, J. E., Prince, R. J., Harris, R. J., & Handmaker, S. D. (1995). Event-related potentials in cross-modal divided attention in autism. *Neuropsychologia, 33*, 225–246.

Collette, F., Salmon, E., van der Linden, M., Chicherio, C., Belleville, S., Degueldre, C., et al. (1999). Regional brain activity during tasks devoted to the central executive of working memory. *Cognitive Brain Research, 7*, 411–417.

Conway, A. R. A., Kane, M. J., & Engle, R. W. (2003). Working memory capacity and its relation to general intelligence. *Trends in Cognitive Sciences, 7*, 547–552.

Crowder, R. G. (1989). Modularity and dissociations in memory systems. In H. L. Roediger, III, & F. I. M. Craik (Eds.), *Varieties of memory and consciousness: Essays in honour of Endel Tulving* (pp. 271–294). Hillsdale, NJ: Lawrence Erlbaum Associates, Inc.

Daneman, M., & Carpenter, P. A. (1980). Individual differences in working memory and reading. *Journal of Verbal Learning and Verbal Behavior, 19*, 450–466.

Engle, R. W. (2002). Working memory capacity as executive attention. *Current Directions in Psychological Science, 11*, 19–23.

Engle, R. W., Tuholski, S. W., Laughlin, J. E., & Conway, A. R. A. (1999). Working memory, short-term memory and general fluid intelligence: A latent variable approach. *Journal of Experimental Psychology: General, 128*, 309–331.

Frith, U. (2003). *Autism: Explaining the enigma* (2nd ed.). Oxford, UK: Basil Blackwell. (Original work published 1989)

Geurts, H. M., Verté, S., Oosterlaan, J., Roeyers, H., & Sergeant, J. A. (2004). How specific are executive functioning deficits in attention deficit hyperactivity disorder and autism? *Journal of Child Psychology and Psychiatry, 45,* 836–854.

Gilbert, B., Belleville, S., Bherer, L., & Chouinard, S. (2005). A study of working memory in Parkinson's disease. *Neuropsychology, 19,* 106–114.

Hasher, L., & Zacks, R. T. (1988). Working memory, comprehension, and aging: A review and a new view. In G. H. Bower (Ed.), *The psychology of learning and motivation* (Vol. 22, pp. 193–225). San Diego, CA: Academic Press.

Heavey, L., Pring, L., & Hermelin, B. (1999). A date to remember: The nature of memory in savant calendrical calculators. *Psychological Medicine, 29,* 145–160.

Hill, E. L. (2004). Executive dysfunction in autism. *Trends in Cognitive Sciences, 8,* 26–32.

Hoeksma, M. R., Kemner, C., Verbaten, M. N., & van Engeland, H. (2004). Processing capacity in children and adolescents with pervasive developmental disorders. *Journal of Autism and Developmental Disorders, 34,* 341–354.

Hughes, C., & Russell, J. (1993). Autistic children's difficulty with mental disengagement from an object: Its implications for theories of autism. *Developmental Psychology, 29,* 498–510.

Klin, A., Jones, W., Schultz, R. T., Volkmar, F. R., & Cohen, D. (2002). Visual fixation patterns during viewing of naturalistic social situations as predictors of social competence in individuals with autism. *Archives of General Psychiatry, 59,* 809–816.

Koczat, D. L., Rogers, S. J., Pennington, B. F., & Ross, R. G. (2002). Eye movement abnormality suggestive of a spatial working memory deficits is present in parents of autistic probands. *Journal of Autism and Developmental Disorders, 32,* 513–518.

Logan, G. D. (1994). On the ability to inhibit thought and action. In D. Dagenbach & T. H. Carr (Eds.), *Inhibitory processes in attention, memory and language* (pp. 189–239). San Diego, CA: Academic Press.

Luna, B., Minshew, N. J., Garver, K. E., Lazar, N. A., Thulborn, K. R., Eddy, W. F., & Sweeney, J. A. (2002). Neocortical system abnormalities in autism: An fMRI study of spatial working memory. *Neurology, 59,* 834–840.

Martin, R. C., Lesch, M. F., & Bartha, M. C. (1999). Independence of input and output phonology in word processing and short-term memory. *Journal of Memory and Language, 41,* 3–29.

Martin, R. C., & Romani, C. (1994). Verbal working memory and sentence comprehension: A multiple-components view. *Neuropsychology, 8,* 506–523.

Martin, N., & Saffran, E. M. (1997). Language and auditory-verbal short-term memory impairments: Evidence for common underlying processes. *Cognitive Neuropsychology, 14,* 641–682.

Ménard, E., Belleville, S., & Fecteau, S. (1999). *Is there a working memory deficit in autism?* Albuquerque, NM: Society for Research in Child Development (SRCD).

Ménard, E., Belleville, S., & Mottron, L. (1998). Evaluation de la mémoire de travail chez des personnes autistes de haut-niveau. *Science et Comportement, 27,* S-156.

Ménard, E., Belleville, S., & Mottron, L. (in preparation-a). Characterization of the working memory processes in persons with high-functioning autism and Asperger's syndrome.

Ménard, E., Belleville, S., & Mottron, L. (in preparation-b). The executive function of working memory and the complexity theory in persons with high-functioning autism and Asperger's syndrome.

Ménard, E., Mottron, L., Belleville, S., & Limoges, E. (2001). *Executive and phono-articulatory processes of working memory in persons with autism.* Paper presented at the international meeting for Autism Research, San Diego, CA.

Minshew, N. J., & Goldstein, G. (1998). Autism as a disorder of complex information processing. *Mental Retardation and Developmental Disabilities Research Reviews, 4,* 129–136.

Minshew, N. J., Goldstein, G., & Siegel, D. J. (1997). Neuropsychologic functioning in autism: Profile of a complex information processing disorder. *Journal of the International Neuropsychological Society, 3,* 303–316.

Minshew, N. J., Luna, B., & Sweeney, J. A. (1999). Oculomotor evidence for neocortical systems but not cerebellar dysfunction in autism. *Neurology, 52,* 917–922.

Miyake, A., Friedman, N. P., Rettinger, D. A., Shah, P., & Hegarty, M. (2001). How are visuospatial working memory, executive functioning, and spatial abilities related? A latent variable analysis. *Journal of Experimental Psychology: General, 130,* 621–640.

Mottron, L. (2004). Matching strategies in cognitive research with individuals with high-functioning autism: Current practices, instrument biases, and recommendations. *Journal of Autism and Developmental Disorders, 34,* 19–27.

Mottron, L., & Belleville, S. (1993a). L'apport de la neuropsychologie cognitive à l'étude de l'autisme. *Journal of Psychiatry and Neuroscience, 19,* 95–102.

Mottron, L., & Belleville, S. (1993b). A study of perceptual analysis in a high-level autistic subject with exceptional graphic abilities. *Brain and Cognition, 23,* 279–309.

Mottron, L., Belleville, S., Stip, E., & Morasse, K. (1998). Atypical memory performance in an autistic savant. *Memory, 6,* 593–607.

Mottron, L., & Burack, J. (2001). Enhanced perceptual functioning in the development of autism. In J. A. Burack, T. Charman, N. Yirmiya, & P. R. Zelazo (Eds.), *The development of autism: Perspectives from theory and research* (pp. 131–148). Mahwah, NJ: Lawrence Erlbaum Associates, Inc.

Mottron, L., Lemmens, K., Gagnon, L., & Seron, X. (2006). Non-algorithmic access to calendar information in a calendar calculator with autism. *Journal of Autism and Developmental Disorders, 36,* 239–247.

Mottron, L., Mineau, S., Martel, G., Saintonge, C. H., Saint Charles-Bernier, C., Berthiaume, C., et al. (in press). Lateral glances toward moving stimuli among toddlers with autism: Early evidence of locally-oriented perception? *Development and Psychopathology.*

Mottron, L., Morasse, K., & Belleville, S. (2001). A study of memory functioning in individuals with autism. *Journal of Child Psychology and Psychiatry, 42,* 253–260.

Mottron, L., Peretz, I., Belleville, S., & Rouleau, N. (1999). Absolute pitch in autism: A case-study. *Neurocase, 5,* 485–501.

Nairne, J. S. (1990). A feature model of immediate memory. *Memory and Cognition, 18,* 251–269.

Nairne, J. S. (2002). Remembering over the short-term: The case against the standard model. *Annual Review of Psychology, 53,* 53–81.

Norman, D. A., & Shallice, T. (1986). Attention to action: Willed and automatic control of behavior. In R. J. Davidson, G. E. Schwartz, & D. Shapiro (Eds.), *Consciousness and self-regulation: Advances in research and theory.* New York: Plenum Press.

Noterdaeme, M., Amorosa, H., Mildenberger, K., Sitter, S., & Minow, F. (2001). Evaluation of attention problems in children with autism and children with a specific language disorder. *European Child and Adolescent Psychiatry, 10,* 58–66.

Ozonoff, S. (1995). Reliability and validity of the Wisconsin Card Sorting Test in studies of autism. *Neuropsychology, 9,* 491–500.

Ozonoff, S., & Jensen, J. (1999). Brief report: Specific executive function profiles in three neurodevelopmental disorders. *Journal of Autism and Developmental Disorders, 29,* 171–177.

Ozonoff, S., & McEvoy, R. E. (1994). A longitudinal study of executive function theory of mind development in autism. *Development and Psychopathology, 6,* 415–431.

Ozonoff, S., Pennington, B. F., & Rogers, S. J. (1991). Executive function deficits in high-functioning autistic individuals: Relationship to theory of mind. *Journal of Child Psychology and Psychiatry, 32,* 1081–1105.

Ozonoff, S., & Strayer, D. L. (1997). Inhibitory function in nonretarded children with autism. *Journal of Autism and Developmental Disorders, 27,* 59–77.

Ozonoff, S., & Strayer, D. L. (2001). Further evidence of intact working memory in autism. *Journal of Autism and Developmental Disorders, 31,* 257–263.

Ozonoff, S., Strayer, D. L., McMahon, W. M., & Filloux, F. (1994). Executive function abilities in autism and Tourette syndrome: An information processing approach. *Journal of Child Psychology and Psychiatry, 35,* 1015–1032.

Pennington, B. F., & Ozonoff, S. (1996). Executive functions and developmental psychopathology. *Journal of Child Psychology and Psychiatry, 37,* 51–87.

Pennington, B. F., Rogers, S. J., Bennetto, L., Griffith, E., Reed, D., & Shyu, V. (1997). Validity tests of the executive dysfunction hypothesis of autism. In J. Russell (Ed.), *Autism as an executive disorder* (pp. 143–178). New York: Oxford University Press.

Petrides, M. (1995). Functional organization of the human frontal cortex for mnemonic processing. *Annals of the New York Academy of Sciences, 769,* 85–96.

Plaisted, K., O'Riordan, M., & Baron-Cohen, S. (1998). Enhanced discrimination of novel, highly similar stimuli by adults with autism during a perceptual learning task. *Journal of Child Psychology and Psychiatry, 39,* 765–775.

Roberts, R. J., Jr., & Pennington, B. F. (1996). An interactive framework for examining prefrontal cognitive processes. *Developmental Neuropsychology, 12,* 105–126.

Rumsey, J. M. (1985). Conceptual problem-solving in highly verbal, nonretarded autistic men. *Journal of Autism and Developemental Disorders, 15,* 23–36.

Rumsey, J. M., & Hamburger, S. D. (1988). Neuropsychological findings in high-functioning men with infantile autism, residual state. *Journal of Clinical and Experimental Neuropsychology, 10,* 201–221.

Rumsey, J. M., & Hamburger, S. D. (1990). Neuropsychological divergence of high-level autism and severe dyslexia. *Journal of Autism and Developmental Disorders, 20,* 155–168.

Russell, J., Jarrold, C., & Henry, L. (1996). Working memory in children with autism and with moderate learning difficulties. *Journal of Child Psychology and Psychiatry, 37,* 673–686.

Scheuffgen, K., Happé, F., Anderson, M., & Frith, U. (2000). High "intelligence", low "IQ"? Speed of processing and measured IQ in children with autism. *Development and Psychopathology, 12,* 83–90.

Sergeant, J. A., Geurts, H., & Oosterlaan, J. (2002). How specific is a deficit of executive functioning for attention-deficit/hyperactivity disorder? *Behavioural Brain Research, 130,* 3–28.

Shallice, T. (1982). Specific impairments of planning. In D. E. Broadbent &

L. Weiskrantz (Eds.), *The neuropsychology of cognitive function* (pp. 199–209). London: Royal Society.

Shimamura, A. P., Jurica, P. J., Mangels, J. A., Gershberg, F. B., & Knight, R. T. (1995). Susceptibility to memory interference effects following frontal lobe damage: Findings from tests of paired-associate learning. *Journal of Cognitive Neuroscience, 7*, 144–152.

Steel, M. G., Gorman, C. R., & Flexman, J. E., (1984). Neuropsychiatric testing in a autistic mathematical idiot-savant: Evidence for nonverbal abstract capacity. *Journal of the American Academy of Child Psychiatry, 23*, 704–707.

Stevens, D. E., & Moffitt, T. E. (1988). Neuropsychological profile of an Asperger's syndrome case with exceptional calculating ability. *The Clinical Neuropsychologist, 2*, 228–238.

Stuss, D. T., Shallice, T., Alexander, M. P., & Picton, T. W. (1995). A multidisciplinary approach to anterior attentional functions. Annals of the New York Academy of Sciences *769*, 191–211.

Van der Linden, M., Bruyer, R., Rolland, J., & Schils, S. P. (1993). Proactive interference in patients with amnesia resulting from anterior communicating artery aneurysm. *Journal of Clinical and Experimental Neuropsychology, 15*, 525–536.

Volkmar, F. R., Lord, C., Bailey, A., Schultz, R. T., & Klin, A. (2004). Autism and pervasive developmental disorders. *Journal of Child Psychology and Psychiatry, 45*, 135–170.

Wechsler, D. (1997). *Wechsler Adult Intelligence Scale* (3rd ed., Canadian form; WAIS-III. Toronto, Canada: Psychological Corporation.

11 Short-term memory in Down syndrome

Christopher Jarrold, Harry R. M. Purser, and Jon Brock

OVERVIEW

Individuals with Down syndrome consistently show relatively poor perform-ance on tests of verbal short-term memory such as digit span tasks. However, poor performance on such tasks does not necessarily imply that individuals suffer from a fundamental impairment to some verbal short-term system, particularly given that hearing difficulties, speech production problems, and language delay are also associated with the condition and would be expected to adversely affect task performance. In fact the work reviewed here suggests that although these other factors may contribute to the low levels of per-formance typically observed on such tests by individuals with Down syn-drome, there is also evidence for a reduction of verbal short-term memory capacity. The implications of this deficit for the development of vocabulary skills in Down syndrome are discussed, although the data currently do not clearly support the suggestion that vocabulary in Down syndrome is constrained solely by individuals' relatively poor verbal short-term memory.

BACKGROUND TO DOWN SYNDROME

Down syndrome owes its name to J. Langdon Down, who published a description of the condition in the mid-nineteenth century (Langdon Down, 1866), but there is clear evidence that the condition was prevalent prior to this time (Stratford, 1996). It is a genetic condition, caused by a triplication of the 21st chromosome (trisonmy 21). Trisonmy 21 is, in fact, not the only form of trisonmy that occurs in humans. However, the fact that chromosome 21 is the smallest of our chromosomes means that the extra loading of genes associ-ated with Down syndrome has less impact than in other triplications, increas-ing the viability of the individual. Indeed, according to some estimates, Down syndrome is the most common single organic cause of learning disability, with a prevalence of approximately 5 per 10,000 live births (Steele & Stratford, 1995). Although pre-natal screening for Down syndrome is increasingly common in developed countries, any reduction in the birth rate as a result appears to be offset in recent years by a trend for mothers to have children later in life coupled with the fact that the incidence of Down syndrome rises steeply with maternal age (Steele, 1996).

Down syndrome is associated with a number of physiological features, which include a characteristic physiognomy, heart defects, hearing difficulties and speech-motor problems often caused by the presence of cleft palate and enlarged tongue size relative to the oral cavity. In addition, individuals with Down syndrome typically suffer from some degree of mental retardation. As little as 30 years ago (and arguably more recently than this) expectations and outcomes for individuals with Down syndrome were relatively bleak. More recently the advent of early intervention programmes, more sophisticated medical care and higher expectations in general, have led to improvements in the educational levels attained by children with Down syndrome. A number of individuals are educated in a mainstream setting, at least over primary school years, and some can show near to age-appropriate levels of ability. Nevertheless, in general individuals with Down syndrome do suffer from some form of intellectual delay (Carr, 1985).

IMPAIRED VERBAL SHORT-TERM MEMORY PERFORMANCE IN DOWN SYNDROME

Given these general intellectual difficulties, it is perhaps unsurprising that early studies showed that individuals with Down syndrome had poor short-term memory skills. For example, Rohr and Burr (1978; see also Burr & Rohr, 1978) found that a sample of children and teenagers with Down syndrome had auditory and visual memory scores that fell below the 5-years age equivalent level on the Illinois Test of Psycholinguistic Development (ITPA; Kirk, McCarthy & Kirk, 1968). Of more interest is whether memory performance is delayed in Down syndrome relative to individuals' general level of intellectual abilities; or in other words, whether memory performance in Down syndrome is specifically impaired. In fact, studies using tests such as the ITPA or the Stanford-Binet test battery (Thorndike, Hagen & Sattler, 1986) showed that the performance of individuals with Down syndrome on visual memory subtests was in line with general intellectual abilities, but that their performance on the verbal memory subtasks was considerably poorer (Bilovsky & Share, 1965; Bower & Hayes, 1994; Burr & Rohr, 1978; Kay-Raining Bird & Chapman, 1994; Rohr & Burr, 1978; see also Marcell & Armstrong, 1982). The tasks used to assess verbal memory in these studies were all versions of digit span, and consequently these studies provide preliminary evidence of a particular problem in verbal short-term memory in Down syndrome.

However, as Marcell and Armstrong (1982) pointed out, it is not clear that test batteries such as the ITPA provide a proper comparison of verbal and visuospatial short-term memory, because the visual memory subtests do not tap immediate serial recall of visuospatial information in a manner analogous to digit span in the verbal domain. In the ITPA visual memory subtest, participants are shown an abstract design and then have to recreate that design by arranging tiles into the correct configuration. Similarly, the nonverbal "bead memory" subtest of the Stanford-Binet test battery involves the recreation of a visual pattern with appropriate props.

In an attempt to counter this concern, and to provide a more meaningful comparison of verbal and visuospatial short-term memory performance in Down syndrome, Marcell and Armstrong (1982) explored the magnitude of the modality effect in immediate serial recall among typically developing children and individuals with Down syndrome. That is, they compared short-term memory for digits that were presented either auditorily or visually. These authors showed that, while typically developing children showed superior performance for auditorily rather than visually presented digits as would be expected given previous research (Dilley & Paivio, 1968), individuals with Down syndrome showed no such advantage. Similarly, McDade and Adler (1980) found that their sample of children with Down syndrome showed impaired recall of auditorily presented digits, but unimpaired recall of visually presented digits relative to mental age matched controls. One potential concern about this approach is that standard models of working memory (e.g., Baddeley, 1986) state that verbal information is stored in verbal short-term memory regardless of its mode of presentation; for example, adults show relatively poor recall of phonologically confusable lists that are presented visually (Conrad, 1964). Given this, manipulations of presentation modality do not tap fundamentally different storage systems among adults. However, there is considerable evidence that young children aged less than 7 do not spontaneously recode visually presented verbal material into a phonological form (Conrad, 1971; Hitch, Halliday, Dodd & Littler, 1989; Hitch, Halliday, Schaafstal & Schraagen, 1988). Consequently, a modality manipulation presented to individuals aged less than 7, or functioning below an age-equivalent level of 7 as was the case for Marcell and Armstrong's Down syndrome sample, may well provide an appropriate comparison of verbal and visuospatial short-term memory.

A recent and elegant extension of this line of research was carried out by Laws (2002) who examined memory for "focal" and "nonfocal" colours among individuals with Down syndrome and controls. She classed focal colours as those that were readily labelable, such as "red", "yellow" or "green" and nonfocal colours as those that were harder to label due to being non-primary (e.g., a "dark blue-green" colour), and presented sequences of these items, which participants then had to recall in serial order by pointing to a duplicate response array. Laws found that individuals with Down syndrome were unimpaired relative to mental age matched controls in their ability to recall nonfocal colours, but showed a deficit in memory for focal colours. She argued that this reflected unimpaired visual short-term memory in Down syndrome, but impaired verbal memory for colours that could be named. Of course, this implies that participants in this instance were able to recode the visually presented focal colours into verbal labels, contrary to the suggestions made above. Indeed, among controls only, memory was superior for focal as opposed to nonfocal colours despite the fact that these individuals were all younger than 7 years of age.

Although these data are clearly suggestive of impaired verbal short-term memory performance in Down syndrome, relative to levels of visuospatial short-term memory performance, they are clearly open to concerns about the extent to which visually presented material is relableable into a phonological form. Consequently, arguably stronger evidence for this dissociation comes from studies that have contrasted digit or word span tasks with more "traditional" measures of visuospatial short-term memory. One such task is the Corsi span test in which participants watch as an experimenter taps a sequence of blocks from among a set of nine possible locations, before having to reproduce the sequence themselves. In many ways this provides a visuospatial analogue of a digit span task, and consequently a direct comparison between these two tests is particularly informative.

Studies that have contrasted Corsi and digit memory in individuals with Down syndrome and ability-matched comparison groups have consistently shown unimpaired Corsi performance among Down syndrome groups (Brock & Jarrold, 2005; Jarrold & Baddeley, 1997; Jarrold, Baddeley & Hewes, 1999; Jarrold, Baddeley & Phillips, 2002; Laws, 2002; Numminen, Service, Ahonen & Ruoppila, 2001; Vicari, Carlesimo & Caltagirone, 1995). In addition, in all bar one of these studies (Vicari et al., 1995) an interaction was indicated by the data, reflecting impaired performance on the digit task among the Down syndrome participants. This clearly supports the claim for a specific deficit in short-term memory for verbal material, but there remains at least one concern as to the comparability of even this pair of tasks. In typical digit span tests, one avoids presenting lists that consist of obvious number "patterns" (e.g., "1, 2, 3, 4", "8, 6, 4, 2"), and consequently individuals need to retain both the items in the list and the order in which they were presented. In contrast, although Corsi span tasks do call for recall of item location in correct serial order, there is some evidence that participants typically remember the shape traced out by the path connecting successive locations in the list. For example, Corsi recall is typically poorer when the traced path crosses over itself than when it describes a single figure without crossing (Kemps, 2001) suggesting that individuals might rely less on discrete representations of every location that are held in appropriate order, and more on a representation of the general path shape. If so, then the relatively strong performance of individuals with Down syndrome on this task might reflect good recall of pattern and form (cf. Stratford & Metcalf, 1982) rather than recall of serial order of the kind involved in digit span; this is an issue we are exploring in our current work. Nevertheless, the existing evidence from studies of Corsi recall, coupled with the data from studies of the effect of modality of presentation on verbal recall and Laws' colour memory experiment, does suggest that individuals with Down syndrome have a specific deficit in verbal, rather than visuospatial short-term memory performance.

A related question is whether this apparent deficit in Down syndrome is specific to verbal short-term as opposed to verbal long-term memory. There is evidence that individuals with Down syndrome showed impaired recall on list learning paradigms in which list of words are repeatedly presented for successive recall in order to test long-term verbal learning (Carlesimo, Marotta & Vicari, 1997; Nichols et al., 2004; Pennington, Moon, Edgin, Stedron & Nadel, 2003; see also Vicari, Bellucci & Carlesimo, 2000). However, these tasks tap recall of information that is learnt over a series of immediate recall trials, and consequently learning in this procedure may depend to some extent on verbal short-term memory skills. Indeed, Carlesimo et al. (1997) found poorer list learning among individuals with Down syndrome than controls, but comparable forgetting rates over time among these groups given the level of learning obtained. In addition, in our own work we have looked at individuals' ability to learn long-term verbal labels using the Names subtest of the Doors and Pictures test (Baddeley, Emslie & Nimmo-Smith, 1994). In this task participants are required to learn the names of four individuals in response to being shown their photograph. Among our sample of individuals with Down syndrome, performance on this test was no poorer than one would expect given individuals' general levels of verbal ability (Jarrold, Baddeley & Phillips, in press).

Carlesimo et al. (1997) did also report poorer prose recall among individuals with Down syndrome (cf. Wilson & Ivani-Chalian, 1995; though see also Seung & Chapman, 2003), a finding not so open to concerns about the involvement of short-term memory in list learning. However, in relatively open-ended tasks such as this it is possible that impaired recall reflects poorer organizational strategies or levels of motivation rather than impaired mnemonic skills; certainly there is evidence of a reduced motivation for task compliance in Down syndrome (Wishart, 1993). Consequently, although there is some evidence of verbal long-term memory deficits associated with Down syndrome, and more work in this area is certainly needed, our current view is that this is considerably weaker than the corresponding evidence for verbal short-term memory problems in Down syndrome.

DO THESE DEFICITS EXTEND TO WORKING MEMORY TASKS?

The distinction between short-term and working memory is not always clearly drawn, after all Baddeley's (1986) "working memory" model readily accommodates performance on "short-term memory" tasks of the form described above. In our research we restrict the term "short-term memory" to situations where information has to be maintained over the short term, without any obvious manipulation of that material and in the absence of any other distracting activity; a digit span task would be an example of such a situation. In line with others (e.g., Daneman & Merikle, 1986; Engle, Tuholski, Laughlin & Conway, 1999) we would argue that working memory involves a similar degree of maintenance or storage of information, but also requires the manipulation or processing of information that can lead to more rapid forgetting of to-be-remembered material. For example, in "complex span" working memory tasks individuals are typically presented with a series of processing episodes which they have to complete, and which often provide a to-be-remembered item of information; in reading span tasks (e.g., Daneman & Carpenter, 1980) individuals read and make decisions about a series of sentences before recalling the final word of each sentence, in counting span tasks (e.g., Case, Kurland & Goldberg, 1982) individuals count the dots on a series of cards and remember these count totals for subsequent serial recall. Although such measures clearly capture something more than "simple span" short-term memory tasks such as digit span (Engle, 2002), they share with them the need to maintain information in correct serial order. Consequently, one might view such tasks as more complex extensions and variants of short-term memory procedures (Bayliss, Jarrold, Gunn & Baddeley, 2003; Engle et al., 1999). As a result, one would expect any individual to perform less well in absolute terms on a complex span task (e.g., reading or counting span) than a corresponding simple span version (e.g., word or digit span).

However, in the only two studies that, to our knowledge, have presented verbal complex span tasks to individuals with Down syndrome, performance was found to be unimpaired relative to controls (Numminen et al., 2001; Pennington et al., 2003). This surprising result might reflect the fact that individuals with Down syndrome carried out the processing aspects of these working memory task more rapidly than controls, and so offset a deficit in recall by reducing the time over which items in memory were subject to decay (cf. Towse & Hitch, 1995). Alternatively, the lack of group effects in these studies may reflect floor effects on performance; indeed, among the individuals with Down syndrome assessed by Numminen et al. (2001) average reading span scores were less than 1. Certainly, to the extent that one could accurately measure verbal working memory in Down syndrome, one would expect it to be impaired to a comparable extent as verbal short-term memory. Indeed, given evidence that the neurophysiological signs of Alzheimer's disease are present in individuals with Down syndrome at an early age (Wisniewski & Silverman, 1996) one might predict additional impairments in aspects of working memory such as dual task coordination (cf. Baddeley, Logie, Bressi, Della Sala & Spinnler, 1986) among older individuals with Down syndrome.

DO VERBAL SHORT-TERM MEMORY DEFICITS REFLECT PROBLEMS OF HEARING AND SPEECH?

The above review suggests that individuals with Down syndrome perform particularly poorly on tests of verbal short-term memory, a conclusion entirely in line with the view that verbal short-term memory is specifically impaired in the condition. However, this conclusion is only warranted if it can be shown that poor performance does not result from some other deficit associated with Down syndrome that particularly affects tasks such as digit span. In fact there are a number of such alternative explanations of poor task performance that follow from the fact that verbal short-term memory tasks are typically presented auditorily, and require spoken serial recall. Most notably, given that individuals with Down syndrome tend to have hearing deficits (e.g., Dahle & McCollister, 1986) and speech production problems (e.g., Dodd & Thompson, 2001) one might expect them to particularly struggle on such tasks regardless of the quality of their underlying memory abilities. Obviously, if an individual cannot hear a presented item it is unreasonable to expect him or her to be able to recall that item. Similarly, speech production difficulties could lead to imperfect and hard-to-interpret responses at recall. In addition, slowed verbal responding to a task will lead to a greater opportunity for time-based forgetting of to-be-produced items (cf. Cowan et al., 1992).

Studies have tended to address these concerns in two ways. One approach has been to measure the degree of hearing loss and speech production problems shown by individuals with Down syndrome, and the extent to which these correlate with levels of verbal short-term memory performance. Cairns and Jarrold (2005) showed that individuals with Down syndrome were impaired relative to controls on a test of nonword repetition, a task that many argue taps verbal short-term memory but which is certainly also affected by speech discrimination and production skills. Indeed, these individuals did have significantly poorer speech production abilities, and somewhat poorer speech discrimination skills, than controls. Nevertheless, neither of these measures was reliably related to nonword repetition score in this sample. In contrast, Laws and Gunn (2004) reported a trend for nonword repetition ability among individuals with Down syndrome to be related to individuals' level of hearing loss.

While one might well expect hearing and speech production problems to be particularly detrimental to nonword repetition, where unfamiliar items have to be identified and repeated, one might expect less of an effect on performance on more standard digit and word span tasks where to-be-remembered items are more familiar and discriminable (cf. Briscoe, Bishop & Norbury, 2001). Indeed, there is even less evidence of correlations between levels of hearing ability and digit span among individuals with Down syndrome. Both Jarrold and Baddeley (1997) and Marcell and Cohen (1992) found no evidence of a reliable relationship between these measures. However, Marcell and Cohen did find an association between hearing thresholds and ability to identify speech that was masked by noise, and it may well be the case that subtle difficulties in item identification that are not picked up by more standard measures such as pure tone audiometry do affect encoding of verbal information in verbal short-term memory tasks in Down syndrome. Having said this, Brock and Jarrold (2005) found that individuals with Down syndrome did not differ from controls in the time taken to identify digits, despite showing poorer short-term memory for them.

A second way of addressing the concern about the influence of hearing and speech problems on verbal short-term memory in Down syndrome has been to manipulate the type of task employed to minimize these potentially confounding factors. Jarrold, Baddeley and Phillips (2002) examined the impact of hearing loss on performance by providing visual support when presenting to-be-remembered verbal information. As discussed above, it is arguable whether words or digits that are only presented visually are stored in a phonological code by individuals of a developmental level less than 7 years; however, if items are presented both visually and auditorily then the visual support may serve to remove any confusion as to the identity of the to-be-remembered phonological trace. Jarrold et al. (2002) did find that providing visual support improved digit spans among individuals with Down syndrome, but it did not remove the deficit in performance relative to controls.

Other manipulations have attempted to reduce or eliminate the need for individuals to produce a full spoken output in response to a verbal short-term memory task. Jarrold, Baddeley and Hewes (2000) employed a probed recall procedure in which individuals were asked to provide the identity of only one item in a three-item list, thereby removing the need for a serial spoken response (see also Purser & Jarrold, 2005). Although individuals with Down syndrome were unimpaired on trials when either of the final two items in the list was probed, they showed impaired performance on the first item in each list, suggesting that reducing output demands did not fully remove the memory deficit. Other studies have employed recognition procedures in which participants simply have to state whether a second list is identical to, or differs from, a target list of verbal items. Individuals with Down syndrome remain impaired on such tasks regardless of whether recognition of order (Jarrold et al., 2002) or item information is required (Brock & Jarrold, 2004). Finally, both Brock and Jarrold (2005) and Marcell and Weeks (1988) employed reconstruction of order tasks in which participants were presented with visual images of the verbal items presented auditorily in a list, and had to indicate the serial order in which they were presented by a nonverbal pointing response. In both cases individuals with Down syndrome were impaired relative to controls despite the absence of a verbal spoken response.

In summary, it is entirely possible that perceptual abnormalities and speech production problems exacerbate the difficulties experienced by individuals with Down syndrome on tests of verbal short-term memory. Indeed, it may be that individuals show such marked impairments on traditional verbal short-term memory measures precisely because these tasks combine the need to encode, remember and reproduce verbal information, all of which may be problematic in Down syndrome. However, the results of the above studies strongly suggest that verbal short-term memory difficulties in Down syndrome cannot be wholly, or even primarily, accounted for by these perceptual and speech production difficulties.

DO VERBAL SHORT-TERM MEMORY DEFICITS REFLECT DEFICIENT LINGUISTIC KNOWLEDGE?

One other possible explanation of poor verbal short-term memory performance in Down syndrome follows from evidence that individuals' scores on short-term memory tasks are typically affected by their familiarity with the to-be-remembered material. So, for example, both adults and children typically show reliably higher short-term memory spans for words than for nonwords (Brener, 1940; Hulme, Maughan & Brown, 1991; Roodenrys, Hulme & Brown, 1993). Importantly, this effect appears not to be mediated by differences in the underlying memorability of these items (Hulme et al., 1991; Roodenrys et al., 1993), but rather is thought to reflect the fact that long-term linguistic knowledge can be used by participants to recreate degraded traces. This process of "redintegration" is clearly more effective for word than for nonword stimuli, as individuals' lexical knowledge allows them to make a "best guess" as to the possible identity of degraded word traces. Nevertheless, there is clear evidence that nonword recall is also influenced by individuals' familiarity with the stimuli as indexed by the similarity of these nonwords to existing known words (e.g., Gathercole, 1995; Roodenrys & Hinton, 2002; Thorn & Gathercole, 2001). Given this, and the fact that the language skills of individuals with Down syndrome tend to be poorer than their other abilities (e.g., Chapman, 1997; Fowler, 1990), it is possible that poor verbal short-term memory performance is a secondary consequence of individuals' relatively impoverished language knowledge (cf. Hulme & Roodenrys, 1995).

In fact, three lines of evidence count against this suggestion. First, individuals with Down syndrome show impaired verbal short-term memory performance even when matched to controls for level of receptive vocabulary (Brock & Jarrold, 2005; Jarrold & Baddeley, 1997; Jarrold et al., 2002; Laws, 2002); and, although the assessment of receptive vocabulary does not give a fully comprehensive index of language familiarity, one would certainly expect it to provide a reasonable estimate of linguistic knowledge. Second, there is evidence that the benefits of lexical knowledge on verbal short-term memory only operate in recall tasks where individuals have to reproduce to-be-remembered items, presumably because redintegrative processes operate to enable recall of partially degraded items. In contrast, lexicality effects – superior memory for words than nonwords – are less marked in paradigms that test recognition of order memory where item information is re-presented at test (Brock, McCormack & Boucher, 2005; Gathercole, Pickering, Hall & Peaker, 2001; Thorn, Gathercole & Frankish, 2002). However, as noted above, individuals with Down syndrome have been found to show impaired verbal short-term memory performance even under these conditions (Brock & Jarrold, 2004, 2005; Jarrold et al., 2002).

Finally, and more directly, studies have examined the magnitude of the lexicality effect shown by individuals with Down syndrome in comparison to that seen among typically developing children. Cairns and Jarrold (2005) showed that although individuals with Down syndrome performed more poorly than typically developing controls on both word and nonword repetition tasks, the magnitude of the lexicality effect, indicated by the difference between these two tasks, was comparable in the two groups. However, these data are somewhat difficult to interpret because of concerns associated with scoring individuals' recall of nonwords. Consequently, in order to obtain a more sensitive index of lexicality effects, Brock and Jarrold (2004) assessed individuals' ability to recognize changes to both word and nonword lists using two recognition tasks. In an order memory recognition task, participants were presented with a list of either words or nonwords that was then followed by a second list in which, on 50% of trials, the same items were presented in a different order (e.g., "ball, fin, gate" – "ball, gate, fin"; cf. Gathercole et al., 2001; Jarrold et al., 2002). In an item memory recognition task two lists were again presented, but in this case on 50% of trials the second list contained an item change effected by altering one of the phonemes of the initial items (e.g., "ball, fin, gate" – "ball, pin, gate". Note that lexical status of the altered item was maintained in each case). Participants simply had to decide whether the second list was the same or different to the first in each case, and a comparison of performance across word and nonword lists provided an estimate of the magnitude of the lexicality effect shown by each group in each task.

Lexicality effects were observed in each task, but were stronger for item than for order memory (cf. Gathercole et al., 2001; Thorn et al., 2002). A direct comparison of the size of this effect in the two groups showed that it was comparable for the order memory task, but that individuals with Down syndrome showed a reliably *larger* lexicality effect than typically developing individuals on the item memory task. In other words, individuals with Down syndrome performed better than expected on the word version of the task than predicted by their performance on the nonword version. This is the reverse of what one would expect if poor verbal short-term memory performance was a consequence of impoverished linguistic knowledge, which instead would predict a reduced lexicality effect. Brock and Jarrold (2004) suggest that particular problems with memory for nonwords in Down syndrome might reflect difficulties of item identification which are likely to be exacerbated for unfamiliar stimuli (see above), but whatever the case these and the related data reviewed here clearly count against the view that poor verbal short-term memory performance in Down syndrome is simply a reflection of individuals' generally poor language knowledge.

INTERPRETING DEFICITS WITHIN THE PHONOLOGICAL LOOP FRAMEWORK

The fact that the poor verbal short-term memory performance typically shown by individuals with Down syndrome cannot be wholly explained away in terms of problems of hearing, speech production and linguistic knowledge suggests that the condition really is associated with a fundamental deficit in verbal short-term storage. Consequently, a number of authors have suggested that this deficit might usefully be defined, and further explored, with reference to Baddeley's (1986) phonological loop model of verbal short-term memory. In fact, the phonological loop is itself a two-component system, consisting of a passive phonological store in which material is maintained in a phonological code but which is subject to time-based decay, and an articulatory rehearsal process that serves to refresh, and therefore maintain, material in the store. Given this, one might ask whether the problems shown by individuals with Down syndrome on verbal short-term memory tasks reflect a fundamental deficit in either phonological storage on subvocal rehearsal.

In fact, the majority of work in this area has focused on the possibility that Down syndrome might be associated with deficient rehearsal. A number of studies have attempted to improve verbal short-term memory performance in individuals with Down syndrome by providing rehearsal training (Broadley & MacDonald, 1993; Broadley, MacDonald & Buckley, 1994; Comblain, 1994; Laws, MacDonald & Buckley, 1996; Laws, MacDonald, Buckley & Broadley, 1995) and although these have tended to lead to some improvements in individuals' performance, these gains are modest and are rarely sustained in the long term (Jarrold, Baddeley & Phillips, 1999). This suggests that rehearsal deficits might not lie at the heart of individuals' difficulties in verbal short-term memory.

Support for this suggestion comes from studies that have examined the rate at which individuals with Down syndrome might be expected to rehearse material in verbal short-term memory. According to Baddeley's model, the efficiency of rehearsal is constrained by its speed – individuals who are able to rehearse more rapidly are able to maintain more memory items in the phonological store (Baddeley, Thomson & Buchanan, 1975; Standing & Curtis, 1989). Furthermore, material which takes longer to rehearse is harder to maintain for the same reason, providing a potential explanation for word length effects in immediate serial recall (Baddeley et al., 1975; Standing, Bond, Smith & Isley, 1980). Consequently, if Down syndrome is associated with atypically slow rehearsal then this could account for individuals' poor verbal short-term memory performance.

This possibility has been evaluated by examining individuals' overt speech rates, based on the assumption that rate of covert subvocal rehearsal equates to rate of overt repetition (Baddeley et al., 1975). Hulme and Mackenzie (1992) found that individuals with Down syndrome had reliably slower mean articulation rates than typically developing controls; however, more recent studies have failed to replicate this difference. In our work we have found no reliable slowing in the average speech rates of individuals with Down syndrome relative to either children with moderate learning difficulties (Jarrold et al., 2000) or typically developing individuals (Jarrold, Cowan, Hewes & Riby, 2004). Similar results have also been reported by Kanno and Ikeda (2002) and by Seung and Chapman (2000). Having said this, a more detailed analysis does suggest some speech production difficulties in Down syndrome, which might account for Hulme and Mackenzie's findings. Seung and Chapman found that, while individuals with Down syndrome produced their response to a digit span task at the same rate as controls once they had begun responding, they took reliably longer to initiate their responses (see also Bunn, Simon, Welsh, Watson & Elliott, 2002). Similarly, Jarrold, Cowan et al. showed that, although individuals with Down syndrome actually articulated words more rapidly than typically developing controls, they left longer gaps between words of a long spoken duration. Both of these results are suggestive of speech planning difficulties in Down syndrome (see above). The extent to which such a difficulty is likely to impact on subvocal rehearsal depends on whether these difficulties are due to planning problems at the internal or articulatory level (Waters, Rochon & Caplan, 1992). At present this is difficult to determine, although the fact that individuals with Down syndrome make more speech errors when repeating words from memory than when reading them (Bunn et al., 2002) suggests planning problems that may go beyond the articulatory level.

Whatever the case, the view that poor verbal short-term memory performance is the result of *slowed* rehearsal is called into serious question by the additional fact that speech rates do not correlate with memory span in Down syndrome. In contrast to data from typically developing adults (see above), and indeed some other developmental conditions (Avons & Hanna, 1995; Jarrold, Cowan et al., 2004; Raine, Hulme, Chadderton & Bailey, 1991), studies have consistently failed to find a relationship between verbal short-term memory performance and rate of articulation of to-be-remembered items in Down syndrome (Comblain, 1996; Hulme & Mackenzie, 1992; Jarrold, Cowan et al., 2004; Seung & Chapman, 2000; Vicari, Marotta & Carlesimo, 2004). This finding suggests that rather than suffering from slowed rehearsal, individuals with Down syndrome might not typically engage in rehearsal at all.

At first sight, this view appears to be challenged by data from studies that have examined the magnitude of word length effects shown in short-term recall by individuals with Down syndrome. Although Hulme and Mackenzie (1992) failed to find reliable word length effects among their sample of individuals with Down syndrome, subsequent studies have shown clear word length effects in immediate serial recall paradigms (Broadley, MacDonald & Buckley, 1995; Comblain, 1996; Jarrold et al., 2000; Kanno & Ikeda, 2002; Laws et al., 1995; Vicari et al., 2004). This difference in results might reflect the relatively poor baseline performance of individuals with Down syndrome, which in turn makes it relatively difficult to observe decrements in performance in "harder" conditions. Nevertheless, the fact that reliable word length effects are observed in serial recall in Down syndrome might appear to suggest that rehearsal is taking place, given the suggestion that the word length effect arises because of differences in rehearsal time required for words of different spoken duration (Baddeley et al., 1975).

However, an alternative explanation of the word length effect is that differences in spoken duration lead to differences in the time taken to produce output responses to verbal immediate serial recall tasks (Cowan et al., 1992); the argument being that the greater time taken to produce long as opposed to short words leads to greater forgetting of still-to-be-recalled list items held in memory (though see Lovatt, Avons & Masterson, 2002). Indeed, both "internal" rehearsal effects and "external" output effects might contribute to the typical word length effect observed in serial recall paradigms with adults (Avons, Wright & Pamme, 1994; Baddeley, Chincotta, Stafford & Turk, 2002). Consequently, one might still expect to see a word length effect in standard serial recall, albeit perhaps a diminished one, among individuals who are not rehearsing. Given this, studies have increasingly employed paradigms such as probed recall, which remove the need for a spoken serial response, in order to test for the presence of word length effects that can be more confidently attributed to internal rehearsal processes. The one study that, to our knowledge, has explored these effects using probed recall among individuals with Down syndrome (Jarrold et al., 2000) found a reliably smaller word length effect under probed recall than serial recall conditions, and showed that the size of this effect was not significantly different from zero in the former case. In other words, although individuals with Down syndrome do tend to show word length effects in traditional recall paradigms, they do not show this effect in a task that removes serial output demands, suggesting that they are not engaging in rehearsal.[1]

One might therefore be inclined to argue that poor verbal short-term memory performance in Down syndrome reflects a rehearsal failure in Down syndrome, such that individuals show impoverished verbal recall relative to their rehearsing peers (cf. Hulme & Mackenzie, 1992). The problem with this suggestion is that there is considerable evidence that individuals with Down syndrome show poorer verbal short-term memory performance than comparison groups who also appear not to be rehearsing. Since Flavell, Beach and Chinsky (1966) showed that children younger than 7 tend not to make lip movements when maintaining lists of verbal items, many have suggested that children younger than 7 do not engage in spontaneous verbal rehearsal (e.g., Gathercole & Adams, 1993). Potential support for this view comes from the evidence reviewed above, which suggests that children younger than 7 do not spontaneously recode visually presented verbal information into a phono-logical code – a process thought to be mediated by the same subvocal "renam-ing" of items than occurs in rehearsal. In addition, Henry (1991) failed to find a reliable word length effect in verbal probed recall among 5-year-old typically developing children (see also Allick & Siegel, 1976; Balthazar, 2003), suggesting that word length effects observed in children of this age with serial recall of auditorily presented information may reflect output rather than rehearsal effects (see above, though see also Note 1). Finally, although reliable correlations are typically observed between individuals' speech rates and their immediate verbal serial recall among adults (e.g., Cowan et al., 1998; Standing et al., 1980; Tehan & Lalor, 2000), the correlations between these measures are often considerably weaker among children aged less than 7 years (Ferguson, Bowey & Tilley, 2002; Gathercole & Adams, 1993; Gathercole, Adams & Hitch, 1994; Jarrold, Cowan et al., 2004).[2]

Consequently when individuals with Down syndrome are compared to typical developing comparison individuals who are aged less than 7 years, or individuals with learning difficulties functioning below the 7-year mental age equivalent level, one would not necessarily expect any individuals to be en-gaging in spontaneous rehearsal. Indeed, Balthazar (2003) found no reliable word length effects in the probed recall of individuals with language impair-ment who, though aged 7, were functioning below this level in mental age terms. More directly, and as noted above, Jarrold et al. (2000) reported similar results among their individuals with Down syndrome who had a mean vocabu-lary mental age of below 5 years, but also found no reliable word length effect under probed recall conditions among both typically developing and learning disabled controls of an equivalent vocabulary level. In addition, neither these individuals with Down syndrome nor learning disabled (Jarrold et al., 2000) or typically developing (Jarrold, Cowan et al., 2004) individuals showed reliable correlations between their speech rates and span perform-ance. In other words, although individuals with Down syndrome showed impaired overall verbal short-term memory performance in these two studies, it appears that this deficit cannot be explained in terms of a selective failure in rehearsal among this group.

If this is the case, and if one still wishes to interpret the poor verbal short-term memory performance of individuals with Down syndrome in terms of Baddeley's phonological loop framework, then one is forced to argue that individuals must suffer from some form of impairment to the phonological store component of this model. In fact, this might take one of two forms (cf. Gathercole & Baddeley, 1990a); individuals with Down syndrome might suffer from atypically rapid loss of information from the store, or forgetting might occur at a normal rate but from a store of relatively reduced capacity. At first sight these two possibilities might appear to be conceptually equiva-lent – more rapid forgetting would appear to lead to a functional reduction in capacity – but we believe they can be distinguished from each other.

For example, in our recent work (Purser & Jarrold, 2005) we have explored whether slowing the rate of presentation of verbal information in a short-term memory paradigm has a particularly detrimental effect on the perform-ance of individuals with Down syndrome. Among adults, slowing presentation rates typically does not reduce verbal serial recall performance (Baddeley, Lewis & Vallar, 1984), but this may well be because individuals are rehearsing and can therefore offset any extra degree of forgetting with the greater opportunities for rehearsal afforded by a more spaced presentation (Baddeley & Lewis, 1984; Brown & Hulme, 1995). However, if individuals are not rehearsing, then one might well expect the longer maintenance intervals associated with slower presentation rates to lead to poorer recall (cf. Vallar, Di Betta & Silveri, 1997). Indeed, in two studies in which we examined probed recall of words from four-item lists under either faster or slower presentation rates, both individuals with Down syndrome and typically developing controls showed poorer recall when presentation was slower. However, the key finding was the fact that, in both experiments, individuals with Down syndrome were no more affected by this rate manipulation than were controls. In other words, although forgetting from verbal short-term memory was occurring, there was no evidence that this loss of information was any more rapid for individuals with Down syndrome.

This leaves the possibility that individuals with Down syndrome suffer from reduced phonological store capacity. One way in which this has been investigated is by examining the magnitude of the phonological similarity effect shown in verbal short-term memory paradigms by individuals with Down syndrome. The standard phonological similarity effect is the finding that individuals show poorer short-term recall of information that is phono-logically confusable than material that is phonologically distinct (Baddeley, 1966; Conrad & Hull, 1964), a result implying that verbal material is held in short-term memory in a phonological code. Following this, some authors have further suggested that the magnitude of this effect might provide an index of the capacity of the phonological store, with a smaller similarity effect indicating reduced phonological store capacity (Vallar & Papagno, 1995; Vicari et al., 2004), although one might equally argue that phonologic-ally similar materials might become more confusable as phonological storage capacity reduces. Indeed, the evidence concerning the size of the phono-logical similarity effect in Down syndrome is mixed. Varnhagen, Das and Varnhagen (1987) found no reliable effect among their sample of individuals with Down syndrome, but presented individuals with four-item lists of either phonologically similar or dissimilar words despite the fact that individuals' average word spans was only two items. Consequently, it is possible that the use of supraspan lists may have discouraged individuals from attempting to hold all items in verbal short-term memory (see Jarrold, Baddeley & Phillips, 1999). Indeed, both Broadley et al. (1995) and Comblain (1996) found a reliable phonological similarity effect among their samples with Down syn-drome. Other studies that have compared the magnitude of this effect among individuals with Down syndrome and controls have produced similarly mixed findings. Jarrold et al. (2000) found comparable phonological similarity effects among individuals with Down syndrome and individuals with moderate learning difficulties in probed recall. However, both Hulme and Mackenzie (1992) and Vicari et al. (2004) found a reliably smaller phonological similarity effect among individuals with Down syndrome than among controls. Once again though, this latter finding might reflect methodological constraints; Vicari et al. report that floor effects operated to limit the variability of individuals' recall of words in their phonologically similar condition. Furthermore, although there may be intraindividual variation in the magnitude of the phonological similarity effect among typically developing adults (Logie, Della Sala, Laiacona, Chambers & Wynn, 1996), neuropsychological patients with clear verbal short-term memory deficits often show a standard sized effect (Vallar & Papagno, 1995). Consequently, although the absence of a phonological similarity effect would appear to be strong evidence for a complete absence of phonological coding in verbal short-term memory provided that floor effects are avoided (Vallar, Di Betta & Silveri, 1997), it may well be that a typically sized effect is observed provided that at least some material is held in the phonological store, regardless of the store's capacity. Consequently, these data fail to provide clear support either for or against the suggestion of a reduced phonological store capacity in Down syndrome.

More direct evidence for a capacity limitation comes from studies that have examined serial position effects in the verbal short-term memory performance of individuals with Down syndrome. In fact, such studies are limited in number, presumably because the relatively poor performance of individuals on immediate verbal serial recall tasks limits the scope for serial position analyses.[3] However, the use of probed recall tasks can potentially extend the range of serial positions over which individuals produce meaningful verbal short-term memory data. In our probed recall study (Jarrold et al., 2000) we found that individuals with Down syndrome were only reliably impaired relative to controls on the first list position of three-item word lists. If one assumes that this does not reflect atypically rapid forgetting of information (see above) one reading of these data is that they reflect a reduced capacity for phonological storage of information in Down syndrome. Put somewhat simplistically, if individuals with Down syndrome were unable to maintain all three items in short-term memory to the same extent as controls, but rather were able to successfully maintain two items, then one would expect them to engage in a successive updating of information as the to-be-remembered list was presented. Consequently the final two items, but not the first, would be maintained in verbal short-term memory at the end of the presentation, leading to unimpaired performance when either of these positions was probed. Support for this reading of the data comes from a more recent experiment reported by Purser and Jarrold (2005, Exp. 2). In this instance, individuals' memory for item information was probed by presenting four-item lists followed by the immediate and rapid re-presentation of three of these items.

The participants' task was to recall the remaining item in the presented list that had not been re-presented. The serial position of this probed item within the presentation list was systematically varied across trials, and the results showed that individuals with Down syndrome were unimpaired when the final position in the four-item list was probed, but performed poorly at all other positions. Once again this suggests a reduced verbal short-term capacity among these individuals, such that only the most recently presented item or items are successfully maintained.

CONSEQUENCES OF A VERBAL SHORT-TERM MEMORY DEFICIT

The research reviewed above confirms that individuals with Down syndrome do perform poorly on tests of verbal short-term memory, and that this poor performance cannot wholly be explained in terms of hearing difficulties, problems in speech production, or reduced linguistic knowledge. There is, therefore, clear support for the view that Down syndrome is associated with a fundamental verbal short-term memory deficit. Furthermore, this deficit appears not to be related to problems of rehearsal, but more likely reflects problems of phonological storage, and potentially, a reduced capacity for the short-term storage of phonological information. In this final section, we consider the broader consequences of this verbal short-term memory deficit for certain aspects of language development in Down syndrome.

Baddeley, Gathercole and colleagues (e.g., Baddeley, Gathercole & Papagno, 1998) have argued that the phonological store component of Baddeley's model plays an important role in the language acquisition process, particularly during children's new word learning. Their suggestion is that verbal short-term memory is required in order to successfully maintain and represent the phonological form of new word sounds when they are first encountered, and to support subsequent learning. This view is supported by evidence from a number of sources. Verbal short-term memory performance is clearly related to children's level of receptive vocabulary, even when potentially confounding measures such as level of nonverbal ability are controlled for (see Baddeley et al., 1998). Indeed, longitudinal and quasilongitudinal designs have shown that, among young children, early measures of verbal short-term memory performance do predict subsequent levels of vocabulary attainment (Gathercole, Willis, Emslie & Baddeley, 1992; Jarrold, Baddeley, Hewes, Leeke & Phillips, 2004). More directly, participants' verbal short-term performance is also correlated with their ability to learn novel phonological forms in experimental word learning paradigms (Baddeley, 1993; Baddeley, Papagno & Vallar, 1988; Gathercole & Baddeley, 1990b; Gathercole, Hitch, Service & Martin, 1997; Papagno & Vallar, 1995).

The clear prediction that follows from this research is that poor verbal short-term memory in Down syndrome should lead to difficulties in vocabulary acquisition. It is certainly the case that vocabulary is delayed in Down syndrome relative to age, or perhaps even nonverbal mental age levels (Chapman, 1995, 1997), and this delay does not appear to be caused by difficulties in the "conceptual" demands of acquiring word meanings. For example, Chapman, Kay-Raining Bird and Schwartz (1990) reported relatively strong "fast mapping" skills in Down syndrome – that is, when faced with a novel word, individuals readily assumed that this must refer to a novel, rather than familiar, object. Nevertheless, vocabulary is certainly not the weakest aspect of the language skills of individuals with Down syndrome, and is often markedly stronger than individuals' syntactic skills (Chapman, 1995; Fowler, 1990; Laws & Bishop, 2004; Vicari, Caselli, Gagliardi, Tonucci & Volterra, 2002). Although it has been suggested that verbal short-term memory impairments might lead on to grammatical difficulties in addition to problems in new word learning (Adams & Gathercole, 1995; Baddeley et al., 1998), the evidence and theoretical rationale for a causal relationship with syntactic development is less strong than it is for vocabulary (see Baddeley et al., 1998). Consequently, the fact that vocabulary is not particularly impaired within the domain of language functioning in Down syndrome is problematic for the view that poor verbal short-term memory leads to poor vocabulary learning.

One possibility is that individuals with Down syndrome are able to compensate for their poor verbal short-term memory and acquire vocabulary primarily through an alternative route. Baddeley (1993) reported the case of an individual (without Down syndrome) who acquired normal vocabulary despite a severe developmental short-term memory deficit and despite poor performance on an experimental nonword learning paradigm. As a result Baddeley suggested that it is "unlikely that phonological short-term memory sets the limit for adult vocabulary, which seems much more likely to be determined by a combination of richness of linguistic environment, coupled with the intelligence to deduce the meaning of unfamiliar words in context" (p. 144). It is possible that individuals with Down syndrome rely more than is typical on contextual information to support their vocabulary acquisition and (perhaps more pertinently) to aid their performance on vocabulary tests.

If individuals with Down syndrome are not relying on verbal short-term memory during vocabulary acquisition, then one might expect that vocabulary knowledge would not be correlated with measures of verbal short-term memory to the extent that it is in typically developing children. Laws (1998) found that receptive vocabulary *was* reliably related to nonword repetition performance in a sample of 33 individuals with Down syndrome even when age and nonverbal ability was controlled. However, she failed to find a significant corresponding relationship between vocabulary and digit span in this group.[4] Nevertheless, a 5-year follow-up (Laws & Gunn, 2004) of 31 of these individuals showed that both Time 1 nonword repetition and Time 1 digit span scores predicted Time 2 vocabulary knowledge even when Time 1 vocabulary and chronological age were controlled for (cf. Gathercole et al.,

1992). As Laws and Gunn (2004) note, these findings are currently the strongest evidence for the presence of the typical relationship between verbal short-term memory and new word learning in Down syndrome.

An important caveat, however, comes from the consideration of developmental changes in the relationship between vocabulary knowledge and verbal short-term memory. Jarrold, Baddeley et al. (2004) proposed that, although verbal short-term memory capacity plays a critical role in early vocabulary acquisition, as the level of vocabulary knowledge increases, the association between vocabulary knowledge and verbal short-term memory is increasingly driven by the top-down influence of vocabulary knowledge on verbal short-term memory performance. Consequently, significant associations between vocabulary and verbal short-term memory reported in Down syndrome are not necessarily indicative of a role of verbal short-term memory in vocabulary acquisition. Indeed, Cairns and Jarrold (2005) reported that a reliable correlation between vocabulary knowledge and nonword repetition in individuals with Down syndrome was not reduced by partialling out individuals' digit spans, suggesting that it was not mediated by verbal short-term memory.

An important unresolved issue, therefore, is whether individuals with Down syndrome rely on an alternative mechanism for acquiring vocabulary or whether measures of vocabulary knowledge used in existing studies are simply insensitive to their difficulties. This question could in principle be addressed by looking at performance on experimental word-learning tasks and on measures of vocabulary knowledge that are sensitive to the strength and accuracy of phonological representations (as opposed to semantic knowledge). Given the aforementioned changes in the relationship between vocabulary knowledge and verbal short-term memory in typical development, it will be important to compare individuals with Down syndrome and those with other forms of learning disability who are of a comparable chronological age and developmental level.

CONCLUSION

The above review has shown that individuals with Down syndrome perform particularly poorly on tests of verbal short-term memory. Furthermore, although it is clear that the hearing difficulties, speech production problems and relatively impoverished linguistic knowledge that are often associated with the condition are likely to affect performance on standard verbal short-term memory tasks such as digit span, there is good evidence to indicate that Down syndrome is associated with a fundamental verbal short-term memory deficit. What is somewhat less clear is how one should conceptualize this deficit in terms of Baddeley's phonological loop model – although there is evidence for a reduction in the capacity of phonological storage – and whether these deficits equally affect performance on more complex working memory tasks as one would expect. These are clearly issues for further research.

However, arguably the most pressing current research issue concerns the possible consequences of a verbal short-term memory deficit in Down syndrome for aspects of individuals' language development. There are clear theoretical and empirical reasons to expect a detrimental impact of such a deficit on language acquisition, and on vocabulary development in particular, but at present there is little firm evidence for these effects in Down syndrome. In the absence of this evidence, the study of verbal short-term memory performance in Down syndrome currently tells us more about the structure of short-term memory in general than it does about the development of individuals with Down syndrome. However, if future research can more clearly specify the consequences of poor verbal short-term memory for other aspects of cognitive development then this would clearly have important implications for the type of educational and remedial interventions that might usefully be applied among individuals with the condition. In particular, if individuals with Down syndrome spontaneously compensate in some way for their poor verbal short-term memory when acquiring vocabulary, then a clearer understanding of the nature of any compensatory strategies might allow these to be applied to other aspects of cognitive development.

NOTES

1   One concern about the comparison of effect sizes in serial and probed recall is that probed recall is likely to be a less sensitive procedure, and therefore may be a less powerful test of a phenomenon such as the word length effect. This reduction in sensitivity follows from the fact that, across trials, probed recall tasks typically probe for recall of items at each serial position in the list. Because probes are provided immediately after test, performance for later serial positions tends to be at or near ceiling (e.g., Waugh & Norman, 1965), reducing the power to find condition effects, particularly when short list lengths are presented.

2   A problem with the view that individuals *begin* rehearsing at around a developmental level of 7 years is that there is no evidence of a qualitative jump in performance levels around this age among typically developing individuals. Indeed, age-based changes in immediate verbal serial recall across childhood appear quantitative and continuous rather than discrete (e.g., Case et al., 1982; Gathercole, Pickering, Ambridge & Wearing, 2004; Hulme, Thomson, Muir & Lawrence, 1984; Nicolson, 1981).

3   Vicari et al. (2004) do report serial position data for free recall of 12 item lists by individuals with and without Down syndrome, and showed comparable recency effects among these groups at positions 10, 11 and 12. However, it is questionable whether the recency portion of the free recall curve reflects the contribution of short-term memory processes as was once thought to be the case (see Baddeley & Hitch, 1977).

4   It is also possible that the failure to find reliable correlations between digit spans and receptive vocabulary in these samples reflects the relatively attenuated range of digit span scores that one tends to observe among individuals with Down syndrome.

REFERENCES

Adams, A. M., & Gathercole, S. E. (1995). Phonological working memory and speech production in preschool children. *Journal of Speech and Hearing Research*, *38*, 403–414.

Allick, J. P., & Siegel, A. W. (1976). The use of the cumulative rehearsal strategy: A developmental study. *Journal of Experimental Child Psychology*, *21*, 316–327.

Avons, S. E., & Hanna, C. (1995). The memory-span deficit in children with specific reading disability: Is speech rate responsible? *British Journal of Developmental Psychology*, *13*, 303–311.

Avons, S. E., Wright, K. L., & Pamme, K. (1994). The word-length effect in probed and serial recall. *Quarterly Journal of Experimental Psychology*, *47A*, 207–231.

Baddeley, A. (1993). Short-term phonological memory and long-term learning: A single-case study. *European Journal of Cognitive Psychology*, *5*, 129–148.

Baddeley, A., Gathercole, S., & Papagno, C. (1998). The phonological loop as a language learning device. *Psychological Review*, *105*, 158–173.

Baddeley, A., Logie, R., Bressi, S., Della Sala, S., & Spinnler, H. (1986). Dementia and working memory. *Quarterly Journal of Experimental Psychology*, *38A*, 603–618.

Baddeley, A., Papagno, C., & Vallar, G. (1988). When long-term learning depends on short-term storage. *Journal of Memory and Language*, *27*, 586–596.

Baddeley, A. D. (1966). Short-term memory for word sequences as a function of acoustic, semantic and formal similarity. *Quarterly Journal of Experimental Psychology*, *18*, 362–365.

Baddeley, A. D. (1986). *Working memory*. Oxford, UK: Oxford University Press.

Baddeley, A. D., Chincotta, D., Stafford, L., & Turk, D. (2002). Is the word length effect in STM attributable to output delay? Evidence from serial recognition. *Quarterly Journal of Experimental Psychology*, *55A*, 353–369.

Baddeley, A. D., Emslie, H., & Nimmo-Smith, I. (1994). *The doors and people test: A test of visual and verbal recall and recognition*. Bury St. Edmunds, UK: Thames Valley Test Company.

Baddeley, A. D., & Hitch, G. J. (1977). Recency reexamined. In S. Dornic (Ed.), *Attention and performance VI* (pp. 647–667). Hillsdale, NJ: Lawrence Erlbaum Associates, Inc.

Baddeley, A. D., & Lewis, V. J. (1984). When does rapid presentation enhance digit span? *Bulletin of the Psychonomic Society*, *22*, 403–405.

Baddeley, A. D., Lewis, V. J., & Vallar, G. (1984). Exploring the articulatory loop. *Quarterly Journal of Experimental Psychology*, *36A*, 233–252.

Baddeley, A. D., Thomson, N., & Buchanan, M. (1975). Word length and the structure of short-term memory. *Journal of Verbal Learning and Verbal Behavior*, *14*, 575–589.

Balthazar, C. H. (2003). The word length effect in children with language impairment. *Journal of Communication Disorders*, *36*, 487–505.

Bayliss, D. M., Jarrold, C., Gunn, D. M., & Baddeley, A. D. (2003). The complexities of complex span: Explaining individual differences in working memory in children and adults. *Journal of Experimental Psychology: General*, *132*, 71–92.

Bilovsky, D., & Share, J. (1965). The ITPA and Down syndrome: An exploratory study. *American Journal of Mental Deficiency*, *70*, 78–82.

Bower, A., & Hayes, A. (1994). Short-term memory deficits and Down syndrome: A comparative study. *Down Syndrome: Research and Practice*, *2*, 47–50.

Brener, R. (1940). An experimental investigation of memory span. *Journal of Experimental Psychology*, *26*, 467–482.

Briscoe, J., Bishop, D. V. M., & Norbury, C. F. (2001). Phonological processing, language, and literacy: A comparison of children with mild-to-moderate sensorineural hearing loss and those with specific language impairment. *Journal of Child Psychology and Psychiatry*, *42*, 329–340.

Broadley, I., & MacDonald, J. (1993). Teaching short term memory skills to children with Down syndrome. *Down Syndrome: Research and Practice*, *1*, 56–62.

Broadley, I., MacDonald, J., & Buckley, S. (1994). Are children with Down syndrome able to maintain skills learned from a short-term memory training programme? *Down Syndrome: Research and Practice*, *2*, 116–122.

Broadley, I., MacDonald, J., & Buckley, S. (1995). Working memory in children with Down syndrome. *Down Syndrome: Research and Practice*, *3*, 3–8.

Brock, J., & Jarrold, C. (2004). Language influences on verbal short-term memory performance in Down syndrome: Item and order recognition. *Journal of Speech, Language, and Hearing Research*, *47*, 1334–1346.

Brock, J., & Jarrold, C. (2005). Serial order reconstruction in Down syndrome: Evidence for a selective deficit in verbal short-term memory. *Journal of Child Psychology and Psychiatry*, *46*, 304–316.

Brock, J., McCormack, T., & Boucher, J. (2005). Probed serial recall in Williams syndrome: Lexical influences on phonological short-term memory. *Journal of Speech, Language, and Hearing Research*, *48*, 360–371.

Brown, G. D. A., & Hulme, C. (1995). Modeling item length effects in memory span: No rehearsal needed. *Journal of Memory and Language*, *34*, 594–621.

Bunn, L., Simon, D. A., Welsh, T. N., Watson, C., & Elliot, D. (2002). Speech production errors in adults with and without Down syndrome following verbal, written, and pictorial cues. *Developmental Neuropsychology*, *21*, 157–172.

Burr, D. B., & Rohr, A. (1978). Patterns of psycholinguistic development in the severely mentally retarded: A hypothesis. *Social Biology*, *25*, 15–22.

Cairns, P., & Jarrold, C. (2005). Exploring the correlates of impaired nonword repetition in Down syndrome. *British Journal of Developmental Psychology*, *23*, 401–416.

Carlesimo, G. A., Marotta, L., & Vicari, S. (1997). Long-term memory in mental retardation: Evidence for a specific impairment in subjects with Down syndrome. *Neuropsychologia*, *35*, 71–79.

Carr, J. (1985). The development of intelligence. In D. Lane & B. Stratford (Eds.), *Current approaches to Down syndrome* (pp. 167–186). London: Cassell.

Case, R., Kurland, D. M., & Goldberg, J. (1982). Operational efficiency and the growth of short-term memory span. *Journal of Experimental Child Psychology*, *33*, 386–404.

Chapman, R. S. (1995). Language development in children and adolescents with Down syndrome. In P. Fletcher & B. MacWhinney (Eds.), *Handbook of child language* (pp. 641–663). Oxford, UK: Blackwell.

Chapman, R. S. (1997). Language development in children and adolescents with Down syndrome. *Mental Retardation and Developmental Disabilities Research Reviews, 3,* 307–312.

Chapman, R. S., Kay-Raining Bird, E., & Schwartz, S. E. (1990). Fast mapping of words in event contexts by children with Down syndrome. *Journal of Speech and Hearing Disorders, 55,* 761–770.

Comblain, A. (1994). Working memory in Down syndrome: Training the rehearsal strategy. *Down Syndrome: Research and Practice, 2,* 123–126.

Comblain, A. (1996). Auditivo-vocal short-term memory's functioning in Down syndrome: Implication for the model of working memory. *Approche Neuropsychologique Des Apprentissages Chez L'Enfant, 8,* 137–147.

Conrad, R. (1964). Acoustic confusions in immediate memory. *British Journal of Psychology, 55,* 75–84.

Conrad, R. (1971). The chronology of the development of covert speech in children. *Developmental Psychology, 5,* 398–405.

Conrad, R., & Hull, A. J. (1964). Information, acoustic confusion, and memory span. *British Journal of Psychology, 55,* 429–432.

Cowan, N., Day, L., Saults, J. S., Keller, T. A., Johnson, T., & Flores, L. (1992). The role of verbal output time in the effects of word length on immediate memory. *Journal of Memory and Language, 31,* 1–17.

Cowan, N., Wood, N. L., Wood, P. K., Keller, T. A., Nugent, L. D., & Keller, C. V. (1998). Two separate verbal processing rates contributing to short-term memory span. *Journal of Experimental Psychology: General, 127,* 141–160.

Dahle, A., & McCollister, F. P. (1986). Hearing and otologic disorders in children with Down syndrome. *American Journal of Mental Deficiency, 90,* 636–642.

Daneman, M., & Carpenter, P. A. (1980). Individual differences in working memory and reading. *Journal of Verbal Learning and Verbal Behavior, 19,* 450–466.

Daneman, M., & Merikle, P. M. (1996). Working memory and language comprehension: A meta-analysis. *Psychonomic Bulletin and Review, 3,* 422–433.

Dilley, M. G., & Paivio, A. (1968). Pictures and words as stimulus and response items in paired-associate learning of young children. *Journal of Experimental Child Psychology, 6,* 231–240.

Dodd, B., & Thompson, L. (2001). Speech disorder in children with Down syndrome. *Journal of Intellectual Disability Research, 45,* 308–316.

Engle, R. W. (2002). Working memory capacity as executive attention. *Current Directions in Psychological Science, 11,* 19–23.

Engle, R. W., Tuholski, S. W., Laughlin, J. E., & Conway, A. R. A. (1999). Working memory, short-term memory, and general fluid intelligence: A latent-variable approach. *Journal of Experimental Psychology: General, 128,* 309–311.

Ferguson, A. N., Bowey, J. A., & Tilley, A. (2002). The association between auditory memory span and speech rate in children from kindergarten to sixth grade. *Journal of Experimental Child Psychology, 81,* 141–156.

Flavell, J. H., Beach, D. R., & Chinsky, J. M. (1966). Spontaneous verbal rehearsal in a memory task as a function of age. *Child Development, 37,* 283–299.

Fowler, A. E. (1990). Language abilities in children with Down syndrome: Evidence for a specific syntactic delay. In D. Cicchetti & M. Beeghly (Eds.), *Children with Down syndrome: A developmental perspective* (pp. 302–328). Cambridge, UK: Cambridge University Press.

Gathercole, S. E. (1995). Is nonword repetition a test of phonological memory or long-term knowledge? It all depends on the nonwords. *Memory and Cognition, 23,* 83–94.

Gathercole, S. E., & Adams, A. M. (1993). Phonological working memory in very young children. *Developmental Psychology, 29,* 770–778.

Gathercole, S. E., Adams, A. M., & Hitch, G. J. (1994). Do young children rehearse? An individual differences analysis. *Memory and Cognition, 22,* 201–207.

Gathercole, S. E., & Baddeley, A. D. (1990a). Phonological memory deficits in language disordered children: Is there a causal connection? *Journal of Memory and Language, 29,* 336–360.

Gathercole, S. E., & Baddeley, A. D. (1990b). The role of phonological memory in vocabulary acquisition: A study of young children learning new words. *British Journal of Psychology, 81,* 439–454.

Gathercole, S. E., Hitch, G. J., Service, E., & Martin, A. J. (1997). Phonological short-term memory and new word learning in children. *Developmental Psychology, 6,* 966–979.

Gathercole, S. E., Pickering, S. J., Ambridge, B., & Wearing, H. (2004). The structure of working memory from 4 to 15 years of age. *Developmental Psychology, 40,* 177–190.

Gathercole, S. E., Pickering, S. J., Hall, M., & Peaker, S. M. (2001). Dissociable lexical and phonological influences on serial recognition and serial recall. *Quarterly Journal of Experimental Psychology, 54A,* 1–30.

Gathercole, S. E., Willis, C. S., Emslie, H., & Baddeley, A. D. (1992). Phonological memory and vocabulary development during the early school years: A longitudinal study. *Developmental Psychology, 5,* 887–898.

Henry, L. A. (1991). The effects of word length and phonemic similarity in young children's short-term memory. *Quarterly Journal of Experimental Psychology, 43A,* 35–52.

Hitch, G. J., Halliday, M. S., Dodd, A., & Littler, J. E. (1989). Development of rehearsal in short-term memory: Differences between pictorial and spoken stimuli. *British Journal of Developmental Psychology, 7,* 347–363.

Hitch, G. J., Halliday, M. S., Schaafstal, A. M., & Schraagen, J. M. C. (1988). Visual working-memory in young children. *Memory and Cognition, 16,* 120–132.

Hulme, C., & Mackenzie, S. (1992). *Working memory and severe learning difficulties.* Hove, UK: Lawrence Erlbaum Associates Ltd.

Hulme, C., Maughan, S., & Brown, G. D. A. (1991). Memory for familiar and unfamiliar words: Evidence for a long-term memory contribution to short-term memory span. *Journal of Memory and Language, 30,* 685–701.

Hulme, C., & Roodenrys, S. (1995). Practitioner review: Verbal working memory development and its disorders. *Journal of Child Psychology and Psychiatry, 36,* 373–398.

Hulme, C., Thomson, N., Muir, C., & Lawrence, A. (1984). Speech rate and the development of short-term memory span. *Journal of Experimental Child Psychology, 38,* 241–253.

Jarrold, C., & Baddeley, A. D. (1997). Short-term memory for verbal and visuospatial information in Down syndrome. *Cognitive Neuropsychiatry, 2,* 101–122.

Jarrold, C., Baddeley, A. D., & Hewes, A. K. (1999). Genetically dissociated components of working memory: Evidence from Down and Williams syndrome. *Neuropsychologia, 37,* 637–651.

Jarrold, C., Baddeley, A. D., & Hewes, A. K. (2000). Verbal short-term memory deficits in Down syndrome: A consequence of problems in rehearsal? *Journal of Child Psychology and Psychiatry, 41*, 233–244.

Jarrold, C., Baddeley, A. D., Hewes, A. K., Leeke, T., & Phillips, C. E. (2004). What links verbal short-term memory performance and vocabulary level? Evidence of changing relationships among individuals with learning disability. *Journal of Memory and Language, 50*, 134–148.

Jarrold, C., Baddeley, A. D., & Phillips, C. E. (1999). Down syndrome and the phonological loop: The evidence for, and importance of, a specific verbal short-term memory deficit. *Down Syndrome: Research and Practice, 6*, 61–75.

Jarrold, C., Baddeley, A. D., & Phillips, C. E. (2002). Verbal short-term memory in Down syndrome: A problem of memory, audition, or speech? *Journal of Speech, Language, and Hearing Research, 45*, 531–544.

Jarrold, C., Baddeley, A. D., & Phillips, C. E. (in press). Long-term memory for verbal and visual information in Down syndrome and Williams syndrome: Performance on the doors and people test. *Manuscript submitted for publication.*

Jarrold, C., Cowan, N., Hewes, A. K., & Riby, D. M. (2004). Speech timing and verbal short-term memory: Evidence for contrasting deficits in Down syndrome and Williams syndrome. *Journal of Memory and Language, 51*, 365–380.

Kanno, K., & Ikeda, Y. (2002). Word-length effect in verbal short-term memory in individuals with Down syndrome. *Journal of Intellectual Disability Research, 46*, 613–618.

Kay-Raining Bird, E., & Chapman, R. S. (1994). Sequential recall in individuals with Down syndrome. *Journal of Speech and Hearing Research, 37*, 1369–1380.

Kemps, E. (2001). Complexity effects in visuospatial working memory: Implications for the role of long-term memory. *Memory, 9*, 13–27.

Kirk, S. A., McCarthy, J. J., & Kirk, W. D. (1968). *Examiner's manual for Illinois Test of Psycholinguistic Abilities.* Urbana, IL: University of Illinois Press.

Langdon Down, J. (1866). Observations on an ethnic classification of idiots. *Clinical Lectures and Reports of the London Hospital, 3*, 259–262.

Laws, G. (1998). The use of nonword repetition as a test of phonological memory in children with Down syndrome. *Journal of Child Psychology and Psychiatry, 39*, 1119–1130.

Laws, G. (2002). Working memory in children and adolescents with Down syndrome: Evidence from a colour memory experiment. *Journal of Child Psychology and Psychiatry, 43*, 353–364.

Laws, G., & Bishop, D. V. M. (2004). A comparison of language abilities in adolescents with Down syndrome and children with specific language impairment. *Journal of Speech, Language, and Hearing Research, 46*, 1324–1339.

Laws, G., & Gunn, D. M. (2004). Phonological memory as a predictor of language comprehension in Down syndrome: A five-year follow-up study. *Journal of Child Psychology and Psychiatry, 45*, 326–337.

Laws, G., MacDonald, J., & Buckley, S. (1996). The effects of a short training in the use of a rehearsal strategy on memory for words and pictures in children with Down syndrome. *Down Syndrome: Research and Practice, 4*, 70–78.

Laws, G., MacDonald, J., Buckley, S., & Broadley, I. (1995). Long-term maintenance of memory skills taught to children with Down syndrome. *Down Syndrome: Research and Practice, 3*, 103–109.

Logie, R. H., Della Sala, S., Laiacona, M., Chambers, P., & Wynn, V. (1996). Group aggregates and individual reliability: The case of verbal short-term memory. *Memory and Cognition, 24,* 305–321.

Lovatt, P., Avons, S. E., & Masterson, J. (2002). Output decay in immediate serial recall: Speech time revisited. *Journal of Memory and Language, 46,* 227–243.

Marcell, M. M., & Armstrong, V. (1982). Auditory and visual sequential memory of Down syndrome and nonretarded children. *American Journal of Mental Deficiency, 87,* 86–95.

Marcell, M. M., & Cohen, S. (1992). Hearing abilities of Down syndrome and other mentally handicapped adolescents. *Research in Developmental Disabilities, 15,* 533–551.

Marcell, M. M., & Weeks, S. L. (1988). Short-term memory difficulties and Down syndrome. *Journal of Mental Deficiency Research, 32,* 153–162.

McDade, H. L., & Adler, S. (1980). Down syndrome and short-term memory impairment: A storage or retrieval deficit? *American Journal of Mental Deficiency, 84,* 561–567.

Nichols, S., Jones, W., Roman, M. J., Wulfeck, B., Delis, D. C., Reilly, J., et al. (2004). Mechanisms of verbal memory impairment in four neurodevelopmental disorders. *Brain and Language, 88,* 180–189.

Nicolson, R. I. (1981). The relationship between memory span and processing speed. In M. Friedman, J. P. Das, & N. O'Connor (Eds.), *Intelligence and learning* (pp. 179–183). New York: Plenum Press.

Numminen, H., Service, E., Ahonen, T., & Ruoppila, I. (2001). Working memory and everyday cognition in adult persons with Down syndrome. *Journal of Intellectual Disability Research, 45,* 157–168.

Papagno, C., & Vallar, G. (1995). Verbal short-term memory and vocabulary learning in polyglots. *Quarterly Journal of Experimental Psychology, 48A,* 98–107.

Pennington, B. F., Moon, J., Edgin, J. O., Stedron, J., & Nadel, L. (2003). The neuropsychology of Down syndrome: Evidence for hippocampal dysfunction. *Child Development, 74,* 75–93.

Purser, H. R. M., & Jarrold, C. (2005). Impaired verbal short-term memory in Down syndrome reflects a capacity limitation rather than atypically rapid forgetting. *Journal of Experimental Child Psychology, 91,* 1–23.

Raine, A., Hulme, C., Chadderton, H., & Bailey, P. (1991). Verbal short-term memory span in speech-disordered children: Implications for articulatory coding in short-term memory. *Child Development, 62,* 415–423.

Rohr, A., & Burr, D. B. (1978). Etiological differences in patterns of psycholinguistic development of children of IQ 30 to 60. *American Journal of Mental Deficiency, 82,* 549–553.

Roodenrys, S., & Hinton, M. (2002). Sublexical or lexical effects on serial recall of nonwords? *Journal of Experimental Psychology: Learning, Memory, and Cognition, 28,* 29–33.

Roodenrys, S., Hulme, C., & Brown, G. (1993). The development of short-term memory span: Separable effects of speech rate and long-term memory. *Journal of Experimental Child Psychology, 56,* 431–442.

Seung, H.-K., & Chapman, R. S. (2000). Digit span in individuals with Down syndrome and in typically developing children: Temporal aspects. *Journal of Speech, Language, and Hearing Research, 43,* 609–620.

Seung, H.-K., & Chapman, R. S. (2003). The effect of story presentation rates on story retelling by individuals with Down syndrome. *Applied Psycholinguistics, 24,* 603–620.

Standing, L., Bond, B., Smith, P., & Isely, C. (1980). Is the immediate memory span determined by subvocalization rate? *British Journal of Psychology, 71,* 525–539.

Standing, L., & Curtis, L. (1989). Subvocalization rate versus other predictors of the memory span. *Psychological Reports, 65,* 487–495.

Steele, J. (1996). Epidemiology: Incidence, prevalence and size of the Down syndrome population. In B. Stratford & P. Gunn (Eds.), *New approaches to Down syndrome* (pp. 45–72). London: Cassell.

Steele, J., & Stratford, B. (1995). Present and future possibilities for the UK population with Down syndrome. *American Journal of Mental Deficiency, 86,* 465–472.

Stratford, B. (1996). In the beginning. In B. Stratford & P. Gunn (Eds.), *New approaches to Down syndrome* (pp. 3–11). London: Cassell.

Stratford, B., & Metcalf, J. A. (1982). Recognition, reproduction and recall in children with Down syndrome. *Australia and New Zealand Journal of Developmental Disabilities, 8,* 125–132.

Tehan, G., & Lalor, D. M. (2000). Individual differences in memory span: The contribution of rehearsal access to lexical memory, and output speed. *Quarterly Journal of Experimental Psychology, 53A,* 1012–1038.

Thorn, A. S. C., & Gathercole, S. E. (2001). Language differences in verbal short-term memory do not exclusively originate in the process of subvocal rehearsal. *Psychonomic Bulletin and Review, 8,* 357–364.

Thorn, A. S. C., Gathercole, S. E., & Frankish, C. R. (2002). Language familiarity effects in short-term memory: The role of output delay and long-term knowledge. *Quarterly Journal of Experimental Psychology, 55A,* 1363–1383.

Thorndike, R. L., Hagen, E. P., & Sattler, J. M. (1986). *Stanford-Binet Intelligence Scale* (4th ed.). Chicago: Riverside.

Towse, J. N., & Hitch, G. J. (1995). Is there a relationship between task demand and storage space in tests of working memory capacity. *Quarterly Journal of Experimental Psychology, 48A,* 108–124.

Vallar, G., Di Betta, A. M., & Silveri, M. C. (1997). The phonological short-term store rehearsal system: Patterns of impairment and neural correlates. *Neuropsychologia, 35,* 795–812.

Vallar, G., & Papagno, C. (1995). Neuropsychological impairments of short-term memory. In A. D. Baddeley, B. A. Wilson, & F. Watts (Eds.), *Handbook of memory disorders* (pp. 135–165). Chichester, UK: John Wiley.

Varnhagen, C. K., Das, J. P., & Varnhagen, S. (1987). Auditory and visual memory span: Cognitive processing by TMR individuals with Down syndrome or other etiologies. *American Journal of Mental Deficiency, 91,* 398–405.

Vicari, S., Bellucci, S., & Carlesimo, G. A. (2000). Implicit and explicit memory: A functional dissociation in persons with Down syndrome. *Neuropsychologia, 38,* 240–251.

Vicari, S., Carlesimo, A., & Caltagirone, C. (1995). Short-term memory in persons with intellectual disabilities and Down syndrome. *Journal of Intellectual Disability Research, 39,* 532–537.

Vicari, S., Caselli, M. C., Gagliardi, C., Tonucci, F., & Volterra, V. (2002). Language acquisition in special populations: A comparison between Down and Williams syndromes. *Neuropsychologia, 40,* 2461–2470.

Vicari, S., Marotta, L., & Carlesimo, G. A. (2004). Verbal short-term memory in Down syndrome: An articulatory loop deficit. *Journal of Intellectual Disability Research, 48*, 80–92.

Waters, G., Rochon, E., & Caplan, D. (1992). The role of high-level speech planning in rehearsal: Evidence from patients with apraxia of speech. *Journal of Memory and Language, 31*, 54–73.

Waugh, N. C., & Norman, D. A. (1965). Primary memory. *Psychological Review, 72*, 89–104.

Wilson, B. A., & Ivani-Chalian, R. (1995). Performance of adults with Down syndrome on the children's version of the Rivermead Behavioural Memory Test: A brief report. *British Journal of Clinical Psychology, 34*, 85–88.

Wishart, J. (1993). The development of learning difficulties in children with Down syndrome. *Journal of Intellectual Disability Research, 37*, 389–403.

Wisniewski, H. M., & Silverman, W. (1996). Alzheimer's disease, neuropathology and dementia in Down syndrome. In J. A. Rondal, J. Perera, L. Nadel, & A. Comblain (Eds.), *Down syndrome. Psychological, psychobiological, and socio-educational perspectives* (pp. 43–50). London: Whurr Publishers.

12 Working memory in Williams syndrome[1]

Melissa L. Rowe and
Carolyn B. Mervis

OVERVIEW

The cognitive profile for Williams syndrome is characterized by relative strength in verbal short-term memory (typically measured by forward digit recall) and language and severe weakness in visuospatial construction. Given this pattern, individuals with Williams syndrome might be expected to have significantly better verbal working memory and significantly weaker spatial working memory than CA- and IQ-matched individuals with other forms of mental retardation. Results are consistent with this expectation for memory tasks that do not require mental manipulation. Thus, children and adults with Williams syndrome perform significantly better on measures of forward digit recall and the first trial of word list recall than do CA- and IQ-/MA-matched groups with Down syndrome or mental retardation of mixed or unknown etiology. Performance is at or above the level expected for MA and is affected by the same semantic and phonological factors as for the general population. Children and adults with Williams syndrome perform significantly worse than CA- and IQ-/MA-matched individuals with other forms of mental retardation on forward Corsi (spatial) recall. When mental manipulation is required, however, between-group differences are considerably reduced. On backward digit recall tasks, groups of individuals with Williams syndrome consistently demonstrate longer spans than CA- and IQ-/MA-matched groups with other forms of mental retardation, but the between-group differences are not significant. In the only study that compared backward Corsi span, mean span for the Williams syndrome and Down syndrome groups was almost identical. In contrast to prior characterizations stressing the independence of language and cognition in Williams syndrome, verbal memory abilities are strongly related to grammatical and vocabulary abilities in Williams syndrome well into adolescence. These relations are stronger than for the general population, suggesting that language acquisition by individuals with Williams syndrome is more dependent on verbal working memory than it is for typically developing children. Methodological issues regarding the use of group matching designs, especially when the groups differ in CA, are discussed and difficulties in interpreting the results of such studies are stressed.

BACKGROUND

Williams syndrome (often called Williams-Beuren syndrome in Europe) is caused by a microdeletion of ~1.6 Mb on chromosome 7q11.23 (Ewart et al., 1993). So far, ~20 genes have been mapped to the deleted region (Hillier et al., 2003). This deletion is the same in about 99% of individuals with Williams syndrome (C. A. Morris, personal communication, 2005); of the remaining 1%, slightly more than half have longer deletions (associated with more severe mental retardation; Morris & Mervis, 2000; Stock et al., 2003). The prevalence of Williams syndrome has widely been assumed to be 1/20,000–1/25,000 live births. However, the results of a recent epidemiological study (Strømme, Bjørnstad, & Ramstad, 2002) indicated a prevalence of 1/7500 live births.

Williams syndrome is associated with distinctive medical, cognitive, and personality phenotypes. The medical phenotype (see Morris, 2005) includes a characteristic set of facial features (Williams syndrome facies), cardiac abnormalities (most commonly supravalvar aortic stenosis), connective tissue abnormalities, failure to thrive in infancy, hypercalcemia, hypersensitivity to sound, early puberty associated with a briefer growth spurt leading to adult height <3rd percentile, and attention deficit hyperactivity disorder. The cognitive phenotype (see Mervis & Klein-Tasman, 2000; Mervis et al., 2000) includes mild to moderate mental retardation, a relative strength in verbal short-term memory and language, and severe weakness in visuospatial construction (e.g., writing, drawing, pattern construction/block design). The personality phenotype includes gregariousness, overfriendliness, high empathy, oversensitivity, and anxiety (Klein-Tasman & Mervis, 2003; Mervis & Klein-Tasman, 2000).

As is true for most syndromes, Williams syndrome has considerable variability for each phenotypic feature. Even though 99% of individuals with Williams syndrome have the identical ("classic") 1.6 Mb deletion (including *elastin*, the gene involved in the cardiac disease associated with the syndrome), only 80% have detectable cardiovascular disease (Morris, 2006) and of these affected individuals, some require only monitoring by a cardiologist, whereas others need lifesaving surgery to relieve obstruction. Similarly, a wide range of intelligence has been associated with Williams syndrome; although most individuals have mild to moderate mental retardation, some have intelligence in the normal range and others have severe mental retardation (Mervis et al., 2000; Morris & Mervis, 2000). Furthermore, although extreme difficulty with visuospatial construction is one of the hallmark characteristics of Williams syndrome, for a few individuals, visuospatial construction is a strength (Mervis et al., 2000). Although verbal short-term memory is a relative strength for most individuals with Williams syndrome, some individuals do not perform any better on verbal short-term memory measures than on measures of spatial cognition (Mervis et al., 2000); this is especially characteristic of very low-functioning individuals. So far, neither genetic nor environmental factors that may alter phenotypic expression for individuals with classic deletions have been identified for Williams syndrome.

Although Williams syndrome was first described in the medical literature in the mid-twentieth century (Beuren, Schulze, Eberle, Harmjanz, & Apitz, 1964; Stapleton, MacDonald, & Lightwood, 1957; Williams, Barratt-Boyes, & Lowe, 1961), the genetic basis for this syndrome was not discovered until 1993 (Ewart et al., 1993) and a genetic test was not commercially available until 1995. Until then, the diagnosis was based on the clinical phenotype, with the result that about 20% of individuals clinically diagnosed with Williams syndrome were later found not to have a deletion. Even after the genetic test became available, many research groups continued to define Williams syndrome clinically; only very recently have most groups begun to restrict the Williams syndrome participants in their studies to individuals with confirmed deletions. This restriction is important; results of a study of individuals who had a clinical diagnosis of Williams syndrome but who did not have a deletion indicated that most of these individuals did not fit the cognitive profile for genetically defined Williams syndrome (Mervis et al., 2000).

In this chapter, we review research on the verbal and spatial working memory abilities of people who have Williams syndrome. Relations between working memory abilities and other cognitive abilities are also considered. We approach working memory ability from the Baddeley and Hitch (1974; Baddeley, 1986) perspective. Thus, working memory is defined as the capacity to hold and manipulate information "online." Working memory enables temporary storage of information while incoming data are actively processed and information from long-term storage is retrieved. Working memory is particularly important for carrying out complex cognitive tasks such as complicated mental arithmetic, in which a person must hold the results of previous calculations in working memory while working on the next stage. Working memory also represents an essential aspect of higher cognitive processes such as language, planning, and problem solving (Baddeley, 1986). According to the Baddeley and Hitch model, working memory contains two complementary slave systems for storing information over the short term: the phonological loop and the visuospatial sketchpad, and a central executive that controls attention. The phonological loop retains and processes verbal material in a phonological code by way of a passive phonological store and an active rehearsal mechanism. The visuospatial sketchpad is involved in temporary maintenance of visual images and visuospatial information. Both slave systems are linked to the central executive, a limited capacity central processor that manages the temporary storage and processing of information from both slave systems.

The literature on memory abilities of people who have Williams syndrome is considerably more limited than the literature on memory abilities of people who have Down syndrome or who have mental retardation either of mixed or unknown etiology. Although Williams syndrome was formally identified in the early 1960s, very little cognitive research was conducted on people who had this syndrome until the late 1980s. In recent years, the pace of research has increased considerably, and most studies of the memory abilities of individuals with Williams syndrome were published within the past 10 years. Because the interpretation of the findings from many of these studies is complicated by methodological difficulties affecting the majority of studies that make comparisons between a group of participants with Williams syndrome and other contrast groups, we begin by characterizing these difficulties and the limitations they place on interpretation of apparently statistically significant results.

METHODOLOGICAL ISSUES

Studies of individuals who have developmental disabilities typically include one or more control groups matched to the target group on one or more control variables. Examples of control variables are mental age (MA), language age (LA), and chronological age (CA). The validity of any conclusions drawn from statistical tests comparing the performance of the groups on the dependent measures rests critically on at least two factors: (1) How closely were the groups matched on the control variables? (2) What are the measurement characteristics of the scores used to compare the groups, whether on the control variables or the target variables? The appropriateness of the commonly made prediction that groups that are matched for a control variable such as MA or nonverbal reasoning ability but are not matched for CA should perform at equivalent levels on the target variable(s) is determined by these measurement characteristics. In this section, we briefly consider these issues. (For a more extensive consideration, see Mervis, 2004; Mervis & Klein-Tasman, 2004; Mervis & Robinson, 2003, 2005.)

Determining if groups are matched on the control variable(s)

Researchers are well aware that if the target group (individuals with Williams syndrome, in the case of this chapter) is not matched to the control group(s) on the control variable(s), then comparison of the performance of the two groups on the target variable(s) is not valid. Determination of whether the groups are adequately matched is typically made based on the results of *t*-tests comparing the groups on the control variable(s). If the groups do not differ significantly, then they are considered matched. Harcum (1990, p. 404) describes this phenomenon as "casual acceptance of the null hypothesis." *P* levels of .06–.15 are commonly reported as evidence that groups are matched (see Mervis & Klein-Tasman, 2004, for examples). The null hypothesis should not be accepted so easily, however. In terms of the group-matching design, the probability of making a Type II error (accepting the null hypothesis that the groups do not differ even though they do) is of primary concern. As the level increases, the probability of making a Type II error decreases. Frick (1995) proposes the following guidelines: Any *p*-value less than .20 is too low to accept the null hypothesis. A *p*-value greater than .50 is large enough to accept the null hypothesis. A *p*-value between .20 and .50 is ambiguous.

Predicted outcomes as a function of measurement characteristics of control and target variables

In many studies, the target and control groups are well matched for CA over a narrow CA range. This is the simplest case; cases in which the groups cover a wide CA range or the groups are not matched for CA are more complex and are considered below. An example of the "simple" case would be a target group of children with Williams syndrome aged 10–12 years matched to a control group of children with Down syndrome of the same mean CA, with a similar standard deviation and range. These children might in addition be well matched for nonverbal reasoning ability; the target variable might be digit recall. If mean digit recall for the Williams syndrome group was found to be significantly better than mean digit recall for the Down syndrome group, and the Down syndrome group was considered to be the standard, it would be reasonable to conclude that children with Williams syndrome demonstrate a relative strength in verbal short-term memory (as measured by digit recall). Alternatively, if Williams syndrome was the standard, it would be reasonable to conclude that children with Down syndrome demonstrate a relative weakness in verbal short-term memory.

Much more commonly, designs are used in which either two syndromes are compared but each group spans a wide age range and the groups are matched for some type of ability (e.g., raw score on a measure of nonverbal reasoning or vocabulary) or children with a syndrome are compared to typically developing children matched for raw score on some assessment (again, examples include raw scores on measures of nonverbal reasoning or vocabulary). If significant between-group differences are found on the target variable (e.g., digit recall), researchers typically interpret these differences as indicating that the target group's ability on the target variable is lower than it should be (assuming that the control group of typically developing children performed better than the target group – the most common finding). This conclusion rests critically on the assumption that development of the control variable and the target variable occurs at the same rate. If this assumption were correct, then it would be reasonable to expect that children of different ages who earned the same raw score on a particular control variable should also earn the same raw score as each other on the target variable. In this situation, the finding that the target group scored significantly lower than the control group on the target variable would indicate that the target group's performance was lower than expected for level of ability on the control variable.

However, the assumption that the target variable and the control variable are developing at the same rate is very often incorrect; abilities in different domains develop at different (often nonlinear) rates. These differences in rates of development are well illustrated in Figure 12.1, which uses age equivalents (corresponding to ability scores – similar to raw scores) from the School-Age form of the Differential Ability Scales (DAS; Elliott, 1990), a commonly used assessment of intellectual abilities. This figure demonstrates the expected variability in age-equivalent scores for language, visuospatial construction, and verbal short-term memory (forward digit recall) as a function of CA, given a constant age-equivalent score of 7 years 10 months on the Matrices subtest (measuring nonverbal reasoning) and equivalent levels of ability relative to peers (same standard score) on each of these measures. As may be seen in this figure, given the same level of nonverbal reasoning ability, young children would be *predicted* to have much better forward digit recall than adolescents if each group's level of forward digit recall relative to same-CA peers was the same as its level of performance relative to same-CA peers on nonverbal reasoning. Thus, the commonly found pattern of better

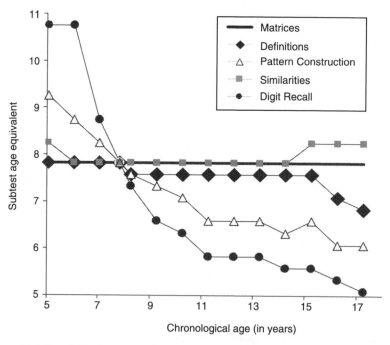

Figure 12.1 Variability in expected age equivalent (ability score – similar to raw score) on DAS verbal, verbal memory, and visuospatial construction subtests as a function of CA, given a constant age equivalent of 7 years 10 months on the Matrices (nonverbal reasoning) subtest and the assumption that the child has earned identical standard scores on all subtests. Reprinted with permission from Mervis (2004).

performance on the target variable for the younger typically developing children than the older syndrome group may well not indicate that the syndrome group has a specific deficit in whatever was being measured by the target variable. To conclude that the syndrome group does have a specific deficit, it is necessary to show that that group performs significantly worse than expected given its performance on the control variable, relative to same-CA peers. This is most easily accomplished by comparing standard scores on subtests of a particular assessment or on two assessments that were conormed or that were well-normed on the same type of norming sample at about the same time (see Mervis & Robinson, 2005, for further discussion). Unfortunately, studies that are designed to permit this type of comparison are rare.

VERBAL WORKING MEMORY IN WILLIAMS SYNDROME

Forward digit recall

The majority of studies of the verbal working memory abilities of individuals with Williams syndrome have been focused on forward digit span tasks. In these tasks, the researcher presents a list of digits (typically at a rate of one digit per second) and the participant is asked to repeat the list verbatim. Initial list length is usually two digits, and two trials for each length are usually presented. If the participant correctly repeats at least one of the two-digit strings, the researcher presents two trials of three-digit lists. This process continues until the participant is not able to correctly repeat the list on either of the two trials of a given list length or until the participant correctly repeats the longest list included in the study (typically eight or nine digits). The participant's span is considered to be the length of the longest list he or she was able to repeat verbatim (correct items in correct order). Comparison groups have included individuals with Down syndrome, individuals with mental retardation of mixed etiologies, and typically developing children.

The results of studies using individuals with Down syndrome as controls consistently indicate that digit recall is a relative strength for both children and adults with Williams syndrome. The first study to make this comparison was conducted by Wang and Bellugi (1994), who compared the performance of a group of adolescents with Williams syndrome to that of a CA- and MA-matched group of adolescents with Down syndrome. The Williams syndrome group was found to have a significantly longer forward digit span. Klein and Mervis (1999) compared the performance of pairs of 9- to 10-year-old children with Williams syndrome and Down syndrome matched for both CA and total general cognitive raw score (GCS) on the McCarthy Scales of Children's Abilities (MSCA; McCarthy, 1972). The children with Williams syndrome had significantly longer forward digit spans. Vicari et al. (2004), in a comparison of the performance of a group of children and adolescents with Williams syndrome to a Down syndrome group matched for CA and

MA, with IQ as a covariate, found that the Williams syndrome group had significantly better forward digit recall. Edgin (2003) compared the forward digit spans of a group of adolescents and young adults with Williams syndrome to a CA-matched Down syndrome group, with IQ as a covariate. Once again, forward digit span was significantly longer for the Williams syndrome group than for the Down syndrome group. (For further discussion of the memory abilities of individuals with Down syndrome, please see Jarrold et al., chapter 11, this volume.)

A possible interpretation of these findings is that rather than individuals with Williams syndrome having a relative strength in digit recall, individuals with Down syndrome have a relative weakness in digit recall. After all, although children with Williams syndrome evidence a relative strength in grammatical ability in comparison to CA- and IQ-matched children with Down syndrome, this apparent strength is actually simply a reflection of the weakness in grammatical ability associated with Down syndrome. When the grammatical abilities of children with Williams syndrome are compared to those of CA- and IQ-matched children with mental retardation of mixed etiologies, no differences are found (see review in Mervis, Robinson, Rowe, Becerra, & Klein-Tasman, 2003). Thus, comparisons of the memory abilities of individuals with Williams syndrome to those of well-matched individuals with other forms of mental retardation are important.

Two studies of forward digit recall by individuals with Williams syndrome have included a well-matched comparison group of individuals with mixed etiologies of mental retardation. Udwin and Yule (1991) compared the digit recall abilities of children with Williams syndrome to those of children with mental retardation of mixed etiology matched for CA and verbal IQ and found that the Williams syndrome group had significantly better digit recall than the mixed etiology group. Devenny et al. (2004) compared the forward digit spans of adults with Williams syndrome to CA- and IQ-matched adults with mental retardation of unknown etiology and found significantly better performance for the Williams syndrome group. The findings from these two studies, combined with the findings from the studies including a matched Down syndrome comparison group, indicate that forward digit recall is indeed a relative strength for individuals with Williams syndrome.

The studies described so far are the only studies of forward digit recall of individuals with Williams syndrome that have matched groups for CA. Groups were also matched for MA and/or IQ. As indicated in the Methodological Issues section above, results for studies that do not match groups for CA and MA/IQ are difficult to interpret unless comparisons are based on standard scores. Three additional studies have been reported in which groups were not matched for CA. Jarrold, Baddeley, and Hewes (1999) conducted two studies of the forward digit recall abilities of individuals with Williams syndrome. In the first study, the two comparison groups included individuals with Down syndrome and individuals with mental retardation of mixed etiology. Mean CA for the Williams syndrome group was more than 4 years older than mean CA for either of the other groups. Mean verbal MA (age equivalent on the British Picture Vocabulary Scale; BPVS; Dunn, Whetton, & Pintilie, 1982) was considerably higher for the Williams syndrome group than for either of the other groups. Mean nonverbal MA (age equivalent on the Pattern Construction subtest of the DAS; Elliott, 1990) for the Williams syndrome group was considerably lower than for the mixed-etiology mental retardation group but higher than for the Down syndrome group. Results of an analysis of covariance controlling for spatial span, nonverbal MA, and verbal MA indicated that the forward digit recall abilities of the Williams syndrome group were significantly better than those of the Down syndrome group but equivalent to those of the mixed-etiology group. In the second study, the Williams syndrome group was matched on nonverbal MA to a mixed etiology group with a mean CA almost 5 years younger and a typically developing group with a mean CA 12 years younger. Mean verbal MA was about 2 years older for the Williams syndrome group than the mixed-etiology group and 4 years older than for the typically developing group. Analysis of covariance controlling for verbal MA indicated no differences among the groups in forward digit recall. As the authors point out, one needs to be careful interpreting results of analyses of covariance when the groups differ considerably on the covariates (as they do in this case). This is especially true when the groups also differ considerably on CA.

Vicari and his colleagues have conducted two studies comparing the performance of children with Williams syndrome to much younger MA-matched typically developing children. Vicari, Brizzolara, Carlesimo, Pezzini, and Volterra (1996) found no differences between the groups in forward digit recall and concluded that for children with Williams syndrome, forward digit recall was at the level expected for MA. Vicari et al. (2004) compared the performance of a group of children and adults with Williams syndrome to that of a much younger group of typically developing children matched for MA and found that the Williams syndrome group performed significantly worse than the typically developing group on forward digit recall. The authors interpreted this difference as indicating that forward digit recall was below MA level for people with Williams syndrome. However, given the very large discrepancy in mean CA for the two groups, a significant difference in forward digit recall, favoring the typically developing group, would be expected assuming the two groups were well matched for MA (see Figure 12.1). Thus, both the significant difference found in the second study and the lack of a significant difference in the first study are difficult to interpret; at a minimum they indicate that forward recall abilities of children with Williams syndrome are at the level expected for MA; it is possible that forward recall abilities are above the level expected for MA (again, see Figure 12.1).

In summary, the results of studies controlling for CA and IQ or MA indicate that forward digit recall is a relative strength for individuals with Williams syndrome relative to both individuals with Down syndrome and individuals with mental retardation of mixed etiologies. Findings from studies comparing younger groups of children to individuals with Williams syndrome are difficult to interpret given the methodological problems inherent in such designs, but at a minimum indicate that forward digit recall abilities of individuals with Williams syndrome are at the level expected for MA.

List learning

The ability of individuals with Williams syndrome to recall supraspan lists of words has been assessed in three studies of list learning. In these studies, lists contained 12–15 words presented at a rate of one word per second. Words did not need to be recalled in the order in which they were presented. CA matching occurred in only one of the studies, and in that study for only one of the comparisons. Nichols et al. (2004) compared the list-learning abilities of adolescents with Williams syndrome to a CA- and MA-matched group of adolescents with Down syndrome, using the California Verbal Learning Test – Children's Version (CVLT-C; Delis, Kramer, Kaplan, & Ober, 1994), a list of 15 words composed of 5 words from each of three semantic categories. The Williams syndrome group recalled significantly more words than the Down syndrome group on both the first presentation of the first list (List A) and the interference list (List B). This finding is consistent with the results for forward digit recall. Nichols et al. also included three additional groups of younger children matched to each other for CA and MA and to the Williams syndrome and Down syndrome groups for MA: typically developing children, children with specific language impairment, and children with early onset focal lesions. The Williams syndrome group did not differ from any of these three groups with regard to number of words recalled on List A or List B. Interpretation of this finding is problematic because the Williams syndrome group is on average 7 years older than the other three groups (again, see the patterns in Figure 12.1).

Vicari and his colleagues (Vicari, Belluci, & Carlesimo, 2001; Vicari, Brizzolara et al., 1996) have conducted two studies of list learning in which adolescents with Williams syndrome were compared to much younger typically developing children matched for MA. In the first study, 12 unrelated high frequency words were read aloud at the rate of one word every 2 seconds. The child was required to repeat as many words as possible. The typically developing group recalled significantly more words than the Williams syndrome group. In particular, there was a significant between-group primacy effect, a marginal mid-list effect, and no recency effect. In the second study, Vicari et al. (2001) presented participants with 12 high-frequency nonsemantically related words one at a time. Each word was accompanied by a picture of the item and the child was asked to repeat the word. After all 12 items had been presented, the participant was asked to recall the list. There was no difference between the groups in the number of words recalled.

In summary, the results of the one study in which CA and MA were controlled indicated that, consistent with the findings from the forward digit recall studies, individuals with Williams syndrome show a relative strength in verbal list learning. The results of the studies comparing adolescents with Williams syndrome to much younger MA-matched typically developing children are mixed, with one study finding Williams syndrome performance significantly lower than the performance of the MA-matched typically developing group and two studies finding equivalent performance for the Williams syndrome and typically developing groups. Once again, interpretation of these findings is problematic because the Williams syndrome group is much older than the typically developing groups, and therefore would be expected to have lower memory abilities, as illustrated in the patterns shown in Figure 12.1. Because age-based standard scores are not available, it is impossible to know if the Williams syndrome group's performance on list-learning tasks is at the level expected for their MA or instead is higher than expected for MA.

Phonological and semantic contributions to verbal working memory

The working memory performance of typically developing individuals varies as a function of the words included on the to-be-remembered list. Factors include word frequency (used as a surrogate measure for word familiarity), word length, and phonological similarity. In general, more words are remembered if the words are high frequency (rather than low frequency), if they are short (rather than long; one syllable rather than multisyllabic), and if the words are dissimilar (rather than similar) phonologically. The word frequency effect has been attributed to the impact of long-term memory (in the form of semantic information) (Hulme, Maughan, & Brown, 1991). The word-length effect is attributed to differences in articulatory time; long words take longer to articulate and/or rehearse than do short words (Baddeley & Hitch, 1974). The phonological similarity effect occurs because phonologically dissimilar words are represented by more distinctive traces in working memory than are phonologically similar words and thus are easier to retrieve (Baddeley, 1986). Recently, each of these factors has been investigated in studies of the verbal memory abilities of individuals who have Williams syndrome.

Vicari, Carlesimo, Brizzolara, and Pezzini (1996) conducted the first study of working memory in Williams syndrome that used words rather than digits as stimuli. In this study, the MA of a group of children with Williams syndrome was determined based on the Leiter International Performance Scale – Revised (Leiter, 1979) and then a comparison group of children whose CA matched the MA of the Williams syndrome group was selected. The two groups differed in CA by a mean of 5½ years. The same procedure was followed as in the digit recall studies, beginning with lists containing two words presented at a rate of one word per second and continuing until the child could not repeat either of the lists of words of a particular length. Six types of lists were included, allowing for a comparison of high-frequency and low-frequency words of two different lengths (two or four syllables) and a comparison of low frequency words that were either acoustically similar or acoustically dissimilar. Results indicated that both groups showed word length, word frequency, and phonological similarity effects. The magnitude of the effects of word length and phonological similarity was similar for the Williams syndrome group and the typically developing group. However, the Williams syndrome group showed a smaller effect of word frequency than the typically developing group. Vicari, Carlesimo et al. interpreted this finding as indicating an impairment in the contribution of long-term memory to short-term memory for the Williams syndrome group, leading to over-dependence on phonological encoding at the expense of semantic encoding. Further evidence of a long-term verbal memory impairment in Williams syndrome is provided by Edgin's (2003) finding that adolescents and young adults with Williams syndrome showed a significantly smaller gain in number of words recalled (relative to initial recall) the fifth time a supraspan list of words was presented than did a CA-matched Down syndrome group; IQ was treated as a covariate in this analysis. Furthermore, although Nichols et al. (2004) found a significant difference between the Williams syndrome group and a CA-matched Down syndrome group in number of words recalled the first time a supraspan list was presented (as described earlier in this chapter), not only was the difference between groups on the fifth trial not significant, the fifth-trial means for the two groups were very similar, suggesting that the Down syndrome group again had gained significantly more words than the Williams syndrome group.

Majerus, Barisnikov, Vuillemin, Poncelet, and van der Linden (2003) compared the performance of 4 10- to 12-year-olds with Williams syndrome to 12 CA-matched typically developing children and 12 vocabulary-age (VA)-matched typically developing children (2 years younger than the WS group) on word span for lists varying in word length (one vs. three or four syllables) and lists varying in phonological similarity (similar vs. dissimilar). On average, the children with Williams syndrome performed as well as the VA-matched children on all of the lists and as well as the CA-matched children on all of the lists except the long words. These findings suggest that verbal working memory is a relative strength for children with Williams syndrome, and that on average these children show normal word-length and phonological similarity effects.

Laing et al. (2005) compared the word spans of a group of children and adults with Williams syndrome to two groups of typically developing con-trols. The first control group was individually matched to the participants with Williams syndrome for raw score on the British Ability Scales–II (BAS-II; Elliott, Smith, & McCullough, 1996) Recall of Digits subtest. The second control group was individually matched to the participants with Williams syndrome for raw score on the British Picture Vocabulary Scale–II (BPVS-II; Dunn, Dunn, Whetton, & Burley, 1997). Participants were asked to recall two sets of lists. The lists in one set varied by phonological similarity (phonologically similar list vs. phonologically dissimilar list) and the lists in the second set varied by concreteness (concrete vs. abstract words). Results indicated significant effects of both phonological similarity and concreteness on the word spans of all three groups, extending the previous finding that children with Williams syndrome show normal phonological similarity effects to adults with Williams syndrome and providing initial evidence of a normal concreteness effect. There were no significant differences between groups in word span for any of the types of lists.

To investigate the role of speech rate in memory performance for individuals with Williams syndrome, Jarrold, Cowan, Hewes, and Riby (2004) compared a group of children, adolescents, and young adults with Williams syndrome to a VA-matched group of typically developing 8-year-olds. Participants were asked to recall two lists of words (words with short spoken durations vs. words with long spoken durations). In addition, to measure articulation rate, participants were asked to repeat pairs of words (two short words or two long words) as rapidly as possible. Analysis of covariance (partialling out the effect of verbal MA) indicated that the control group recalled significantly more words than the Williams syndrome group, but that both groups showed equivalent word-length effects. Analyses of articulation time showed a marginal effect ($p = .07$) favoring the typically developing group. Further analyses indicated that for the Williams syndrome group, but not the control group, number of words recalled was significantly negatively correlated with articulation time and with pause time between words. Once the effect of articulation rate and pause duration were partialled out, the difference between the Williams syndrome group and the control group in the number of words recalled was no longer significant, suggesting that the initially identified significant between-group difference was due to differences in articulation rate and pause duration.

In summary, the results of the studies reviewed in this section suggest that the verbal working memory performance of individuals with Williams syndrome is affected by the same factors as for individuals who are developing typically. In particular, people with Williams syndrome show normal effects of word length, phonological similarity, and concreteness. Word frequency has been considered in only one study; results suggested that although there was an effect of word frequency, it was reduced relative to that for typically developing individuals. Vicari, Carlesimo et al. (1996) interpreted this difference as suggesting an impairment in verbal long-term memory; this possibility is consistent with the results of more recent studies of verbal long-term memory for lists of words.

Nonword repetition

The nonword repetition task is another measure of verbal working memory. In this task, participants are asked to repeat individual nonsense words designed to fit the phonotactics of the language that the participants speak.

Judgments of correct or incorrect are made by listening to the response; an incorrect score is given if there is any deviation at all from the presented nonword (excluding speech sound production problems). In principle, nonword repetition tasks provide a measure of verbal working memory that is not confounded by familiarity (Gathercole & Baddeley, 1989). In practice, nonword repetition tasks vary from those for which familiarity is not a factor (e.g., Montgomery, 1996) to those for which increased syllable length is accomplished by adding English morphemes such as -ually or -ation, which leads to a confound with familiarity (e.g., Children's Test of Nonword Repetition; CNRep; Gathercole & Baddeley, 1996).

Grant et al. (1997) administered the CNRep to 18 children and adults with WS (mean CA 18 years 7 months). The Williams syndrome group showed a normal pattern of performance on this measure, including an effect of syllable length, with decreasing performance as syllable length increased from two to three to four syllables but no further decrease for five syllables. The lack of difference between performance on four and five syllable words, also found for typically developing children, was attributed to the fact that the inclusion of familiar morphemes in the five-syllable nonsense words likely offset the expected increase in difficulty as a function of increase in number of syllables. The effect of syllable length remained significant even after the effect of wordlikeness was partialled out. As for typically developing children, there was no effect of the presence or absence of consonant clusters. Performance was significantly better on the high wordlikeness words than the low wordlikeness words. However, the pattern of relations between VA and age-equivalents (AE) for CNRep and digit recall differed significantly from that found for much younger children matched on either VA or nonverbal MA (as determined by performance on the Raven's Colored Matrices; Raven, 1986). In particular, VA was much higher than AE for CNRep and AE for digit recall for the Williams syndrome group, whereas the opposite pattern was found for typically developing five-year-olds. Note that once again, this pattern is to be expected, given the relations shown in Figure 12.1 between verbal ability, nonverbal ability, and memory ability, when CA varies widely.

Grant et al. (1997) also compared the performance of a subset of the Williams syndrome group to groups of five-year-olds matched for either VA or nonverbal MA. The MA-matched groups performed at the same level on the CNRep. However, the typically developing VA-matched group performed significantly better on the CNRep than did the Williams syndrome group. In contrast, Laing, Hulme, Grant, and Karmiloff-Smith (2001), also using the CNRep as the measure of nonword repetition, found that a group of children, adolescents, and adults with Williams syndrome (mean CA 15 years 1 month) performed equivalently to a group of much younger typically developing children matched for single-word reading AE as measured by the BAS Word Reading achievement test and VA as measured by the BPVS.

As part of the study described above, Majerus et al. (2003) also considered performance on a nonword repetition task that did not include French morphemes. Two types of nonwords were included: words that fit high-frequency phonotactic patterns for French and words that fit low-frequency phonotactic patterns for French. Performance of the Williams syndrome group was at or above the level of the VA-matched group of typically developing children. For two of the four measures (number of high-phonotactic frequency nonwords repeated correctly and number of low-phonotactic frequency nonword syllables repeated correctly), the Williams syndrome group did not differ from the CA-matched group. Barisnikov, van der Linden, and Poncelet (1996), in a case study of an adult with Williams syndrome using a nonword repetition task in which the nonwords did not include morphemes, found that this individual performed at the same level as CA-matched adults with normal intelligence.

In summary, the pattern of factors that affect the nonword repetition ability of individuals with Williams syndrome is the same as the pattern for typically developing individuals: Effects are found for syllable length and for native-language frequency of the phonotactics used in the nonwords. Performance is at least at nonverbal MA level and in some studies is at CA level, although the possibility of ceiling effects for the typically developing CA-matched participants has not been ruled out. When apparent differences in patterns of strengths and weaknesses have been found between the Williams syndrome group and much younger children matched for VA, the patterns have fit those expected based on differences in rate of development of the different skills, as illustrated in Figure 12.1.

Backward digit recall

Tests of backward digit recall follow the same format as those for forward digit recall, except that the participant is required to repeat the digits in reverse order. Success on this task requires the participant to remember the string of digits presented and then to mentally reverse the order of items in the string before repeating the digits aloud.

There have been very few studies of the backward digit recall abilities of individuals with Williams syndrome. Mervis, Morris, Bertrand, and Robinson (1999) reported data on the backward digit recall abilities of 36 adults with Williams syndrome. Four of the participants were not able to repeat even two digits in reverse order. At the other end of the ability range, three participants were able to repeat five digits in reverse order. Mean backward digit span was 2.67, which was 1.16 standard deviations below the mean reported by Banken (1985) for a sample of adults who had low average intelligence (mean WAIS-R IQ = 91).

The backward digit spans of adolescents and adults with Williams syndrome have been compared to those of adolescents and adults with Down syndrome in two studies. Wang and Bellugi (1994) found that although the mean backward digit span was higher for the Williams syndrome group than for the CA- and IQ-matched Down syndrome group, the difference in backward digit span between the groups was not significant. Similarly, Edgin (2003) found that the Williams syndrome group had a higher mean backward digit span than the CA-matched Down syndrome group but that, when IQ was treated as a covariate, the two groups did not differ significantly in backward digit span. Across the three studies, very similar backward digit spans were obtained for the Williams syndrome group, with a range from 2.61 to 2.67.

Devenny et al. (2004) compared the backward digit recall abilities of adults with Williams syndrome to those of CA- and IQ-matched adults with mental retardation of unknown etiology. Groups were split into younger (<50 years) and older (≥50 years) subgroups. The younger subgroups had significantly better backward digit recall than the older subgroups. Both the younger and older Williams syndrome subgroups performed better than the corresponding unknown etiology groups, but once again, the differences were not significant. The rate of decline as a function of CA also did not differ between the groups.

In summary, a similar pattern emerged from all three studies comparing the backward recall abilities of individuals with Williams syndrome to CA-matched groups with mental retardation. The Williams syndrome group consistently had a higher mean level of performance, but the between-group difference was not significant. It is possible that the lack of significant difference is due to low statistical power. However, since significant between-group differences were reliably found in the same studies for forward digit recall, at a minimum group-differences are more reliable for forward digit recall, which does not require mental manipulation of items in memory, than for backward digit recall, which does require mental manipulation.

SPATIAL WORKING MEMORY IN WILLIAMS SYNDROME

Visuospatial construction (e.g., drawing, pattern construction/block design) is widely considered to be the area of greatest weakness for individuals with Williams syndrome (e.g., Bellugi, Marks, Bihrle, & Sabo, 1988; Mervis et al., 1999, 2000). Given this finding, one would expect that individuals with Williams syndrome would have considerable difficulty with spatial working memory, and the results of most studies are consistent with this prediction.

The most commonly used measure of spatial working memory in studies that include people with Williams syndrome is the Corsi block-tapping task (Milner, 1971). The Corsi task involves a board on which nine neutral-colored blocks are fastened in a random arrangement. The participant is asked to tap a set of blocks in the same sequence that was presented by the researcher. The presentation of blocks begins with a sequence of two blocks tapped at a rate of one block per second and increases incrementally, exactly as in the forward digit span task described earlier in this chapter. Span is calculated the same way as for forward digit span.

Forward Corsi recall

Several of the previously described studies of forward digit recall also included the forward Corsi recall task. Wang and Bellugi (1994) found that adolescents and adults with Williams syndrome performed significantly worse on Corsi forward recall than did a CA- and IQ-matched Down syndrome group. Edgin (2003) replicated this finding for adolescents and adults with Williams syndrome compared to a CA-matched Down syndrome group; IQ was treated as a covariate in her analyses. Vicari et al. (2004) also reported poorer performance for a group of children, adolescents, and adults with Williams syndrome than for a CA- and MA-matched Down syndrome group, although the difference was not statistically significant.

Vicari and his colleagues have also performed several studies of forward Corsi recall using typically developing children as a control group. The Vicari et al. (2004) study just described included a considerably younger group of typically developing children matched to the Williams syndrome group for MA on the Italian version of the Stanford-Binet Intelligence Scale Form L-M (Bozzo & Mansueto Zecca, 1993). This group performed significantly better on forward Corsi recall than did the Williams syndrome group. Vicari, Brizzolara et al. (1996) also compared the performance of a group of children with Williams syndrome to a VA-matched group of typically developing children; the typically developing group performed better on forward Corsi recall than did the Williams syndrome group. Vicari, Bellucci, and Carlesimo (2003) compared the performance of a group of children with Williams syndrome to a younger typically developing group matched for MA on the Stanford-Binet using a computerized version of the Corsi task. Once again, the typically developing group performed significantly better than the Williams syndrome group. In this study, Vicari et al. also included a measure of visual span, in which increasingly long series of nonsense forms were presented at the same rate as the Corsi task; at the end of the presentation, the child was shown a set of nonsense forms and was asked to touch the correct forms in the order in which they were presented. The two groups had virtually identical visual spans. This pattern of findings was interpreted by Vicari et al. as evidence for impairment of the dorsal stream and a relative sparing of the ventral stream. While a variety of other evidence supports this conclusion (e.g., Meyer-Lindenberg et al., 2004), performance on the visual span task by the typically developing group was poor enough that the lack of significant between-group difference on the visual span task may be due to a floor effect.

Jarrold et al. (1999) compared the performance of a group of adolescents and adults with Williams syndrome to that of younger groups of individuals with either Down syndrome or mental retardation of unknown etiology. The groups were not matched for CA or MA; these factors were treated as covariates in the analyses. Results indicated significantly better performance on the forward Corsi task for the unknown etiology group than for either the

Down syndrome group or the Williams syndrome group. As mentioned earlier in this chapter, it is difficult to interpret the results of this study because the groups were not matched.

Racsmány, Pléh, and Lukács (2005) compared forward Corsi recall by a group of children and adolescents with Williams syndrome (mean CA: 13 years 4 months) to three typically developing control groups: a group matched for CA, a younger group matched for VA (mean CA 7 years 1 month) as determined by the Hungarian version of the PPVT (Csányi, 1974), and a still younger group (mean CA: 4 years 6 months) matched for raw scores on the Block Design subtest of the Hungarian version of the WISC-III (Wechsler, 1991) and the Arrows subtest from the NEPsy (Korkman, Kirk, & Kemp, 1998). The Williams syndrome group performed significantly worse than each of the control groups.

Backward Corsi recall

Only one study of backward Corsi recall by individuals with Williams syndrome has been conducted. Edgin (2003) compared backward Corsi recall by adolescents and young adults with Williams syndrome to a CA-matched Down syndrome group. In contrast to the significant advantage for the Down syndrome group over the Williams syndrome group for forward Corsi recall, performance on backward Corsi recall was virtually identical for the Williams syndrome group and the Down syndrome.

In summary, the performance of individuals with Williams syndrome on forward Corsi recall was considerably and reliably weaker than the performance of a variety of control groups. In contrast, performance on backward Corsi recall was highly similar to that of a CA-matched Down syndrome group. Because several of the studies included measures of both forward digit recall and forward Corsi recall, researchers were able to compare performance across verbal and spatial memory tasks. Results consistently indicated that the Williams syndrome group performed significantly better on the verbal memory task than on the spatial memory task, paralleling findings that verbal abilities are considerably stronger than visuospatial constructive abilities for individuals with Williams syndrome.

RELATIONS BETWEEN VERBAL MEMORY ABILITY AND GRAMMATICAL ABILITY

Verbal working memory is associated with the acquisition of both vocabulary (Gathercole & Baddeley, 1989, 1993) and syntax (Kemper, Kynette, Rash, & O'Brien, 1989; Norman, Kemper, & Kynette, 1992) for individuals who are developing typically. Similarly, the nonword repetition task has been proposed as a phenotypic marker for specific language impairment (SLI; Bishop, North, & Donlan, 1996). These and other studies suggest that verbal working memory plays an active role in the acquisition of words and grammatical structures by diverse populations.

Robinson, Mervis, and Robinson (2003) hypothesized that given the Williams syndrome cognitive profile, verbal working memory may play a *more important* role in the language acquisition of individuals with this syndrome than in language acquisition by typically developing children. To address this possibility, they compared the relations between forward digit recall, backward digit recall, phonological memory (Montgomery's nonword repetition task, 1996), and receptive grammatical abilities (raw score on the Test for Reception of Grammar; TROG; Bishop, 1989) for a group of children and adolescents with Williams syndrome (mean CA 10.24 years, range 4.5–16.7 years) to those of a younger typically developing group (mean CA 6.01 years, range 4.08–10.26 years) closely matched for TROG raw score.

As expected, the correlations between the memory measures and TROG raw score were significant for the Williams syndrome group. Forward digit span, nonword repetition, and backward digit span shared partial correlations (controlling for CA) of .33, .48, and .52 with TROG respectively. Taken together, the memory variables accounted for 26% of the variance in the TROG raw scores in the Williams syndrome group above and beyond CA. However, regression analysis indicated that forward digit span alone did not uniquely contribute to variance in the scores once CA, nonword repetition, and backward digit span were taken into account. Nonword repetition, by contrast, did account for additional unique variance even after CA and the other memory measures were controlled for. Thus, phonological memory may account, in part, for the grammatical skills of individuals with Williams syndrome. This finding fits with those of Grant et al. (1997), who reported that nonword repetition scores were significantly related to receptive vocabulary for individuals with Williams syndrome. One would therefore expect that the ability to encode and store small speech units, such as bound morphemes and function words, would similarly be related to grammatical ability. Backward digit span accounted for the largest proportion of variance in TROG scores for the Williams syndrome group. Even after controlling for CA, forward digit span, and nonword repetition, backward digit span accounted for an additional 10% of variance. Thus, the ability to manipulate verbal items, not just store them, seems to be important to grammatical ability.

After controlling for CA, there were no significant differences between the Williams syndrome group and the typically developing group in the strength of relation between either forward digit span or nonword repetition and TROG raw scores. The Williams syndrome group, however, showed a significantly stronger relation between backward digit span and receptive grammar than did the typically developing group. Therefore, it is possible that individuals with Williams syndrome may have to rely more heavily than typically developing children on verbal working memory abilities in order to puzzle out complex grammatical structures. Comprehending phrases, and, presumably, learning grammatical constructions, requires more than the storage of linguistic items in short-term memory. A child must extract the meaning of a phrase from the context of the utterance and then associate it with the linguistic item that is stored in short-term memory. The interpretation of nonlinguistic cues to meaning would involve perceptual, social, and cognitive analysis. For a typically developing child much of the process of extracting meaning from context is effortless and not limited by verbal working memory ability. For a child with deficits in one or more of the domains necessary to the processing and integration of the nonlinguistic cues, however, more effort and time is required for meaning extraction; therefore verbal working memory ability, particularly the ability to manipulate items in verbal working memory, might be more important for language acquisition.

Further evidence that verbal memory ability plays an important role in grammatical ability for children with Williams syndrome is provided by a study comparing the performance of a group of 13 9- and 10-year-olds with Williams syndrome on the subtests of the MSCA to the performance of a group of 13 children with Down syndrome closely matched for both CA and MA (as measured by total raw score on the MSCA) (Klein & Mervis, 1999). As expected, the Down syndrome group performed significantly better than the Williams syndrome group on subtests measuring visuospatial construction. Interestingly, the Williams syndrome and Down syndrome groups performed virtually identically on subtests measuring verbal (non-memory) ability. However, there were significant and large differences in favor of the Williams syndrome group on the subtests that measured verbal memory ability. Consistent with these differences in verbal memory ability, there were large differences in the proportion of children who typically spoke in complete, grammatical sentences: 9 of 13 children with Williams syndrome vs. 4 of 13 children with Down syndrome. Thus, despite being closely matched for level of overall cognitive ability and showing virtually identical verbal conceptual ability as measured by the verbal nonmemory subtests of the MSCA, the Williams syndrome and Down syndrome groups clearly differed on productive grammatical ability. Comparisons of the original samples of children from which the matched pairs had been selected revealed an even larger difference: 19 of the 23 children with Williams syndrome but only 4 of the 25 children with Down syndrome typically spoke in complete grammatical sentences.

The relation between verbal memory ability and language ability also has been addressed in two studies of children acquiring native languages other than English. Pléh, Lukács, and Racsmány (2002) compared the morphological abilities of a group of children and adolescents with Williams syndrome (mean CA 13.2 years) to a VA-matched group of younger typically developing children (age range: 7–10 years; mean not reported). A picture description task was used to elicit regular and irregular plural and accusative forms. Participants also completed a forward digit recall task. The Williams syndrome group made significantly more errors than the typically developing group. A relation between verbal working memory and morphological ability was found for the Williams syndrome group but not for the control group. In particular, results based on a median split of the Williams syndrome group based on digit span (span of three or less vs. span of four or more) indicated that the longer span group performed significantly better than the shorter span group on both the regular forms (97% vs. 77% correct) and irregular forms (90% vs. 61% correct). This memory effect remained even after controlling for CA. On the basis of these findings, Pléh et al. suggested that some of the variability among children with Williams syndrome on cognitive and behavioral measures may be due to differences in verbal working memory capacity. This suggestion is supported by Mervis, Robinson, Rowe, Becerra, and Klein-Tasman's (2004) finding that for a sample of 50 children and adults with Williams syndrome, both forward and backward digit span are significantly and strongly related not only to vocabulary ability (raw score on the Peabody Picture Vocabulary Test – Revised; PPVT-R; Dunn & Dunn, 1981) and grammatical ability (number of blocks correct on the TROG), but also to nonverbal reasoning ability (raw score on the Matrices subtest of the Kaufman Brief Intelligence Test; Kaufman & Kaufman, 1990) and pattern construction ability (ability score on the DAS Pattern Construction subtest), even after partialling out the effects of CA.

Volterra, Caselli, Capirci, Tonucci, and Vicari (2003) compared the language and verbal memory abilities of six younger children with Williams syndrome to those of six children with Down syndrome matched for CA and expressive vocabulary size on the Italian version of the MacArthur Communicative Development Inventories (CDI; Fenson et al., 1993) and six younger typically developing children matched for expressive vocabulary size. The grammatical ability of the children with Williams syndrome, as assessed by the Early Sentence Checklist component of the CDI, was similar to that of the typically developing control group; these groups also performed similarly on the sentence repetition task. In contrast, the Down syndrome group performed considerably (but not significantly) less well than the Williams syndrome group on the Early Sentence Checklist and significantly worse than the Williams syndrome group on the sentence repetition task. For all three groups, grammatical ability was strongly and significantly correlated with sentence repetition ability, suggesting an important role for verbal working memory in early grammatical development, independent of etiology.

CONCLUSION

Based on the initial studies of intellectual abilities in Williams syndrome, people with Williams syndrome were characterized as having a relative strength in verbal memory in contrast to considerable weakness in visuo-spatial construction (e.g., Udwin & Yule, 1991). More recent research, as reviewed in this chapter, has corroborated this initial impression. Children and adults with Williams syndrome perform significantly better on tests of forward digit recall and list recall than do CA- and IQ-matched individuals with either Down syndrome or mental retardation of unknown etiology. Furthermore, verbal working memory for people with Williams syndrome is affected by the same semantic and phonological factors (word frequency/ familiarity, word length, phonological relatedness, degree of concreteness) as for the general population. Comparisons between people with Williams syndrome and CA- and IQ-matched participants with Down syndrome or mixed etiology on tests of backward digit recall, although not resulting in significant differences, consistently favor the Williams syndrome group. Although the lack of significant between-group differences on backward digit recall may be due to low power, the fact that the same studies yielded significant differences on forward recall suggests that at a minimum, between-group differences are considerably more robust for rote recall ability than for manipulation of items in verbal memory.

In contrast, as might be expected given the great difficulty that individuals with Williams syndrome have with visuospatial construction, children and adults with Williams syndrome perform significantly worse than CA- and IQ-matched individuals with Down syndrome on forward Corsi recall. In the one study that included backward Corsi span, the performance of the Williams syndrome and CA- and IQ-matched Down syndrome groups was virtually identical. Thus, when mental manipulation is needed, the spatial working memory capabilities of individuals with Down syndrome and individuals with Williams syndrome are similar.

Early research on Williams syndrome often focused on apparent dissociations between language abilities and cognitive abilities, arguing that Williams syndrome was the paradigmatic example of the independence of language and cognition (e.g., Bellugi et al., 1988; and Bates', 1990, presentation of Bellugi's research); more recent and extreme instantiations of this claim are provided by Piattelli-Palmarini (2001) and Pinker (1999). In contrast, other researchers (e.g., Bates, Tager-Flusberg, Vicari, & Volterra, 2001; Karmiloff & Karmiloff-Smith, 2001; Mervis, 1999; Mervis & Klein-Tasman, 2000; Mervis et al., 2003, 2004) have argued that cognitive (particularly verbal memory) abilities and language abilities are strongly interrelated. As reviewed in this chapter, results of studies that measure the relations between cognitive abilities and language abilities have consistently indicated a very strong relation between these abilities. In particular, verbal memory abilities are strongly related to grammatical ability and vocabulary ability for children with Williams syndrome. Furthermore, although these relations are also significant for typically developing children early on but not as children get older, they continue to be significant and strong for people with Williams syndrome at least through adolescence. This pattern of findings has led several research groups to argue that in stark contrast to the claim that Williams syndrome provides the paradigmatic example of the independence of language from cognition, language acquisition is more dependent on verbal working memory for individuals with Williams syndrome than it is for typically developing children (e.g., Karmiloff & Karmiloff-Smith, 2001; Mervis, 2006; Mervis et al., 2003, Pléh et al., 2002; Robinson et al., 2003).

NOTE

1 Preparation of this manuscript was supported by grants from the National Institute of Child Health and Human Development (HD29957) and the National Institute of Neurological Disorders and Stroke (NS35102) to CBM.

REFERENCES

Baddeley, A. D. (1986). *Working memory*. Oxford, UK: Oxford University Press.

Baddeley, A. D., & Hitch, G. (1974). Working memory. In G. Bower (Ed.), *The psychology of learning and motivation* (Vol. 8, pp. 47–90). New York: Academic Press.

Banken, J. (1985). Clinical utility of considering digits forward and digits backwards as separate components of the Wechsler adult intelligence scale – revised. *Journal of Child Psychology*, *41*, 686–691.

Barisnikov, K., van der Linden, M., & Poncelet, M. (1996). Acquisition of new words and phonological working memory in Williams syndrome: A case study. *Neurocase*, *2*, 395–404.

Bates, E. (1990, April). *Early language development: How things come together and how they come apart*. Paper presented at the international conference on Infant Studies, Montreal, Canada.

Bates, E., Tager-Flusberg, H., Vicari, S., & Volterra, V. (2001). Debate over language's link with intelligence. *Nature*, *413*, 565–566.

Bellugi, U., Marks, S., Bihrle, A., & Sabo, H. (1988). Dissociation between language and cognitive functions in Williams syndrome. In D. Bishop & K. Mogford (Eds.), *Language development in exceptional circumstances* (pp. 177–189). London: Churchill Livingstone.

Beuren, A. J., Schulze, C., Eberle, P., Harmjanz, D., & Apitz, J. (1964). The syndrome of supravalvular aortic stenosis, peripheral pulmonic stenosis, mental retardation, and similar facial appearance. *American Journal of Cardiology*, *13*, 471–483.

Bishop, D. V. M. (1989). *Test for the Reception of Grammar* (2nd ed.). Manchester, UK: Chapel Press.

Bishop, D. V. M., North, T., & Donlan, C. (1996). Nonword repetition as a behavioural marker for inherited language impairment: Evidence from a twin study. *Journal of Child Psychology and Psychiatry*, *37*, 391–403.

Bozzo, M. T., & Mansueto Zecca, G. (1993). *Adattamento italiano della Scala d'Intelligenza Stanford-Binet Forma L-M nella revisione Terman-Merill*. Firenze, Italy: Organizzazioni Speciali.

Csányi, F. I. (1974). *Peabody Szokincs-Teszt*. Budapest, Hungary: Barczi Gusztav Gyogypedagogiai Foiskola.

Delis, D. C., Kramer, J. H., Kaplan, E., & Ober, B. A. (1994). *The California Verbal Learning Test – Children's version*. San Antonio, TX: Psychological Corporation.

Devenny, D. A., Krinsky-McHale, S. J., Kittler, P. M., Flory, M., Jenkins, E., & Brown, W. T. (2004). Age-associated memory changes in adults with Williams syndrome. *Developmental Neuropsychology, 26*, 691–706.

Dunn, L. M., & Dunn, L. M. (1981). *Peabody Picture Vocabulary Test* (Rev. ed.). Circle Pines, MN: American Guidance Service.

Dunn, L. M., Dunn, L. M., Whetton, C., & Burley, J. (1997). *The British Picture Vocabulary Scale* (2nd ed.). Windsor, UK: NFER-Nelson.

Dunn, L. M., Whetton, C., & Pintilie, D. (1982). *British Picture Vocabulary Scale.* Windsor, UK: NFER-Nelson.

Edgin, J. O. (2003). A neuropsychological model for the development of the cognitive profiles in mental retardation syndromes: Evidence from Down syndrome and Williams syndrome. *Dissertation Abstracts International: Section B. The Sciences and Engineering, 64*(3-B), 1522.

Elliott, C. D. (1990). *Differential Ability Scales.* San Antonio, TX: Psychological Corporation.

Elliott, C. D., Smith, P., & McCulloch, K. (1996). *British Ability Scales II.* Windsor, UK: NFER-Nelson.

Ewart, A. K., Morris, C. A., Atkinson, D., Jin, W., Sternes, K., Spallone, P., et al. (1993). Hemizygosity at the elastin locus in a developmental disorder, Williams syndrome. *Nature Genetics, 5*, 11–16.

Fenson, L., Dale, P. S., Reznick, J. S., Thal, D., Bates, E., Hartung, J. P., et al. (1993). *The MacArthur Communicative Development Inventories: User's guide and technical manual.* Baltimore: Paul H. Brookes.

Frick, R. W. (1995). Accepting the null hypothesis. *Memory and Cognition, 23*, 132–138.

Gathercole, S. E., & Baddeley, A. D. (1989). Evaluation of the role of phonological STM in the development of vocabulary in children: A longitudinal study. *Journal of Memory and Language, 28*, 200–213.

Gathercole, S. E., & Baddeley, A. D. (1993). *Working memory and language.* Hillsdale, NJ: Lawrence Erlbaum Associates, Inc.

Gathercole, S. E., & Baddeley, A. D. (1996). *The children's test of nonword repetition.* London: Psychological Corporation.

Grant, J., Karmiloff-Smith, A., Gathercole, S. A., Paterson, S., Howlin, P., Davies, M., & Udwin, O. (1997). Phonological short-term memory and its relationship to language in Williams syndrome. *Cognitive Neuropsychiatry, 2*, 81–99.

Harcum, E. R. (1990). Methodological vs. empirical literature: Two views on the acceptance of the null hypothesis. *The American Psychologist, 45*, 404–405.

Hillier, L. W., Fulton, R. S., Fulton, L. A., Graves, T. A., Pepin, K. H., Wagner-McPherson, C., et al. (2003). The DNA sequence of chromosome 7. *Nature, 424*, 157–164.

Hulme, C., Maughan, S., & Brown, G. D. A. (1991). Memory for familiar and unfamiliar words: Evidence for a long-term contribution to short-term memory span. *Journal of Memory and Language, 30*, 685–701.

Jarrold, C., Baddeley, A. D., & Hewes, A. K. (1999). Genetically dissociated components of working memory: Evidence from Down syndrome and Williams syndrome. *Neuropsychologia, 37*, 637–651.

Jarrold, C., Cowan, N., Hewes, A. K., & Riby, D. M. (2004). Speech timing and verbal short-term memory: Evidence for contrasting deficits in Down syndrome and Williams syndrome. *Journal of Memory and Language, 51*, 365–380.

Karmiloff, K., & Karmiloff-Smith, A. (2001). *Pathways to language: From fetus to adolescent*. Cambridge, MA: Harvard University Press.

Kaufman, A. S., & Kaufman, N. L. (1990). *Kaufman Brief Intelligence Test*. Pines, MN: American Guidance Services.

Kemper, S., Kynette, D., Rash, S., & O'Brien, K. (1989). Life span changes to adults' language: Effects of memory and genre. *Applied Psycholinguistics, 10*, 49–66.

Klein, B. P., & Mervis, C. B. (1999). Cognitive strengths and weaknesses of 9- and 10-year-olds with Williams syndrome or Down syndrome. *Developmental Neuropsychology, 16*, 177–196.

Klein-Tasman, B. P., & Mervis, C. B. (2003). Distinctive personality characteristics of 8-, 9-, and 10-year-old children with Williams syndrome. *Developmental Neuropsychology, 23*, 271–292.

Korkman, M., Kirk, U., & Kemp, S. (1998). *NEPSY: A developmental neuropsychological assessment*. San Antonio, TX: Psychological Corporation.

Laing, E., Grant, J., Thomas, M., Parmigiani, C., Ewing, S., & Karmiloff-Smith, A. (2005). Love is . . . an abstract word: The influence of lexical semantics on verbal short-term memory in Williams syndrome. *Cortex, 41*, 169–179.

Laing, E., Hulme, C., Grant, J., & Karmiloff-Smith, A. (2001). Learning to read in Williams syndrome: Looking beneath the surface of atypical reading development. *Journal of Child Psychology and Psychiatry, 42*, 729–739.

Leiter, R. G. (1979). *Leiter International Performance Scale* (Rev. ed.). Chicago: Stoelting.

Majerus, S., Barisnikov, K., Vuillemin, I., Poncelet, M., & van der Linden, M. (2003). An investigation of verbal short-term memory and phonological processing in four children with Williams syndrome. *Neurocase, 9*, 390–401.

McCarthy, D. (1972). *McCarthy Scales of Children's Abilities*. New York: Psychological Corporation.

Mervis, C. B. (1999). The Williams syndrome cognitive profile: Strengths, weaknesses, and interrelations among auditory short-term memory, language, and visuospatial constructive cognition. In E. Winograd, R. Fivush, & W. Hirst (Eds.), *Ecological approaches to cognition: Essays in honor of Ulric Neisser* (pp. 193–227). Mahwah, NJ: Lawrence Erlbaum Associates, Inc.

Mervis, C. B. (2004). Cross-etiology comparisons of cognitive and language development. In M. Rice & S. F. Warren (Eds.), *Developmental language disorders: From phenotypes to etiologies* (pp. 153–186). Mahwah, NJ: Lawrence Erlbaum Associates, Inc.

Mervis, C. B. (2006). Language abilities in Williams-Beuren syndrome: A review. In C. A. Morris, H. M. Lenhoff, & P. P. Wang (Eds.), *Williams-Beuren syndrome: Research, evaluation, and treatment* (pp. 159–206). Baltimore: Johns Hopkins University Press.

Mervis, C. B., & Klein-Tasman, B. P. (2000). Williams syndrome: Cognition, personality, and adaptive behavior. *Mental Retardation and Developmental Disabilities Research Reviews, 6*, 148–158.

Mervis, C. B., & Klein-Tasman, B. P. (2004). Methodological issues in group-matching designs: Alpha levels for control variable comparisons and measurement characteristics of control and target variables. *Journal of Autism and Developmental Disorders, 34*, 7–17.

Mervis, C. B., Morris, C. A., Bertrand, J., & Robinson, B. F. (1999). Williams syndrome cognitive profile: Findings from an integrated program of research. In

H. Tager-Flusberg (Ed.), *Neurodevelopmental disorders: Contributions to a new framework from the cognitive neurosciences.* Cambridge, MA: MIT Press.

Mervis, C. B., & Robinson, B. F. (2003). Methodological issues in cross-group comparisons of language and cognitive development. In Y. Levy & J. Schaeffer (Eds.), *Language competence across populations: Toward a definition of specific language impairment* (pp. 233–258). Mahwah, NJ: Lawrence Erlbaum Associates, Inc.

Mervis, C. B., & Robinson, B. F. (2005). Designing measures for profiling and genotype/phenotype studies of individuals with genetic syndromes or developmental language disorders. *Applied Psycholinguistics, 26,* 41–64.

Mervis, C. B., Robinson, B. F., Bertrand, J., Morris, C. A., Klein-Tasman, B. P., & Armstrong, S. C. (2000). The Williams syndrome cognitive profile. *Brain and Cognition, 44,* 604–628.

Mervis, C. B., Robinson, B. F., Rowe, M. L., Becerra, A. M., & Klein-Tasman, B. P. (2003). Language abilities of individuals with Williams syndrome. In L. Addeduto (Ed.), *International review of research in mental retardation* (Vol. 27, pp. 35–81). Orlando, FL: Academic Press.

Mervis, C. B., Robinson, B. F., Rowe, M. L., Becerra, A. M., & Klein-Tasman, B. P. (2004). Relations between language and cognition in Williams syndrome. In S. Bartke & J. Siegmüller (Eds.), *Williams syndrome across languages* (pp. 63–92). Amsterdam: John Benjamins.

Meyer-Lindenberg, A., Kohn, P., Mervis, C. B., Kippenhan, J. S., Olsen, R., Morris, C. A., & Berman, K. F. (2004). Neural basis of genetically determined visuospatial construction deficit in Williams syndrome. *Neuron, 43,* 623–631.

Milner, B. (1971). Interhemispheric differences in the localization of psychological processes in man. *British Medical Bulletin, 27,* 272–277.

Montgomery, J. (1996). Examination of phonological working memory in specifically language-impaired children. *Applied Psycholinguistics, 16,* 355–378.

Morris, C. A. (2005). Williams syndrome. In S. B. Cassidy & J. E. Allanson (Eds.), *Management of genetic syndromes* (2nd ed., pp. 655–665). New York: Wiley.

Morris, C. A. (2006). Dysmorphology, genetics, and natural history of Williams-Beuren syndrome: An overview. In C. A. Morris, H. M. Lenhoff, & P. P. Wang (Eds.), *Williams-Beuren syndrome: Research, evaluation, and treatment* (pp. 3–17). Baltimore: Johns Hopkins University Press.

Morris, C. A., & Mervis, C. B. (2000). Williams syndrome and related disorders. *Annual Review of Genomics and Human Genetics, 1,* 461–484.

Nichols, S., Jones, W., Roman, M. J., Wulfeck, B., Delis, D. C., Reilly, J., & Bellugi, U. (2004). Mechanisms of verbal memory impairment in four neurodevelopmental disorders. *Brain and Language, 88,* 180–189.

Norman, S., Kemper, S., & Kynette, D. (1992). Adult reading comprehension: Effects of syntactic complexity and working memory. *Journals of Gerontology, 47,* 258–265.

Piattelli-Palmarini, M. (2001). Speaking of learning: How do we acquire our marvelous facility for expressing ourselves in words? *Nature, 411,* 887–888.

Pinker, S. (1999). *Words and rules: The ingredients of language.* New York: Basic Books.

Pléh, C., Lukács, A., & Racsmány, M. (2002). Morphological patterns in Hungarian children with Williams syndrome and the rule debates. *Brain and Language, 86,* 377–383.

Racsmány, M., Pléh, C., & Lukács, A. (2005). Spatial working memory in Williams syndrome. *Manuscript submitted for publication.*

Raven, J. C. (1986). *Raven's progressive matrices and vocabulary scales.* London: H. K. Lewis.

Robinson, B. F., Mervis, C. B., & Robinson, B. W. (2003). Roles of verbal short-term memory and working memory in the acquisition of grammar by children with Williams syndrome. *Developmental Neuropsychology, 23*, 13–31.

Stapleton, T., MacDonald, W. B., & Lightwood, R. (1957). The pathogenesis of idiopathic hypercalcemia of infancy. *American Journal of Clinical Nutrition, 5*, 533–542.

Stock, A. D., Spallone, P. A., Dennis, T. R., Netski, D., Morris, C. A., Mervis, C. B., & Hobart, H. H. (2003). Heat shock protein 27 gene: Chromosomal and molecular location and relationship to Williams syndrome. *American Journal of Medical Genetics, 120A*, 320–325.

Strømme, P., Bjørnstad, P. G., & Ramstad, K. (2002). Prevalence estimation of Williams syndrome. *Journal of Child Neurology, 17*, 269–271.

Udwin, O., & Yule, W. (1991). A cognitive and behavioral phenotype in Williams syndrome. *Journal of Clinical and Experimental Neuropsychology, 13*, 232–244.

Vicari, S., Bates, E., Caselli, M. C., Pasqualetti, P., Gagliardi, C., Tonucci, F., & Volterra, V. (2004). Neuropsychological profile of Italians with Williams syndrome: An example of a dissociation between language and cognition? *Journal of the International Neuropsychological Society, 10*, 862–876.

Vicari, S., Bellucci, S., & Carlesimo, G. A. (2001). Procedural learning deficit in children with Williams syndrome. *Neuropsychologia, 39*, 665–677.

Vicari, S., Bellucci, S., & Carlesimo, G. A. (2003). Visual and spatial working memory dissociation: Evidence from Williams syndrome. *Developmental Medicine and Child Neurology, 45*, 269–273.

Vicari, S., Brizzolara, D., Carlesimo, G. A., Pezzini, G., & Volterra, V. (1996). Memory abilities in children with Williams syndrome. *Cortex, 32*, 503–514.

Vicari, S., Carlesimo, G. A., Brizzolara, D., & Pezzini, G. (1996). Short-term memory in children with Williams syndrome: A reduced contribution of lexical-semantic knowledge to word span. *Neuropsychologia, 34*, 919–925.

Volterra, V., Caselli, M. C., Capirci, O., Tonucci, F., & Vicari, S. (2003). Early linguistic abilities of Italian children with Williams syndrome. *Developmental Neuropsychology, 23*, 33–59.

Wang, P. P., & Bellugi, U. (1994). Evidence from two genetic syndromes for a dissociation between verbal and visuospatial short-term memory. *Journal of Clinical and Experimental Neuropsychology, 16*, 317–322.

Wechsler, D. (1991). *Wechsler intelligence scale for children* (3rd ed.). New York: Psychological Corporation.

Williams, J. C., Barratt-Boyes, B. G., & Lowe, J. B. (1961). Supravalvular aortic stenosis. *Circulation, 24*, 1311–1318.

Author index

Subject index